PUBLIC ADMINISTRATION: EMERGING PERSPECTIVES

PUBLIC ADMINISTRATION : EMERGING PERSPECTIVES

(Essays in Honour of Prof. S.P. Verma)

EDITORS

PARDEEP SAHNI
ALKA DHAMEJA
UMA MEDURY
E. VAYUNANDAN

GYAN PUBLISHING HOUSE

NEW DELHI - 110002

PUBLIC ADMINISTRATION :
EMERGING PERSPECTIVES
(Administration, Crime/Law/Police, Economics, Industry, Management, Rural Development)

ISBN : 81-212-0604-9

Published in 1999 in India by
Gyan Publishing House
5, Ansari Road
New Delhi 110 002
Laser Typesetting: Grow Computers, Delhi.
Printed at Mehra Offset Press, New Delhi.

Contents

Acknowledgements

Facilitation volumes are brought out with a specific purpose of recording appreciation for the scholarly output of renowned academicians. These see the light of the day with the active help and cooperation of the noted scholars and professionals who contribute through their writings. We contacted some close friends and admirers of Prof. S.P. Verma for their articles, and it goes without saying that our request was readily adhered to. It is our duty to bring on record the encouragement we have received from our esteemed contributors. We shall always remain obliged to them.

It has been very kind of Prof. A.W. Khan, Vice-Chancellor, Indira Gandhi National Open University for acceding to our request to write a Foreword to this volume. His interest in academics, more particularly his intense involvement in the different aspects of Public Administration gets amply reflected in the meaningful and thought provoking foreword penned by him.

Last but not the least, it is Mr. Amit Garg of Gyan Publishing House, New Delhi who has taken immense pains to bring out this volume expeditiously. We express our heartfelt gratitude to him.

Pardeep Sahni
Alka Dhameja
Uma Medury
E. Vayunandan

Foreword

Public Administration as a discipline has always intrigued me. I have often pondered over its enormity, integrity and range. A generalistic perspective and a negative attitude is what everyone seems to have towards administration. From 'cradle to grave', it is said, the vicious circle of encounters with administrative hurdles, formalities and insensitivity goes on. But, this is only one side of the picture. The more serious issue is the dependency of overall development of the country on an efficient and responsive administration. There is a need for a more optimistic conception for the future. This book initiates a debate that may facilitate the achievement of such a vision. There is no dearth of erudite books on Public Administration but I feel that rarely does a copious account of wide ranging issues gets compiled as done in this volume.

The changing socio-economic and political scenario has thrown up many potent questions regarding different aspects of Public Administration. The relationship between government, industry and labour is witnessing a metamorphosis. Theory and practice of administration are now expected to complement each other. We must therefore take a fresh look at the constraints of bureaucracy, rigid administrative structure, obsolete policy-making and implementation mechanism and inadequate benchmarks of evaluation. This book makes an attempt to satiate the queries of all voracious readers pertaining to liberalisation, privatisation, organisational reforms, work environment, ethical code, research, training, democratic decentralisation, people's participation, leadership qualities, advancement of technology, rural uplift and urban planning.

I have never been a formal student of Public Administration, however, as an area of practice, I have always been confronted with dilemmas related to decision-making, policy enforcement, monitoring and assessment at different levels in my long career as an administrator. This book has in fact made me look deeper into the complexities of this interesting subject. I would like to congratulate my colleagues who have made unceasing efforts in editing this useful volume. Their endeavour is indeed commendable. It is heartening to note that the book is dedicated to Prof. S.P. Verma with whom I have had some very memorable years of interaction. He has not only contributed towards the enrichment of the discipline but has been instrumental in laying the foundation of the Faculty of Public Administration at IGNOU. I think this is the most decorous way of paying tribute to his endowments. I am confident that the rich array of thoughts and ideas presented in this volume would be of great utility to the theoreticians and practitioners in the field of Public Administration and its allied areas.

25th March 1999 **(A.W. Khan)**
New Delhi Vice-Chancellor
Indira Gandhi National Open University

Professor Suresh Prasad Verma: An Appreciation

Born on May 8, 1926, Professor S.P. Verma had his higher education at Nagpur (the then capital of C.G. & Barar). At intermediate level (1949) he got first class IInd position in order of merit from Nagpur University. While being the student of SBCT College Nagpur and Department of Political Science, Professor Verma obtained his B.A. Honours and M.A. degrees in Political Science and was also enrolled at University Law College.

A fulbright scholar (1962-65), Professor Verma was awarded Ph.D. degree of state University of IOWA, USA and had been a Visiting Professor, Augustana College, Illinois, USA, 1965. Prior to that he started his teaching career at Government Robbrtson College, Jabalpur (1954-56) and later on while teaching at Government Morris College, Nagpur, was appointed by Nagpur University as a part-time lecturer in the University, Department of Public Administration, the first department to start M.A. Public Administration, under the leadership of late Professor M.P. Sharma.

Professor Verma later on shifted to Delhi and served as senior faculty member (Reader/Professor) at Indian Institute of Public Administration, New Delhi from 1962 to 1987. He was also Professor of Public Administration in Indira Gandhi National Open University (1988-91). From 1995 to 1997 Professor Verma was the Senior Director and Dean EMPI Business School, New Delhi.

A renowned scholar of Political Science and Public Administration Professor Verma, apart from innumerable research papers, have authored/edited nearly a dozen and half books. Some of the important ones of them are *Comparative Public Administration, Development Administration, Managing Public*

Personnel System: A Comparative Perspective, Indian Parliamentarians : A Study of Socio-Political Background, etc.

While at IIPA, Professor Verma directed Management and Executive Development Programmes for senior administrators including the Programme Director of Fourth Advanced Professional Programme in Public Administration. He had also been the head of the training activities at the Institute. He was also associated with several government committees and commissions e.g. Administrative Reforms Commission, Third Pay Commission, Railway Board, Indian Council for Agricultural Research, Sikkim and Gujarat State Pay Commission, etc. A Life Member of various professional organisations e.g. Indian Political Science Association, Indian Public Administration Association, Indian Institute of Public Administration etc. Professor Verma was elected President, Indian Public Administration Association (1987), President, New Public Administration Society of India (1998) and elected member of the Executive Council of Indian Institute of Public Administration since 1986 till date.

Professor Verma's areas of specialisation are Indian Government and Politics, Personnel Management, Organisational Behaviour, Communication, etc. He continues to be associated with the various universities of India e.g. Board of Studies, Selection Committee, Governing Board, etc. He is also associated with the various committees of UGC and NCERT. He has had the opportunity to represent the country on various international fora e.g. EROPA (Eastern Regional Organisation for Public Administration) in 1987 and Beijing in 1991.

Presently, Professor Verma is actively engaged in promoting the objectives of IIPA by encouraging younger Public Administrationists in developing the Discipline in Universities, participating in the Management Programmes of IIPA and Central and State Training Institutes and members' activities in Regional/ Local Branches of IIPA.

Introduction

For any academic endeavour, to add to the ocean of knowledge, there has to be an inspiration. We have had several, but our strongest inspiration has been the eternal reverence that we all hold towards Professor S.P. Verma. An eminent scholar of Public Administration, he needs no introduction. His contribution to the discipline has been enormous and noteworthy. We have immensely enriched ourselves over the years from our interaction with this veteran academician and a remarkable human being. Though no work of praise can befit his charisma and magnanimity, this book at least gives us an opportunity to commemorate his service to the discipline and also record our heartfelt gratitude to him.

Public Administration as a discipline has come a long way since the Wilsonian era. In India, it is facing new challenges which need to be grappled with if the subject has to sharpen its tentacles. The privatisation debate is posing the most crucial question mark, forcing the scholars to look for endogenous responses within the discipline. The exercise may entail restructuring at the organisational level, decentralising at the operational level or even debureaucratising at the decision making level. This calls for a fresh introspection of the subject that would enable us to analyse the impact of globalisation on the economy, repercussions of haphazard urbanisation and the debacles of grass-root planning. This volume is an attempt to throw light on varied pertinent aspects of Public Administration keeping in view the changing perspective and the growing dimensions of the discipline. While it is not feasible to summarise each and every argument put forward by the distinguished contributors to this volume, a little reflection on a few important issues may be in order.

Indian administrative system is reeling under the impact of global economic liberalisation which has initiated a process of reforms in the public sector since 1991. A good number of articles in the book deal with this issue. Broadly speaking, liberalisation or deregulation in the Indian context implies policy initiatives that have radically changed the existing balance between the public and private sector, by reducing the scope, role and status of public sector in the economy. The main thrust is to create a more competitive environment between private, state and foreign capital leading to better quality of goods and services. This point has been clearly brought forth in the book. It has also been mentioned that India with a share of only 0.5 per cent of the world trade still stands to benefit if other factors like the extension of liberalisation in sectors like, agriculture, textiles, services, professional manpower, global competition and reduction of tariffs are given due regard.

Attention has been drawn to the fact that India is one of the few countries where macro-economic restructuring has turned out to be a success. The Stabilisation and Structural Adjustment Programme has outlined a comprehensive package of reform measures for the public sector. There is a need for a reappraisal of the role of the State. The multitude of micro and macro adaptations often put the capacity of government to severe test. As the State tries to promote the process of adjustment and economic development, it requires supportive environmental policies, strong government intervention, reforms in the non-market institutional structures and privatisation of all non-core public enterprises. Above all, an adaptable and flexible system rendering non-standardised services is the call of the hour.

It has been reasserted that the reforms have indeed altered the context and quality of relations between the government, private industry and labour. There is an urgent need to introduce crucial changes in the areas of disinvestment, deregulation, equity pattern, market and client requirements, accountability and responsiveness of public enterprises, labour relations, user charges on public utilities, exit policy and boards of management. The point of debate is why go for privatisation at all? The inefficiency of a few enterprises has brought this query to the fore. The objective is not to reduce the role of public sector in an absolute sense but increase the role of private enterprises in the nation's development. The public sector is demanding a level playing field in order to compete with the private sector. A case has therefore been made for restructuring of public enterprises, reorientation of their objectives, enhancing the autonomy of boards of management and conferring 'Navratana' status to nine select public sector enterprises.

The growth of public sector necessitates a concomitant development of technology. Though modernisation of technology is not a new phenomenon, it has received reassertion through the recent package of liberalisation. It has been pointed out that the stress on the role of technology in rural development and organisational arrangements for transfer of technology to the people would only make sense if the governmental efforts for technological advancement are accentuated, development strategies for rural development are streamlined and nature and characteristics of organisations for dissemination of technology are made more responsive and autonomous.

It has been reiterated that the fundamental characteristic of modern societies is their functional differentiation under relatively independent sub-systems and spheres of action. Public administration in the post-industrial State would be efficiency-driven with accent on autonomy and accountability but a complete shift to a totally new set-up is not yet in sight. Certain super-optimising solutions need to be sought via a new and useful form of public policy evaluation for India's Industrial Policy. The object is to evolve a highly productive system which is skillful as well as humane.

The changing scenario has brought home the need to improve the technological infrastructure, research and development and training orientation. It has been clearly brought out that Research and Development (R&D) system in the country does not do justice to our expectations. The leaps in science and technology fronts that are planned and anticipated are almost beyond comprehension today. Paramount significance has to be laid on training and development in computer technology, applied technology in rural areas, ecological development, land reforms, legal system, and poverty eradication. Innovative ideas are needed if the pace of development has to be quickened.

In operational terms, development administration is viewed as the process of guiding an organisation towards the achievement of progressive socio-economic goals. The managerial planning, regressive development and insurrectional approaches to development administration focus on its goal and action-oriented nature. In today's context, an interface between concepts and social action has to be established. The recent trends in development administration that emphasise on the paradigmatic shift from a blue print approach to a learning process approach and from a production-centred approach to people-centred approach have been highlighted. Through administrative decentralisation, it is possible to bring about standards to deal with national problems, while at the same time to allow for adjustments to meet particular local needs.

Panchayati Raj Institutions (PRIs) are the prime instruments of decentralisation at the grass-root level. They assume importance due to the need to contain the relentless demographic pressures and optimum use of scarce resources for development. In the wake of economic liberalisation, the PRIs are the most rational way of meeting the challenges of development. Their grip has been tightened with the promulgation of 73rd Constitution (Amendment) Act, 1992 as almost all the states have completed the process of enacting fresh legislation. It has been mentioned that there is a need for decentralisation of power into the hands of people so that they could be brought into the mainstream of decision making process. More teeth can be provided to this legislation by establishing linkages between panchayats and cooperatives. This would resolve conflicting interests of the people and facilitate sustainable development.

Reforms are also called for even in the urban areas which are succumbing to the offshoots of ill-planned development strategies. The problems of population growth, slums, housing, health, law and order and environment have been a cause for concern. These areas have been discussed in the book. There is a need to strengthen public administration in order to meet the challenges posed by accelerated growth of urbanisation. In the past the policy directives have not been seriously implemented. Population explosion, absence of national urban policy, financial crunch and lack of political will have negated all sincere efforts in the areas of housing for poor and provision of basic amenities. Similar has been the plight of health administration. There is a need to treat hospitals as institutions of promotion of health and prevention of diseases, the concepts of complex hospital organisation and community health have to be evolved. The futurological perspective on hospital organisation must accompany curative, preventive as well as rehabilitative dimensions with enhanced focus on development of human resources, work accomplishment through mutual confidence, increased decentralisation of decision making and quality assurance of services.

The unabated deterioration of our environment base poses a major threat. The need of the day is not only to dwell on the effects of environmental pollution but also on sources and causes of the same. This problem has been discussed in some detail. What is being followed is a reactive approach to the issue which gives scant regard to preventive measures and changes in institutional coordination, policy adjustments and structural adaptations. Stress is therefore needed on adequate regulatory mechanism, strategy on effluent charges, national environmental standards, quality control procedures, public participation and environmental education and training.

It would be worthwhile to note at this point that a stable law and order situation is a prerequisite to all round development. Serious law and order situations could arise from student agitations, communal disturbances, caste conflicts, industrial unrest, state sponsored bandhs and strikes by public servants etc. Moot questions have been raised in the book that relate to the autonomy of police, selection of police officers, training of cops and most importantly the dilemma behind the use of force. It has been suggested that public cooperation is a must to handle law and order problems, public help can be sought in the area of road accidents too. The role of the traffic police also assumes importance and needs to be streamlined for best results.

In-depth analysis has been made on the complexity of administrative corruption which is a major obstacle in the pursuit of developmental goals. It has been stressed that every country has its own specific forms and patterns of corruption and it is hard to generalise about the experiences of different countries within a common framework of analysis, yet it would not be inappropriate to place the concept of corruption under the broad categories of power and authority; law and policy. There is a strong need to unravel the causes of preventable public maladministration in administrative ethics.

A case study of Tanzania reveals that due to the prevalence of nepotism, regionalism, ethnicity and religious considerations, administrative corruption has assumed acceptable dimensions.

Despite sincere efforts to restore honesty and accountability, our administrators tend to operate in a culture that is tolerant of unethical behaviour. A plea has been made to evolve a code of ethics and enforce it earnestly. It is not an impossible task if certain broad guidelines are agreed upon. To demystify the ethical dilemmas in the changing context, it is necessary to define ethics and ethical behaviour. This will help the administrators in confronting the issues of problem solving and decision making in order to formulate policies more resolutely.

There is, therefore, a need to carry out the policy implementation task without tearing the socio-cultural fabric of the country. The success of such an exercise would depend on the relationship between politics and administration, the complexion of electoral reforms, amendments in several legal enactments and training of professionals and semi-professionals. Innovative changes need to be introduced in the economic, social, political, labour, administrative and educational policies. Much would depend on political will and administrative leadership. The questions that become pertinent are; Is leadership culture free? Is it capable of being transferred from one social context to another? The situational leadership is based on the interplay among the amount of guidance a leader gives, the amount of socio-economic support the leader provides and the readiness level the followers exhibit in performing a specific task.

Leadership models exude a lot of flexibility, it is possible to learn from other country's experiences and even imbibe them if these fit into the socio-economic and political set up. We could as well learn from the budgetary system in China, and the calculations, causes, impact and future of China's budgetary process. Making use of different concepts and approaches to study administrative system is another area that has been highlighted. China's budgetary system is peculiar as it is linked with cultural and Constitutional contexts. The debt disbursements in the country constitute revenue rather than a means of financing deficits, it underestimates the size of deficits and overestimates the performance of the government. It has been mentioned that even modern economic analysis has to offer several tools such as for studying the internal organisation of bureaux (such as the game theory...). These could be adopted to deal with the individual and group; decision goals and objects; and information incentives and motivation. Though Weber's approach to nature of organisation and the concept of rationality is still the starting point in the study of bureaucracy, some extant approaches in the area could be adopted with advantage; suitable allowances however should be made for the differences between the functions, objectives and constraints of the business firms and the bureaux.

As it enters the future era with a great potential for bringing about significant reforms, Public Administration needs to sincerely define its domain. The priorities have to be judiciously selected and the constraints have to be plugged. India's growing participation in the world market is a welcome sign and so is the zest to improve the administrative system. Yet, a national vision seems to be missing, we are merely seeking short-term solutions to the age-old maladies. It is high time that we recognise the pressures that the administration is wilting under, the 'obsolete' must give way to the 'novel'. The areas that require utmost attention are policy guidelines, structural reforms, infrastructural facilities, technological advancement, comparative analysis, rural management, research, training and development. Any slowdown in the process of liberalisation and development now will push us behind the times and seriously jeopardise our projections. While planning this book, we have tried to cover a gamut of emerging perspectives so that comprehensive solutions could be found to some of these wide-ranging issues.

List of Contributors

1. **Alka Dhameja**
   Senior Lecturer-Public Administration
   Indira Gandhi National Open University
   New Delhi
2. **B.S. Bhatia**
   Professor and Coordinator-Enterpreneurship
   Development Cell
   Department of Business Management
   Punjabi University
   Patiala
3. **C.H. Balaramulu**
   Professor of Public Administration
   University Post-Graduate Centre
   Nirmal (A.P.)
4. **C.V. Raghavulu**
   Vice-Chancellor
   Nagarijuna University
   (A.P.)
5. **Charanjeev Singh**
   Lecturer
   Department of Public Administration
   Punjab University
   Chandigarh
6. **D.R. Sachdeva**
   Former Professor of Public Administration
   Punjabi University
   Patiala

7. **Dhrubajyoti Bhaumik**
Department of Political Science
University of North Bengal
Darjeeling

8. **Dolly Mathew**
Senior Lecturer-Public Administration
Indira Gandhi National Open University
New Delhi

9. **G.S. Batra**
Department of Business Management
Punjabi University
Patiala

10. **H.R. Bangia**
Administrative Officer
National Institute of Public Cooperation and Child Development
Siri Institutional Area,
Hauz Khas
New Delhi

11. **Huaping Luo**
Franklin College of Arts and Science
Department of Political Science
Baldwin Hall
University of Georgia

12. **Lokesh Kumar**
Assistant Professor of Political Science
Government College of Arts and Commerce
Lakhnadon (M.P.)

13. **M. Bapuji**
Professor
Department of Political Science and
Public Administration
Nagarjuna University
Andhra Pradesh

14. **M. Gopalakrishnan**
Former Special Chief Secretary to Govt. of Andhra Pradesh
Hyderabad

15. **N.J. Sola**
Lecturer-Institute of Development Management
Mzumbe
Tanzania

16. **Nawal Kishor**
Reader
School of Management Studies
Indira Gandhi National Open University
New Delhi

17. **O.P. Dwivedi**
Professor of Public and Environmental Administration
Department of Political Studies
University of Guelph

18. **P.N. Sharma**
Consultant
CEMPRES
LBS National Academy of Administration
Mussoorie

19. **Paul Hersey**
California American University
California

20. **R.K. Mishra**
Professor and Chairman Financial Management Division
Institute of Public Enterprise
Hyderabad

21. **R.K. Tiwari**
Professor of Public Administration
Indian Institute of Public Administration
New Delhi

22. **Robert T. Golembiewski**
Franklin College of Arts and Sciences
Department of Political Science
Baldwin Hall
University of Georgia

23. **Saugato Sen**
Senior Lecturer-Economics
Indira Gandhi National Open University
New Delhi

24. **S.L. Kaushik**
Professor of Public Administration
Punjab University
Chandigarh

25. **S.N. Mishra**
Professor of Indian Institute of Public Administration
New Delhi

26. **Stuart S. Nagel**
University of Illinois
And the Developmental Policy Studies Consortium

27. **Uma Medury**
Senior Lecturer-Public Administration
Indira Gandhi National Open University
New Delhi

28. **V. Bhaskara Rao**
Professor of Public Administration and
Dean, Faculty of Social Sciences
Kakatiya University
Warangal

29. **V.S. Murthy**
Professor (Retd.)
Department of Public Administration
University of Nagpur

1

Privatisation: An Indian Experience

S.L. Kaushik
Charanjeev Singh

The planning model adopted in many of the developing countries including India relied mainly on the Soviet pattern, which emphatically was based on the public sector, to bring about accelerated development to reduce regional imbalances and for equitable distribution of wealth and resources. However, since 1980, the ineffectiveness and inefficiency of public sector spread across the world has been a major area of public policy concern. As a consequence many countries have revised their policies towards privatisation. Today privatisation itself is a many faceted phenomenon referred to as "people-isation", "market-isation" , or "de-government-isation". Privatisation, though seemingly a hurried step, was necessitated due to the "chronic ills that plagued state-owned enterprises (SOEs) around the world, a resurgence of economic liberalisation during 1970's resulted in the dismissal of economic models based on the public monopolies". *(Schwartz and Lopes, 1993)* Privatisation was motivated in many countries due to the realisation of the "worldwide collapse of State socialism and this has created a new inevitability—the rise of free economic institutions." *(Moore, 1992)*

Multiple meanings of the word 'privatisation' can be witnessed but "essentially, it refers to a process through which the direct involvement of the State or the public sector is reduced through transferring the ownership, control, and/or managerial responsibility for government enterprises, functions and activities, fully or partially, to the private sector corporations, individuals or group of individuals, such as employees, customers and citizens, domestic or foreign." *(Venkata Ratnam, 1993)*

Why Privatisation?

Before going into the details of the Indian experience, it is imperative to answer a few fundamental questions regarding privatisation, the major thrust being on why privatisation at all? The economics of public ownership emerged as a response to the incapability or failure of the private market to provide equitable, efficient and effective distribution of resources. But a similar picture can be portrayed even when majority of the enterprises are State owned; moreover these circumstances have also led to lack of competition and inefficiency. It is worth mentioning that the key objective of private organisations is profit maximisation whereas State owned enterprises have multitude of objectives which hinder its profit maximisation. Moreover, "when public and private sectors are compared in terms of cost of producing similar outputs in a competitive environment, the private sector usually outperforms the public sector. Often, State-owned enterprises need to be kept afloat at taxpayers' expense, either through explicit government subsidies, such as direct cash grants, or through implicit subsidies, such as subsidised credit, guaranteed sales to government at fixed prices, reduction of tax liabilities, government equity injections, or preferential exchange rates." *(Shwartz and Lopes op.cit)*

Thus, privatisation is often viewed as the best option to bring in more competitiveness, improvement in efficiency and generation of resources. The mere notion that privatisation will serve as a catalyst for economic and social transformation may not hold good, as a nostrum for all economic ills unless it is accompanied by industrial restructuring. The entire industrial structure will have to be revamped and revitalised to bring in more efficiency gains and it will be necessary to introduce some type of regulations and supervision to reproduce healthy competition. If otherwise, the private enterprises will reap substantial monopoly profits and leave the consumer worse off.

Privatisation in India: A Saga of Reforms

The theoretical models of economic reforms, their rationale, their objectives and their designs may differ from country to country on the basis of the economic pattern which the country had adopted and thus, no uniform model is possible. However, there are mainly three components of these reforms, namely, deregulation, competition and strong budget constraints. Deregulation allows the market forces to have a free play. But allowing freedom of market forces does not necessarily result in a competitive economy and efficient allocation of resources. The budget constraints are present not just in government enterprises, even the private sector could suffer from inadequate finances and resource constraints, such problems are applicable to all agents in an economy. *(Sengupta, 1995)* The privatisation through the New Economic Policy, in India differs from that of other countries where reforms had been initiated since late 1970's. "The privatisation moves in India are largely a part of the conditionalities of Structural Adjustment Loans (SALs) and for Sectoral Adjustment Loans (SECALs). Unlike many other developing countries, India seems to be following a cautious and selective approach, than taking recourse to rapid privatisation. The basic thrust is not on reducing the role of the public sector in absolute sense but to allow an increasingly greater role for the private sector in the national economic development." *(Economic Survey 1992-93)* These conditions hold good for economic reforms which have been introduced in India since July1991. It would be pertinent here to highlight the initiatives of the New Industrial Policy, which represent renewed efforts towards consolidating the gains of national reconstruction. They are:

— Private sector to enter all industrial and manufacturing activities; industrial licensing has been done away with for all industries except a few strategically sensitive areas such as defence, atomic energy, etc., irrespective of the level of investment.

— Compulsory licensing to continue in areas like coal, petroleum, sugar, cigarettes, motor cars, hazardous chemicals, drugs and pharmaceuticals and some luxury items.

— Reservation of items for small scale to continue so as to promote the industrial and agro-industrial employment base.

— Public sector to retain its monopoly existence in the 8 core areas like defence, atomic energy, mineral oils, rail transport and mining.

— Import of capital goods shall be automatically cleared where the foreign exchange requirement is ensured through foreign equity.

— Import of capital goods w.e.f. 1.4.92 shall be automatically approved if the c.i.f. value of the import is less than 25 per cent of the total value of the plant and machinery, subject to a maximum limit of Rs. 2 crore.

— All existing and new industrial units to be broad banded, so as to enable them to produce any article without requiring any additional investment in plant and machinery.

— All substantial expansions of existing units exempted from licensing.

— Term loans to be granted by financial institutions for new projects shall no longer be convertible into equity.

— The limit for foreign investment in equity has been raised to 51 per cent from existing level of 40 per cent in high priority industries. Consequential amendments to the Foreign Exchange Regulation Act, 1973, to follow.

— Dividends to be expatriated by companies with foreign equity to be met through export earnings over a period of time.

— Foreign equity proposals delinked from foreign technology agreements.

— Companies with foreign equity upto 51 per cent to act as trading houses primarily engaged in export.

— Automatic clearance for foreign technology agreements in high priority industries upto a lump sum payment of Rs. 1 crore, 5 per cent royalty for domestic sales and 8 per cent for exports, subject to a total payment of 8 per cent of sales over a 10 years period from the date of agreement or 7 years from the commencement of production.

— Government's shareholding in public sector units to be offered to mutual funds, financial institutions, general public and workers, in consonance with the partial disinvestment policy to be implemented in a phased manner.

— Workers participation in management and revival of sick units, to be encouraged.

— MRTP Act to be amended to remove the threshold assets limits in respect of the MRTP companies and dominant undertakings, and to eliminate requirements of prior approval of Central Government for establishment of new undertakings, expansions, mergers, amalgamations and takeovers and appointment of Directors under certain circumstances. *(Venkata Ratnam, op. cit)*

Public Sector Reforms: Disinvestment—The Last Straw

During the 70's public sector was ascribed a dominant role to play, by several countries including India, "Government in its unrestricted enthusiasm to meet social objectives like maintaining employment, nationalised many a loss making units, not realising the enormous burden (both managerial and financial) involved in such an action and as had been assessed by all discerning observers, failed utterly in the task of reviving them." *(Economic Times, 1994)* The dismal performance of these PSUs, despite honourable exceptions led to huge accumulated losses. Above all, the potential patronage perpetuated the difficulty to dismantle them.

As a precursor to the New Economic Policy (NEP) several expert committees were set up in 1980's to review the performance of public sector undertakings. These included those headed by Mohd. Fazal (1980-82), L.K. Jha (1983-84), and Arjun Sengupta (1986) and the reports of the Committee on Public Undertakings of 1981-82 and 1987-88. But only a lip service was extended to implementing the recommendations of these committees. The announcement of the Industrial Policy, 1991 and the subsequent reforms brought about major changes in the policy towards the PSUs.

In order to mobilise funds and to provide wider ownership the disinvestment typically became one of the main-stand of the new policy concerning the public sector. "Controversial from the very beginning, disinvestment was never a strategy of reforms. It was later conceived of as an easy way of raising money to close the government's budget deficits." *(Business Today, 1995)*

The process of disinvestment started in 1991-92 when Rs. 3038 crore was realised against the targeted Rs. 2500 crore from the disinvestment of 20 per cent share holdings. During the years 1992-93 and 1993-94 the target of disinvestment was set up at Rs. 3500 crore each. The modus operandi of disinvestment was altered keeping in view the criticism and experience. This time a reserve price was fixed, not being the average of the net asset value and profit earning capacity value as in 1991-92, by the three merchant bankers. In the first round in October 1992, 5 per cent of the shareholdings of 16 companies accounted for Rs. 1912 crore and by March 1993, 11.4 per cent of shareholding of 31 companies mobilised Rs. 4950 crore. In 1993-94, the policy of disinvestment was revised and restricted to lowering of the minimum bid amount of Rs. 25,000 from Rs. 2 lakhs in 1992-93. The government hoped to raise Rs. 2500 crore (it got only Rs. 2292 crore) from 11 PSUs chosen for this round. These were part of the 31 profitable PSUs selected for disinvestment in 1991. In 1992-93 the government managed to raise a mere Rs. 1913 crore as against the target of Rs. 3500 crore. While no amount was realised as against the target of Rs. 3500 crore in 1993-94, Rs. 4843 crore was secured in 1994-95 against the target of Rs. 4000 crore and Rs. 168 crore has been realised in 1995-96 from disinvestment of PSU shares while the government targetted an amount of 7000 crore (Public Enterprises Survey 1996-97) since the beginning of disinvestment in 1991-92, so far, a total amount of Rs. 10,341.06 crore has been realised by disinvestment in 39 public sector enterprises. The list of PSUs whose shares have been disinvested since 1991-92 is given in the Table 1.

Table 1

PSEs-Wise Percentage, Disinvestment and Present Govt. Shareholding

S. No.	*Name of the PSE*	*As on 31.3.1997* *Percentage Disinvestment*	*As on 31.3.1997* *Percentage Govt. Holding*
1.	Andrew Yule	9.60	62.84**
2.	Bharat Earth Movers Ltd.	39.16*	60.81
3.	Bharat Electronics Ltd.	24.14	75.86
4.	Bharat Heavy Electricals Ltd.	32.28	67.72
5.	Bharat Petroleum Corp. Ltd.	33.80	66.20
6.	Bongaigaon Refineries & Petro Chem. Ltd.	25.54	74.46
7.	CMC Ltd.	16.69	83.31

8.	Cochin Refineries Ltd.	6.12	55.04**
9.	Container Corp. of India Ltd.	23.07	76.93
10.	Dredging Corp. of India Ltd.	1.44	98.56
11.	Engineers India Ltd.	5.98	94.02
12.	Fert. & Chem. (Travancore) Ltd.	1.70	97.38**
13.	Gas Authority of India Ltd.	3.40	96.60
14.	HMT Ltd.	8.44	91.56
15.	Hindustan Cables Ltd.	1.04	98.96
16.	Hindustan Copper Ltd.	1.24	98.76
17.	Hindustan Organic Chemicals Ltd.	41.39*	58.61
18.	Hindustan Petroleum Ltd.	48.94*	51.06
19.	Hindustan Photofilms Mfg. Co. Ltd.	9.87	90.13
20.	Hindustan Zinc Ltd.	24.08	75.92
21.	Indian Oil Corp. Ltd.	8.74	91.14**
22.	Indian Petro Chemicals Corp. Ltd.	40.05	59.95
23.	IRCON International Ltd.	0.27	99.73
24.	Indian Telephone Industries Ltd.	22.98	76.67**
25.	Indian Tourism & Dev. Corp.	10.03	89.97
26.	Kudermukh Iron & Ore Comp. Ltd	1.00	99.00
27.	Madras Refineries Ltd.	16.92	53.80**
28.	Mahanagar Telephone Nigam Ltd.	34.27	65.73
29.	Minerals & Metals Trading Corpn. Ltd.	0.67	99.33
30.	National Aluminium Ltd.	12.85	87.15
31.	National Fertilizers Ltd.	2.35	97.65
32.	National Mineral Dev. Corp. Ltd.	1.62	96.36**
33.	Neyveli Lignite Corp.	6.01	93.99
34.	Oil & Natural Gas Corp.	3.86	96.14
35.	Rashtriya Chemicals & Fert. Ltd.	7.50	92.50
36.	Shipping Corp. Ltd.	19.88	80.12
37.	State Trading Corp.	8.97	91.03

38.	Steel Authority of India Ltd.	14.18*	85.82
39.	Videsh Sanchar Nigam Ltd.	33.04*	66.96

* Including dilution of Govt. Share holding by Public Issue/GDR Issues.

** The balance equity is held by State Govts./other collaborators.

PE Survey 1996-97

The sale of PSU equity can play a strategic role in bringing the fiscal imbalance under control. But revenue from this source cannot be used indefinitely to plug the hole in the budget. This is precisely what the Government is doing : selling small portions of family silver each year without working towards the restoration of the viability of PSUs *(Financial Express, 1994)*. The major challenge for PSUs at present is to improve their profit generating capacities and competitiveness so as to be attractive to the bankers and investors — domestic as well as foreign. The key areas where attention needs to be focused are:

— Improving productivity and efficiency;

— Upgradation of technology, be it in manufacturing or in services;

— Redefining and clearly understanding the market and client needs;

— Improving customer orientation within the organisation; viewing competition as a positive, efficiency-building factor rather than as an irritant;

— Creating the ability to assess and respond speedily to rapidly changing business environment which is increasingly entering a globalised setting; and

— Acquiring, preserving and harnessing human resources appropriate for organisation. *(Basu, 1994)*

Privatisation Options *(Business Today, 1994, p. 82)*

Disinvestment, if assumed a panacea for problems of public sector will lead to same results what nationalisation did when it was thought a panacea in the private sector.

What needs to be done is to conduct a study on a case to case basis in the public sector and identify specific problem areas of each enterprise. More disinvestment is not the only solution for the government and various options could be tried to get better returns.

Instead of disinvestment of the shares of the PSUs, following options could be tried to improve the performance of the PSU's:

Selling PSE equity to a world level competitor. Appropriate where domestic markets cannot absorb large public offerings and where the PSE faces uncertain prospects.	Trade Sale	Air India Indian Airlines Indian Telecom Industries
Where the PSE has good future prospects and excellent financials	Public Floatation	Indian Oil Bharat Petroleum
Where the PSE is making losses because of mismanagement, a turnaround calls for a new management	Management buy-out	Transport Companies Public Works Highways
In services where government wants to retain ownership, the PSE management can be contracted or leased to private companies	Management Contract	BHEL-HMT HMT-Titan IPCL-NOCIL
In case where the PSEs need for new skills and capital is matched by the private sector's wish to enter new markets for expanding their business.	Joint Ventures	

Memorandum of Understanding

Another innovative feature dawned after the initiation of economic reforms is the MOU. Though MOU is not an indigenous method, it can strengthen the public sector's capabilities and compel them to perform better.

In order to improve the performance of the public enterprises, the Government of India has introduced the concept of performance contracts called 'Memorandum of Understanding' (MOU). MOU is an annual document based on a long term corporate plan in which the government (represented by the administrative ministry) and the public enterprises lay down their mutual obligations and responsibilities. The concept of MOU was "derived from the French experiment with the performance contracts, the MOU could never succeed because it is an agreement between two unequals : the public sector manager can be held accountable but not the owner, the government. Even the French have abandoned their performance contract system and have initiated privatisation." *(Business Today, 1995, p. 41)*

Although the protagonists, the French have discarded their experiment with the performance contracts, in India we are ardently holding onto the losing ground. During 1992-93, 98 PSEs signed MOUs as against 71 in the year 1991-92. Based on their audited accounts, performance of 67 PSEs was evaluated, out of which 28 were rated excellent (41.8 per cent), 22 as very good (32.8 per cent), 10 as good and 7 fair. *(Economic Survey, 1993-94, p. 101)* 101 PSEs signed MOUs in 1993-94 as against 98 in the preceding year. Based on their audited accounts, performance of 100 PSEs was evaluated, out of which 46 were rated excellent (46 per cent), 29 as very good (29 per cent), 12 as good and 10 fair. In 1994-95, 106 PSE s have signed MOU s which is five per cent higher than last year. *(Economic Survey, 1994-95, p. 109)*

During 1995-96, 104 public sector enterprises signed MOUs. As per the latest evaluation, out of these, 51 were rated as excellent, 31 as very good and 2 as poor. *(Economic Survey 1995-96, p. 121)* While in 1996-97, 110 PSEs signed MOUs, out of these, 46 have been rated excellent, 27 very good, 19 as good, 11 as fair and 7 as poor (Economic Survey 1996-97, p. 121)

Safety Net — National Renewal Fund (NRF)

The disinvestment policy of the government has raised many eyebrows. The initiatives to remove the road blocks to set in a more free economy involves complex social and labour issues. The criticism of this policy came in from various sections of society: politicians, academicians, bureaucrats and trade unions. The fear of the trade union were not miscalculated. The over-staffing of the public enterprises would be pruned and majority of them would be retrenched or declared surplus. Keeping in view this criticism, Government of India has setup a NRF in February 1992 to deal with sickness in the public and the private sectors, particularly in the former. The objectives of the fund are as follows :

— Provide assistance to firms to cover the costs of re-training and re-employment of employees as a result of modernisation and technological upgradation of the existing capacities and from industrial restructuring.

— Provide funds for compensation to employees affected by restructuring or closures of industrial units, both from the public and the private sectors.

— Provide funds for employment generation schemes in the organised and unorganised sectors in order to create a social safety net for labour. The Department of Industrial Development which administers NRF has now taken up first set of cases relating to the National Textile Corporation (NTC) units; and

— Provision of fund through NRF also exists for cases where workers retire voluntarily or are declared surplus.[19] *(Econimic Survey, 1992-93, p. 102)*

To implement the NRF schemes an authority has been created with a provision of Rs. 700 crore in the 1993-94 budget. An additional amount of Rs. 320 crore was approved for NRF in the supplementary budget in December, 1993. An amount of Rs. 786.24 crores was disbursed from NRF (upto October, 1993) and an estimated number of 60,000 workers had opted for voluntary retirement under this scheme. A major portion of the amount has been utilised in the textile sector. *(Economic Survey 1993-94, p. 100)*

To implement the NRF schemes, an empowered authority has been created. An amount of Rs. 542.29 crore was released from NRF during 1993-94. During 1994-95, Rs. 217 crore, Rs. 252 crore during 1994-95 and 1995-96 were released. An estimated 87,800 workers had opted for voluntary retirement under the scheme. A major portion of the amount has been utilised in the Textiles Sector. *(Economic Survey 1996-97, p. 121)*

"NRF does have a role to play in initiating activities that are not immediately bankable and in providing seed capital for demonstration projects." *(Business Today, 1995, p. 41)* But NRF must not supplement or deviate from its objectives for which it has been created on a sustained basis. Moreover, NRF should not be treated as merely a retirement fund. Keeping in view its highly specialised tasks i.e., of renewal and regeneration of employment it should be managed by a team of professionals and for this a more independent and separate body must be created.

Notwithstanding the benevolence of NRF, it should not be given a status of a sacred cow and treated as a permanent solution as it is not meant to withstand the entire burden of restructuring.

Conclusion

The experience shows that the privatisation programme and its via media have been low on the government agenda. The selective and very cautious moves were aimed at distracting the keen attention of the observers mainly the pressure groups. Thus, we can see that there is no clear cut policy of disinvestment. Whatever disinvestment was made, was not accompanied by the immediate and meaningful changes in the management boards of the enterprises. The disinvestment programme, which was to play the role of "economic powerhouse for the adverse balance of payments" has only resulted in relieving the government from its short term fiscal deficit. Its impact has been limited to the extent to reduce the budgetary dependence of the public enterprises.

Moreover, the critics have labelled the reforms as anti-poor, as no benefits have eventually trickled down, the empiricists have professed to insulate the poor from the adverse effects of the privatisation moves of the government. The present day government is trying to adopt the 'middle path' of reforms where the theory of 'hire and fire' does not become the order of the day and the poor and unemployed will be shielded from the brunt of the structural reforms. In fact, the microscopic evaluation of the so called 'middle path' policies accounts to nothing more than treading down the trodden path for clutching the political power, have drifted the funds from disinvestments and other portfolio investments to the populistic policies, thus, giving a constipated look to the policies of disinvestment.

REFERENCES

1. Basu D., 'PEs and Reforms : Challenges Ahead', *The Economic Times,* March 3, 1994.
2. *Business Today,* December 22, 1994 to January 6, 1995, p. 41.
3. *Business Today,* December 22, 1994 to January 6, 1995, p. 41.
4. *Business Today,* February 22 to March 6, 1994, p. 82.
5. *Economic Survey,* Government of India, 1992-93.
6. *Economic Survey* 1992-93, Ministry of Finance, Government of India, p. 102.
7. *Economic Survey* 1993-94, MInistry of Finance, Government of India, p. 100.

8. *Economic Survey* 1993-94, Ministry of Finance, Government of India, p. 101.
9. *Economic Survey* 1994-95, Ministry of Finance, Government of India, p. 109.
10. *Economic Survey* 1995-96, Ministry of Finance, Government of India, p. 121.
11. *Economic Survey* 1996-97, Ministry of Finance, Government of India, p. 121.
12. *Financial Express*, August 11, 1994.
13. Moore John. 'British Privatisation — Taking Capitalism to the People', *Havard Business Review*. Jan-Feb, 1992, p. 115.
14. Public Enterprise Survey 1996-97, Department of Public Enterprises, Ministry of Industry, p. 203.
15. Schwartz Gred and Paulo Silva Lopes, 'Privatisation : Expectations, Trade-offs and Results'. *Finance and Development*, June, 1993, p.14.
16. Sengupta Arjun, 'Sustainable Economic Reform', *The Indian Economic Journal*, Jan.-March, 1995, p. 15.
17. *Business Today*, December 22, 1994 to January 6, 1995, p. 41.
18. *The Economic Times, Special Issue on Public Sector Companies*, June 23, 1994.
19. Venkata Ratnam C.S., 'Adjustment Through Privatisation : The Indian Agenda' *ASCI Journal of Management*, Vol. 22, No. 4, March 1993, p. 165.

2

New Economic Policies and Reforms in Economic Administration

V.S. Murthy

When the spectre of privatisation haunted the country after the government accepted the conditionalities of IMF(International Monetary Fund) and the World Bank to receive the loans in foreign exchange, students of Public Administration (P.A.) were concerned about the future of P.A. with apprehensions. A reference is necessary to 'Big Democracy' of Paul Appleby where he established that the frontiers of P.A. will expand and extend when the private enterprise prospers, the country undergoes social reconstruction and registers economic development. Therefore, the future of PA is safe and secure. Now it is only for the students of PA to rise to the occasion to convince people of their worth and utility.

After 1980 the country experimented with liberalisation in economic policy and an era of consumerism was inaugurated. The government raised short-term loans in the foreign money markets to defray their expenditure in foreign exchange for Utsavs, foreign jaunts,etc. These loans were due for repayment alongwith interest. The country could not increase exports as targetted and hence no foreign exchange was available for repayment by 1990s. The government faced the prospect of defaulting on this count. At this juncture the government approached IMF and the World Bank for assistance. They imposed their conditions to which the Government of India submitted. This led to privatisation of public sector undertakings and invitation of private capital from the advanced countries.

In order to comply with the conditions of IMF and World Bank, the Government of India liberalised the regulations and controls in existence for economic development. The Americans insist that the bureaucratic machinery and set-up for regulation and control should be dismantled and the Japanese persist that the laws passed by the legislature for regulation and control should be revoked. The reformist lobby is also advocating the adoption of the policy followed by the People's Republic of China— the socialist market economy— which recorded 10-11per cent growth rate. The Communist Party of China has tight control over all activities except economic endeavours, which are free from control and regulation. The Government of India has been promising everything to everybody. They are not using the powers vested in government agencies and institutions in response to the demands of the creditor countries.

New Economic Policy and its Impact on Public Administration

Parkinson's Law

"Work in Bureaucracies expand in proportion to time available for its completion."

When he came forward with his law by 1959, it created a sensation and became quite popular, as it was useful to condemn the creation of new posts.

It is a matter of regret to note that his methodology to declare his findings is not properly scrutinised. He studied the Office of the Admirality in Britain in 1950s. He noted that the number of warships was quite high before 1918 but their number was negligible by 1950s. He said that to his surprise he discovered the number of employees in the Office of the Admirality considerably increased. According to him the employees had no work but created the posts so that they all can ensure promotions for themselves. Thus the interests of the country were subordinated to those of the bureaucracy.

But the significant flaw in his finding is that he did not take into account the total work-load of the Office of the Admirality. After the First World War, the number of warships decreased, as the importance of the Navy declined as an instrument of Defence strategy. Since the role of Air Force became prominent a separate agency was established for the Air Force. After the First World War, the importance of merchant navy increased because of the growth of trade and commerce and London was an important centre for world finance, commerce and trade. Though merchant navy was privately owned, the government assumed supervisory and regulatory powers to protect and promote public interest, with regards to the safety of goods, passengers, standards and quality of work etc. In view of the large number of ships in merchant navy, the work-load for supervision, regulation and control also registered a rise. Hence the number of employees to perform those regulatory functions increased. All these employees were placed under the administrative control of the Office of the Admirality. Parkinson saw only the increase in the number of employees but did not notice the cause of it . He only exposed the fall in the number of warships and enacted his law to make a name.

It may also be stated that Parkinson worked in Malaya. This may be interpreted to mean he could not secure a proper placement in Britain where he was educated. Thus he suffered from home sickness and had a longing for an opportunity to return home. Therefore he developed a cynical approach to men and matters, persons and problems, individuals and issues. His cynicism is also revealed in his law.

Parkinson's law is relevant to our new economic policy and the future of PA in India. When the Government of India announced the policy for privatisation, it spread shockwaves among the present and future government employees as they feared their prospects for employment and promotion would be adversely affected. This reading of the position is not correct. Therefore a detailed analysis of the Parkinson's law proves that the importance of Public Administration is not in any way affected because of the New Economic Policy. It may also be noted that the government will not like to enhance the areas of government ownership and if possible reduce them. But the objectives of State policy as enshrined in the Indian Constitution will oblige the government to oversee the organisation and working of privatisation so that public interest is promoted. Therefore the scope for employment potential in government agencies and institutions will be as good as it has been and with the expansion of privatisation it will also expand. Further the task of government employees will be more responsible than what it has been in the past for they have to supervise the work of the employees of private sector which takes pride in the standards of quality, efficiency of their goods and services.

Economic Reforms at a Glance

A list of policy changes were brought about like de-licensing of all but fifteen industries, introduction of current account convertibility of rupee, devaluing of rupee by 22 per cent, abolition of monopoly laws, dilution of the rigours of foreign exchange control, counter-guarantee given to seven foreign private sector projects which are expected to bring into country Rs.12,000 crores in the next three to four years, NRIs can repartriate part of the profits if they participate in joint ventures for housing or real estate. Amendment to Mineral Regulation and Development Act is made to give effect to March, 1993 policy allowing foreign holding in prospecting and extracting minerals. Public sector giant Hindustan Machine Tools (HMT) is allowed to go in for joint ventures with foreign companies, capital restructuring of Hindustan Antibiotics Corporation is done (both in trouble and ailing), twenty seven land reform laws passed by state legislatures put in the IXth Schedule of the Constitution taking them out of judicial purview, amending Trade Union Act of 1926 to put an end to multiplicity of Unions and seeking to bring discipline among Trade Unions, Repeal of Air Corporation Act allowing IA and AI to become limited companies and ending their monopoly of the skies, amending the Banking Regulation Act to let banks employ non-executive Chairmen, Macro-economic stabilisation (except for fiscal deficit), partial reform of tariff system, partial shift to VAT (Value Added Tax) regime, partial reform of direct tax system, incentives for foreign direct investment, allowing foreign participation in capital markets; these were some major policy changes done.

Economic Reforms: Yet to be Done

Full convertibility including capital account, completion of tariff system and direct tax reforms, complete shift to VAT system, implementation of Narasimham Committee Report on financial sector reforms, implementation of Malhotra Committee Report on insurance industry reforms, strengthening the legal system to enforce Intellectual Property Rights, substitution of FERA with a simpler, more liberal law reflecting convertibility and greater integration with world economy, announcement and implementation of clear policy on privatisation, announcement and implementation of clear policy to downsize government; these policy pronouncements are yet to see the light of the day.

Impact of Economic Reforms: Foreign Trade and Investments

1. Exports increase, encouraged by 'liberal trade and tax policy'
2. Imports grow as industry expands.
3. Trade deficit narrows but depends on rate of import growth.
4. Rupee remains strong in Rs. 38-39 range.
5. Foreign exchange reserves continue to grow.
6. Foreign direct investment flow increases.
7. FII participation increases.

Industry

1. Delicensing makes expansion / new projects easier.
2. Term loans cheaper by one per cent.
3. Import of latest equipment easier and cheaper.
4. Excise duty formalities simpler.
5. Shift to MODVAT and VAT speeded up; eliminates cascading of duty.
6. Foreign tie-ups easier.
7. Corporate tax reduced, more incentives to expand, restructure and modernise.
8. Even greater incentives to launch new projects and businesses.

Forecast : Overall industrial output expands by 4 to 6 per cent in 1994-95.

Common Person

1. Short term tension from slight price increase but relief over medium term.
2. Increase in disposable income resulting from tax reliefs.
3. Greater choice of better products and services.
4. Shift from job security to better productivity on the job.
5. Easier availability of goods and services.
6. Better career prospects.
7. Easier availability of loans especially housing loans.
8. More avenues for investment and capital gains especially in the stock market.

9. Easier foreign travel, education and trade.

Prices

1. Large fiscal deficit puts upward pressure.
2. Lower import duties reduce pressure.
3. Lower excise duties reduce pressure.
4. Good harvest and large buffer stock reduces pressure.

Forecast : Price rise around 9 to 11 per cent (Source:The Weak, published from Kochi, Kerala) (March-April,1994).

India on the Eve of Economic Reforms

The atmosphere was surcharged with tension and uncertainty, with vehement criticism of the reforms programme, and cries of sell-out of the country's sovereignity to multinationals and financial institutions. It was alleged that India's budget was dictated by the IMFor the budget had the prior approval of the IMF etc.

In any case the situation was such that India had hardly any option of the matter when the country was on the verge of collapse. The last straw came in the form of a possibility that repayment of instalments be defaulted—a more-than-life-time sin in world affairs. The country was compelled to mortgage gold to avert the crisis.

Philosophy of Economic Reforms

During his Guildhall speech in London, the Prime Minister, P.V. Narasimha Rao in March, 1994 revealed his ideas on Indian Economic Reforms which were initiated by him in 1991.

"Our problems are very simple—food, clothing and shelter. But it is the magnitude, not the complexity, that is so forbidding—we are speaking of 900 million people." He views India's economic reforms as a pyramid. "Little by little, the pyramid goes up. We do not want to distinguish between the top, middle and bottom. It is the Government alone that can take care of the bottom, no multinational is going to do that— I am convinced of that no industry is going to come and open up primary health centres — I am sure of that."

"I look after the base, they (the industries) look after the top. This is the pattern we have accepted and I am sure it is going to work because no one is going to be hurt by this." *(Indian Express, 1994).*

"The Guild Hall speech certainly appears to have contributed to a more robust understanding of the aims of India's economic reforms. It is probably the first time, the Prime Minister publicly made a distinction between the values of the marketplace and the "social good". Contrary to the impression Manmohan Singh and, more so, the reformist lobby have created, Rao does not see the market as an end in itself but as the best available instrument for the efficient allocation of resources. But market forces are inefficient in that they do not recognise need unless there is purchasing power to back it; the Government must therefore act at the base of Rao's "pyramid" to ensure that the essential needs of food, housing, primary health centres, etc. are met. There should be no quarrel at home with such an exposition of the 'middle way' and the role of the Government in the economy. It is a pity though that Rao has not found the occasion yet to explain his ideas to domestic audiences who, weary as they are of all kinds of ideology, should be more than ready to embrace common sense. The country also waits to hear more about the Government's role higher up the socio-economic pyramid." *(Indian Express, 1994).*

Public Sector—Disinvestment—Privatisation

The Member-Secretary of the Planning Commission favoured handing over of even some of the core public enterprises to private sector as a part of radical economic reforms. He called for privatisation of all non-core public enterprises to herald a new phase of social justice based on efficiency.

Since mere disinvestment did not amount to privatisation, public enterprises should be handed over to private sector, as there was no rationale behind continued government control, ownership and management of public enterprises.

Though the VOODOO economics peddled by Reagon and Thatcher, was discredited in both the U.S.A. and the U.K., it is sad that the Government of India still reposes faith in tax cuts and reduced public investment.

All over the world, it is now recognised that private investment does not always respond to tax cuts and that instead of replacing public investment, it tends to fall when the latter is cut. For this reason there is a need to increase public investment in infrastructure and higher direct taxes to reduce the revenue deficit.

The first round of disinvestment in public sector created its own scandal, where allegations were made of favouritism and corruption while the sale prices of shares of public sector units were fixed.

GATT - W.T.O.

On April 15,1994, Pranab Mukherjee signed the Uruguay Round Agreements at Marrakesh commiting India to a series of multilateral obligations and activities. A section of the public and Parliament, it seems, have doubts over India being a party to these accords. It is to be conceded that the Uruguay Round Agreements are not entirely fair or just. They do not meet a number of our aspirations and concerns. Though we have joined in this international economic process, we must remain aware of the suspect politico-economic and strategic motivations which animate the great powers to put such arrangements in place.

The more powerful industrially and the technologically advanced countries have the objectives of: (a) ensuring their domestic economic well-being safe from pressures of recession and inflation, (b) aspiring to free market and investment access globally while being protectionist about their own markets to the extent possible, (c) remaining interested in maximising their control over raw materials and natural resources, as well as the world's main trade routes, (d) desiring, to the extent possible, exclusive control on advanced technologies and scientific information, (e) since direct politico-military means cannot be used (normally) to meet these objectives, the tactical use of environmental, ecological, socio-political and intellectual property rights arguments.

Signing the Uruguay round agreements does not involve signing away our right and capacity to chart our future course of action keeping in mind the above constants in the policies of the more important economic powers. The current public and parliamentary debate on the "Dunkel Agreements" serves the purpose of keeping India alert about future choices and challenges. *(Dixit, 1994)*

Level Playing Field

Indian industrialists asked for equality of treatment for foreign and Indian managements as regards taxes etc. The Indian industrialists complained to the then Finance Minister (Dr. M. Singh) that favours were then offered to foreigners and the Indians were denied the same. Hence free competition and private enterprise in

India will be to the advantage of foreign investors. The Finance Minister pontificated that in real life there is nothing like level playing field as every country is in the process of globalisation.

The developed countries registered an increase in their GNP consequent to protectionist policies. They progressed behind protectionist walls and became economically stronger. But the developing countries are denied the infant industry benefits. After GATT agreement was signed, the advanced countries raised the issues of social justice and environmental protection so that the advantage of low labour cost is not available to Indian exports.

Exit Policy

The fact that economic reforms will make the existing work-force surplus has been conceded by all the reformers. But none of the advocates for the economic reforms has any action plan to rehabilitate the surplus workers. The IMF-World Bank made provision for a safet ynet for them so that they can be absorbed by the industry after they are given training to improve their skills.

The private sector has been asking for powers to hire and fire their employees and the government has been promising that the Industrial Disputes Act will be amended accordingly. But the Trade Unions have been opposing the dilution of the provisions of the Industrial Disputes Act. Protests are already made by the Trade Unions against the impending unemployment.

Social unrest is apprehended and the government has no programmes at present to face it. The spokespersons for the government only declare that there will be no retrenchment because of economic reforms.

New Trends in Trade Unionism

The new economic policy introduced a new culture in the Trade Union Movement. The Trade Unions, in the sick industries which are closed, for whatever reason, are breaking away from the established Central Trade Union Organisations like INTUC, AITUC etc. They are forming their own adhoc organisations to arrive at an understanding with the employers who opened the workshops with new agreements with their workers, who are not affiliated to any Central Trade Union Organisation. This took place in Bombay and also in Calcutta where the Leftist government was a helpless spectator to the new trend in trade unionism, which is not to the liking of the State Government.

This development has a great potential for the future growth of economic progress in the country. Till now Trade Unions are front organisations for political parties, who have their own Trade Union Organisations. If the Trade Unions are free from outside leadership, it can promote the professional trade union movement in India and this may have its impact on the political parties bidding for power at General Elections.

Foreign Institutional Investors (FIIs)

Government permitted them to enter Indian money market. Hence the prices of Blue Chip shares registered a rise as floating funds are available. This is not money which moves wherever returns are high. It is said that the rate of interest is only 4 per cent in advanced countries but is 13 per cent in India. This alone attracts foreign funds, whose stay in India is unpredictable.

Because of the influx of these foreign funds, the foreign exchange position is stated to be comfortable. At the same time the rupee value has appreciated which is causing anxiety on the export front which is already not very promising.

If the FIIs decide to shift their funds from India suddenly, it will lead to economic destabilisation. Since the government gave up their powers to control and regulate the money market, they will be helpless spectators to the free play of economic forces who have no soft corner for India.

Development Bureaucracy in an Era of Decontrol and Deregulation

A serious pitfall of India's emerging liberalised economic regime is that precious little has been done to make the bureaucracy shed its dilatoriness and obstructionism. While former Finance Minister Manmohan Singh waxed eloquently on the challenge before the private sector in combating foreign competition by improving quality and price competitiveness, the bureaucracy continued to function under very weak accountability. The hangover of the "licence-permit raj" under which the bureaucrat wielded extraordinary clout, is still very strong with most civil servants unreconciled to the dilution of their power, they used to enjoy. The government is yet to shake off the inertia in the system and to deter those who are unresponsive to change. In a study by S.R. Maheshwari published in the recent past, it was suggested that an enterpreneur still faced as many as 18 agencies of clearance and 51 inspectors from as many statutes relating to industrial laws.

Overstaffing and lack of work culture continue to be the bane of our bureaucracy. A Finance Ministry study pointed out last year that about a fifth of the Government's 10.2 million employees were surplus. With increased privatisation one expected some ministeries to shed their flab. Yet, there is not even a token effort to reduce numbers or to put the surplus manpower to some better use. An *India Today* study revealed that 53,000 new posts had been added to the already bloated bureaucracy since the inception of reforms.

While relieving surplus staff on a big scale would increase unemployment and cause social tension to aggravate, there is scope for redeploying government staff as part of the decentralisation process and the recent Panchayati Raj amendments to the Constitution. A seminar on the Panchayati Raj Act at the Centre for Development Studies in Thiruvananthapuram in Kerala suggested that departments like agriculture, animal husbandry, irrigation, public works, rural development, social welfare, cooperation, education and health could be broken up in such a way that a director was stationed at the district level with a supporting staff. This sounds worthwhile.

The crucial element in any decentralisation would be to identify the functions, responsibilities and powers a state government decides to devolve on the local bodies and what financial resources are placed at their disposal. The present vertical hierarchy in the bureaucracy is ill— suited to devolution. Consequently, a restructuring of the bureaucracy would be an essential part of any process of decentralisation.

There would inevitably be some resistance from the bureaucracy to any attempt at restructuring. But the government cannot evade its own responsibility much longer while expecting heroics from other sectors. A greater degree of accountability, redeployment of staff and pruning of non-developmental wasteful expenditure are imperatives that cannot be ignored. *(Kanwar, 1994)*

The American, The Japanese and The Chinese Approaches to Economic Reforms

Since India declared her free objectives to move towards privatisation and globalisation, three schools of thought have been proposed. The Americans ask for debureaucratisation, the Japanese for their townships where they enjoy diplomatic immunities and the Chinese for free enterprise and open competition in economy but tight grip over all non-economic activities of the people. The policy advisers have been opting for one of these three alternatives. It is a regret that no Indian indigenous approach for our economic development and social reconstruction is advocated by Indian Think Tanks.

Galbraith 1960s and 1990s

After Avadi Congress, the socialist pattern of society was accepted by India. The government decided to control the commanding heights of the economy through public sector undertakings. The average Congressman and as a matter of fact all politicians could not understand and much less appreciate the socialist pattern advocated by Nehru.

Prof. Galbraith from Harvard University was invited to deliver a lecture to the Members of both the Houses of Parliament in the Central Hall of the Parliament House, on the subject. He was fresh from the limelight focused on him for his work on the Affluent Society where he pleaded for government intervention and public spending to maintain employment and to provide social justice to the unprivileged and underprivileged sections of society in the U.S.A.

Because of Galbraith's reputation as an academic who argued for public sector expansion, he was also requested to advise the Government of India on the management of our public sector undertakings. He gave a report to the Government of India and found fault with the top level administrators, both political and professional, as they had no intention or inclination to delegate authority to functionaries on the spot in the field or factory. He cited the case where an engineer who in those days was paid Rs.30 per day and a truck costing Rs.50,000 were both idle as the engineer had no powers to spend more than Rs. 300 to purchase the spareparts for the truck. He was awaiting for financial sanction from the Finance Department to incur an expenditure of Rs.1000 to see that the truck could move and he could perform his work.

Because of the plain speaking, Galbraith's report on Public Sector Undertakings was not given the publicity which Appleby's reports received.

In 1992, Prof. Galbraith was invited by Rajiv Gandhi Foundation to deliver a lecture under its auspices. He advanced three ideas. For economic progress he said political stability, price stability and agricultural development are essential prerequisites. He dealt with the bad conditions prevailing in South American and African countries. He complimented on the achievements made by India till now but warned that India cannot afford to be complacent. He felt India can join the developed world provided she manages her affairs properly. The important point to be noted is that Prof. Galbraith advocated a trusteeship management for countries in Africa as they could not administer their countries. The standards of administration are so low and bad that these countries cannot repay the loans given by the IMF, World Bank and other agencies. Hence the UN should take over the administration of these countries till their conditions are improved. When the USA is the only super power after 1991, the UN will depend on her for its own existence. It is evident from the resolutions passed by the UN through the Security Council as regards Iraq, Kuwait, Yugoslavia etc.

During the British regime we had the Managing Agency System to operate industries in the private sector in India. How can this be different from it? We are now faced with the prospect of UNO Trusteeship Management of our country till we repay our huge loans to IMF, World Bank and other financial institutions in the USA and the developed countries.

When the British told us that they would leave India, the moment Indians could prove their abilities to rule themselves, we became angry. We took it as an insult, acquired the required skills and talents to prove that we were no worse than the British. During the Gandhi—Irwin talks, they both agreed on the contents of the pact. They both sat down to reduce their talks to writing. In one particular point, Lord Irwin suggested a number of words to convey the idea of their agreement. Gandhi was not satisfied with the wording. When Irwin was tired of drafting, he gave the paper to Gandhi to do the job. Gandhi rewrote the complete sentence and showed it to Irwin, who expressed his surprise to say that it was better than all his drafts. He also complimented Gandhi for the draftsmanship.

As a contrast Lord Wavel can be cited. When he had negotiations with Congress leaders, they agreed on certain points. The Congress leaders went back from the Viceregal Palace to their places where they stayed, and reduced to writing the gist of their talks with Wavel. To be fair they sent a copy to Wavel who complained that what they wrote was not what they agreed to and they were talking and writing like lawyers. Nehru wrote back to tell him that it was true they were all lawyers but they were taught law by the Britishers only. Hence Wavel could not object to what they wrote in the language of the British. The purpose of refering this is to convey as to how fragile freedom is. Our freedom is in danger. We have to remember that the East India Company also was given the right to collect revenue by the Moghul emperor as he could not manage his economic affairs.

It may be stated that India is going Iran's way. The Anglo-Iranian oil company was controlling the economics and politics of Iran till the time the Second World War was over. Dr. Mossadiq nationalised the oil company and this naturally was opposed by the British Government. Because of the social and cultural problems in Iran, the socialist experiment through nationalisation of the oil company failed. The King of Iran returned to his throne after the pre-nationalisation party was removed from power. Meanwhile the fundamentalists were marking their time. They managed to build up sufficient disaffection between the king and the people. They demanded democracy and a bigger and greater say in the affairs of the State. All the efforts made by the King, with advice and guidance from American experts and specialists, to improve social and economic conditions of the people through provision of social services measures like education, health etc. could not succeed to turn the tide in his favour. Ultimately Ayatollah Khomaini staged a come back and established a theocratic State.

The policies and programmes advocated by Nehru were not commended by the Rightists in the Congress Party and these people claimed the patronage of Sardar Patel. After the demise of Patel, Nehru became the supreme leader whose word was the law both in the Government and the Party. Nehru continued to pursue his path of socialism.

Shyama Prasad Mukherjee did not agree with the policies of Nehru and resigned from Nehru's Cabinet. He later formed the Jan Sangh, a Rightist Party by 1952. Jan Sangh maintained its identity till the Janata Party was formed in 1977. After the collapse of the Janata Party government, the Bharatiya Janata Party came into existence.

A perceptible decline in the economic conditions of the people was evident by 1980 because of the populist programmes executed by the government. Hence the people were disenchanted with the socialist policies of the Government as the 'Garibi Hatao' programme was not successful anywhere.

By 1990s, the BJP sidelined the liberals in the party and religion overtook politics. As the living conditions of people became deplorable and intolerable they turned to religion and God for relief and solace. Failure of economic policy is mainly responsible for these developments in the country.

Conclusion: The Need for an Indigenous Solution

India has its own culture and civilisation. In her own special way she found solutions to her problems in the past. During the British regime, the national spirit and enthusiasm prompted the thinkers encouraged by Mahatma Gandhi to search for indigenous solutions to Indian problems in all walks of life.

After the country became free, industrialisation for all practical purposes was construed to be a synonym for westernisation, though the policy-makers underlined the need for labour-intensive techniques of production to provide employment to the teeming millions and to overcome the paucity of capital goods. The constructive programme of Mahatma Gandhi, the work of National Planning Committee under the Chairmanship of Nehru during 1937-39 and the efforts of those who discovered the new methods of production to suit Indian ethos, were of no avail, when the national government after 1947 began to look for the turn-key projects from the developed countries of the West.

The policies of the Government of India were influenced by the techniques adopted in the West, where every country did her best to create a favourable balance of trade. If every nation does everything to increase exports, who is going to absorb these imports? This leads to hegemony and other forms of imperialism and colonialism in sophisticated forms and shapes. The concept of balance of power and spheres of influence are rejected by the Government of our country. The first Prime Minister of India brought the areas of cooperation to the notice of the powers in this world of conflict and tension. The third Prime Minister of India gave the world a concept of 'Vasudhaika Kutumbam' (the world is a family). In spite of our attempts to think of problems of all people, all over the universe, we have not been able to formulate concrete policies for economic development and social re-construction.

After India attained independence, the USA and other advanced countries came forward to aid and assist our programmes for economic progress. Therefore, science and technology in India have been modulated to conform to the conditions in the USA and other Western democracies. Until Stalin passed away, India was not recognised as a free nation. It was only after Khruschev came to power that India began to enlist support from the USSR. Because of international factors and other causes, India was able to enter into a Peace Treaty with the USSR and to this extent, the relations between India and the U.S.A. had deteriorated. After the collapse of the Soviet Union, which under wrote some of our development programmes, it became necessary to evolve a new economic policy.

The role of village and small scale industries is to be appreciated in the context of full employment, social justice, decentralisation of economic power and the government is aware of their potential for the future of the country. After P.N. Haksar assumed office as the Deputy Chairman of the Planning Commission, he spoke of indigenous technology. In 1946 the then Madras Government took up the Firka Development Scheme inspired by the work of Mahatma Gandhi (and this was later merged) with the Community Development Programme) and did not permit the sale of mill-made cloth in the province. But the premier of Madras was removed from office using the influence of textile-mill owners and their friends in the Congress Party in power.

Unless a bold policy decision is made, we will have in the market, goods in abundance but out of the reach of the common man. On the other hand the essentials for life will be scarce as the profit margin is not attractive in these lines of products. The export drive will deprive the nation of the opportunity to consume goods produced in our own country. The position may be grave in some cases and the government will be forced to ban exports of certain goods and commodities. This happened in the case of onions in seventies in Maharashtra as well as recently in the country.

The present crisis in our economy is to be utilised to re-orient our policies in all fields of activity so that indigenous solutions can be found for our problems. As an illustration it may be stated that the Gobar gas plant was advocated since 1930s by Gandhiji but it is only after the energy crisis, created by the oil politics, that this is taken up by our scientists, technologists and Government in India.

REFERENCES

1. Dixit J.N., *Indian Express,* Hyderabad 26th April, 1994.
2. *Indian Express,* Hyderabad, 16th March, 1994.
3. *Indian Express*— Editorial, Hyderabad 17th March, 1994.
4. Kanwar Kamlendra, *Indian Express,* Hyderabad 4th May, 1994.

3

Administrative Reforms in the Context of New Economic Policy

C.V. Raghavulu

The new economic policy, as reflected in structural adjustment, implies a reappraisal of the relative roles of the State and the market. This has the obvious implications for the governmental systems and administrative procedures, not to speak of the attitudes of the bureaucracy. Unfortunately, these are a few of the most enduring and hard-to-change elements of our system. In the success stories of both Japan and South Korea, State intervention or regulatory measures were used to promote enterprise. However, governmental controls were not based on the belief, as has been the case in India, that anyone with a profit-making proposition needs to be controlled. In the wake of liberalisation and privatisation, such belief systems, the command-centred structures and regulatory mechanisms are surely counter-productive. The top-down approach of the generalist bureaucracy tends to be equally outmoded in the context of an overt dilution of the doctrine of infallibility of State controlled economic activity. The orientation should be one of direction rather than control. It should also be noted that indecisiveness and sluggish implementation by the bureaucracy highlight the greatest dangers of the economy falling apart. This study is addressed to the need for a conscious effort to take stock of concomitant reforms in the policy apparatus and the public administrative systems.

Policy, Bureaucray and Concomitant Reforms

Nations have followed different models of structural adjustment. Each model of adjustment implies different political and administrative strategies for industrial promotion. They also imply different political vulnerabilities as they raise questions about the distribution of costs and benefits among different social groups and political constituencies. The multitude of macro and micro adaptations often put the capacity of a government to severe test when it attempts to promote the process of adjustment. In the East Asian cases one finds stable macro-economic policies, strong government intervention to promote competitiveness and a high degree of consensus among the stakeholders—government, industry and labour. Also strengthening their cause are political health standards and supportive legal and administrative framework. In Japan and France, while trade, agriculture and industry got protection, labour was squeezed. In South Korea and Taiwan, labour had to give in because of its weak bargaining position. In Germany, the distributional questions were resolved by bargain and mutual accommodation rather than marketplace conflict.

In the Indian context, structural adjustment was adopted, as noted earlier, in a "crisis" context. In the middle of 1991 when the Union Ministries of Finance, Commerce and Industry, launched a programme of structural adjustment the programme was essentially 'crisis-driven' and 'Finance Ministry-driven'.

The process is no longer crisis-driven. Precisely because it was crisis-driven in 1991, and because the agenda was narrower and focussed on areas where the domestic consensus was wider, the support base for structural adjustment was fairly wide both within the Union Government and within the ranks of the opposition political parties. Now, precisely because it is no longer crisis-driven and many crucial elements of the 'next stage' of economic reforms have as yet failed to acquire wider support within the government, it remains even more Finance Ministry-driven. A number of expert committees, notably the Narasimham Committees on Banking Reforms, the Raja Chellaiah Committee on Tax Reforms, the Rangarajan Committee on Foreign Investment and the Goswami Committee on Industrial Sickness and Corporate Restructuring, have been appointed to study and make recommendations on various policy measures associated with structural adjustment. Besides the World Bank, the IMF, the Asian Development Bank, foreign institutional investors, potential foreign investors including a many non-resident Indians, domestic business groups, etc., were involved in dialogues and continuous interaction with Government functionaries in shaping public policy. Although the Planning Commission and the Ministries of Industry and Commerce played a prominent role in policy outcomes, the main mission rested all through with the Ministry of Finance. The confidence reposed by the then Prime Minister, in Dr. Manmohan Singh, the Finance Minister in his cabinet, has been a significant element in the political and administrative process associated with the shaping of India's economic policy. The Labour Ministry is credited to have been acting as a pressure front for the trade unions and espousing the cause of labour. Similar inferences were drawn about other Ministries and Departments as they seem to display sub-unit identifications and are averse to attempts at reforming the regulatory mechanisms under their control. As such, policy making tends to be highly fragmented in the absence of a concerted and coherent approach.

Potential foreign investors have a plethora of complaints, about the inadequacies of the legal framework in particular. The Japanese insistence on statutory sanction to ensure greater certainty and policy stability for potential investors deserves appreciation. They are unsure of the current exemptions being granted by the Government by way of administrative decisions as these could be reversed. While investors appreciate the country's impeccable record of automatically permitting repatriation of dividends once the conditions are satisfied, they have a feeling of discomfort because this is in the nature of relaxation of a regulation rather than right available to them under law. A point thrown up by the Rangarajan report relates to the fear foreign investors have over nationalisation. The Committee is of the view that while it is generally appreciated that India does not indulge in nationalisation unless it is in public interest and that too with adequate compensation, a formal incorporation of that provision into a law or treaty would provide the necessary assurances to shareholders of the investing companies. A National Investment law is a must in the opinion of the Rangarajan Committee to get the foreigners interested in India. This law should codify the existing policy and practices relating to dividend repatriation, disinvestment, non-discrimination subject to conditions that may be specified, employment of foreign nationals, non-expropriation and sanction and servicing of external commercial borrowings. Such a law could also provide for enabling policy procedures and institutional framework for approval of investments under non-automatic route, according pioneer status or domestic investor status, new instruments of private commercial inflows and applicability of local or international laws, etc.

Foreign investors also raise doubts over the complex reporting needs and long-winding procedures which upset them because they are governed by exemption from regulations. To ensure political and administrative sanctity for effective implementation, the assessment of a number of dimensions is considered necessary. They include :

(a) The formulation of clear rules/regulations well in advance;

(b) Efficient and expeditious application and enforcement of the rules;

(c) Creation of institutional mechanisms in the application of rules;

(d) Provision of machinery for the rapid resolution of conflicts, preferably through prompt judicial decisions; and

(e) Procedures for amending the rules when they become irrelevant.

True that deregulation and liberalisation have to an extent reduced the need for enterpreneurs to depend on clearances and approvals in some areas. But there are powerful stumbling blocks. Thinning the jungle of regulations is not all that simple. In a study conducted for the Federation of Indian Chamber of Commerce and Industries, Dr. Amit Mitra has calculated that after an investor has his sanction in principle, he must comply with 51 industrial statutes, covering 2,030 pages, maintain 16 separate registers, pay fourteen separate fees, and fill 160 forms. In his operations, he has to comply with 67 provisions of the Monopolies and Restrictive Trade Practices Act, 298 provisions of the direct taxation laws, 81 provisions of the Foreign Exchange Regulation Act and 385 rules of the Central Excise Collectors. All this is supervised by 51 inspectors and all of them have power to stop production. However, the proposed changes in the company law will reduce the number of forms to be filled by companies from 86 to 2.

Over the years, the regime of controls was nurtured on mistrust and suspicion of viewing everyone who has a money making proposition. The bureaucracy at the Union and state levels was delighted in putting spokes and framing rules that were designed to cause interminable delays. There was also 'speed money' in it, for those in the lower rungs of the bureaucratic ladder. As a result, vested interests have grown up around controls. Moreover, little has changed in the procedures and behaviour of the bureaucracy, especially at the state and local levels where investors must still depend on bureaucrats for certain facilities and services like land, power, water, etc. The implications of the reforms for the structures, procedures and decision-making processes in relation to the tasks of different agencies operating at different levels have not been analysed in a systematic manner to rationalise the procedures and operations. There is still little realisation that the challenge of structural adjustment would affect the entire gamut of Government. As one management analyst notes :

> "...When there is inertia in the system, streamlining of the public agencies and their rules and reorientation of the bureaucracy will take place only when it is undertaken as a serious exercise. Reforms of this type are more complex and qualitatively different from the macro-economic reforms the country has just gone through. The East Asian Tigers have somehow been able to achieve this transition. Their public agencies seem to be able to adapt and respond to the change effectively, thus reducing the transaction costs of enterpreneurs. This is in sharp contrast with what one observes in many public agencies in India. To aspire to be a tiger and yet ignore this aspect of reform is certainly inconsistent" (Samuel Paul, *The Economic Times,* Nov. 2, 1992).

At a Round Table on Foreign Institutional Investors (FIIs), sponsored by the *London Economist* and the Government of India, the foreign investors expressed concern that the changes have not trickled down to the levels that matter. Red tapism and bureaucracy, or rather the hassles associated in dealing with them, are cited by most participants as the single most important factor that stops them from taking the plunge into the Indian markets. Similar views were expressed by Indian observers of the scene. Abid Hussain, who worked as a member of the Indian Administrative Service, Indian Ambassador to USA and a member of the Indian Planning Commission, was more forthright in his comments :

> "... The present administrative system... was incapable of delivering the goods. Even today, the system is oriented towards direct government intervention in all spheres and

that proposals for a study of the changes required met with resistance" (Hussain, *The Indian Express*, Vijayawada, Aug. 22, 1993).

In a sense, the emphasis has to shift toward reforming the non-market institutional structures. The policy regime in the present context has to achieve synergy between the government and the enterprise. It has perforce to be an entrepreneurial government in which government intervenes actively to promote investment and the growth of enterprise to usher in an internationally competitive set of industries. But the existing apparatus limits the effectiveness of policies. There has also been a growing reluctance to accept two attributes of India's generalist civil service : neutrality and competence. Declining faith on both these dimensions has undermined the legitimacy of the higher echelons of the bureaucracy in regard to economic policy making. Firstly, there is a declining expectation of objective analytical inputs for decision making and increasing expectation of anticipatory compliance to the wishes of the politicians and rationalisation of their decisions. Neutral competence, the stock-in-trade of the higher generalist civil service, has been increasingly questioned on empirical grounds as well. Secondly, the details of economic administration are so complex that a generalist background is considered inadequate to supply the requisite policy inputs. Moreover, expertise in economic issues is now commonly seen as flourishing abundantly outside the confines of the tenured civil service. Policy expertise, it appears, has been "privatized". The bottomline here is that the Indian bureaucracy has its own organisational characteristics, procedural and 'craft' patterns which sharply delineate it from its counterparts in the West or East Asia. One is left with the realisation that other national bureaucracies though with very similar organisations and identical task structures, would often act altogether differently and with more "maximising" outcomes. In India, bureaucratic reform involves a fundamental qualitative change, a non-economic transition far more significant than the macro-economic reforms the country has been going through. Ministerial and bureaucratic interests are believed to be averse to what they perceive as a threat to their power. The control mania of the masters constitutes a key impediment. In this respect, the political universe itself needs considerable self-restraint.

Economic development is a complicated phenomenon and not amenable to simple and clear cut formulae. It needs a supportive environment, with the interweaving of sophisticated technology, skill diffusion, social ethics and values and a State structure with specific forms of mediation in the direction of capital-labour relationship. The increasing globalisation of the market place will be forcing the government as well as individual enterprises to pay more attention to international developments and to adjust their structure and methods of operations to a broader and more rapidly shifting economic environment. In a world in which efficiency is measured in terms of productivity, capacity for innovation and technology absorption take precedence. The accent is also on meeting the administrative challenges by integration of specialists and coordination of interdependent decisions. To cope with the challenges of uncertainty of the environment and competitiveness, the quality of management has to undergo a major change with an entrepreneurial drive. The quality of products and services matters most. It appears as though the managerial challenges to new economic reforms are not fully grasped. These challenges pertain to the government as well as the private sector. To reiterate the point made earlier, the standard set of administrative arrangements presently in vogue are not adequate to meet the challenges of structural adjustment. The reforms have altered the context and the quality of relations between the Government, private industry and labour. Considering the tardy implementation of liberalisation and privatisation it is suggested that greater focus be laid on policy management (Khandwalla, 1992). Some critical requirements of policy management are effective information systems, highly responsive organisation structures, a culture of innovation rather than of bureaucratic rigidity, appropriate networking of governmental organisations with non-governmental enterprises and institutions to attain policy objectives. There is an immediate need to evolve an information system for the Union Cabinet with regard to the progress of implementation of the new economic reforms. The information charts should provide aggregate figures as well as figures disaggregated by sectors, major industries, product groups, trade regions, etc. along with figures for other leading Third World nations. The information system should be able to pinpoint the results of specific measures such as relaxation of controls, reduction of import duties and excise levies, abolition of export curbs or other deregulatory aspects.

The present system also suffers from the handicap of sequential, multilayered scrutiny and excessive preoccupation with copious noting, resulting in endless delays in clearing files. The system needs to be changed to delivering files straight to the officer concerned, who in turn, can seek advice only where it is needed. This will have the indirect effect of flattening the hierarchy or creating an officer-oriented administrative system.

Another aspect of the reforms consists of setting up of autonomous responsibility centres or agencies in the place of departments with their unwieldy hierarchies. Such centres would be manned by professionals, drawn on a contract basis, from industry or other non-governmental organisations, instead of by career civil servants. When technology and economics are outpacing traditional ways of thinking in a competitive world the decision-making structures which are reminiscent of the pre-industrial era, need alteration. Setting up of product-based industry groups with enterprise chiefs and professionals from the concerned fields is yet another step. In many areas of decision making relevant to promotion of economic growth, governments at all levels must shed their powers.

This discussion has drawn attention to the fact of many loose ends in the policy framing, largely due to the habit of fragmented response patterns from each of the Economic Ministries. It also notes that archaic bureaucratic systems constitute a major impediment to the implementation of economic reforms. A century ago, the word bureaucracy meant something positive, a rational and efficient method of organisation, as opposed to the arbitrary exercise of power by the authoritarian regimes. Hierarchy and functional specialisation made possible the efficient undertaking of large, complex tasks. Today's economic environment demands public systems that are extremely flexible and adaptable so that they respond to an enterpreneurial culture, rendering non-standardized services, in a competitive setting. When the preference is for market mechanisms, the bureaucracy has to catalyze all sectors. Unfortunately, old habits die hard. The bureaucracies at various levels seem to be preoccupied with the trivia of the old culture which permits every petty official to have the power of life and death over the investor. Structural adjustment has not only altered the technical relations between private industry and the State, but it has also profoundly altered the administrative context.

In order to demonstrate full faith in the doctrine of liberalisation, rational and comprehensive changes in administration are imperative. A basic requirement in the context of the economic reforms is the dismantling of the regulatory structure. Besides, it is also necessary to shake off the sloth of public administrators to provide a vigorous response to the challenges posed by the economic reforms.

REFERENCES

1. Esman, Milton, J., 'The Maturing of Development Administration', *Public Administration and Development*, 8, 1988: 125-34.
2. Khandwalla, Pradip, 'Management Imperatives for Liberalisation', *The Economic Times*, April 23, 1992.
3. Paul, Samuel, 'Privatisation : A Review of International Experience , *Economic and Political Weekly*, 23, 1988: 273-76.
4. Rose, Richard, 'Toward a Civil Economy', *Journal of Democracy*, 3, 1992: 16-18.

4

Public Enterprises in India Under the Stabilisation and Structural Adjustment Programme

R.K. Mishra

In this paper we discuss the background of the Stabilisation and Structural Adjustment Programme (S&SAP), the need for launching the S&SAP as a corrective measure to revitalise the Indian economy and the impact of this programme on the performance of public enterprises and their future.

Why S&SAP?

By July 1991 India had completed forty-four years of freedom. During this period, a number of other countries also attained independence within Asia. Some of its neighbours such as China, Sri Lanka, Afghanistan and Myanmar, who were under alien rule for a very long period also became free states around the same time that India achieved its freedom. Japan, a great economic power, and the ASEAN countries such as Malaysia, Singapore and Indonesia, having similar problems which the Indian nation had during the last 200 years, having achieved their freedom in the 1940s, made a spectacular progress. However, in the case of India, the macro-economic management having done well till the 1960s passed through an era of continuous deterioration in the 1970s and 1980s so much so that in the early 1990s its rate of growth fell to a mere 3 per cent per annum, Gross Domestic Product (GDP) rose at a pace of 1 per cent per annum, rate of growth of exports declined, balance of payments problems became very acute, the number of unemployed work force increased at a fast rate and the economy was on the brink of disaster in that the Government had no money to pay the interest on international economic obligations, let alone the payment of principal. Internationally, the industrial production was not touching the previous performance. Till the 1960s, the rate of growth of industry was 8-10 per cent per annum with a perception of stepping it up to 15 percent per annum by the turn of the century. The rate of growth of industry slipped down to 2.5-3 per cent per annum in the late 1980s. On top of this, the rate of inflation hovered around 16-20 percent per annum and despite a number of measures initiated by the Government, there was no let up on this front.

To introduce new vigour in the country internally and to save the country from the international default of payments, the government approached the International Monetary Fund (IMF) and the Industrial Bank for Reconstruction & Development (IBRD) to extend huge assistance of the order of about US $3 billion. The international institutions, as in the past, were very accommodative to India's request. However, they were apprehensive that if some corrective measures were not taken by the Indian policymakers to set right the course of the economy, the problems would increase, and in such a situation, would aggravate so much that even they could not be of any help to bring the Indian economy back on the rails. While agreeing in principle to grant the financial package of the desired order, they brought home their point of view to the Indian policymakers that there was a need to restructure the Indian economy in toto and thereby unleash forces of a free market economy which could consistently monitor the progress of the Indian economy to an upward path.

Long parleys took place between the international institutions and the Indian policymakers. The Indian policymakers had the full support of the administrative machinery at the national and sub-national levels and political leaders of the country. In the course of dissecting the ailing Indian economy, the international institutions and the policymakers on the Indian side came to agree to the fact that the phenomenon was the result of both short-term and long-term problems and that it was essential that a concerted effort be made to take on both the kinds of problems at one go. In order to implement this concept, a package was prepared which contained a number of palliatives to ensure that the short-term and long-term problems were tackled in such a way that their recurrence was averted in future. As a measure of foresight, it was decided that in the immediate run a greater emphasis would be placed on tackling the short-term problems and the measures suggested to eliminate these problems were termed as the "Stabilisation Programme". The long-term problems required wholesale changes in the functioning of the Indian economy and its readjustment with the external environment to eliminate these problems. An approach was built up which was termed as the "Structural Adjustment Programme".

It is thus obvious that the Indian economy was in a very bad shape at the beginning of the 1990s. To prevent any further deterioration, it was necessary to take curative measures of far-reaching proportions, failing which the world would have seen yet another economic and political disaster of much greater magnitude than what happened by the disintegration of the then USSR.

What is S and SAP?

In April 1994, India completed three years of its Stablisation and Structural Adjustment Programme (S&SAP). The Indian experiment is being watched with keen interest by many. Several other countries had also launched similar adjustment programmes. There is no unanimity about the outcome of such efforts. However, the weight of the opinion lies in favour of the assertion that these programmes have not been able to improve the performance of the various economies where they were launched. The instances given to support this argument relate to most of the countries in Africa and Latin America. Even in Asia, the performance of such programmes in Bangladesh and Pakistan remains questionable. However, some countries have done very well on this front. The Turkish experience is quoted very widely. The Indonesian experience has also drawn admiration. It seems that despite severe discomfort felt by the different components of the Indian economy, India's persistence to continue with this programme and successes in its orderly implementation has given great support to the international financial institutions in prescribing this sort of remedy to the many ailing economies coming forward to stake their claim for international financial assistance. The S&SAP in India is a comprehensive effort to have a fresh look at the policy prescriptions and the procedures governing the major elements of the Indian economy. These elements include, in main, the industrial policy, trade policy, monetary policy, fiscal policy, agricultural policy and the policies pertaining to the functioning of its financial sector. An implementation of this package also had an associated question as to which sector to start with for reforms. As is known, the sequencing of economic reforms is a major policy decision which can make or mar the success of any such programme. There has been no agreement on the precise sequencing and that is why in a number of countries where the programme has not made much headway, both the international institutions and the policymakers in such countries have jointly blamed the wrong sequencing as being responsible for the failure.

In India, the S&SAP started with reforms in the area of industry. Though the programme was launched in 1991, the changes in the industry were conceived right in 1985, the seeds of which were sown sometime in the early 1980s. Though the government started in a big way to change its approach towards industry in 1991, it was in 1984 that the policy of delicensing, broadbanding and deregulation of industry became a part of its programme to lift the rate of growth of industry to a higher level. However, the order of change was so small that the industrial sector felt there was no momentum. Thus, in 1991 the whole issue of readjustment between the boundaries of public and private sectors was looked at. The regime of permits, licences and controls was unshackled. A number of industries for the first time were allowed not to seek permission to increase their installed capacities for production. The barriers to entry were withdrawn. These were imposed by the strict legalistic regime in operation in the form of legislations like the Monopolies & Restrictive Trade Practices (MRTP) Act, the Industrial Development & Regulation Act and various policy statements including the Industrial Policy Statements of 1948, 1956 and 1977.

The industries were given a free hand to have their own arrangements with regard to decisions about the selection of raw materials, capital mix, market arrangements, acquisition of plant and location of industry. The restriction about setting up industries in specific districts of the country which are known as "Zero Industry Districts" has been withdrawn in as much as it was restricting the setting up of industries necessarily in a particular district. Now those who propose to set up an industry in a backward district are given a capital subsidy but the element of compulsion stands withdrawn. There is an awakening within the government even on the front of industrial relations. The trade unions have been asked to become more constructive and this even they have learnt by the pressure of the economic changes. The culture of work-to-rule, wild-cat strike and pen-down has come to a grinding halt. "Gheraos" (the act of keeping an executive immobile until such time the demand of the workers is accepted) now take place few and far between. The trade union movement now listens to talk of productivity with some reverence. On the whole, the entire burden of the national economic policy in the realm of the industrial sector is to make the Indian industry competitive on the international scale. The industrialists have been permitted to tap the international capital markets. The various curbs on international investment have been withdrawn and the international investors have been permitted to have a major equity stake in the Indian firms. These have certainly reduced the capital input cost and made financial resources available in a greater magnitude to the Indian firms. The culture of collaboration is replacing the monopoly strongholds. This industrial restructuring has given a new turn to the conventional thinking of domination of the public sector. It has in a way also given a go by to the concept of mixed economy in its traditional sense as the industrial policy changes ought to result in a substantial share of private sector in the Indian economy and the share of the public sector is likely to decline from the present so-called commanding heights to a supportive fraction of say 5 per cent of the GDP in another 20 years.

In the field of agriculture, the policy of opening up has been adopted. The General Agreement on Trade and Tariffs (GATT) reflected in the negotiations at Marrakesh in 1994 have only contributed to the further speeding up of agricultural reforms. Now the agriculturists will have to stand on their own feet in that the subsidies to agriculture would have to be contained to the limits spelt out by the recent round of multilateral trade talks. The agriculturists will also have to abide by the Intellectual Property Rights Convention. The government support will be through the availability of infrastructure on an increasing scale. The old approach of market interventions and financial reliefs has to take a back seat.

Another very important element of the new economic policy in the field of trade is the emphasis on reduction of tariffs. The Indian economy had built a very high wall of protective tariffs ranging from 100-300 percent which was unseen and unheard of anywhere in the world. It resulted in depressing the consumer's choices and also in disallowing him to get goods worth the value of his money. It also indirectly affected the growth of industry and the supply of various goods as a response to the demand factor. Simultaneously, the curbs on exports are also being lifted gradually to allow the Indian industry and other sectors of the economy to have a wider choice in regard to inputs. The number of items banned for import and export included in the "red book" is decreasing. A number of measures have been taken to improve exports. This includes even the devaluation of the Rupee and readjustment of the exchange value of the Rupee vis-a-vis foreign currencies. An effort has been made to introduce the convertibility of the Rupee into foreign currencies in the trade account. Now it remains to be extended in respect of certain other heads which may take some more time in view of the instability of the Indian economy in so far as its foreign exchange earnings are concerned. However, it is worth mentioning that the foreign exchange reserves increased from US$ 17.0 billion at the end of 1995-96 to US$ 22.4 billion at the end of 1996-97. It rose further to reach US$ 26.4 billion at the end of August 1997. The total foreign exchange reserves of the country (including gold and SDRs) at the end of March 1998, according to the *Economic Survey 1997-98* amounted to US$ 29.4 billion. The foreign direct investment at the end of 1996 stands at $ 0.2587 billion.

The Chelliah Committee was appointed to simplify the direct taxation structure and systematise it. The Raina Committee was set up to look into the revision of indirect taxes. The tax practices at the state and local levels are also undergoing restructuring. The entire exercise of the tax reforms is attempted to scale down the excessive details to comfortable levels and bring them on par with the international norms. So far as direct taxes are concerned, the effort is to hike them to a level where they lose the present character of being regressive and make the tax administration strong so that the dishonest may not escape. An effort is also on to widen the tax base. The reforms in taxation include reduction in corporate taxes and personal income tax to bring them on par with the international levels of taxation.

The fiscal policy has been in for a total revamp. Former Finance Minister Dr. Manmohan Singh brought about these changes and received accolades which can be seen from the recognition given by "Euro Money" and also the "Best Finance Minister Award" given by an Asian organisation. To recount some of his successes, we can start with his attack on the concept of budgetary deficit. The Indian budget in 1991 had a deficit of about 10 per cent which was much beyond the benchmark provided by any fiscal organisation/ economist. Through concerted efforts this deficit has been brought down to a manageable limit of 5 per cent. In fact, this deficit should have come down to a mark of 3.5 per cent but for the political adjustments which were necessitated to allow the government to remain in power in the year 1993-94. Another very important step as an exercise in fiscal reforms, had been his consistent efforts to put a cap on the growth of government expenditure. He tried very hard to contain the level of subsidies. The subsidies put together amount to a resource transfer of about $3 billion per annum. Some of the beneficiaries of these subsidies include rich farmers and prosperous industrial groups. Though the abolition of subsidy has created a hue and cry in the country, the government has more or less succeeded in impressing upon the different constituencies that it is difficult to live beyond one's means and any further deterioration in this aspect will bring bankruptcy to the country. The benefits of subsidy have never been enjoyed by the public sector in the form of the subsidisation of cash losses and creating townships, etc. The Indian monetary policy was out of tune prior to the launching of the new economic policy. To bring it in line with international norms, the interest rates were deregulated. Earlier, the central bank of country, viz., the Reserve Bank of India, used to prescribe an interest rate structure providing no leeway for any manipulation to adjust to market needs. Since July 1991, a new interest rate structure has evolved at the ebb of which is the prime bank rate. The credit policy has undergone a great deal of transformation. Prior to July 1991 the credit policy used to be one of an administered nature. The RBI, in consultation with the Finance Minister, used to announce a credit policy twice in a fiscal year, viz., in March and October. Though this policy is still prevalent, a lot of flexibility has been built up around it.

The financial sector reforms are presently in full swing. These include reforms in the fields of commercial banking, capital market, financial instruments and unorganised financial market. The banking industry in India became a monolith in terms of bank branches, deposits, advances and its access to different sectors of the Indian economy. It became a purveyor of funds so much so that the end growth of a sector became dependent finally to the extent that an accommodation was extended by the bank to it. The financial sector reforms have swept off the insensitive banking industry. Now new banks could be opened in the private sector which will be governed by the same law applicable to the public sector banks. The strings on them in the form of a minimum cash reserve ratio and the statutory liquidity ratio have been significantly loosened. This has resulted in greater availability of funds with these institutions. This measure has benefited them further in realising the cost of funds to be provided to the economy. Now the banks have greater latitude in making lending decisions. To be internationally competitive, they have embarked on a gigantic computerisation programme. They are mechanising their operations and improving their productivity. They are extending their portfolio business from one of lending and depositing to one of providing personal services and merchant banking. The dormant capital markets are now bustling with feverish activity. Instead of fragmented control by several bodies, a new organisation was created and vested with vast powers known as the Securities & Exchange Board of India (SEBI). The domination of the Bombay Stock Exchange, also known as Dalal Street, was balanced by the creation of National Stock Exchange which has taken off in June 1994 to deal with the debt instruments which amount to $30 billion. The stock exchanges have been asked to take care of the investors. Self-regulating organisations have been created to protect the investors' interests. The foreign financial institutions have been permitted to appoint their brokers on the Indian stock exchanges. The repatriation limits on dividends have been withdrawn and the previous curbs on withdrawing investments do not exist now. The membership of the stock exchanges is no more the preserve of an exclusive class of riggers and specialist businessmen. Now even foreign financial institutions and banks can also become members of the stock exchanges. The non-banking finance companies, the expiates of which made a number of innocent investors suffer have now been brought under the control of the State.

It is thus clear that the S&SAP was launched to bail out the economy from its fast deterioration. The stabilisation element of the programme as mentioned earlier was to arrest the immediate downslide and this was done through concentrating on containing, and if possible arresting the trend, both in absolute and relative terms, the demand phenomenon. Some of the measures adopted to do this were to increase the bank margins substantially on lendings for the commodities and services which were in short supply, increasing the interest rates, both at the macro and micro levels, import of goods and services, reduction in the rate of growth of money supply, impounding dearness allowance of a certain class of employees and assiduously controlling the government expenditure. The structural adjustment programme on the other hand related to the adjustment of the Indian economy to long-term responses signalled by the economy. As discussed earlier, this was done through the deregulation of industry and capital market and initiating appropriate fiscal measures as evidenced in the steps taken with regard to the control of budgetary deficits and subsidies.

S&SAP and Public Enterprises

Public Enterprises (PEs) are a formidable component of the Indian economy. They have an investment of about $100 billion. Their performance has a lot to do with the overall performance of the Indian economy. To make a success of the S&SAP, the Government took both short-term and long-term measures in the context of PEs. As a part of the stabilisation programme, the Government decided to stop all subsidies to PEs. An effort was made to bring down the budgetary support also. They were asked to enhance the rate of dividends in order and to make it happen they were advised to improve their profitability. The capital expenditure in these enterprises was frozen. They were asked to fend for their foreign exchange requirements through stepping up the level of exports. The interest rate subsidy which these enterprises were enjoying in the form of a lower interest both for short-term and long-term loans was withdrawn. They were asked to have such financial accommodation either on the market rates of interest or to raise such resources alternatively on their own on commercial basis. It was made clear to them that while fulfilling social objectives they had to ensure a reasonable rate of profitability of their operations. They were also told to pay taxes and the exemptions which some PEs enjoyed in regard to the payment of taxes were withdrawn. To make them productive and competitive, an effort was initiated to bring all PEs under one organisational umbrella, i.e. company form of organisation. This was intended to be done to create a level playing field for the public and private sector enterprises. However, what is important is the impact of the

S&SAP on the long-term performance of PEs. The S&SAP has found many pointers which have a great relevance to the issues connected even with the future existence of PEs and their working methods and patterns. The S&SAP has opened the debate on the portfolio of investments in PEs. While the industrial restructuring, an important part of the SAP, suggests a stop on the setting up of any new PEs, it also reduces the number of areas reserved for setting up of PEs between 1947 and 1991. Now the PEs have an exclusive monopoly only in areas which stretch from the manufacture of strategic arms and ammunitions to the railways. It may be mentioned here that the Indian Railways has started considering a number of permutations and combinations to farm out its activities to the private sector, including foreign private institutions. Some of the activities which are being considered for privatisation include the running of special trains, promoting new projects, conversion of metre gauge lines to broad gauge and maintenance and upkeep of railway stations. Many state governments forming part of the Indian Union have taken a decision not to add any new PEs. In fact, in many states, the process of amalgamation or merger of PEs has commenced. Even the central government is toying with the idea of not setting up any new PEs, and if possible reducing the present number to a manageable few. From the point of view of effective governance and administrative control by its various ministries and departments, some state governments are even closing down their enterprises which are sick or incurring high cash losses.

The approach to the retention of PE portfolio has triggered an interesting debate in India. There are some who suggest that all loss-making enterprises should be closed down. Some others say that it will be appropriate to sell out the profit making enterprises. Those who view this as a problem related to market, suggest the division of PEs in terms of monopoly and competitive units. They plead that the competitive PEs should be handed over to the private sector. Whatever may be the modality, there is a case to look afresh at the present number of PEs and retain only the few which have to be necessarily run and managed by the government. Some models have been presented to solve this growing problem of portfolio to be retained. Sankar, Mishra and Nandagopal have suggested in the Indian context, a three-dimensional matrix including public performance, mobilisation of resources from financial institutions and profitability to judge whether an enterprise is worth being retained in the public sector. The enterprises which score high on all the three counts deserve to be retained in the public sector and those which score low on these counts need to be off-loaded from the public sector portfolio. An application of this matrix in the case of sub-national enterprises, known as the State Level Public Enterprises (SLPEs) in India, reveal that out of 874 enterprises studied, only 25 scored high on all the three parameters, whereas 200 scored low. The rest fall in between the two categories and a different action needs to be suggested in their context. An application of this matrix in the case of the Central Public Enterprises (CPEs) may not give very different results. Another model developed by Sankar and Mishra classifies the CPEs in terms of market-financial performance and market structure. The application of the model points out that 83 PEs in the competitive sector need to be hived off from the portfolio as they have been unsuccessful year after year. There were 15 enterprises in the non-competitive sector which required to be off—loaded from the PE portfolio as they were also unsuccessful in financial terms. The model further suggested that 76 competitive and successful enterprises need to be divested from the PE portfolio as the private sector can come forward to take over these enterprises as there was nothing very specific suggesting their continuation in the PE portfolio in future. In other words, the model singled out the retention of non-competitive successful enterprises only in the public sector portfolio in future.

The debate has assumed a serious turn in the wake of the views contained in the reports of the World Bank which have suggested to the government the winding up of all the CPEs in the course of ten years. The report has suggested the retention of only infrastructural PEs in the future with the government. As the World Bank is suggesting the extension of the process of economic reforms from the central to state governments, it is obvious that it will take the same line in the case of SLPEs numbering more than 1,000 and having an investment of about $20 billion. It is interesting to mention here that in the centrally held annual convention of the Congress (I), the same sentiments were expressed about the public sector. According to the resolution, all manufacturing PEs, whether central or state, may not be run and managed by the central and state governments and only infrastructural PEs operating in key sectors of the economy should be a part of the public sector. Interestingly, the Government of India has made some efforts to put this line of thinking into practice. The government has decided to close down about 108 sick textile mills as they were neither in the preferred social sector, nor financially successful, nor did they have any support of the masses in favour of their continuation. When it comes to the question of the portfolio of PEs, the experiences of the state governments reveal that they have had more such cases of closure or hiving off and that they have made greater progress in this direction. However, it is no indication of the trends which one could foresee for the future in the sense that the state governments in the country are much more politicised and are accused of less political will to come out with a policy in this respect. Though the central government, as pointed out by the World Bank in its recent reports, has been indecisive for very long, it may be easier for them to formulate a clear and concise policy in this regard. If the present developments are any indication, one can suggest that as long as there is no clear-cut policy on the PE portfolio for retention, it will be useful to go on a case by case basis to decide the status of a particular unit when it comes up for a decision for continuation or closure.

Restructuring of the Equity Patterns of PEs

The issue of restructuring of the equity patterns has assumed significance both from the point of view of the continuation of a PE or its closure. Most of the PEs in the country have not been able to fare well financially because of an imbalance in their debt-equity ratio. For the last 30 years when a discussion on debt-equity ratio has taken place, it has been the unanimous view that it has resulted in high interest cost, so much so that even the gross margins earned by these enterprises have not been adequate to meet the interest cost and resultantly they have been in minus at the level of profits before interest and taxes. However, this kind of analysis and understanding of the debt-equity ratio is outdated now. With the privatisation and liberalisation and the pressure of PEs to get their shares listed, the question of maintaining and upgrading the Earning Per Share (EPS) in positive terms has become a matter of life and death. It is in this context that most of the PEs have been talking of the conversion of equity into debt. Interest being a chargeable expense it allows PEs, the profitable ones, to gradually increase their EPS. The question of restructuring of the equity patterns has resulted in one or the other way thus enabling PEs to raise new sources of finance, restructure their debt-equity pattern and go in for joint ventures in which case asking the foreign partners to make a capital contribution of a specific kind having a favourable impact on the EPS. Since a large number of PEs are capital-intensive, their capital charge is also of a very vast order. In order to increase the earnings per share they have to perform the magic of reducing the capital stock to manageable proportions. Thus the problem has been solved in a very queer way, by the disinvestment of their shareholdings, helping both the government and PEs. The government, as noted earlier, was bitten very badly by the deficit bug so much so that it has almost earned notoriety in the financial circles. As suggested by the World Bank, the government decided to reduce the fiscal deficit though the World Bank never intended to take the accruals arising out of disinvestment as sums to offset the fiscal deficits on capital account.

The Industrial Policy Statement of 1991 envisaged disinvestment of part of government share holdings in the case of selected public sector enterprises to provide financial discipline and improve the performance of public enterprises. Since the beginning of disinvestment in 1991-92, 9 rounds of disinvestment of PSU shares had taken place till 1995-96. In the process 153.45 crore shares in 39 PSUs have been disinvested and an amount of Rs. 9962.07 crore have been realised. However, the World Bank is not satisfied with the speed on this score and has suggested that the Government should go to the furthest extent to implement the Rangarajan Committee Report on Disinvestment in PEs which has suggested disinvestments ranging from 25 to 51per cent in a number of areas. All this leads us to surmise that the disinvestments will be a continuing activity in future. Taking a cue from this, it was felt that both the government and the PEs should set up appropriate systems to disinvest effectively and in such a way that the best value is received and the tax payers money is not frittered away due to lack of information of bungling by those who are involved in handling the disinvestment programme.

The Disinvestment Commission was set up in August 1996 with a chairman and four part time members and a member secretary for suggesting the modalities for undertaking disinvestment of equities for select public sector enterprises. Fifty public sector enterprises were referred to the Commission for advice and recommendations. It recommended disinvestment at varying levels for twelve public sector enterprises, strategic sales in various proportions for twenty one enterprises. The state governments have also awakened and started taking some positive measures with regard to disinvestments.The Tamil Nadu government has disinvested its equity in many joint ventures in the state. It is in the process of identifying some PEs where disinvestments could be made. The Kerala government has identified ten SLPEs for this purpose. The government of Assam has disinvested its equity in some textile mills. The disinvestment programme has had a halting progress at the Centre because of lack of political will on the one hand and the government's lack of concern about formulating a suitable policy in this area. The government has kept mum about keeping its hands off from handling the programme and giving it over to an autonomous organisation. The government has also been charged by the press, researchers, Comptroller & Auditor General of India and the Estimates Committee of the Parliament about selling the shares cheaply and in the process allowing the benefits to be passed on at the cost of the State to the middlemen.

Sooner or later many PEs will attain the status of autonomous organisations. Disinvestments are not new to corporate enterprises, they are an ongoing phenomenon. Thus, even PEs in future will have to master the art of managing disinvestments. This will require them to have a close interaction with the capital market and get each one of their staff educated about the dynamics of the capital market and the way PEs can benefit from them to increase their EPs.

As discussed elsewhere, the restructuring of the equity patterns will mean a higher dependence on non-budgetary sources for PEs and a continued reduction of the governmental support to them in future. This means that in the years to come the PEs will have to resort to the various instruments of financing, operating on the Indian and international capital markets. Even for the working capital support they may have to look to capital markets as the fund-based financing for working capital need not come in the proportion it was available earlier since the nationalised commercial banks under the new economic reforms will not be bound to fulfil 100 per cent of the working capital support to these enterprises.

Interface between the Government and PEs

The Government—PE interface has been a cause for great concern and has resulted in influencing the performance of PEs in a negative way. It is said that PEs in India are over-administered and under-managed. There are too many controls which these enterprises are subjected to. A study completed by the Institute of Public Enterprise (IPE) for the World Bank on Investment Management for PEs points out that an investment clearance for a PE needs some 84 approvals. There have been changes in procedures but things have not changed radically. The controls are imposed from all around. For instance, for financial matters the approvals have to come from the Finance Ministry, Planning Commission, Administrative Ministry, etc. On labour issues an enterprise has to approach, besides its Administrative Ministry, the Home Ministry and Ministry of Labour. On the one hand, the controls are not supportive of the operations in PEs and on the other hand the controlling agencies question their performance. There has been an all round misconception about the performance of these enterprises in the sense that they have been accused of a low rate of return. On an investment of $100 billion, the return is less than $1 billion per annum. However, as seen earlier, performance is the end product of a number of factors. Therefore, according to one study, PEs should be held responsible only for managerial performance and not for the enterprise performance.

Despite the lack of a unified perception on the issue relating to performance, it is crystal clear that in the years to come some unified measure of evaluating performance has to be developed to satisfy the various stakeholders of these enterprises. The new economic policy in its various assertions has very clearly pointed out that the Memorandum of Understanding (MOU) (performance contracts as they are known in some other countries) will be used as a mechanism to evaluate the performance of PEs and to provide a basis for further discussion on the performance issues between the Government and the PE. In 1996-97, 110 PSEs at the Centre, negotiated a MOU with the Government. These MOUs specify the obligations of PEs, the targets to be achieved by them in a financial year, the support to be provided by the Government to these enterprises and the parameters on which their performance is assessed. The performance of PEs is assessed on a five-point scale ranging from the lowest performance to the outstanding performance. The enterprises having an average or high performance are given greater financial autonomy whereas the enterprises having poor showing have to explain the reasons and accept the government's advice in order to do better in the ensuing year. Interestingly, some state governments, such as Assam and Gujarat, have also introduced a system of performance evaluation for their enterprises. Some other state governments are seized with this idea and they include the governments of Karnataka and Madhya Pradesh. The World Bank and other international financial institutions have also lent their support to these instruments of performance evaluation in the Indian context. The MOU as a system is still under the process of evolution. It has a number of irritants and it will take quite some time to overcome them. The results of this system need to be watched carefully for a complete assessment of its success in the Indian context.

Boards of Management

Under the new economic regime, it has been decided to make PE Boards an effective institution and allow them to be the decision-making centres for PEs. The government plans to empower them to take decisions on all matters connected to the internal operations of the PEs and also act as a buffer between the enterprise and the Government. The New Economic Policy (NEP) intends to do away with the widespread belief that the PE Boards in India are a rubber stamp of the government and they are no more tea and coffee clubs where the Board members act on a brief and say "yes" to all that is being suggested by the Managing Directors of the Government. The Government has decided to (i) restrict the number of nominees to an organisation; (ii) bring one-third of the Directors from the various professions of the country; (iii) have workers' representation on the Boards of Directors; and (iv) give greater freedom to the Boards in the matters of investment management, selection of product mix, negotiation on wage-related matters and tying up collaborations with foreign firms. In other words, the government proposes to empower the Boards for taking all strategic and operational decisions. The Boards will have to really face very complex challenges in the future in view of the privatisation of PEs through disinvestments therein and withdrawal of budgetary support to these enterprises gradually by the government. Further, in many cases, the government as it used to do hitherto will not provide guarantees to foreign firms or financial institutions in India. This will mean that the Board members will have to take collective responsibility to fulfil the deeds of contract. Both the Indian corporate laws and the international corporate laws fix clear-cut responsibility on the members of the Board for a number of things, the non-fulfilment of which attracts punishment and penalty collectively and individually for the Board members. Thus, in the changed context, Board membership is no longer personal decoration. The NEP outlines a longer tenure for the Board members, a five-year tenure for the chief executive, greater freedom to the Administrative Ministry to appoint the Board members, and may be in future a much reduced role for the Public Enterprises Selection Board (an institution which recommends the names of the Chief Executives and Board members for appointment) and the Cabinet Committees on Appointments and Economic Affairs.

Environment of PEs

The NEP proposes to bring PEs on par with the private sector enterprises. It also intends to create a level playing field between Indian and foreign firms in India. In other words, it does not want any special treatment to be given to any sector in terms of such enactments or provisions. Following from this, the government has amended the MRTP Act, the provisions of which are now equally applicable to PEs. The Sick Industries Companies Act, 1985, has been suitably amended to incorporate the inclusion of the public sector firms within the scope of the Act. Now those PEs having wiped out their net worth to 50 per cent, or incurring cash losses continually for five years, whichever is earlier, will have to report the incidence of sickness to the Board for Industrial and Financial Reconstruction. The Board in such cases will have to decide about their closure or continuation. In the case of the latter, the Board has to develop a rehabilitation package which has to have a consensus of the enterprise management, owners and the financial institutions. The Board has a list of 300 sick SLPEs. It is also looking into the problems of more than 75 sick CPEs.

The PEs will now have to be closer to the consumers as the Consumer Protection Act allows the consumers to report against cases of non-performance of the products and fraudulent advertising. The consumer courts can levy heavy penalties and punish the officials of PEs held responsible for cheating the consumers or not fulfilling the conditions stipulated in the contract mutually agreed to by the consumers and the PEs.

The work force in PEs will now be subjected to readjustments. This implies a heavy retrenchment and redeployment of the staff under the various PEs but this has to be done with a human face. This has hampered the progress of restructuring the work force in PEs in that a large-scale retrenchment has not been made effective. To overcome this problem, the government in the NEP has come out with the scheme of safety net for workers, according to which a National Renewal Fund (NRF) has been set up with a base of $0.3 billion. The international financial institutions had suggested a sum of $3 billion for the purpose, as they were expecting a readjustment of a colossal order in the work force of PEs. About 75,000 workers have been retrenched through the "Golden Handshake" scheme, a voluntary retirement plan evolved which promises an attractive sum to workers taking voluntary retirement. However, there have been counter claims on this and there have been suggestions to increase the sum given for voluntary retirement substantially. It is estimated that if PEs have to readjust their work force to the required level, they will have to retrench about one million workers in the CPEs alone, which will require a stupendous sum of about $2 billion. The international financial institutions have been toying with the idea of providing larger sums for the NRF. However, this alone will not help PEs meet this challenge as the NRF has been used not only for retrenchment but also for redeployment and retraining. To undertake the latter two tasks successfully and then to achieve the reduction in the work force to the required levels, the government and international agencies will have to pump a huge sum into the NRF. It may be mentioned that the GOI has published guidelines to manage the NRF and has also brought into the network of managing the funds the representatives of the various state governments and the trade unions. As a corollary to the extension of the NEP from the Centre to the States it is but natural that such readjustments may be taking place in the SLPEs. This will require additional sums for the NRF. PEs environmentally will be bound by the government's new policy of greening the areas around and not polluting them. This may require them to have special allocations to change the design of their plant and machinery, and product, and make their activities environment-friendly.

Conclusion

The S&SAP was taken up by the government out of sheer necessity. The country had reached the brink of disaster in terms of its external obligations and domestic economic management. Since the launch of the programme in 1991, the country has achieved a tremendous turnaround from various economic parameters. India is one of the few countries where the macro-economic restructuring has turned out to be a success. The restructuring of PEs is an important component of the macro-economic restructuring in India. The S&SAP outlined a comprehensive package of reform measures for PEs. As a result of the implementation of the package, the PE portfolio has become trim, the equity patterns have undergone a great alteration, the PE-Government interface is controlled by a new equation, the PE Boards have got greater empowerment, and the PEs have to complete with private enterprises because of the level playing field concept. To sum up, the PEs will now have to act as autonomous organisations in the true sense of the term.

5

The Industrial Policy of 1991 and Boards of Management in Public Sector Enterprises

Uma Medury

Public sector reform/restructuring has assumed a global phenomenon in recent times necessitated by the ongoing wave of globalisation and liberalisation. We are witnessing serious efforts being made by many governments world over to rejuvenate public or state owned sector which forms a significant component of their respective economies. Indian public sector is also undergoing the process of restructuring to face the challenges of national and international competition. The public enterprise management is required to exhibit the necessary innovativeness, dynamism to discharge the new tasks. But an important question is whether the top management which is to provide the necessary leadership fully equipped to take up this onerous task? What sort of restructuring of corporate governance is required ? This paper tries to focus on the present status of the boards of management of central public sector enterprises and their role especially in the light of the New Industrial Policy of 1991. It also highlights the features of the concept of 'Navaratna' public sector enterprises introduced by the government in 1997.

State intervention in economic activities, its ownership and distribution of means of production remained a necessity in the beginning of the century in many of the developed and developing countries. It arose as a result of interplay of several factors like industrial catching up, achieving economic sovereignty and social equity, establishing supremacy of the State over private sector and so on. A general view that prevailed globally in the early 20th century was that the private sector is weak and more prone to promote its interests than keeping the national interests in view. Hence the State had to assume the role of an entrepreneur. This took the shape of public sector resulting in setting up of State owned public sector enterprises. The Post-World War II period witnessed an enormous expansion of governmental intervention in national economies, especially in 1960s and 1970s whereupon public sector was seen as a major contributor to economic growth.

Public sector had been accorded a pivotal role in India's economic and social development at the time of independence. It was assigned the stupendous task of controlling the commanding heights of the economy to give it a sense of direction and development. Huge investments made in the public sector to a great extent contributed in strengthening of our country's technological and industrial base. This resulted in phenomenal growth of central public sector enterprises from five units in 1950 with an investment of 29 crore to 242 units with an investment of 193121 crore by the end of March 1997. This, however, includes not only the newly set up enterprises, but also nationalised and taken over sick enterprises. In addition to central public sector enterprises there are around 800 enterprises operating in various states.

The eighties had witnessed a slow but growing disenchantment with public sector, world over. This was due to mainly low productivity and poor returns on investment. The net profit on capital employed in public sector enterprises has been just around 2 per cent. In addition to growing fiscal deficits, overmanning, unprofessional management, poor project management have contributed to the deteriorating performance of public sector enterprises. The bureaucratised functioning of State owned enterprises which bred inefficiency and uncompetitiveness led to enormous dissatisfaction. Hence considerable debate took place during the eighties regarding the restructuring of public sector. This was a phenomenon that occurred in developed countries also like the U.K. and U.S.A. where restructuring of public sector took the form of privatisation. The public sector reform has been influenced by the successful economic performance of Japan and newly industrialised countries like Asian Korea, Singapore, Taiwan, which have all followed a model of growth characterised by intense competition, a global approach to production and international competitiveness and a significant role for the private sector (Suresh Kumar, 1994). The collapse of a command economy like the former Soviet Union also brought to fore the consequences of uncompetitive State controlled economies. The influence of market forces in the generation and distribution of wealth became quite strong. There emerged a tide globally towards the need for formulation of economic policies directed at promoting competitive, productive and efficient State-owned or public enterprises.

In India also, the various industrial policy statements made between 1948 and 1991 though had specific mention of public sector, its main fabric was left untouched. All the policies aimed at the maintenance of status quo. This has been compounded by other problems in late 80's. The rate of growth of industry expected to touch nearly 15 per cent per annum slumped to 2.5 to 3 per cent per annum, Gross Domestic Product (GDP) rose to 1 per cent per annum. There has been an acute balance of payments problem and the Indian economy was on the brink of disaster. The financial assistance provided then by the International Monetary Fund and the World Bank to the tune of about US $3 billion, also made it necessary to bring about an economic policy with a new focus to activate the economy. It was an attempt by the policy makers to undertake a comprehensive restructuring of public sector, as it constitutes a formidable component of the Indian economy.

Features of New Industrial Policy

The New Industrial Policy announced by the Government of India on July 24, 1991 was a significant departure from the concept of State controlled economy towards a market based economy with the intention of boosting the economy. It prescribed changes in financial, trade and public sectors. The major features of industrial policy were :

1. Deregulation of the licensing systems.
2. Automatic approval for technology imports.
3. Easy access to direct foreign investment.
4. Import relaxation.

The main elements of the new policy pertaining to the public sector are :

1. Narrowing down of the areas reserved for public sector from seventeen to six.

2. Reviewing of the portfolio of public sector investments with a view to focusing of public sector on strategic, hitech and essential infrastructure. Whereas some reservation for the public sector is being retained, there would be no bar to areas of exclusivity being selectively opened up to the private sector. Similarly the public sector will also be allowed entry into areas not reserved for it.

3. Referring chronically sick public enterprises and which are unlikely to be turned around to the Board for Industrial and Financial Restructuring (BIFR) or other similar high level institutions created for the purpose, for the formulation of revival/rehabilitation schemes. A social security mechanism will be created to protect the interests of workers likely to be affected by rehabilitation measures.

4. Raising resources and encouraging wider public participation, with a part of the government's shareholding in the public sector being offered to mutual funds, financial institutions, the general public and workers.

5. Professionalising the boards of public sector companies and giving them greater powers.

6. Providing greater thrust on performance improvement through the Memoranda of Understanding (MOU) system, through which managements are to be granted greater autonomy and will be held accountable. Technical expertise on the part of the government will be upgraded to make MOU negotiations and implementation more effective.

7. Facilitating a fuller discussion on performance of public enterprises with placing of the MOU signed between the government and the public enterprise in the parliament. While focusing on major management issues, this would also place the day to day operations of public enterprises in their current perspective.

The New Industrial Policy with its thrust on deregulation and decentralisation of industry has thrown new challenges before the public sector. It has become imperative now for the public sector to imbibe the necessary drive, dynamism, innovativeness required to withstand competition in the present day market economy. The *World Development Report* has indicated three key characteristics for enterprises running on commercial lines of operation or on business principles either in public or private sectors. They include:

clear and coherent goals focused on delivering services, autonomous management and financial independence.

The public sector as such over the years has been devoid of any competition. They could not function on commercial lines as they were deprived of necessary functional, operational autonomy and professional management. The drastic reduction in the number of areas reserved for public sector, has opened wider avenues for the private sector. In this changed business environment, restructuring of public sector enterprises is being undertaken to achieve higher operational outcomes. The restructuring is taking place on various fronts i.e. organisational, ownership, financial, personnel etc.

The New Industrial Policy of 1991 requires public sector to assume new responsibilities of:

- Reformulation of objectives in the light of changed business environment.
- Adoption of commercial lines of operation.
- Generation of its own internal resources for its continuous growth.
- Development of technology internally or acquiring it from domestic or external markets.
- Enhancement of entrepreneurial skills, competitive abilities.
- Inducing dynamic corporate leadership.
- Ensuring professional management by board of directors.
- Introducing a new work culture in the organisations with the aim of working towards productivity and profitability.

One of the significant aspects of the Industrial Policy of 1991 is the emphasis placed on professionalising the boards of management of public sector enterprises. This is the first time that an intention to restructure the boards has been formally expressed by the industrial policy statement. There has been lack of serious efforts earlier, towards enhancing the quality of top management of public sector enterprises, which for a long time remained a neglected area. Proper constitution of boards of public enterprises received least attention of the government.

An examination of the constitution and functioning of boards of directors in Indian public sector since its evolution in 1950s brings out that to ensure the autonomous functioning of the enterprises, they were constituted in the form of public corporations and companies with the responsibility for the management of the affairs of the enterprises vested in the board of directors. Though the board was envisaged as an instrument of autonomy, the paradox had lied in inducting civil servants to the boards with the intention of injecting experience and integrity in the field of management. This in years to come, had become one of the deterrent factors for effective functioning of boards which for a long time remained the domain of bureaucrats.

The attempt made by the government during the second half of the fifties to create an Industrial Management Pool met with little success. The pool which drew personnel belonging to ICS\IAS, Indian Audit and Accounts Service, Indian Revenue Service, could not provide the much needed professional expertise in various areas to public enterprises.

By the end of 1960s, to meet the growing complexity of operations of public enterprises, trend towards having whole time directors on the board had become visible. To begin with predominantly two functions were represented namely production and finance. Slowly other areas like marketing personnel found place on the board. But most of the boards still comprised directors and chairmen drawn from civil service (retired as well as those in service) with the result the boards functioned more or less like extensions of government departments which defeated the very purpose of providing autonomy to public enterprises. A 'secretariat culture' which crept in the functioning of public enterprises (continuing till date) marred its performance. The management of an enterprise calls for not only knowledge, experience but also a certain amount of creativity, flexibility and a vision. A suitable blend of these ensures the success of an organisation. The management of an enterprise involves taking crucial decisions pertaining to location of project, investment, technical aspects, production, distribution, pricing, marketing etc. The growing complexity of operations necessitates reinforcing the practice of having more whole time functional directors on the board representing critical areas. Their involvement in arriving at crucial board decisions ensures effective implementation.But the issue of providing for inclusion of more whole time functional directors on the board could not garner the much needed support from the government.

This is evident from the policy guidelines issued by the government in 1972 which stated that for large multi-unit enterprises and trading organisations, the Chairman cum Managing Director (CMD) should be assisted by "at least two functional directors, one of whom would be incharge of Finance." For smaller enterprises, the CMD was to have one or two "senior officers of the undertaking itself as functional directors ..... One of the functional directors could if, necessary, be designated as Executive Director or Director (Coordination)". The Economic Administration Reforms Commission in 1984 expressed that it was somewhat fallacious to adopt the principle that the "smaller" public enterprises do not really need full time directors other than the Chief Executive. Even the smaller public enterprise is not really very small in comparison with units in private sector and in any case not too small for a sound corporate organisation. Any organisation which has been given an independent corporate existence should have a proper board. It may be "small" in comparison with large public enterprises but internally its relative "smallness" is of little significance from the point of view of proper management pattern and organisation. The Committee recommended a minimum, of three functional directorships in a public enterprises board regardless of the size of the organisation. In bigger enterprises there can be five or six or even larger number on the board.

But the evasive attitude on the part of the government to take suitable steps to implement this recommendation had led to a situation where in some enterprises apart from the Chairman and Managing Director, there has been just one director on the board. The strength of the public enterprise board has no correlation with either the size or investment of the enterprise. The New Industrial Policy also failed to touch upon this aspect of boards of management.

The Public Enterprises Selection Board (PESB) created in 1974 with the responsibility of spotting talent for top management of public enterprises has of late seens to have lost its importance. The PESB which was to consist of four members including a Chairman had at times functioned without its full strength of members. A body entrusted with the task of providing top management personnel to nearly 246 public enterprises has been devoid of personnel. With the result in many of the public enterprises there have been frequent discontinuities of top management, prolonged delays in making appointments affecting the efficiency, productivity, morale of the enterprises. The once mighty PESB seems to have lost much of its significance not just because of the inadequate attention paid to its strength but also because its recommendations no longer seem to remain sacrosanct. There have been instances of its recommendations being ignored frequently by the administrative ministries.

How can professionalism which is very essential for the functioning of the boards in the prevailing competitive environment be brought about? One possible way could be by reasons of experience and professional competence of the directors. The composition of board has a lot to do in making an enterprise board managed in a true sense. This is required especially keeping in view the multi dimensional functions of the boards like determining the corporate policy, strategic planning, dealing with major expansion, collaboration projects, their resource allocation etc. The New Industrial Policy calls for emphasis on growth, diversification quality control, entrepreneurship, efficiency, customer satisfaction, export orientation etc. The required professionalism necessary for making the boards effective deliberating and decision making bodies could be brought about by inducting alongwith functional directors non-official directors for providing the much needed specific managerial, technical expertise to the board. This is possible as the non-official directors would assume only directorial responsibilities being not part of the management, responsible for the execution of decisions. This has become a common feature of British and American enterprises. Hugh Parker, who has examined the board room effectiveness over many years in US , UK and Europe questions the effectiveness of a board wholly constituted of executive directors (i.e. insiders of the company). According to him "A Board consisting wholly of executive managers will understandably be preoccupied with the day to day problems of running the business." He recommends the inclusion of non-executive directors to make the board balanced and effective. He specifies three roles for non-executive directors. The first and foremost is to bring to the deliberations of the board a measure of independence and objectivity. Another is to provide special skill or expertise that may be lacking on a particular board. A third role that has taken on growing importance in the US and is likely to do so in other countries is to serve on special committees to which executive directors cannot be appointed on grounds of perceived self interest (Chakraborty, 1983).

On the face of it in Indian public sector boards though the emerging scenario in professionalising managerial cadres in public enterprises appears to be bright, still at the board level, bureaucrats and interest groups other than managers and employees dominate (Venkataratnam, 1985, 51). The Economic Administration Reforms Commission reiterated the need for making the functioning of the board professional, managerial and decisive and the part time directors be people who can contribute with their knowledge and experience to the efficient management of their enterprise. Experts in fields like management and accountancy, industrial relations, economists etc. need to be appointed as part time directors. In pursuance to this recommendation, the Government's communication in 1986 to all the ministries/departments emphasised the need for broad basing public enterprise boards by the "induction of scientists, technologists, senior and reputed industrialists or officials from other public sector undertakings."

The Rangarajan Committee on Disinvestment also recommended imparting a new dynamism in the management of public enterprises. With diversified ownership coming into effect after disinvestment, reconstitution of boards of public enterprises with appropriate representation for non-government directors has been favoured by the Committee.

The recent guideline issued by the Department of Public Enterprises in 1992 in the light of New Industrial Policy (BPE O.M. No.18(6)/91-GM dated 16 March, 1992) stipulated that the number of non-official part time directors on a board should be at least one-third of its total strength. The panel of suitable persons who could be considered for appointment of non-official directors was to be maintained centrally by the Department of Public Enterprises, prepared by PESB and the Secretary of Administrative Ministry.

This again had vested the power in the government instead of leaving it to the concerned public enterprise, with the result the boards of many enterprises did not have representation of non-official directors.

Providing continuity of top management can strengthen the professionalism of the boards of management. Discontinuity in the appointment of Chief Executive Officer or the Chairman cum

Managing Director of the enterprises at the apex of the organisation has far reaching effects. For example between 1973 and 1987, India had 12 Ministers and 8 Secretaries in the Steel Ministry. The Chairman of the SAIL was changed six times during the period while the Chairman cum Managing Director of IISCO was changed about 14 times (*Business India* 8-16 23/87:50). A policy of proper succession planning at all levels needs to be evolved.

A related issue that needs to be examined is the question of the autonomy of the enterprises. It is ridiculous that when we speak of public enterprises becoming entrepreneurial, does the present liberalisation tide going to reduce the multiple controls imposed on the enterprise ? It has been estimated that in India, a typical project proposal of a State Owned Enterprise requires 637 days to move through the approval procedure. There are key supervisory bodies at various stages that can block the investment which include the Public Investment Board, Budget Division of the Ministry of Finance, the Planning Commission, Foreign Investment Board and Reserve Bank of India (Waterbury, 1993). Does these ensure entrepreneurial behaviour on the part of public enterprise ? In early years of development of public sector its association was restricted to only government and parliament. In contrast the present day witnesses multifarious interaction of the enterprise with other organs of government. An analysis by Rama Murthy revealed that the State owned sector is controlled by 7-10 Ministers, 36-40 senior bureaucrats, 20-30 people in media, 10-20 union leaders and 20 members of Lok Sabha *(Ravi Ramamurthi, 1990).*

Another important question that needs to be considered keeping in view the varied functions the board has to perform with the changing environment, is that whether the boards have sufficient autonomy to discharge its tasks or not ? Arjun Sengupta observed that "It is recognised by all that on paper, managements' of public enterprises enjoy large autonomy, sometimes much more than even by the private sector management. However, in practice, formal and informal involvement of Ministries and Departments take place in areas wholly within the decision making powers of public enterprises." On one hand while rolling back of state in many spheres is advocated, on the other, this does not seem to be possible with respect to public enterprises. This is due to government still holding more than 50 per cent of the equity of public enterprises, as disinvestment has been effected only to the tune of 20 per cent. With the result the government as a majority shareholder continues to exercise its power of constituting and representing in the boards of enterprises. There is also no dilution of the role of Joint Secretary in a Central Ministry who is a nominee of the central government on the board of directors.

In a democratic set up like ours, where public enterprises are considered national property, it is of course not a practical or feasible proposition to have the government totally absolved of its control over public enterprises. But the points of intervention can always be minimised. A certain amount of corporate democracy needs to be ensured. As commented by Arjun Sengupta Committee "The government should primarily be concerned with overall strategic planning and policy, rather than with day to day functioning of enterprises. Greater freedom needs to be given to boards in matters of investment management, selection of product mix, negotiation on wage related matters and collaborations with foreign companies. Otherwise it is difficult to ensure superior effective performance."

The continuing debate on public sector restructuring in particular the boards of directors, has led to the Government of India embarking on an experiment of devolving autonomy on few enterprises. In June 1997, the government decided to grant financial and functional autonomy to nine select public sector enterprises considered as 'Navaratna enterprises'. This has been in tune with a commitment made by the then government in their Common Minimum Programme of identifying public sector undertakings with growth potential and turning them into global giants. These nine enterprises are those select companies, whose performance in terms of sales, profits, turnover over the past five years has been high. These include the (1) Indian Oil Corporation, (2) Hindustan Petroleum Corporation Limited, (3) Bharat Petroleum Corporation Limited, (4) Oil and Natural Gas Corporation Limited, (5) Indian Petrochemicals Limited, (6) Steel Authority of India Limited, (7) Bharat Heavy Electricals Limited,(8) National Thermal Power Corporation Limited and (9) Videsh Sanchar Nigam Limited. This has been considered as one of the steps towards public sector reforms that will act as the basis for further restructuring.

Financial Autonomy

The Navaratna public sector enterprises have been granted the freedom to incur capital expenditure without any monetary ceiling. Further they are exempted from seeking clearances from the Public Investment Board, the Cabinet or the Cabinet Committees for capital expenditure incurred on new projects.

Operational Freedom

The Navaratnas have been conferred the freedom to enter into technology joint ventures and to obtain by purchase or other arrangements technology and know-how. The freedom to establish financial joint ventures and wholly owned subsidiaries in India or abroad has been granted to these public sector undertakings with certain stipulations. They are the equity investment of the public sector undertaking is to be limited to : (a) Rs. 200 crore in any one project, (b) Five per cent of net worth of the public sector undertaking in any one project, and (c) 15 per cent of the net worth of the public sector undertaking in all joint ventures / subsidiaries put together.

Human Resource Development

These public sector undertakings have been given the autonomy to structure and implement schemes relating to personnel and human resource management, voluntary or compulsory retirement schemes. Also they have the freedom to effect the organisational, restructuring including establishment of profit centres, opening of offices in India and abroad, creating new activity centres etc.

Corporate Boards

The Navaratna boards are to be restructured with induction of eminent non official part time directors. At least one third of the board of directors are to be the non-executive directors. Each of the navaratna boards is to induct initially at least four non official directors.

The government through this experiment intends to make at least nine blue chip public sector enterprises board managed. But the question that remains unanswered is whether this autonomy will mean anything positive to them, as these remain majority government owned enterprises. They continue to remain within the writ jurisdiction of the judiciary, the ambit of parliamentary questions. These issues remain unanswered.

The problem of unprofessional management of public enterprises is prominent due to overlapping of their ownership and management. In private enterprises, with separation of ownership and management, the appointed professionals entrusted with the task of management are responsible for the performance. But in a public enterprise, with the government assuming the role of promoter, investor, entrepreneur, it has indirectly assumed the responsibility of management with its involvement in setting up the Board of Directors. Though the Indian Companies Act makes the board a representative body of the shareholders or owners of company, with the government being the majority shareholder, it gives the legitimacy to exercise overriding powers. The role of the boards has been reduced to that of executing policies determined by the government.

Ayub and Hegstad (1986) in their analysis of the different roles of owners and management of private enterprises have clearly demarcated between ownership, strategic and operating roles. Of these three roles, while the ownership role is performed by the owners of enterprises, the strategic role is the responsibility of the Boards of Directors. It includes deciding upon strategic plans, monitoring performance against targets and appoint, advise and dismiss the Chief Executive Officer. The operating role is performed by the Chief Executive Officer and his top management. According to the authors, in public enterprises there is a breakdown in the demarcation of the major functions with government encroaching on the strategic and operations functions of public enterprises resulting in their poor performance "when governments take over the strategic role traditionally played by the Boards of Directors and get entangled in operating decisions, problems surface quickly. The board's principal functions of providing strategic guidance and effective control are generally replaced by inadequate guidance, weak or no controls and slow and politicised decision making."

It has been the common feature of all public enterprises in developing countries, that the government in its capacity as 'owner' of the enterprise in a sense usurped the ownership, strategic and to a certain extent the operational roles. With the result the boards of enterprises are not able to exercise initiative, autonomy in dealing with strategic issues. There was hardly any scope for evolving a professionalised approach in dealing with key issues. But the much talked about restructuring taking place at present, envisages to restrict the shareholding of government to 51 per cent with partial disinvestment taking place. The partial disinvestment also is resulting in transforming of equity within the government as it is offered to financial institutions, mutual funds. The government needs to realise the seriousness of the malady and make all possible efforts to make public enterprises truly board managed.

The present day scenario compels adoption of a new managerial approach by the public enterprises to exhibit the necessary drive, initiative, dynamism to face competition at both domestic and international fronts. The top management is entrusted with onerous responsibility to provide the necessary thrust to the enterprise. The need of the hour is distancing of public enterprises from government to enable them show positive results. The boards have to emerge as true decision making bodies, implementors of policies of the enterprise rather than deliberating and executing government policies.

The necessary initiatives to be taken in this direction include:

1. Clear demarcation of the roles of the government and board of directors.
2. Broad-basing the boards in tune with process of disinvestment and restructuring of equity.
3. Enhancing the powers of the boards of directors, through necessary changes in the articles of association of companies.
4. Democratising the functioning of the board with its percolating down to the shop floor-level.
5. Ensuring fixed tenure for the members of the boards upto five years.
6. Introducing succession planning at the top level to ensure continuity of activities.
7. Reducing the gap in remuneration of board of directors between public and private sectors.
8. Appropriate delegation of authority commensurate with accountability.
9. The remuneration of chief executives and board members to be linked with the performance of the enterprise.

Conclusion

The time has now come to have a fresh look at the government public enterprise interface as their respective roles are undergoing a change. Prompted by developments ushered in by liberalisation, the government has taken a little initiative to have a relook at governance of public sector enterprises by restructuring the boards of management. This experiment will meet with success only when apart from structural changes, there is change in the attitude on the part of government towards public sector, in conferring them proper autonomy. Professionalism needs to be ushered in the boards of management by way of not just inducting competent persons on the board, but also by empowering them in a true sense. The public enterprises need to be made board managed companies.

REFERENCES

1. Administrative Reforms Commission, *Report on Public Sector Undertakings*, Government of India, New Delhi, 1967.
2. Chakraborty S.K. ed., Boards of Directors in India : Their Statics and Dyanmics, All India Management Association, New Delhi, 1983.
3. Committee on Disinvestment of Shares in Public Sector Enterprises, *Report on Disinvestment of Shares in Public Sector Enterprises,* New Delhi, 1993.
4. Department of Public Enterprises, *Public Enterprises Survey* 1996-97, Ministry of Industry, Government of India, New Delhi,1998.
5. Dhamija Nand, Reforming Public Enterprises, *Productivity,* Vol. 35, No. 1, April-June 1994.
6. Laxmi Narain, *Boards of Directors of Public Enterprises—A Study,* SCOPE, New Delhi, 1990.
7. Mahmood Ali Ayub and Sven Olaf Hegstad, *Public Industrial Enterprises: Determinants of Performance,* Washington D.C., World Bank, 1986.
8. Nigam, Raj K.,*Policy Referencer for Public Sector Enterprises,* Vols. I & II, D.C. Publications, New Delhi, 1993.
9. Ramamurthi, Ravi and Raymond Vernon, *Privatization and Control of State Owned Enterprises,* World Bank, Washington D.C., 1991.
10. Standing Conference of Public Enterprises, *Reports/ Recommendations of Various Committees on Public Enterprises,* New Delhi, 1990.
11. Strategic Options for Restructuring Public Sector in India, *Public Enterprise,* Vol.14, No.1-2, March-June 1994.
12. Venkataratnam C.S. and Ramu Naidu, *Public Enterprise Boards: Explorations in Indian Experience,* Himalaya Publishing House, Bombay, 1985.
13. Waterbury John, *Exposed to Innumerable Delusions—Public Enterprise and State Power in Egypt, India, Mexico and Turkey,* Cambridge University Press, USA, 1993.
14. *World Development Report,* World Bank, Washington D.C.,1996.

6

GATT and India

Nawal Kishor

The General Agreement on Tariffs and Trade (GATT) is a multilateral treaty, subscribed to by 123 countries which account for more than 90 per cent of the world trade. India is the founder member of this treaty. It was established in 1948 to enhance the market access of goods and services and facilitate smooth flow of international trade by gradual reduction of tariffs. In order to streamline the world trade, the need for GATT was felt since long time. Of late, it has become inevitable for unfettered operation of world trade. Fredie A. Mehta (1994) highlights the need of GATT due to the following developments:

(i) With the exit of Soviet Union as the leading supporter of most developing countries, particularly of India;

(ii) With the OPEC no longer a powerful player, with most of its major members currently bleeding with budgetary deficits;

(iii) With UNCTAD having now been totally marginalised; and above all

(iv) With the most powerful Third World Country China in the queue to join GATT.

GATT is the most important set of multilaterally agreed rules to govern international trade. It is a forum for trade negotiations for opening markets, reducing tariffs and finding solutions for their trade problems. GATT also functions as an international court to resolve trade disputes with other members. Several rounds of meetings have already taken place. The recent Uruguay Round of Multilateral Trade Negotiations was launched at Punta del Este in September

1986, and concluded successfully in Geneva on December 15, 1993. These talks were the most ambitious and complex so far conducted. Negotiations covered not only traditional subjects such as tariff and non-tariff measures and the improvement of GATT rules and disciplines on subsidies, safeguards, etc. but also extended to new areas not dealt with by GATT earlier, such as Trade Related Intellectual Property Rights (TRIPS), Trade Related Investment Measures (TRIMS) and Trade in Services, agriculture, textiles etc. The main objective of GATT treaty is to reform world trade which is highly distorted because of direct and indirect subsidies that flow to various sectors of the economy in various countries of the world. (Gulati Ashok & Anil Sharma, 1994).

GATT treaty is a very positive direction in the development and expansion of world trade. It provides immense potential for member countries to keep pace with the growing world trade. It is estimated that beyond 2005, world trade is likely to increase by about US $ 200 to 300 billion per year as a result of GATT accord. India with a share of only 0.5 per cent of world trade is likely to enhance her exports as a result of this treaty. The quantum of benefit depends upon the extent of liberalisation in sectors like agriculture, textiles, services and the reduction in tariffs.

Economic Survey (1993-94) highlights the following major gains of GATT Treaty :

General

(i) India can increase her exports by $1.5 to 2.0 billion per annum due to a general expansion of world trade following substantial lowering of tariffs.

(ii) India will benefit from a multilateral trading system. Most Favoured Nation (MFN) treatment will be accorded to member countries. Rule-based trade will ensure transparency.

(iii) India will be protected by a multilateral dispute settlement system. Unilateral trade action will be subject to multilateral review.

Textiles

It was agreed to phase out Multi-Fibre Arrangement (MFA) within a definite time frame of ten years. Pressures were resisted to open our markets on reciprocal basis and to increase the time span of phasing out of MFA to 15 years. Agreement on textiles will strengthen the areas of comparative advantage for India.

Agriculture

(i) The reduction in export subsidies on agriculture by developed countries will make Indian agricultural exports more competitive in world markets.

(ii) Clubbing of product and non-product agricultural subsidies will allow much greater flexibility to provide subsidies for agricultural production. The agreement provides for a subsidy level of 10 per cent of the value of agricultural produce which is far higher than the current level of subsidy in India.

(iii) Under the Uruguay Round agreement, consumer subsidies under the Public Distribution System (PDS) for the rural and urban poor are legitimate and are permitted. Our PDS can therefore continue.

Services

Access of service personnel into markets of member countries will henceforth be possible on a non-discriminatory basis under a transparent and rule-based system. India can now open services sector on MFN basis as opposed to bilateral arrangements. Under the agreement, India will gain in skilled services exports such as computer software, consultancy, medical services, films, etc.

The opening of world economy and dismantling of tariff and other restrictions will provide the scope for developing countries in general and India in particular to increase their exports. The major provisions of GATT, under which India can accrue benefits are:

Trade Related Intellectual Properties (TRIPs)

(i) The accord provides for ten years transition period of introduction of product patents in drugs, chemicals and food products. Product patents would not affect majority of drugs and for the rest, the government can undertake compulsory licensing for non-commercial public use as well as to prevent situations of either inadequate availability or exhorbitant pricing.

(ii) Adoption of international standards in IPR protection would enhance flow of Foreign Direct Investment (FDI) and technology.

iii) While providing for plant-breeder's rights, farmers and researchers rights can be protected under the *sui generis* system to be adopted by us. Farmer's right to produce and exchange seeds will not be affected. Moreover, Indian laboratories engaged in path breaking research in plant varieties and seeds for tropical regious would benefit.

Market Access

In order to streamline world trade the members of GATT countries are supposed to replace all types of non-tariff barriers with tariff barriers and reduce the levels of tariffs under a time bound programme. These tariff levels are to be reduced by 24 per cent in case of developing countries and by 36 per cent in case of developed countries within a period of 10 years and six years respectively.

Minimum access opportunity will be provided from the countries which are not importing significantly. They are required to import at least 3 per cent of their domestic consumption of farm products to be stepped up to 5 per cent over a period of 6 years. Developing countries are required to import agricultural commodities to the extent of 2 per cent of domestic consumption in the first year of GATT, to be stepped up to 3.33 per cent at the end of 6 years. Minimum level of access is not to be granted by the country facing balance of payment crisis. India has not undertaken any commitments in regard to market access because she is under a balance of payment cover in GATT. Therefore, India is free to maintain quantitative restrictions on imports.

Domestic Subsidies

Developed countries provide high level of subsidies to their farmers. For example, United States and European Union provide 20-50 per cent of subsidies to their farmers. Hence, the farmers of developed countries are in a much better position than that of their counterparts in the developing countries. Developing countries can not afford to provide such a huge amount of subsidies to their farmers. Hence, as a result of subsidies reduction the farmers of developing countries will gain. According to GATT, all domestic support in favour of agricultural producers with exemption of exempted measures shall be reduced by 20 per cent in six years in case of developed countries and two-thirds of general commitments (i.e. 13.33 per cent) in case of developing countries over a period of 10 years. The reduction commitments are expressed in terms of the total Aggregate Measurement of Support (AMS). This includes both product specific and non-product specific.

The domestic supports are to be reduced if the total AMS given to farmers exceeds 5 per cent of the value of the total agricultural production of the country in case of the developed countries and 10 per cent in case of the developing countries for the base period of 1986-88. The least developed countries have been exempted from this reduction.

India provides market price support and the support in the form of input subsidies to the farmers. According to Ministry of Commerce, during the base period of 1986-89, India had market price support for 22 products, out of which 17 products had negative AMS and only two had positive AMS. When both product specific and non-product specific AMS were taken into consideration, the total AMS came to the tune of minus 18 per cent of the value of total agricultural output. The negative AMS of 17 products reflects that international prices of these products were higher than the domestic price. Hence, India does not have any commitment to reduce any support. In fact, India does not at all give any product-specific support. India provides non-product specific support which is much less than the stipulated 10 per cent for the developing countries. Therefore, the country can increase subsidies substantially if she has resources to do so.

Export Subsidies

According to GATT the direct export subsidies should be reduced up to a level of 36 per cent below 1986-88 level in case of developed countries over a period of six years. The quantity of subsidised exports by the developed countries is to be reduced by 21 per cent during the same period. In case of developing countries direct export subsidies are to be reduced by 24 per cent and the quantity of subsidised exports is to be reduced by 14 per cent. These reductions are to be carried out over a period of 10 years in case of developing countries.

The developing countries will have to phase out export subsidies in products where they have reached export competitiveness. Export competitiveness in a product exits if a country's exports of that product have attained a share of at least 3.25 per cent in world trade of that product for two consecutive calendar years. Developing countries that have attained a per capita income of $1,000 and are export competitive in a product, have to phase out export subsidies on that product within two years from 1995. Those that have not attained the benchmark of $ 1,000 have eight years from 1995. India is competitive in only diamonds where subsidies have to be phased out beyond 2003. In other products, export subsidies can be retained. Hence, reduction in export subsidy will provide an opportunity to increase India's exports.

The major sectors of beneficiaries are:

Textiles

Textile industry is one of the leading growing sectors of the world. A recent GATT report on developing countries states that textile and articles of clothing are the most important industrial category among the third world countries 'exports' accounting for 22 per cent of the total. The textile industry is the largest industry of India. According to Debroy Bibek (1994) "The textile sector is India's largest foreign exchange earner. Thirty per cent of the export basket is accounted for by textiles and garments. Eighty million people are employed in the textile industry and twenty per cent of industries originate in this sector. Despite the large size of this industry and significant contribution in the India's total export, India's share in total world trade is marginal at about 2.5 per cent."

Rigid quota system was one of the important factors of the slow growth of textile sector. The GATT accord envisages a ten year phasing out of the Multi-Fibre Arrangement (MFA). Hence, by the end of 2005 the quota system will disappear. The withdrawal of MFA will be in phases having begun from January 1995. The bulk of 49 per cent of the total quota volume will be withdrawn during the year 2002-2005. This means that the real jump in the textile sector will be during these last three years (2002-2005).

Textile being a labour intensive industry, India has comparative advantage of cheap labour in this sector. Debroy Bibek (1994) highlights various advantages of Indian textile industry. They are: the availability of cotton, cheap labour, educated supervisory staff, technical and managerial skills and lax pollution norms. India also has one of the finest varieties of raw cotton in the world and one of the largest acreage of land under cotton.

Despite these competitive advantages, India's textile industry is suffering from the monster of poor infrastructure, outdated technology, lack of quality consciousness, non-adherence of strict delivery schedule and less automation of the plant. Needless to say that with the elimination of the quota system and subsequent opening up of the world economy, India will face stiff competition from China, Vietnam, Pakistan, Bangladesh, Indonesia, Malaysia, Sri Lanka, Hong Kong, Taiwan, South Korea and others. Since the major growth of this sector is expected during the last three years (2002-2005), it is high time for India to modernise the textile sector so that the country could produce the international quality products. Increasing efficiency and productivity are to be accorded paramount importance for the development of this sector. Moreover, new international environment standards of developed countries will accept eco-friendly textile products. This requires immediate attention of manufacturing environment friendly products. In order to reap the benefits of this highly growth potential sector, India needs to remove the bottlenecks of this sector and at the same time, international quality standards have to be brought in the fabric of the manufacturing process. In this connection, the ground reality of ISO 9000 certification should be highlighted which is the most important mark of excellence in the world market. It certainly requires a new approach towards manufacturing and delivery process.

Agriculture

India is primarily an agricultural economy. Agriculture is the backbone of the economy. The agricultural sector in India accounts for about 30 per cent of GDP and two-thirds of Indian population is dependent on agriculture. India ranks second in the world in rice, vegetables, sugarcane, groundnut and fruits production and the country is the third largest producer of wheat, cotton and rapseed mustard. Agriculture sector is the third largest foreign exchange earner after textiles and gems and jewellery. Despite this fact, India's share in the world farm produce is less than 1 per cent. The long term trend growth rate in Indian agriculture at present is a little over 2.2 per cent per annum. In order to accelerate the GDP growth, long term agricultural growth rates need to be raised to 3 to 4 per cent.

After textiles, agricultural commodities have largest scope to enlarge exports. The GATT agreement allows minimum access of the markets of developed countries for the agricultural commodities. As a result, the market of European Union countries, Japan, South Korea and other countries will provide an opportunity for India's agriculture produce. On the other hand, developed countries provide huge amount of subsidies to protect the interest of their farmers. Somya Kanti Mitra (1994) also expresses the same view; "The intensity of OECD support to agriculture can be gauged by the fact that positive support for farmers in Japan stands at 72 per cent, 37 per cent within EU countries and 20 per cent in the USA. India typically will stand to benefit since its own pattern of support works out to being largely negative, and the amounts are in any case tiny compared to those which the OECD dole out. The reduction of export subsidies in the developed countries will push up the prices of these commodities in the international market. India may benefit from the price advantage and the agricultural products will be competitive in the global market. This allows greater avenues to boost India's agricultural export.

The reduced support levels and rationalisation of trade barriers will increase production and export of various commodities in those countries which have comparative advantage in the production of agricultural commodities. India is endowed with diverse agro-climatic conditions, fertile soil and cheap workforce. Moreover, Indian agriculture sector consumes less import content compared to other sectors. Thus, India has large potential to expand agricultural exports. The competitive advantage of agriculture sector coupled with the opening up of the world economy will provide enough scope for India to boost agricultural exports. Needless to state that Indian agricultural sector needs immediate modernisation to compete in the global market."

Services

The General Agreement on Trade in Services (GATS) is the first set of multilaterally-agreed and legally-enforceable rules and disciplines. In regard to trade in services, preamble to GATT states 'The objective is to establish a multilateral framework for trade in services with a view to expansion of such trade under conditions of transparency and progressive liberalisation and as a means of promoting growth of all trading partners and the development of developing countries".

In broad, the agreement contains:

(i) A framework of general rules and disciplines;

(ii) Annexes addressing special conditions relating to individual sectors; and

(iii) National schedules of initial liberalisation commitments.

The most important provisions of GATS are:

(a) It covers all internationally traded services.

(b) Both domestic and foreign services should be accorded national treatment.

(c) Echoes most favoured nation treatment under which no member may discriminate among services exporters from other countries.

(d) Each country must have a transparent policy.

(e) The inclusion of market access under which each government shall accord services and services providers of other governments treatment no less favourable than that of its schedule.

(f) Free flow of current payment and transfers.

(g) Economic integration agreements and safeguards concerning balance of payments.

(h) Progressive liberalisation of services.

Services sector play a very significant role in the development of the economy. With the advent of liberalisation, this sector has been growing at a faster rate. This sector accounts for 41 per cent of India's GDP and it is estimated that it will contribute 50 per cent of GDP by the end of Eighth Plan. Despite substantial contribution of services sector to GDP India's share in the world services trade is a negligible to 0.5 per cent. India enjoys competitive advantage in the service sector due to her large reservoir of physical and natural resources. Ramchandriah V, (1994) echoes 'India's competitiveness in the service sector reflects specific characteristics either in the form of national endowments such as physical and cultural resources or through special relations built up with neighbouring countries. There is a revealed competitive advantage for Indian services sector such as professional services, manpower exports, construction, engineering, computer services, banking and insurance'.

The National Seminar on Trade in Services—The Uruguay Round and After organised by Indian Institute of Foreign Trade (1994) concludes the gains of GATS as follows:

(i) India, endowed with large physical and cultural resources, enjoys competitive advantage in sectors such as computer software, engineering and design services and professional services like legal and accountancy. GATS is expected to facilitate an fuller exploitation of these capabilities in terms of increased international trade.

(ii) India stands to gain from the services agreement because of her intrinsic strength due to the large reservoir of highly professional manpower who can provide services of international standards at globally competitive rates.

(iii) Indian software exporters have already emerged as one of the leading lights in the services sector. Strategic alliances between hardware manufacturers and software suppliers will further strengthen this sector.

(iv) Financial reforms and opening up of the banking sector may lead to efficiency enhancement of domestic banking industry.

(v) In order to get the benefit of construction contracts and project exports the bottlenecks of this sector needs to be removed.

(vi) The world tourism industry is increasing at a faster rate than the world economy. This country endowed with natural resources has great potential to enhance tourism business provided the infrastructure and marketing strategies are strengthened.

(vii) The threat perception is due to the nascent stage of the services sector in India and the fear of getting exposed to international competition from global giant companies.

In fact, the gradual opening up of the economy and market forces will force the skill upgradation and enhance the efficiency of the domestic sector. Moreover, India will directly gain in the area of labour intensive services. The time is ripe to meticulously handle the impediments of the services sector and improve the infrastructure to reap the benefits of the GATS.

Trade Related Intellectual Property Rights (TRIPS)

Trade Related Intellectual Property Rights is the most controversial area of the GATT agreement. The agreement encompasses seven areas of intellectual property rights. They include: copyrights, trademarks, trade secrets, industrial designs, geographical appellations, integrated circuits and patents. Out of these areas, in patents our policies are not in conformity with the TRIPS agreement. In this connection, GATT now stipulates that a new patents act on par with international standards should be framed in India. For this purpose a transition period of ten years is allowed from 1995 to 2005. The new GATT provisions state that (i) patents should be available for both the products and the process, (ii) The life of patents should be fixed at 20 years, and (iii) The burden of proof is shifted to the accused.

India's main apprehension is that the drug prices will shoot up as a result of TRIPS. This is not fully true. The prices of patented drugs and the indigenous pharma industry following process patent will be affected. Shah R. A. (1994) expresses views that the extent of price impact depends on a number of factors. They are :

(i) The TRIPS regime applies only to patent applications filed after July 1,1995. It takes anywhere between seven to ten years for a patented drug to come into the world market from the date of the patent application.

(ii) It is unlikely that the share of patented drugs in our market will be more than 10 to 15 per cent of the total drug market. Hence, there is no reason why the prices of drugs that are not covered by patents should shoot up.

(iii) Except for drugs that have spectacular breakthrough, alternative previous generation off-patent drugs are usually available in the market. Their prices would act as a check on the newly introduced patented drugs.

(iv) It is open to use the compulsory licensing system to introduce competition in the market where an essential drug is widely needed by the common man and it is not available at reasonable prices.

Another important apprehension is regarding plants and seeds. In this connection, TRIPS agreement mentions that every country has to protect plant varieties either by *patent* or by *sui generis* system. Sui generis system will protect rights of the plant breeders, farmers and researchers. Farmers will be able to save and use their own seeds and also exchange them with other farmers.

World Trade Organisation

The world trade has so far been conducted by the rules and regulations of the General Agreement on Tariffs and Trade. World

Trade Organisation (WTO) has come into force since January 1995 to reiterate the objectives of GATT. This is an organisation to have privileges and immunities similar to those accorded to the specialised agencies of the United Nations. The principal institution will monitor world trade under the Agreement, which was opened for signature at Marrakesh.

The WTO will :

* Facilitate implementation and operation of all the agreements and legal instruments negotiated in connection with the Uruguay Round.
* Provide a forum for all negotiations.
* Administer the Undertanding on Rules and Procedures Governing the Settlement of Disputes and the Trade Policy Review Mechanism.
* Co-operate with the IMF and IBRD with a view to achieve greater coherence in global economic policy making.

The Preamble

The agreement establishing a WTO reiterates the objectives of GATT: Raising standards of living and incomes, ensuring full employment, expanding production and trade, optimal use of world's resources, at the same time extending the objectives to Services and making them more precise:

* Introduces the idea of 'Sustainable Development' in relation to the optimal use of World's resources, and the need to protect and preserve the environment in a manner consistent with the various levels of national economic development.
* Recognises the need for positive efforts designed to ensure that developing countries, especially the least developed ones, secure a better share of growth in international trade.

Decision Making

The WTO will continue the decision making practice followed under the GATT

* Decision by Consensus which is deemed to exist if no member formally objects.
* Recourse to voting, where a decision cannot be reached by consensus, is now institutionalised, whereas earlier it was exceptional.

* Decisions continue to be taken by a majority of the votes cast, on the basis of "one country, one vote".
* In case of interpretation of provisions of the agreements and waiver of a member's obligations the majority required is three-fourth of the members, unlike the earlier two-third of the votes cast representing at least half of the members under the GATT. The granting of waivers will be more strictly controlled.

  Any member of WTO may submit a proposal to amend the provisions of the Agreements to the Ministerial Conference and the General Council. The quorum required to implement changes will depend on the nature of the amendment.
* Amendments relating to general principles such as MFN treatment must be approved by all members.
* For all other amendments only a two-third majority is required.

Conclusion

GATT accord provides immense opportunity for developing countries in general and India in particular to boost their exports. India has huge potential and will be a major gainer in many areas due to her physical and natural competitive advantage. This is the ripe time for India to strengthen the infrastructure and enhance efficiency and productivity in Indian industry. The apprehensions of pharmaceutical sector and interference of multinational may be handled through the meticulous planning and adequate level playing by the Indian domestic industry. India has to catch up with the race of the world economy. Hence, Indian trade and industry need to be equipped with enough strength to face the global challenges. GATT has opened avenues, the benefit depends upon the right initiative taken by the country.

REFERENCES

1. Debroy Bibek, Textile Exports—Need for Greater Thrust, *World Trade Review,* November 1994.
2. *Economic Survey,* Ministry of Finance, Government of India, 1995.
3. GATT Secretariat— *An Analysis of the proposed Uruguay Round Agreement with Particular Emphasis on Aspects of Interest to Developing Countries,* November 29, 1994.
4. Gulati Ashok and Anil Sharma, Agriculture under GATT—What It Holds For India, *Economic and Political Weekly,* July 16. Indian Institute of Foreign Trade (1994) Trade in Services — The Uruguay Round and After, 1994.

5. Mehta Fredie A, *GATT and India—Economic Implications,* Forum of Free Enterprises, May 17,1994.
6. Mitra Soumya Kanti, No Time to Relax after GATT, *The Economic Times,* October 6,1994.
7. Ramachandriah, V GATT: Gains For India, in Trade in Services, —The Uruguay Round and After, Indian Institute of Foreign Trade, 1994, pp. 45-58.
8. Shah, R.A., *Intellectual Property Rights,* Forum of Free Enterprises, May 17,1994.
9. United Nations Conference on Trade and Development (1989 and 1990) Uruguay Round —Papers on Selected Issues.

7

Annual Reporting as a Tool of Control and Accountability of Public Enterprises: Emerging Dimensions

Prof. B.S. Bhatia
Dr. G.S. Batra

Introduction

Public enterprises have been set up by the government with huge investments of public funds and certain well-defined objectives. Pannikar has emphasised this issue from the constitutional point of view. He opines that "As long as government funds are invested in public enterprises their responsibility to Parliament cannot be overlooked or ignored on the ground that these enterprises are being run on commercial lines as autonomous units. Such control is important in Indian context as it is a developing economy and has scarce resources". These enterprises owe a great public accountability to the masses in order to ensure regularity, productivity and honesty in the employment of funds. This is particularly important in an under-developed country where corruption and malpractices are rampant. This responsibility to the House or any public authority has been called by Robson as 'accountability'. According to him, to account for one's actions means that one gives a report of what one has done in a specified period of time, with whatever explanations may be necessary to justify the actions performed or ends pursued. In other words, accountability to the government, the legislature and the general public regarding their efficiency and progress is essential through various channels such as questions raised in the House, debates, examination by the Committee on Public Undertakings, annual reports, etc. This paper attempts to examine the reporting system as an effective tool of public accountability.

In private corporate sector, the function of reporting is governed by the provisions of the Indian Companies Act, 1956. Hence the annual accounts of the joint stock company are presented to its members and other interested parties on a uniform basis. The shareholders avail this opportunity to satisfy themselves about the manner in which the affairs of the company are being managed. In this respect they seek guidance of professional experts like the auditors who are appointed by them to examine these accounts. In case of public enterprises there are practically no shareholders. A public enterprise is owned by the nation and the House (Parliament or Assembly as the case may be) is expected to exercise the rights of members and to control their working and operations and obtain information from them. The performance of these enterprises may be reported to other groups only through their published annual reports. Thus, these reports become the only medium of communication to the outside world. As such, the annual report of an enterprise is generally the most read public document and serves as an important instrument of public accountability and public relations.

Rationale of Annual Reporting as an Instrument of Control

A study of the annual report is also important for the report serves as an instrument of control in as much as through it the enterprise gives an account of itself to the public at large, the achievements during the year are displayed and non-achievements are accounted for. The extent to which this objective is achieved lessens the executive's responsibility and monitors ministerial and legislative control over the state enterprises.

It provides an opportunity to the members to discuss and criticise their working. These reports contain comprehensive statements of the activities, results, programmes and policies of these enterprises. While describing the importance of annual reports Laxmi Narain states that "The annual report is an important medium through which an enterprise gives an account of itself. It is the only document issued by every public enterprise which provides to the public and Parliament information on a continuous basis about the activities of the enterprise and thus helps in judging its performance. Carefuly prepared and sufficiently detailed annual reports also help to raise the standard of parliamentary discussions and obviate the need of routine questions and thus save valuable Parliamentary time. In private concerns, the annual report is essentially a means through which directors seek and the shareholders extend their confidence to them every year. Legislature which is often considered analogous to the body of shareholders for government companies is not only interested in financial returns, but also in ensuring that public enterprises support and enhance the declared social values and economic objectives". They provide a continuous stream of information of varied nature like output, productivity, finance, labour, development and research, commercial policy, etc. which is much comprehensive than that provided by the commercial companies. An important function of annual accounting is to provide the results of the working of the enterprise for the period under review and thereby provide an objective and quantified measure of the management's success for the period. Pylee in this context opines that "The annual accounts is the principal means by which the management of the corporation can seek and Parliament and the public can decide to accord or refuse their confidence in the board as managers of the enterprises."

Objectives of Study

The study has been undertaken to examine:

1. The problem of public accountability viz., annual reporting, control of state enterprises with a view to study the legal framework of public accountability and the deviations emerging therefrom in the actual practice; and
2. The effectiveness of annual reporting control as a channel of ensuring public accountability over state enterprises in Punjab.

Thus the primary objective of the study here is to examine the nature, adequacy and impact of the reporting system over state enterprises in Punjab. An attempt has been made to evaluate in broad terms whether the level of such control is optimum considering the requirements of their functional freedom and operational efficiency.

Research Methodology

In view of the main objectives of this study viz., to look into the problem of annual reporting as a tool of control over state enterprises in Punjab, an exploratory research design has been followed for the purpose of this study.

The present study is confined to the companies/corporations set up under the Industries Department of the Punjab Government from the year 1966 till date. In all, eight companies/corporations have been set up under the Industries Department of the Punjab Government.

The study is based on primary and secondary data. A questionnaire was prepared and administered to the members of the Committee on Public Undertakings and the Chairman and Managing Directors of the selected enterprises. The opinion of the respondents was obtained through the questionnaire on different aspects of the reporting as a tool of control over state enterprises.

The secondary data has been collected from the annual reports, memoranda of association, articles of association, Director's reports, reports of the Accountant General (Punjab), the reports of the Committee on Public Undertakings and the proceedings of the Punjab Vidhan Sabha. Further the information has been obtained through discussions with the senior executives/managers of state enterprises and those having experience in management, business and accounting profession etc.

These reports and accounts are debated in the Parliament from time to time. In the British House of Commons, the usual practice is that every year three days are allocated by the government for a debate on the reports of the nationalised industries. In India, the reports are placed before the House, but no special time is allocated regularly for debates on them. In India there has been no practice of allocating some days in every session for discussion on the annual reports, as in the case of U.K.

As the number of public enterprises and the amount invested in them has been increasing at a fast rate, it is quite necessary that the government should allocate more time for debates and discussions on the working of these enterprises. Lord Morrison also advocated that "When the number of nationalised industries increases, a case will arise for increasing the number of days provided for debate. They are useful and valued by the boards not less than by Parliament. If some grave happening raised an issue of urgent public importance in connection with the work of nationalised industry, it is quite likely that the government would find it necessary to give facilities for debate in addition to the established arrangement. Laxmi Narain in this context stated that "Public enterprises have a long way to go to provide a fuller account of their operations, problems and achievements in their annual reports. Many public enterprises are in a new and difficult field of activity. It requires to be clearly stated in the reports. At present the tendency generally is to gloss over difficulties or to merely state problems without adequate explanation. Detailed information might in some cases create complications but the easier attitude of indifference or secrecy is bound to harm the long-term interest of public enterprises. Taking the public and Parliament into confidence and educating them about various problems would generally lead to better understanding and appreciation of the situation by them".

Dimensions of Public Accountability and Reporting

Successful working of any public undertaking controlled by the government founded on democratic principles largely depends upon well-informed public opinion. It is, therefore, essential to keep people continuously informed of what is happening in these enterprises. In a democratic community like ours the government should tell people as much as possible within the limits of prudence. As per specific characteristics of public sector, in a public enterprise accountability is not to the shareholders but to the House (Parliament or State Assembly, as the case may be) and through it to the public at large. This body does not meet only once a year, but is in session more or less continuously. Again, unlike in private firms, the achievements of public enterprises cannot be reflected in terms of profits alone. Other aspects are equally, if not more, important. In their case, the main purpose of the annual report would be to:

(a) indicate clearly the efficiency with which an enterprise is operating;

(b) provide a record of the activities of the period under review;

(c) fulfil the statutory requirements;

(d) provide as complete an account of the policies and programmes of the enterprise as possible; and

(e) project the future course of action and indicate the trends in its growth and development

The Committee on Public Undertakings in its 40th report had also observed that it should be possible for government to ensure that meaningful reports giving the performance data of such undertakings reach them at least once every quarter so that it can be monitored and suitable measures may be initiated as required for the efficient functioning of these undertakings. So it is essential not only for enterprises' internal interest but also for society as a whole, that there must be "an effective reporting system" in all organisations. Robson remarks "The annual report of a public undertaking is a document which is or should be of first class importance. It affords an opportunity to the board to explain and justify their policy and to show the results of their administration. It forms the main source of public information on which debates in Parliament can be founded."

Public enterprises are not accountable to their shareholders but to the House, being the representative of the public at large. The House not only thinks in terms of profit margins but has wider horizon and broader standpoint. For instance, how is the enterprise behaving as an employer? How far is it helping in the achievement of the declared socio-economic goals. And above all, to what extent is it financially viable? The annual reports of the public enterprises could greatly help the Parliament by providing a correct perspective of their operations.

It is in the light of this background that a study of the existing reporting system of the state enterprises of Punjab has been undertaken.

Statutory Requirements of State Enterprises Regarding Annual Reports

Every state enterprise is required to submit to the legislature its annual report and accounts of its activities, policies and programmes for scrutiny and debate. The annual reports on the working of each government company are made available to the members of the House. Section 619 of the Indian Companies Act requires that all government companies must in addition to their balance-sheets and profit and loss account, also submit annual reports on their working to the legislature. This provides an opportunity to the legislature to take stock of the operations of the government companies.

Similar provisions are also made in the acts of various statutory corporations and their reports are laid before the legislature. For government companies, the provision regarding the annual reports of the board of directors and the accounts are contained in Sections 210 to 219 of the Companies Act. The report of the board of directors is required to deal, among others with:

(a) The state of company's affairs;

(b) The amount of reserves to be created and dividends to be declared;

(c) Material changes in the financial position of the company falling between the end of the financial year and the date of the report;

(d) Any changes during the year in the nature of business of the company or in the class of business in which the company has an interest, so far as it is necessary for the appreciation of the state of the company's affairs by its members; and

(e) The board shall also be bound to give the fullest information and explanation on every reservation, qualification or adverse remarks of the auditor.

There is no time limit prescribed within which the government has to submit the reports received by it to legislature. For a government company, the provision is that the government shall cause an annual report, prepared on the working and affairs of the government company, to be placed before the legislature alongwith the audit report. There is no specific mention for placing company's annual reports before the legislature, though this may be implied because the audit report almost always forms part of the director's report and the annual accounts.

Though there are sufficient statutory requirements about reporting aspect of the state enterprises, yet its effectiveness depends upon the enforcement machinery and consciousness on the part of the management boards regarding the timely and faithful reporting to public. Under the Companies Act, 1956, the board of directors enjoy the discretion to provide as much information as in the board's opinion is not harmful to the business of the company. This provision often provides an alibi for withholding useful information.

Reporting System of State Enterprises in Punjab

Having gone through the framework of reporting system in the state enterprises, it is now proposed to study some aspects regarding preparation, presentation and mechanism of preparing the annual reports. These issues have been evaluated on the basis of a brief questionnaire which was administered to state industrial enterprises of Punjab.

Preparation of Annual Reports

The respondents indicated that in all the state industrial enterprises under study, the preparation of the annual report is the joint responsibility of the Chairman, the Managing Director, the Chief Accounts Officer, the Financial Controller and the Company Secretary. As a normal practice, the Director's report is looked after by the Company Secretary and accounting part of the report is taken care of by the Chief Accounts Officer. However, the initiative for preparation of the report is taken by the Secretary. The necessary information from various departments is gathered, a draft is prepared and put up for the approval of the higher authorities. Sometimes formal consultations may also take place with the senior officers depending upon the needs and circumstances of the case, otherwise some informal help is sought from the Chairman, the Managing Director and other senior departmental officers. However, the final approval of the Chairman and the Managing Director is essential before sending it for the final printing.

Time Taken in Preparation of Report

The time taken in the preparation of annual reports is of great importance. A report prepared long after the period to which it relates is unlikely to serve much purpose except as a document of historical record. But it does take some time to compile the results of a year's operation and as such the management of the enterprise has to reconcile both the ends.

Viewed from this angle, the position of state enterprises in public is not very satisfactory. In most of the cases, state enterprises generally take six to eight months after the closing of the accounting year in finalising, auditing and adopting the annual accounts of the entity. In addition to it, on an average 45 to 90 days are taken in planning, preparing and printing the annual reports.

The time span depends upon the efficiency and size of the enterprise. Normally delay occurs due to the late preparation and delayed audit of the accounting part of the report. In the case of government companies, after the professional auditors have submitted their report to the Auditor General and the company concerned, the former may choose to scrutinise the accounts with a view to comment or supplement the auditor's report. This process requires extra time. None of the state enterprise seeks the assistance of mechanised accounting in their accounting process which may reduce the time spent in the process.

Presentation and Discussion of Annual Report in the House

It is the obligation of a government company to submit its report to the minister concerned and it is the minister's responsibility to submit it to the House. The enterprises under study pointed out that they do not know when their report is submitted and discussed in the House. In normal practice, state enterprises think that after sending their reports to the ministry concerned, their job is over, so they are least interested in ascertaining whether their report is discussed in the House or not. Moreover, the House also does not have sufficient time to discuss all the annual reports. The senior managers of the undertakings under study were mostly ignorant and indifferent about the legislative discussion on the annual reports of the companies.

Distribution of Annual Reports to Legislature

The respondents indicated that annual report is not sent to every legislator of the state. Only some copies are sent to the Vidhan Sabha Secretariat for its distribution amongst the members of legislative assembly. The decision regarding the distribution of annual report is taken normally by the Managing Director or sometimes by the Secretary of the enterprise. Some enterprises send copies of their annual reports on exchange basis also. This, however, is a good practice. The respondents pointed out that they get a few queries (ranging from 4 to 8 in a year) from Vidhan Sabha Secretariat about the working of enterprise concerned.

Viewpoint of the Committee on Public Undertakings on Annual Reports

The annual report is a document of crucial importance for state enterprises. A well-drafted annual report is an important medium of communication between the enterprise and the public.

It is the only authoritative document by which a state enterprise gives an account of itself before the state assembly and the public at large.

The annual reports should aim at providing a correct, comprehensive and coherent picture of the problems and achievements of the public enterprises. These reports should contain sufficient and adequate information. Carefully prepared reports help in raising the standard of debates and discussions in the House and ensure a constructive criticism. However, the Punjab Legislative Assembly has never expressed its views on the annual reports of these enterprises, whereas the Committee on Public Undertakings (CPU) has discussed these in detail. The members of the CPUs were of the view that the annual reports of state enterprises is discussed by the CPU every year. The major limitations in this regard are that, first of all, the report of a company or a corporation is received generally two years behind. As a result all the topical interest goes and it becomes a post-mortem case which one does not like to indulge in because members are preoccupied with so many other things. Secondly, the tenure of CPU is for one year and the CPU has to pick and choose only a few enterprises for study, hence annual reports of rest of the state enterprises are not discussed due to shortage of time. Lastly, rarely any action has been taken on the recommendations of the CPU in the Punjab Vidhan Sabha.

The CPU also takes up for examination the objections contained in the audit reports of the Comptroller and Auditor General (CAG). A detailed plan of key points is presented to the CPU by the CAG on the matters raised in the audit paras. Hence it provides a background of the case and the government's explanation and audit's viewpoint. Questions as per requirement are framed on the basis of material contained in the audit report for examination by representatives of the undertakings or the ministry concerned.

Out of 39 reports on the state enterprises in Punjab, 14 reports were based on the reports of the CAG. This type of dependence by the CPU may convert it into Public Accounts Committee which examines the reports of the CAG in order to ascertain that the money granted by legislature has been spent by the government within the scope of the demand.

The CPU has from time to time also recommended that the annual reports should be detailed and the specified details should be included depending upon the nature of the undertaking.

Conclusion

An analysis of the reporting system of state enterprises in Punjab leads to the conclusion that the annual reports presented to legislature are not of much use. The prepared and submitted reports are very short. They present only achievements without mentioning any defects or shortcomings.

On the basis of reports which are scanty and one sided it is not possible to form an objective and balanced idea about the working of state enterprises. The reports should state the working of state enterprises without concealing mistakes and failures. There is a tendency of window dressing i.e. depicting only profits and not showing the losses. Such a tendency is not very appropriate and the board should not feel shy in making correct position known to the public through the medium of annual reports. There is no standard form of accounts and the reports are heterogenous in character. Some reports give comparative figures of the last few years while other reports do not give such figures.

Reporting practice is also not uniform since directives issued by the ministers are important matters for which they are responsible to the legislature and these therefore must be published in the annual reports. The reports should also mention the circumstances necessitating the issue of the directives and the different views of the board, if any, for public information.

The experience of past few years, shows that no annual report of the state undertakings has been discussed in the Punjab Vidhan Sabha. It is true that reports of a large number of enterprises cannot be discussed due to shortage of time but it would serve the purpose even if three or four enterprises come up for discussion every year or the reports of a group of similar or allied enterprises are taken together for this purpose. However, a purposeful discussion is possible if some time is allotted for discussion of the annual reports of these enterprises in every session. In view of time constraint, a convention must be developed to cover at least some important enterprises, if not all. On the lines of the British House of Commons, the government should allocate every year three or four days for a debate on the reports of the state enterprises and opposition should be allowed to choose the enterprises which are to be debated.

A bare adherence of statutory requirements has been noticed by the authors in the attitude of the management. They have not accepted it as an effective tool of ensuring their public accountability. The government has also not paid attention to improve the annual reports of these enterprises in any manner content-wise; quality-wise, presentation-wise and so on. Apart from long time taken in finalising the accounts and reports, the disclosure of information in these reports is also not satisfactory and upto the mark.

Suggestions

The annual report is a document of crucial importance for any state enterprise. A well-drafted annual report serves as an important channel of communication between the enterprise and the public at large. The annual accounts which form an essential part of the report should be clear, simple and informative. The legal requirements with regard to preparation and presentation of the accounts do not come in the way of meeting the requirements of the average reader of the annual report. The non-disclosure of certain information should not be based on the predilections of the management, but on the grounds which could be defended publicly. If some important information is necessary to be withheld, the reason for that could be given.

The legislator is not merely interested in the rate of dividend declared by the public undertakings but is concerned with key aspects of their working such as physical and financial programme, productivity, cost of production, price structure, employment trends, labour relations, organisational changes etc. It is suggested that all the undertakings may be advised to describe in their reports their programmes and achievements in greater details. The industrial undertakings may indicate in their reports, inter alia, their unit cost of production, the rate of output per person or per unit of capital employed. Other undertakings also may be encouraged to indicate, wherever possible similar co-efficients of efficiency appropriate to their business.

The basic purpose of reporting system is to provide a correct, comprehensive and coherent picture of the working and performance of the enterprises.

In this direction the following suggestions, if implemented, will be very useful :

1. A distinction should be made between the past results and the policies for the future, a summary of the operational results should be published in tabular form at the beginning of the annual report. The summary should include the following points :

(a) It should start with details of the physical operations;

(b) It should proceed in a logical order e.g. an order of descending magnitude of importance;

(c) It should end with the financial results which are consequences of physical operations; and

(d) It should provide adequate comparison between the results of past year so as to reveal long-term trends. Such comparison can be of three kinds, namely, over different periods of time, between different parts of the organisation and between one organisation and the other.

2. To judge the progress of state enterprises in the use of indigenous or local raw materials and components from year to year, the complete information should be disclosed in the annual report of the concerned undertaking. Disclosure like this, if made, would certainly expose many facets of their working to public scrutiny, and will generally be for the good of all concerned.

3. The utility of the annual reports to the state assembly both as an instrument of information and control is greatly affected by the time taken in submitting them. The accounts and reports for the previous year should be presented to the legislature before the general budget for the following year is presented.

4. At present, the government, in general, exercises no control over the contents of annual reports, However, the concerned ministers draw attention of the state enterprises to the recommendations and observations of the Committee on Public Undertakings regarding contents, form and presentation of annual reports. No specific attempt is however, made by the government to ensure that the reports from public enterprises contain necessary and basic information and comply with the statutory requirements. Such indifferent attitude cannot be said to be desirable. The government should play an effective and decisive role in this direction.

5. The uniformity in the treatment of various items also requires to be re-stressed. Generally accepted accounting principles should be strictly followed in treating the various items so that valid comparisons are made and useful aggregates obtained.

The annual report is an important medium through which an enterprise gives an account of itself. It should be adequately detailed and exhaustive and describe every aspect of the functioning of the enterprise e.g. organisational, operational, productive, financial and personnel etc. Carefully prepared and sufficiently detailed annual reports help raise the standard of legislative discussion and obviate the need of routine questions and thus save valuable time of legislature. Therefore, there is a need for careful preparation and timely presentation of the annual report. It is hoped that the above suggestions would attract the attention of those concerned with the bringing out of the annual reports.

REFERENCES

1. Albu, A., Ministerial and Parliament Control in M. Shanks, ed. *Lessons of Public Enterprises*, London, Jonathan Cape, 1963.
2. Bhatia, B.S. and Batra, G.S., "Legislative Control over Public Enterprises", *Journal of Institute of Public Enterprise*, Hyderabad, 1993.
3. Brown, C.C., "Restructuring the Board : A Director's Perspective", *Management Review*, American Management Association, New York, Sept. 1976.
4. Davies, Earnest, "Ministerial Control and Parliamentary Responsibility of Nationalised Industries", *Political Science Quarterly*, London, Vol. 21, 1950.
5. Dholakia, Bakul, H. *The Changing Efficiency of Public Enterprises in India*, Somiya, New Delhi, 1980.
6. Gillis, Malcolm, "The Role of State Enterprises in Economic Development", *Social Research*, New York, Vol. 47, No. 2, Summer 1980.
7. Jakhar, Balram. "The People, the Parliament and the Administration", *Metropolitan*, New Delhi, 1982.
8. Khera, S.S., *Management and Control in Public Enterprises*, Asia Publishing House, Bombay, 1963.
9. Singh, Gurdeep, "Balancing Autonomy and Accountability in Public Enterprises", *Indian Management Studies Journal*, Punjabi University, Patiala, Vol. I and III, 1990.

8

Economic Liberalisation and Public Administration: The Changing Scenario

R.K. Tiwari

After Independence in India the role of the State in economic development became prominent not only due to ideological reasons but also due to the fact that private capital and markets were not developed and the level of industrialisation was low. As such, it became imperative for the Government to directly produce goods and services and also develop infrastructural facilities which in turn helped in the development of the private sector. It is also important to mention here that ours is a mixed economy and a large number of activities are undertaken in the primary, secondary and tertiary sectors by the private sector. In all these sectors the decisions are taken within a macro-economic environment influenced by economic policy and planning.

There are certain important consequences of this development:

The role of the State in national economy laid the foundation of rapid industrialisation. However, due to multiplicity of objectives, overmanning, etc., a number of public sector enterprises failed to provide reinvestable surplus.

In a large number of developmental schemes, it was observed that there exists a gap between the policy objectives and their outcomes.

With the passage of time, the role of the State and its activities in the social and economic spheres became all pervasive. This resulted in rising deficits on the balance of payments, heavy national debts and problems in the financial sector. The financial problems led various countries to have a more critical outlook and undertake reappraisal of the respective roles for the market and the State.

The role of the State in economic development has been one of the major topics of debate and discussion since many decades. More importantly since 1930s, the role of the State in the economy became more prominent as it mitigated the Great Depression of 1930s. Governments continued playing a major role in the economy and upto 1970 was an era of 'Big Government' which helped in the social and economic development. However, due to the financial problems mentioned in the preceding section, 'privatisation', de-regulation and minimal government have become current watchwords. The concept of privatisation or market mechanisms refers to a whole range of reformative actions designed to subject administrative activity to the disciplines of the market place. In North America and some of the European countries since late 1970s, the objective has been to subject government programmes, wherever possible to competition and market discipline. The main techniques which are employed in these countries to bring the State activities under market discipline are deregulation, disposal of publicly-owned agencies to the market sector, contracting-out the services formerly performed by public authorities, imposition of user charges for services previously rendered without charge. Besides, there have also been attempts to reduce the number of civil servants and bring the concept of performance measurement in the civil service.

Aspects of Liberalisation in India

This section surveys the range of policy initiatives taken in India from July, 1991 and the different forms it has taken. It shows that in the Indian context, liberalisation involves much wider and deeper changes than usually undertaken by other countries. The Union Budget 1992-93, the industrial policy, the trade policy and devaluation constitute pillars of the new economic policy. Broadly, liberalisation or deregulation in the Indian context implies policy initiatives that have radically changed the existing balance between the public and the private sectors, by reducing the scope, role and status of the public sector in the economy. In other words, this means contraction or reduction of the role of the State in the economy. This fact has been very clearly spelt out in the policy initiatives mentioned above and the budget proposals of the Government. The main thrust in all these measures is to create a more competitive environment between private capital, state capital and foreign capital leading to better quality of goods and services. However, in the new economic policy the major thrust is not so much to change the ownership of the public sector enterprises but to increase their efficiency in functions similar to their counterparts in the private sector. Basically by deregulating the industrial sector and liberalising foreign investment and technology imports, the Government is trying to achieve this objective. The following are the important elements of liberalisation in the Indian context.

De-regulation of Industries

Under the New Industrial Policy, industries like iron and steel, electricity, air-transport, ship building, heavy machinery industries such as heavy electrical plants and telecommunication cables and instruments have been opened up for the private sector participation. Earlier, these industries were reserved for the public sector under Industrial Policy Resolution, 1956. Now only, six industries continue to be so reserved. These industries are in areas where nation's security and strategic concerns predominate. The new policy on the one hand provides a greater degree of participation by the private sector in important areas of the economy and on the other hand, the public sector investment has now become more focussed and its role clearly identified. The focus in the public sector will now be on strategic, high technology and essential infrastructural areas. The Planning Commission's Directional Paper has clearly identified the principles governing public sector investment :

The public sector should make investments only in those areas where investment is of an infrastructural nature which is necessary for facilitating growth and development as a whole and where private sector participation is not yet likely to come forth to an adequate extent.

The public sector may also withdraw from areas where no public purpose is served by its presence. The public sector should come in where the investment is essentially for preservation and augmentation of basic resources of the country like land, forest, water and ecology, science and technology etc. The public sector will have responsibility for meeting social needs or for regulating long-term interests of the society like population control, health, education etc.

In large parts of public sector operations where commodities or services are produced and distributed unless it is necessary for protecting the poorest in the society, the principle of market economy should be accepted as the main operative principle. It means charging as per cost and costing with full efficiency in operations.

Abolition of Industrial Licensing

Except for a small number of industries where strategic or environmental concerns are paramount or where industries produce goods with exceptionally high import content, requirement of licensing has been totally dispensed with. In 1997-98, the number of industries subject to industrial licensing has been reduced from 14 to 9. Besides all restrictions on the expansion of large houses have been removed. The new trade policy has made the expansion of industries in the field of exports and even import substitution more attractive. Government clearance for the location of industries is dispensed with, though certain locational guidelines remain.

Removal of Investment Controls on Private Sector

Monopolies and Restrictive Trade Practices Act, 1969 made statutory that all firms with assets above Rs.100 crore have been classified as MRTP firms governed by MRTP Act. The new industrial policy has relaxed the norms of industrial approval. In the amended MRTP Act such firms do not require prior approval of the Government for investment in the de-licensed industries. However, the amended MRTP Act has given more emphasis to the prevention and control of monopolistic, restrictive and unfair trade practices, so that the consumers are adequately protected.

Foreign Investment and Foreign Technology

The limit of foreign equity holding was raised from 40 per cent to 51 per cent in the case of high priority industries. For this purpose, the Foreign Investment Promotion Board which was constituted has been revamped in 1995-96 for making rules and regulations pertaining to foreign investment more transparent. Similarly, automatic approval is being given for foreign technology agreements in high priority industries. The industries eligible for foreign direct equity investment under the automatic approval route by the RBI has been expanded in 1997-98. Foreign Investment Promotion Council has been constituted to prepare project reports in selected thrust areas and thereby facilitate the flow of foreign investment in the country.

Public Sector

Public enterprises which are chronically sick would be referred to the Board for Industrial and Financial Reconstruction for rehabilitation purpose. A social security machanism has been created to protect the interests of workers likely to be affected by such rehabilitation packages. A National Renewal Fund has been set up to assist the employees in re-training, redeployment and counselling. This fund would be used to provide safety net to workers in sick and non-viable public sector enterprises. The Government has also undertaken to divert part of equities of selected public sector enterprises through public financial institutions and mutual funds in order to raise non-inflationary finance for development.

There is a greater emphasis on performance improvement of public sector enterprises through the Memorandum of Understanding (MOU) route through which management would be given greater autonomy to facilitate the fuller discussion on performance. The MOU signed between the Government and public enterprises would be placed in the Parliament.

Contracting-Out

The Eighth Plan document has emphasised on initiating some basic improvements in the administrative system so as to increase efficiency and reduce public expenditure and bring improvements in the services to the public. Instead of creating departmental units within the Government for specialised services, contracting out services to outside agencies has been emphasised.

User Charges on Public Utilities

The Eighth Plan document has also stressed the need for increase in the 'user charges' on public utilities such as irrigation, electricity, water and higher education. This in a way means application of commercial approach to more traditional public goods and recovering their costs by charging the user rather than from general revenues. As a consequence of this, there is an element of market principle in administrative activities and economic evaluation of their outputs.

It is evident from the broad aspects given above that in India, by and large, there has been policy initiatives in the direction of liberalisation as well as application of a commercial approach in administrative activities mainly through user charges and contracting out of services.

Implications of Liberalisation and the Role of the Government

The analysis of the changing role of the Government in the wake of liberalisation indicates a new role of public administration in the national economy. The role of the Government in the economic development has been mitigated by giving more space to the private sector. In short, the Government after the recent policy initiatives has more influence than control in the economic development. As a consequence of all these developments, the role of the Government has become promotional. Government would be playing this role well if there is a timely clearance of private investment proposals. However, no amount of policy change will produce expected results unless the bureaucratic mind-set is in tune with the new liberalisation policy. As such, there has to be a change in the attitude of bureaucracy. It is quite understandable that the bureaucracy will continue to play an important role in the economy of the country. However, for achieving good results qualified and trained personnel capable of analysing policy options and designing a consistent set of macro-economic and sectoral policies are needed. Another related aspect regarding the role of bureaucracy deals with providing the conducive environment to the public and private sector activities that will operate in competitive spirit. Besides, the public sector enterprises have to be run in an efficient manner. This requires expertise and professionalism of a different kind. On the whole, the bureaucracy should have an analytical capability to execute its tasks in an effective and efficient manner within the parameters of policy initiatives. There is also a need to pursue aggressively foreign investment drive and for this purpose it is essential to set-up public relations efforts in major investing countries to make them aware of the policy changes. For this purpose, it is necessary to post officials who have certain amount of expertise in industries and trade policies.

Another area of concern in the changing role of the public administration relates to infrastructural development. It has been pointed out that lack of infrastructure is a big obstacle in the industrial growth. There are problems in areas like power, railways, shipping and communications requiring immediate attention. The *Economic Survey 1991-92* pointed out that the performance of the infrastructure sectors shows mixed trends. This report also pointed out need for improved planning and management practices to avoid time and cost over-runs, better inter-sectoral coordination etc. *The Economic Survey* 1994-95 commented both on the policy thrust as well as problems in the transitional phase of transformation.

The new development strategy attaches a high priority to the development of efficient infrastructure services so that the existing bottlenecks in transport, power, telecommunications and other infrastructure areas do not retard the overall economic growth and export dynamism. *The Economic Survey* 1997-98 also emphasised upon the need for assigning high priority to infrastructure development which is necessary to accelerate the pace of growth and sustain high levels of productivity in all sectors of the economy. Infrastructure Development Finance Company (IDFC) is to be set up as a private company with public funding to provide long-term finance for the infrastructure sector. An ordinance for setting up Central Electricity Regulatory Commission (CERC) at the centre and State Electricity Regulatory Commissions (SERCs) in the states was promulgated on 25 April, 1998. Inadequate and poor quality of existing services, technological changes, financial pressures on public entities and the needs of the external sector are crying for change. The basic issue is how we can expand private participation in infrastructure development so as to improve efficiency and reduce pressure on public finances. However, the scope of privatisation should also encompass other factors such as allocative efficiency, employment generation, and conservation of scarce resources. Deregulation and privatisation also need to be supplemented by the establishment of suitable regulatory frameworks for ensuring fair competition among different operators and protecting consumer interests, needs of vulnerable and weaker sections, public safety, internal and external security and environmental protection. The success of the present transitional phase of transformation also depends on the sustained commitment of the Government to private sector participation with more and more openness and transparency of policies and regulations. The shift from a State monopoly to a competitive environment can be effectively managed through various measures such as guaranteeing the compliance, commitment of contracts, deregulating prices, wherever necessary, and implementing commercial principles in the operation of public entities providing infrastructural services.

Similarly, various states and union territories have to play an important role in investing in infrastructure. The state governments will have also to devise policies consonant with the Union Government's new policies. The state governments have also to simplify some of the procedures for setting up of industries. There are a number of formalities for which clearance has to be taken from various authorities at the local level. Some of these are land acquisition clearance, urban land ceiling clearance, registration with pollution control board and environmental clearance, sanction plan approval from local bodies for factory building, registration with central excise and income-tax authorities, power connection from state electricity boards, formalities relating to industrial relations such as provident fund, employees state insurance, inspector of factories and labour inspector, reserve bank regulations on exchange control, imports, exports etc. Needless to say that these procedures should be simplified, time spent shortened and delays eliminated.

There is also a need to protect the environment. Industry is the biggest source of environment pollution. *The Economic and Social Survey of Asia and the Pacific,* 1991 pointed out that industrial growth diversification in many developing economies have often been accompanied by activities which make a heavy dent in the energy and quality of environmental capital. It further pointed out that the expanding micro electronics industry can create a new type of environmental contamination including heavy metals and other hazardous wastes through air and water borne discharges, which are not so well known. As a consequence, the environmental implications of industrialisation should be a subject of concern. This implies promoting an environmentally sound industrial development. *The Economic Survey* 1994-95, pointed out:

> Environment protection and ecological balance, both are essential to sustained development in the long run. The establishment of a diversified industrial structure, based

on a combination of heavy, medium and small scale industries and growing urban and rural population in the country, have produced resultant pressures on air, water and other natural resources. These pressures are largely reflected in the increased incidence of air and water pollution.

A major development in the area of industrial pollution has been the Industrial Pollution Control Project under the aegis of the World Bank. This aims to provide technical and financial assistance to clusters of Small Scale Industrial units for setting up of connection Effluent Treatment Plants (ETPs). Environmental clearance of development projects based on import assessment has been made mandatory for 29 specified categories of industries.

Consumer protection is another area in which the Government has to play an important role. The Government has to oversee that in the name of industrialisation the business firms should not have a freedom to earn profits by selling products which lack quality. It is necessary that legal measures related to restrictive trade practices, product liability, product advertising will need to be suitably strengthened. This is all the more necessary in our country where a high percentage of population is living below the poverty line. For effective consumer protection there is a need to strengthen the existing laws and improve consumer awareness.

Another important area relates to exit policy. It has been calculated that if the existing norms of sickness are applied to sick units and if such units are allowed to be closed down, it is estimated that 6 lakh workers in the public sector and 4 lakh workers in the private sector would be rendered jobless. Such a big dislocation would create a serious problem. In view of this, there is a need to formulate a well designed and comprehensive social security network so as to make the industrial restructuring workable. Another important aspect of exit policy relates to training and re-training of the existing work force. In order to make these training programmes successful, such programmes should be supplemented with enough stipend and giving subsidy to the industries and also guaranteeing availability of an adequate number of jobs so that there is no mis-match between the new jobs and the training given to the displaced workers.

A related aspect concerns reorganising of the Industrial Development Ministry in view of the reduced responsibilities. There is also to be a clear delineation of responsibilities between Foreign Investment Promotion Board and Project Approval Board. The role of the Planning Commission has also to be clearly spelt out. It has been pointed out that phenomenal success of Japan in industrial production would not have been possible without the promotional role of Ministry of International Trade and Industries (MITI). The experience of MITI suggests that the agency that controls industrial policy also needs to combine atleast planning, energy, domestic production, international trade and a share of finance particularly supply and tax policy. It is worthwhile to examine the set-up of MITI and draw lessons for restructuring the set-up in the Indian context. There is also a need to set up autonomous regulatory systems in various areas of concern to protect the competitive character as well as the interests of consumer. In this connection, G.V. Ramakrishna has rightly pointed out:

> The history of industrialised countries shows that a free market economy does not altogether do away with the role of government but imposes new responsibilities on the government. In its new role, the government should focus on setting up impartial autonomous regulatory systems to ensure that a free market does not degenerate into a "free for-all -market", that competition takes place under conditions of a level playing field and the interests of the small consumer and common man are also adequately protected.

Along with the change in the role and responsibilities of the Government in the national economy, there is also a need for a greater concern on human development. It has rightly been pointed out by Amartya Sen "Market forces create opportunities for some people. But equally they do little for the disabled or for those who are socially in such a disadvantageous position that they cannot participate in the market. It has been rightly observed thus :

> As the economy emerges from a major economic crisis and transits to the path of a strong, broad-based growth, it is vital to reinforce the process of social sector development and take special care to protect the weakest and poorest segments of the society from the rigours of structural adjustment and stabilisation policies during the transition...

As such emphasis has to be given to issues pertaining population control, literacy, urban development, housing etc. and employment generation programmes for the poor to maintain a high rate of economic growth.

Concluding Remarks

The analysis of the changing role of public administration in the context of economic liberalisation signifies that the role has become more regulatory in thrust i.e., environmental protection, consumer protection, exit policy for workers, safety to workers. Besides the other important role is to design and formulate right kind of macro-economic as well as sectoral policies consistent with the overall objectives of economic liberalisation. The policies should enable the private sector to participate in the industrialisation of the country. The other important aspect concerns participation of foreign direct investment in the economy. Besides there has to be a change in the attitude of bureaucracy both at the central level as well as at the local level with regard to the industrial development. The other important need is effective coordination among various central ministries and departments dealing with the infrastructural facilities. Another dimension relates to closer cooperation between the Government and the private sector for rapid industrialisation and globalisation of the economy. This is all the more important because as membership of various regional groups have altered the business by subjecting it to supranational legislation. As a consequence of these developments, the civil servants are required to handle delicate issues relating to domestic business and to collaborate with civil servants of other countries managing joint business and coordination policies. The public sector has to compete with the domestic private sector and the foreign private sector. It is logical that the public sector functionaries need to be professionalised in order to play their role efficiently.

Along with the change in the role and responsibilities of public administration in the national economy, there is simultaneously a greater concern and emphasis on 'human development'. The Eighth Plan emphasised that the main focus during the plan period would be on employment generation, population control, literacy, education, health, potable water and provisions of adequate food and basic infrastructure which are listed as priorities of the Eighth Plan. The State and its public administration will continue to play an important role in the national development by performing functions like maintenance of law and order, collection of revenue, planning, coordination, building infrastructure and as mentioned above, education, health and managing public sector.

The ninth five year plan emphasised on achieving growth with equity within four important dimensions of State policy i.e. quality of life of the citizens, generation of productive employment, regional balance and self reliance. It's focus is on provision of basic minimum services, social infrastructure and services, economic infrastructure, energy, agricultural development, food security, industrialisation. In the Indian context, the Constitution enjoins on the State through the Preamble and the Directive Principles of State Policy, certain obligations so as to provide social and economic justice to the people of India. As mentioned earlier, it is difficult to secure social and economic justice through market forces. As such State intervention is necessary in a large number of areas of human concern.

REFERENCES

1. Chaudhuri Mrinal Datta, 'Market Failure and Government Failure'. *Journal of Economic Perspectives*, Vol. 4, No. 2, 1990, p. 34.
2. Esman Milton J., "The Maturing of Development Administration". *Public Administration & Development*, Vol. 8, 1988, p.127.
3. Government of India, Planning Commission, *Planning Objectives. Trends and Macro-Dimensions of the Eighth Plan*, New Delhi, December 1991, pp. 6-7.
4. Government of India, Planning Commission, *Eighth Five Year Plan*, 1992-97, Vol.1, New Delhi, 1992, p. 477.
5. Government of India, Planning Commision, *Eighth Five Year Plan*, 1992-97, Vol. 1, p. 84.
6. Government of India, *Economic Survey*, 1991-92, Part-2 Sectoral Development, 1992, p.124.
7. Government of India, *Economic Survey*, 1994-95, p.153.
8. Government of India, *Economic Survey*, 1994-95, p.151
9. Government of India, *Economic Survey*, 1994-95, p. 155.
10. Government of India, *Economic Survey*, 1997-98, p. 112.
11. Government of India, *Ninth Five Year Plan*, 1997-2000.
12. Rao Hanumantha C.H., "Public Sector has a Role—Need for Change in Orientation", *The Times of India*, 27th August, 1991.
13. Hendrik J. de Ru and Roger Wettenhall, "Progress, Benefits and Costs of Privatisation" : An Introduction, *International Review of Administrative Sciences*, Vol. 56, 1991, p. 8.
14. *India Today*, December 31, 1991, p.11.

15. "Government Policy Restrictive". *The Indian Express,* December 22, 1991.
16. Johnson Chalmers, *MITI and the Japanese Miracle,* Stanford University Press, Stanford, p. 320.
17. Singh S.S., Consumerism : Concept, Concern and Consumer Care, Theme Paper for the *35th Members, Annual Conference* October, 1991, IIPA, New Delhi, p. 20.
18. Ramakrishna G.V., Regulation required to ensure free market does not become free for all, *The Times of India.* February 9,1992.
19. United Nations, *Economic and Social Survey of Asia and the Pacific,* 1991-1992, New York, 1992, p. 237.
20. Verma Kewal, First Safety net, then exit policy. *Business Standard,* 22nd October, 1991.
21. World Bank, *World Development Report,* 1991, Challenge of Development, Oxford University Press, Delhi, 1991, p. 9.
22. Wise Charles R., "Public Service Configurations and Public Organisations : Public Organization Design in the Post-Privatisation Era". *Public Administration Review,* March/April, 1990, p.146.

Technology, Development and Organisational Building

Dr. Ch. Balaramulu

Although there has been remarkable achievements in the fields of agriculture, industry, science and technology, the kind of development we have had, has led to growing disparities and inequalities. This, in turn has produced widespread discontent and unrest that have fanned the forces of violence and disorder in the society. Attention to glaring socio-economic issues and engagement in a rational political debate to resolve the outstanding problems have suffered in consequence (Ramakrishna Hegde, *Seminar*, 1990). Today there seems to be a growing consensus that the Indian economy needs to be restructured through liberalisation. This model emphasises on liberalisation of import and export rules, modernisation of agriculture, industry and technology, freedom to market forces, privatisation, higher growth rate etc., (Azit Mazoomdhar, Seminar, 1991). It is pertinent to point out that the decades of 1980's and 1990's are called the decades of worldwide economic liberalisation, which is sponsored by World Bank and IMF. In India this model is in operation since more than a decade.

Modernisation of technology — both industrial and agricultural— which is a major package of liberalisation model, is not a recent phenomenon. During pre and post-Independence period, efforts were made to modernise the existing local technology by way of carrying out research. Until the entrance of East India Company, India's local technology was much superior to British technology. The writings of British Administrators reveal that India's technology— particularly in the fields of agriculture, veterinary, irrigation, health etc.— was based on modern scientific principles. Ignoring this fact, Nehru saw the salvation of nation in the development of technology, and the role of the scientific and 'technological community', not only for developing and introducing technology but also as a conscience keeper of the nation in the manner of its use. The successive governments also gave highest priority to the modernisation of technology through importing the technology for economic development (Alvares 1979). This type of development would raise certain fundamental questions. One, whether the Western technology is socio-culturally neutral when seen in the cross national context. Two, whether the Western or modern technology and local technology have a space for co-existence or are they contradictory to each other so much so that the Western technology destroys the local technology. Three, whether there is any need for bringing about changes in the socio-economic system and cultural values to adopt to the modern technology goals of the Indian State. Four, whether there is correlation between the State and mode of production and the level of technology. Lastly, whether the existing administrative organisations can cope with the modern technology or there is need for restructuring the old organisations to carry modern technology to the people. Among these factors organisational arrangement for technological advancement and effective use of technology for economic development are most important.

Let us examine the impact of technology vis-a-vis the organisational arrangements. More particularly the paper seeks to examine the role of technology in the rural development and organisational arrangements for transfer of technology to the people. The major hypothesis, of this study is that, unlike the Western countries, in India, the organisations are not modernised to cope up with the technological advancement. Further, we are importing the technology or modernising the technology without taking into account the socio-economic and cultural constraints. This type of development would result in widening the gap between the rich and the poor, unemployment, subordination of human beings to technology, destruction of indigenous technology, centralised authority, wastage of money, energy, domination of a few over the market forces, paving the way for capitalistic tendencies, strengthening of private property etc. Further, this would also lead to domination of International Government Organisations (WB &

IMF), which are providing aid and assistance for modernisation of technology in our country, over the market and later on every aspect of the human beings. Of these a few aspects are analysed here.

The analyses are mostly based on the secondary sources and personal observations. Section-I briefly touches on government efforts for technological advancements in India. Section-II deals with the developmental strategies for rural development (which includes technology) and examines the nature and characteristics of organisations for dissemination of technology. The impact of modern technology on the rural society is examined in the third section. The last section presents the concluding observations.

I

The most powerful and ubiquitous of social organisations is the government. A government interacts with technology in a variety of ways, sometimes deliberately seeking and encouraging certain aspects and rejecting, delaying or hindering others. Such involvement of the government with technology is a comparatively recent phenomenon and shows trends of increasing interaction in the future. While the interaction between technology and society is as old as human history, the relationship of technology with the government developed increasingly as a historical necessity, mainly in the last couple of hundred years. There was a certain logic in the process. As technology began to regulate wider areas of social life, they also began to take a greater interest in the nature of technological developments and their social consequences. More recently, particularly since the Second World War, societies and governments have been seriously concerned with technology and its consequences in a comparative manner through the articulated science and technology policies (B.D. Nag Chaudhuri, 1979 p. 45).

The speed of technological developments increased significantly after the Second World War not only in military technology but in many areas of human needs. Soon after the World War-II many third world countries, which gained independence from the colonial rule, followed the developmental models of Western industrialised countries, including the technology and also tried to modernise the technology for economic development. In India, after the independence, the central government also established several research organisations for advancement of science and technology. Most important of them are Indian Council of Agricultural Research (ICAR, 1947), the Council of Scientific and Industrial Research (CSIR, 1947), the Department of Atomic Energy (1951), Defence Research and Development Organisation (1958), which account for nearly 80 per cent of the research and development expenditure of the government (B.D. Nag Chaudhari, p. 52). To cope with rapid advances in the field of science and technology in India and around the world, the Government of India formulated a new science and technology policy in 1958. In the same year Nehru initiated the Scientific Advisory Committee (SAC) of the Cabinet through a Cabinet resolution. Later, several organisations like Geological Survey of India (GSI), Indian Meteorological Department (IMD), Indian Standards Organisation and the Test Laboratories (ISOTL), the Railway Design and Standards Organisation (RDSO), Indian Council of Medical Research (ICMR), etc. were also established for the development of science and technology. Apart from these organisations, there are other agencies of research in communications, energy, health, housing, transport, environment and education for the promotion of technology.

In the initial stages, the Government of India did not enter all the fields of technology and industry. It entered the iron and steel, copper, zinc and aluminium, the heavy chemicals, the antibiotics and the petroleum industries. The government's thinking influenced by the scientific advisory committee in the early sixties, resulted in certain kinds of broad policies. For example, the government took the view that it would be of advantage to encourage the import of technology in certain specified directions. Such import would be backed up by setting up laboratories, organisations, agencies and by allocating funds to absorb and adopt these technologies for indigenous use (B.D. Nag Chaudhari, p. 54).

If we closely examine the rural development strategies in India, we find that the modernisation of technology started by early 1950's and continued even to date. During 1950's, for effective implementation of Community Development Programme (CDP) the Government of India sought aid and assistance from American Government. This assistance was mostly in the form of technology.

During sixties the Green Revolution was considered as an important strategy for development. During this period IAAP, Integrated Area Development Programme (IADP), High Yield Variety

(HYV) Programmes were launched to improve the production. In all these programmes the technology was almost considered either independent or neutral to all classes. Further, it was realised that the developmental strategies widened the disparities between the individual and the regions (G. Parthasarathy, 1971).

During seventies several anti-poverty programmes like Small Farmers Development Agency (SFDA), Marginal Farmers and Agricultural Labour Development Agency (MFALDA), Integrated Rural Development Programmes (IRDP), National Rural Employment Programme (NREP) etc., were launched to improve the living conditions of the poor. Through these programmes the state also intended to introduce a new technology i.e., White Revolution, in the rural areas. For this purpose Operation Flood I and Operation Flood II programmes were sponsored by the Netherland Government. In this context, it is also important to note that the International Governmental Organisations (IGO) like World Bank, FAO, ILO etc. have advocated the importance of equity and the involvement of the rural poor in the development process by the provision of redirections of investments or inputs—a new style approach to the poor. This new styled approach advocated for redirecting the investments towards basic needs, agrarian reforms, Training and Visit System (T & V system) Programmes. Of these programmes Training and Visit System, was considered as an important communication method for dissemination of the technology and a core project for poverty alleviation. In India, this programme is in operation since 1974 with the active involvement and financial assistance of the World Bank. This approach is based on use of appropriate technology, close supervision and proper management of the information flow to the farmers, more particularly to the small farmers, who are poor. It is also based on the assumption that this approach would increase the productivity on all farms despite the socio-economic and political structures acting against the interests of small farmers.

1980's is the period of bio-technological revolution. Several research projects were carried on this aspect. Under these projects new vegetables and fruit seeds were invented or imported for economic development.

II

The above discussion indicates that the technologies—Green Revolution technology, White Revolution technology and Biotechnology revolution — are considered as important instruments for rural development. All these measures are aimed at modernising the technology and thereby improving the economic conditions of the people in general and the poor in particular. The success of these measures, to a large extent, depends on the organisational structures devised for rural development. Therefore, there is a need to review the strengths and weaknesses of the organisations which are created for implementation of rural development programmes. Further, it is also necessary to analyse the impact of technology on the rural society.

The major problem in the developmental strategies, during the last four and a half decades has been evolving suitable administrative structure to meet the challenges of the society. The problem was further compounded by the continuity of the old traditions and institutions. The organisations tend to be based on pre-colonial or colonial value system. The major legacy of the British which has been preserved intact in independent India is the tradition of the Generalist Administrative Service (IAS) which is often regarded as a successor to the Indian Civil Service (ICS). All the top positions in the Secretariat, several positions of heads of technical departments and positions of district collectors are held by them. The British view was that an ICS Officer could hold any position and discharge the duties effectively. The supreme belief here is that an officer at the higher level need not have any technical knowledge. That the technical man should be on tap and not on top continues to influence the administrative division of work. Since he has a narrow view, it is argued, his advice and proposals should be subjected to a lay secretary (a Generalist) who is the Chief advisor to the Government. As a result of this supremacy of generalist the technical man is relegated to the background. In this age of exploding knowledge and technological advancement such an age old concept dominating the Indian administrative culture is only an indication of the grip of colonial past on the development administration (G.Ram Reddy and G.Haragopal, 1987, p. 9)

The studies on the rural development programmes reveal that the administrative structures are not suitable for the effective implementation of the programmes. Centralised authority, lack of free and frank communication, absence of proper communication, too much of paper work, manipulation of records, rigid rules and regulations, frequent change of programmes or priorities, inadequacy of extension machinery, frequent transfers of the officials, assigning unrelated work to the technical staff, defective personnel policy, inadequate training to the technical staff, creation of multiple agencies for a single activity, lack of accountability in the organisations, lack of coordination between various departments and functionaries, dominance of bureaucracy, etc. are some of the important administrative problems which are hampering the progress of development process in the rural areas (Ch. Bala Ramulu, 1991).

The behaviour and values of bureaucracy incharge of development, play significant role in realising the goals. It is, however, noticed that value orientation of these personnel is no different from those working in non-development departments. The studies on values of bureaucracy reveal that a large portion of the officials have more bureaucratic attitude which hinder the process of change and development. Among the behavioural values it seems the strict observance of rules and regulations has been the cherished goal of the officials. While from the point of view of officials such values ensure them protection from unnecessary public criticism, the developmental work which is most often situational does need some flexibility in the strict observance of letters of rules and regulations (R.B. Jain and O.P. Dwivedi, 1990, p. 435). Further, the studies pointed out that, in the rural areas the total developmental effort is guided neither by any concern for the poor nor by any clear-cut social purpose (G.Ram Reddy and G. Haragopal, 1985).

An examination of literature on Indian bureaucracy reveals that Indian bureaucracy does not operate on Weberian norms (Kuldeep Mathur, 1986). Although, theoretically, it is the Weberian form that has been accepted, the Indian bureaucracy including rural bureaucracy does not confirm to the form. It is this gap between the form and content that needs to be analysed. One of the possible explanations is that Weberian model is essentially Euro-Centric. The model acquired its own 'unique' character in its interaction with entirely different setting. In a country like India, where the structural-functional differentiation is low, the organisations cannot enjoy relative autonomy as they do in industrially advanced societies. Given in this context, the economy, polity and culture overlap and influence each other. Consequently, no institution can escape the ubiquitous influence of the deeper underlying and interconnected societal processes (G. Hara Gopal and V.S. Prasad, 1990).

The above brief discussion indicates that the existing administrative structures are not suitable for effective implementation of the rural development programmes. On the other hand they are the major strumbling blocks for transformation of technology or development. This situation, perhaps, strengthens the argument of privatisation of public organisations and services. In this context, it is important to note that the State is slowly withdrawing its welfare activities and privatising the services and public organisations. The underlying assumption of this strategy is that private organisations are more efficient than the public organisations either in dissemination of technology or bringing about development.

III

As mentioned earlier, it was believed that technology could be a substitute for the structural changes to bring development in the rural areas. Keeping this in view the new technologies — the Green Revolution, White Revolution, Bio-technology Revolution — have been introduced for rural development.

An examination of Green Revolution reveals that adoption of technology is associated with size of the family, literacy, size of the land, land utilisation pattern, sources of irrigation, temperature, soil conditions, rainfall, and socio-economic conditions of the locality or area. Further, it is also associated with the extension agencies of the government. An analysis of impact of Green Revolution indicates that it has disturbed the economy of farming. The new technology in the shape of electricity, pumpsets, tractors, rigs, high yielding variety seeds etc., have deepened the process of capital penetration in certain pockets of the rural economy. While this has improved the production, it has hit the rural poor which includes small and marginal farmers and agricultural labourers. Further, this has resulted in increasing polarisation of the classes in rural areas creating conditions for major structural transformation. It is this consideration, perhaps, that has made the people in power to express their concern and initiate some action through conscious intervention. The intervention is intended to blunt the polarisation of process and raise overall production. Thus, the concept of SFDA, IRDP and other anti-poverty programmes have to be essentially viewed from this perspective (Ch. Balaramulu, 1984, 1991).

In the case of White Revolution technology, i.e., under operation Flood-I, II and III programmes we have achieved considerable progress. Under these programmes, several Dairy Cooperative Societies and Dairy Development Corporations are established for the promotion of milk production. Apart from this, under IRDP programmes several thousands of poor farmers and agricultural labourers are given jersey cows, murra buffaloes, sheep to improve the milk production in the country.

An examination of Dairy Cooperative Societies and Dairy Development Corporations indicate that neither they are helpful to the consumers nor producers of milk (Bharat Dogra, 1985). An analysis of animal husbandary schemes, under IRDP, reveals that the medium and small farmers, who have some land and other assets have derived benefits from the schemes. The marginal and agricultural labourers, who are poor, could not retain the schemes due to large scale death of animals. The animals, which were non-local, could not withstand the local conditions. Besides the socio-economic necessities and outstanding debts compelled the poor to dispose off the schemes. Considerable percentage of the beneficiaries have resorted to artificial purchasing. The main reasons for non-utilisation of the schemes by the poor are mostly related to cumbersome rules and regulations, poor socio-economic conditions of the beneficiaries, lack of freedom to the beneficiaries in selecting the schemes, negative attitude of officials towards the poor, involvement of pyraveekar (middle men) in implementation of schemes etc. Thus, there are inherent weaknesses in the formulation and the execution of the schemes (Ch. Balaramulu, 1991).

Another implication of White Revolution technology is that it has disturbed the social relations in the rural areas. Prior to the Operation Flood-I, II and III programmes the villagers, irrespective of the caste, religion and economic status, used to exchange the milk, butter milk, free of cost, whenever there was a shortage. Further, the members of the household used to consume milk and ghee which have nutritive value. Today all these are slowly disappearing because of dairy technology. The milk vendors, milk centres are collecting the milk from the rural areas and supplying to the Dairy Development Corporation or to the urban people directly.

The dairy technology is used for preservation of milk, separation of fat from milk and making by- products from it. These by-products—milk powder, ghee, baby foods, skimmed milk, biscuits, chocolates, ice-creams etc. — strengthened the hands of industrialists and multinational corporations. The contribution of Operation Flood - I, II and III programmes, is that about 2600 companies have been established which are owned by Indian Industrialists and multinational corporations (*Indian Express*, 1988). After the announcement of delicensing of dairy sector several multinational and big Indian companies are making a 'beeline' for dairy units. Among these companies, most prominent are Glaxo, Nestle, Cadbury, Noble Soya, Kwality Ice-cream, Kissan Foods, Smithkline Beecham (makers of Horlicks), General Foods, Raymonds Woollen, Apple Industries, Godrej Foods etc. which are competing with each other. Dairy sector sources say that, after delicensing, these companies are making huge profits, which are atleast three times that of liquid milk. They also point out that the natural fallout of this could be a flood of milk-based products in the Indian markets on one hand but an acute shortage of liquid milk on the other (Arindam Mukherjee, *Indian Express,* March 19, 1992). Thus, the White Revolution technology instead of improving the socio-economic conditions of poor, has disturbed the social harmony in the rural areas. Further, it has also helped petty traders, industrialists and multinational corporations in expanding their market and earning profits.

The Bio-technological revolution also resulted in expansion of market of multinational corporations. The vegetable and fruit seeds, which are high yielding and non-local, are prone to diseases. To protect the crops, orchards, the farmers are compelled to use fertilisers and pesticides. This is also true in the case of food grains. In India about 80 per cent of fertilisers and pesticides that are used in the agricultural sector are produced by multinational corporations. The farmers, who are better-off can afford the use of fertilisers and pesticides and increase the production (J.S. Bara, 1981). The studies on Training and Visit system also indicate that, the medium and large farmers — progressive farmers — derived more benefits from Green Revolution and Bio-technology revolution. The marginal and small farmers, who are poor, could not compete with the medium and large farmers in using modern inputs to increase the production. Further, the extension staff which supply inputs and information, found it easier and more rewarding to work with progressive farmers than with the poor farmers. This situation widened the gulf between the progressive and the poor farmers. (Ch. Balaramulu and Hussain Khan, 1984). Thus, the organisation and technology are not neutral to all classes.

IV

The technology is basic to human nature and interacts deeply with human society to produce an impact on the directions and pace of social evolution. The interaction between technology and society, perhaps, is about one million years old. In the process of evolution of society the technology has not remained uniform and static, but variegated and dynamic. It is well informed through a variety of inputs—inputs from science, through social interactions, through perceptions or pre-conceptions of what society might need. Technology today is very informed technology as compared to what it was even a hundred years ago. This is partly due to utilisation of technology and new innovations and partly due to importing the technology. Today, modernisation of technology is considered an important strategy for development, all over the world. In India, during post-independence period, several measures were taken up by the Government and it is giving,top priority to modernise the technology by way of importing it from western societies for economic development.

But modernisation of technology, as mentioned earlier, in any society leads to diversification of technology, specialised skills, division of work, breakdown of communications between divisions and individuals, monotony of extremely specific jobs, alienating individuals from the group, creation of hierarchies, concentration of technical know-how in the hands of a few, centralised decision-making, making workers delinked from the fruits of their own labour, specifying special norms for specific job etc.

Further, this type of technology strategy would raise certain fundamental questions like, whether the imported technology is neutral to countries marked by different socio-cultural fabrics, different classes, different modes of production, and can co-exist with local technology or destroys it. Most important question is whether the existing administrative organisations can cope with the modern technology or there is need for restructuring the old organisations. The organisational theories — classical, human relations, behavioural etc., have all emerged in the Western societies to meet the challanges of advanced technology. A critical examination of these theories reveal that they make the worker subordinate to the technology and management and less developed countries to the developed countries. Further, these theories also aim at expansion of capitalism and private property.

The origin of organisations in India was more a result of the role nature of the State rather than the demands of technology. An examination of functioning of administrative organisations, particularly in the post-Independence period, indicates that they are based on pre-colonial, colonial and neo-colonial value systems. The result has been continuation of old institutions, cumbersome rules and regulations, unproductive work, centralised authority, grip of traditions over the administrative system etc. The colonial bureaucratic structures and pre-colonial hierarchical social structures reinforce each other. In this process changes introduced either are internalised or feudalised.

An analysis of impact of modern technology on the rural society reveals that the Green Revolution technology has widened the gap between the rich farmers and the poor. The White Revolution and Bio-Technological Revolution, instead of creating better conditions for the poor are disturbing social harmony in the rural areas. Further, these technologies help petty traders, industrialists and multinational corporations in expanding their market and in earning profits. The poor and the working class people are being thrown to the mercy of underdeveloped market forces. These technologies are sharpening contradictions among various classes and creating conditions for major structural transformation. The people's movements that are taking place in the rural areas are indicative of contradictions among various classes. The State, instead of positively resolving these contradictions is either withdrawing its services or privatising the services and the public organisations. The focus of power is shifting from the development to the regulatory department. Thus, the above analysis reveals that the application of modern technology has indeed resulted in erosion of indigenous technology and the concomitant harmonious social fabric in atleast certain spots of social life. Further, it has also resulted in increased poverty and unemployment and aggravation of tensions in otherwise harmonious social relationships in the rural areas. However, here it is to be noted that these observations are based on secondary sources of information and personal observations of the researcher in certain areas of Andhra Pradesh, India and it is difficult to generalise it. To gain more insights into phenomenon, there is a need for more systematic empirical studies in different parts of the country. Such studies acquire importance in the context of greater interaction in the aftermath of the collapse of bipolar world system and the consequent opening up of developing societies for modernisation with the help of technologically developed western world.

REFERENCES

1. Alvares Claude, Homo Faber, Allied Publishers, New Delhi, 1979.
2. Bala Ramulu Ch., Administration of Anti-Poverty Programmes, KASPA, Warangal, 1984.
3. Bala Ramulu Ch. and P. Hussain Khan, Poverty Eradication Through Transfer of Technology A Study of Training Visit System, Paper presented to Indian Association of Public Administration, Sambalpur, 1985.
4. Bala Ramulu Ch., Public Policies : An Evaluation of IRDP, Ajanta Publications, New Delhi. 1991.
5. Bara J.S., The Political Economy of Rural Development, Concept, New Delhi, 1981.
6. Chaudhuri B.D. Nag, Technology and Society—An Indian View, Indian Institute of Advanced Study, Simla, 1979.
7. Gopal S.K., Bureaucratic Administration in India, Chugh, Allahabad, 1985.
8. Mukherjee Arindam, *Indian Express,* Hyderabad Edition, March 19, 1992.
9. Haragopal G. and Ch. Bala Ramulu, "Poverty Alleviation programmes : IRDP in an Andhra Pradesh District", *Economic & Political Weekly* Vol. Nos. 35 & 36, Sept., 2-9, 1989, p. 2025.
10. Haragopal G. and V.S. Prasad, "Social Bases of Administrative Culture in India", *Indian Journal of Public Administration (IJPA),* Special Issue on Contemporary Administrative Culture of India, Vol. XXXVI, No. 3, 1990.
11. Haragopal G. and C. Chandra Shekar, The State Apparatus in the Third World, The Theoretical and Methodological Dimensions, Paper presented at a Seminar on Theoretical and Methodological Problems in the Study of State and Society in the Third World, Organised by Nehru Memorial (NMM) Library and University of Delhi, 25-28 Nov., 1991.
12. Haragopal G., Technological Changes and Organisational Development : Some Observations in K. Murali Manohar and others ed., Administrative Theory, Trends & Perspectives, Book Bird, 1991.
13. Hegde Ramakrishna, The Eighth Plan, *Seminar, 376,* December, 1990.
14. *Indian Express,* Hyderabad Edition, June 11, 1988.

15. Jain R.B. and O.P. Dwivedi, "Administrative Culture and Bureaucratic Values in India", *Indian Journal of Public Administration*, Vol. XXXVI, No. 3, July-Sept. 1990.

16. Karanath, "New Technology and Traditional Rural Institutions : Case of Jajamani Relations in Karnataka", *Economic & Political Weekly, 1987*.

17. Mathur Kuldeep, ed. A Survey of Research in Public Administration, 1970-79, Indian Council of Social Science Research, New Delhi, 1986.

18. Mazoomdhar Azit, "Freeing the Economy, *Seminar*", *380*, April, 1991.

19. Parthasarathi G., Green Revolution and Weaker Sections, Bombay, 1971.

20. Pugh D.S. ed., Organisation Theory, Penguin, Harmondsworth, Middlesex, England, 1985.

21. Reddy G. Ram and G. Haragopal, Public Policy and Rural Poor in India, Concept, New Delhi, 1985.

22. Reddy G. Ram and G. Haragopal, "Rural Development : Implementation is the Crux", Asian Survey, 1987.

23. Shah Ghanshyam ed., Capitalist Development : Critical Essays, Popular Prakashan, Bombay, 1990.

24. Tilak B.D., Technology Planning for Rural Development, 1989.

25. Venkateswarlu B., "Theories of Organisation and Development", in Susheela Kaushik ed., Public Administration, An Alternative Perspective, 1990.

10

Administration in the Post-Industrial State

Klaus Konig, Speyer

I. Approaches to a "New" Kind of Administration

The fundamental characteristic of modern societies is their functional differentiation under relatively independent sub-systems and spheres of action, with the concomitant rationalization of these fields in accordance with their specific principles (Luhmann, 1985). Prominent fields of action for such a historic change are the economic system governed by principles like private property, market and competition and, on the other hand, the politico-administrative system which is ruled by principles of, for example, public earmarking with priority over the order of property rights, regularization or hierarchy. Socialism in practice, however, did not keep to this course of development. Society was subjected to the system ideology of one single party. De facto, the economy was nationalized. A cadre administration was clapped over State, economy and society (Konig, 1991 (a)). This Marxist-Leninist modernization effort failed. Practised socialism had to declare bankruptcy.

At the end of the 20th century, the occidental administration thus happens to be without its secular counterpart and, on its part, now appears to brush aside the "basic optimality" of the various system rationalities depending on the sphere of action concerned. To some minds, the market economy's "victory" over the centrally planned economy seems to be transformed into a victory won by the principles of economy over those of the State. More and more ideologies and model concepts are emerging which demand competition in the public sector, a private enterprise culture within the civil service or at least the simulation thereof (Moe, 1994). The forms of manifestation of such postulates differ. They include a simple international marketing of model management concepts such as, for example, Lean Management (Bosenberg/Metzen, 1993) or Total Quality Management (Peters, 1993). There are scientific conceptions such as Reinventing Government that combine ideas on free market economy with the popular Business Motivation literature (Osborne/Gaebler, 1992). There are labels like, for instance, New Public Management (Hood, 1991) lumping together the recent public sector reforms in countries like Britain, Australia, and New Zealand (Mascarenas, 1993). And finally, administrative policy has drawn up sets of claims that list elements from all of these doctrines, model concepts, and draft conceptions, in some cases quite regardless of their inner compatibility.

If we consider the term of paradigm change (Kuhn, 1978), not according to the opinions of scholars, advisors and propagandists but to the attitudes and viewpoints of those engaged actively in politics and administration, there is probably no country where this change has taken place all along the line. Yet it is true that there has been considerable interference in administrative traditions in the name of an enterpreneurial spirit, in particular, in Great Britain (Ridley, 1993); and there are a number of enterpreneurial simulations, mainly at local administration level (Banner/Reichard, 1993). The prize-winning acme would seem to be a municipal waste disposal utility that can consider itself competitive with private bidders. This, however, will make some people ask why such a utility is not privatized outright. A complex beset with even greater difficulties than implementation is practical performance measurement or assessment — unless we are prepared to content ourselves with the judgement of politicians and top executives in the civil service. So far, assessment from outside has been realized only in a few exceptional cases, one of them being Australia, where this was done by parliamentary committees (Kouzmin, 1993). All things considered, the empirical foundation for a scientific judgement as regards a paradigm that goes beyond individual reforms and isolated administrations appears rather slender. Yet this does not preclude criticism being levelled at the underlying ideology by administrative scientists. It strikes one in this context that the model concepts of entrepreneurial management in public administration do not adequately reflect such administration's social environment (Laux, 1994).

Public administration may be interpreted as a social system existing and functioning in accordance with its own order but, on the other hand, it also depends on environmental conditions in a complex and changing society. Enterpreneurial administration concepts are oriented above all to the order concept inherent in the system itself. Administrative precepts, management instruments, result-oriented approaches, production cost accounting, agreements on operational targets, production-related units of organization, decentralized resourcing, and many other issues are involved (Timmermann, 1993). Being one part of the administration's environment, the economic system is of interest in that it appears appropriate to provide precepts for an entrepreneurial culture in the civil service.

Quite apart from the privatization discussion with its multiplicity of facets (Klaus Konig, 1992), many questions relating to a differentiated society are left open: from the primacy of politics over organizational learning in a legally controlled administration to market failure in the supply of goods. The limited view of the world becomes particularly evident where citizens are turned into customers (Moe, op.cit : III). The multifarious differentiation of their roles as voters, tax payers, pupils and students, troublemakers, welfare recipients, juveniles or trade people according to the respective politico-administrative context, gives way to an attitude anticipating uniform behaviours. With the postal services, local water utilities and local public transport one may be satisfied with the role of customer. As regards youth welfare offices, criminal investigation departments, fiscal administration or the foreign office, there are likely to be further demands made on the patterns of performance.

II. Industrialism and Post-Industrialism

Accordingly, curtailment of an entrepreneurial esprit de corps in public administration require the discussion on the modernization of the administrative system to be widened. Environmental conditions can be interpreted in political, legal and economic terms. If we revert to the modern times theory, this means starting with the socio-cultural connections between society, state and administration. From the social development such environmental conditions result that are decisive for the design of a civil service system (Bohret, 1988).

One of the still decisive fundamentals of modernity lies in the term "industrial society" (Klages, 1991 (a)). It relates to a mode of safeguarding social needs that extend beyond the economic sphere and embrace other social system ranges such as public administration, for instance. The wide use of machinery as the focal point of industrialization and new division-of-labour patterns also include clerical functions. Industrial growth also involves the expansion of state activities. New forms of organization with a changed division of labour do not only develop in private production but also in the provision of public goods. Social differentiations regarding, for instance, work and leisure time, places of work and housing, family and safeguarding of social needs, etc. also impinge upon the civil service. Vertically divided civil service career grades from police constable to senior executive officer, supplemented by horizontally structured professions in technical and scientific branches, reflect the change that has occurred in the order of social grades and in the professional melange. Technical and scientific modes of work are characteristic for both the administrative and economic spheres of action. In both sectors, the processes of operation are formalized and controlled. The degree of rationalization is rising in both economic and administrative institutions.

From numerous different viewpoints criticism has been levelled at society's industrial texture. This debate includes disputes which overlap one another mainly due to the widely discussed capitalism issue (Habermas, 1973). Yet, once again, it was industrialism which, in convergence theories, had been credited with greater influential power than the political differences, between a free and constitutional democracy and the rule of socialism in practice (Aron, 1962). Criticism of the industrial society extends from early alienation these pointing to the fragmentation and specialization of human activities in the goods production process that make their mark on the people's everyday consciousness (Marcuse, 1984), to "risk society" theories laying stress on self-imperilment and man-made catastrophes in nuclear, chemical or genetical production in the late industrial age (Beck, 1986, 1991).

Public administration is included in such doubts. Alienation phenomena can be laid at the door of the state bureaucracies, blaming them for impersonal attitudes, rule-based formalism, incomprehensible officialese, obscure distribution of competence, procedural schematism, etc. (Hoffmann-Riem, 1979). In the theoretical approaches as regards the industrial risk society, on the one hand, there is no confidence in the ability of public welfare politics to avert imperilments, and, on the other hand, it is feared that the politico-administrative decisions may themselves trigger off dangers. Critical opinions are directed at the administration in particular when a separate power of rule and the state's functional capacity are questioned at the same time. This is true at least for continental Europe, where the classical modern administrations are by nature state-oriented (Heady, 1984).

The public administration is implicated accordingly when the State in industrial societies is regarded with scepticism (Forsthoff, 1971). Critics fear a loss of state control, of sovereignty. The State is considered unable either to avoid or dominate the factual necessities and the autonomy inherent in industrial conditions. Ultimately, the logic of technical processes seems to govern politics and administration is stated to have been infected by the mentality of technical progress. As proof, reference is made, for example, to the penetration of technical and scientific professions into the civil service, displacing lawyers in their classical role as all-rounders while the specialist spirit is gaining ground.

From another viewpoint, attention is drawn to the dangers arising for the State and administration in highly industrialized societies from the compensation of technical, economic and social consequences. The State is undertaking more and more functions of social safeguarding, intervention in markets and enterprises, consultancy, assistance, education of the population, of precautions against risks not only from natural dangers but technical and man-made perils as we1 l. This appears to result in a welfare bureaucracy, which — reminiscent of Sisyphus — produces ever poorer and more problematic results in spirit of steadily growing efforts and dedication. Confronted with the dynamism of social claims, State and administration seem to have developed into a stability risk. Categories like ungovernability, apathy towards the State, and legitimation crisis characterize the critical consideration of public affairs (Klages, 1975: Hennis/Kielmannsegg, 1977/79). "Over-burdened State-disaffected people?", is one of the questions asked to the accompaniment of the discords in the welfare society of the late industrial era (Klages, 1981).

Where there are so many sceptical diagnoses, an optimistic prognosis will not be lacking. It manifests itself in the concept of the post-industrial society (Fourastie, 1954), according to which, in the wake of the industrial society, a new phase of social development has begun (Bell, 1975). Nonetheless, this kind of extrapolated subsequency need not be interpreted as implying a rupture in history. On the contrary, the industrial society's rationality is extended beyond its classical range of definition. From this viewpoint, the continued scientific and technological progress means growing productivity, more leisure time, a welfare economy, highly qualified professionals and personal prosperity. Natural sciences and technology enable the tensions between new needs and new scarcities to be relieved (Hugger, 1987 : 88). The centricity of theoretical knowledge as the source of innovation and also as the starting point of social policy programming is considered an "axial principle" (Bell, op.cit : 115).

The post-industrial society is a services society. It is presumed that the preponderance of the services sector over the production of material goods is continuing to grow. Developments in education and research are leading to the creation of a "quaternary" sector (Hugger, 1987 : 88). Changes are occurring within the system of social strata and the structure of rule (Klages 1991a : 555). A class of professionalized occupations requiring technical qualifications is beginning to develop and is replacing the outdated status-based strata with a performance-oriented system. The increasing claim to power on the part of this new class manifests itself in the fact that both politics and the economy are increasingly governed by science (Bell, op.cit : 247 ff.). Such subsequent projections of the industrial society then extend up to the image of an "information society" (Deutsch/Sonntag, 1981). This society features a dominance of information technologies, the information professions consolidating their position in the social system structure and then gaining majorities.

III. Aspects of Post-Industrial Administration

The characteristics of the post-industrial society embody, in socio-cultural terms,the environmental conditions for public administration that form part of the justification for that administration's existence and its functioning as a social system. Accordingly, they give an idea of the development lines to be expected in advancing the formation of the system. If post-industrialism does not constitute a break with the old industrial society but its extrapolation. There is little or no likelihood in the near future of a break with the welfare state system of provisions for technical, economic and social emergencies by the public administration — at least not for socio-cultural reasons. Existing differentiations like those between family and social security are maintained. New differences do appear. Growing prosperity makes welfare expectations rise, too. Where human lifespan is prolonged, not the least due to the progress of medical science and technology, people expect material provision for infirmity, and allowance is being made for such expectations by instituting a nursing insurance.

When changes occur in the industrial production system in the direction of information processing technologies, there are not only the new industries : old industries are still there as well. According to all experience, the consequences of such an industrial change are not provided for by market mechanisms, at least not at a short notice. Compensation by State action is needed. When a new quality of technical and scientific professionalization determines the occupational life, there are not just new professions in evidence : old occupations persist as well. And here again, it is in the public sector that the consequences of such changes have to be compensated for. The post-industrial administration will thus continue to be governed by the programmes, organizations, civil service employees and budgets of labour and social policies (Klages, 1994 (a)).

Post-industrial changes make the problems of location and local mobility more acute. For there are old as well as new locations. State and administration are called for in both instances. In one case, it is a matter of redevelopment, revitalization of outdated facilities and putting them to new uses. Mere decay is not tolerated politically (Hesse, 1988). In the other case, a new infrastructure needs to be installed. Simultaneously, the post-industrial society does not only feature social mobility but spatial mobility as well. From traffic routes to communication networks, adequate facilities and equipment must be made available and controlled. A gradient of supply standards from municipal to rural areas no longer appears acceptable. The administration is obliged to ensure comparable standards of performance (Wagener, 1974).

If increased productivity due to technical progress makes the post-industrial society develop into a "leisure-time society", this will not only lead to a new branch of economy, but it will also make the planning and organization of recreational activities a new and expanding sector of public administration. Thus, the beginning of school holidays may mean a ban on leave for traffic policemen. Public authorities undertake to work out plans for tourism, recreation, sport and leisure-time activities for youth. An infrastructure of swimming pools, sports grounds, amusement and playing facilities, footpaths, youth centres, etc. is built up. Leisure-time turns out to be a sphere of life in the need of regulation, if only to protect nature from man. Regulations will extend from the need of official permits in specific cases to the general preservation of the countryside.

If one of the principal features of industrialism is to turn the post-industrial society into a "risk society", social self-endangerment and man-made catastrophes call for increased government activities (Bohret, 1990). A multiplicity of functions need to be fulfilled in the fields of disposal, monitoring and control as well as safety. Public emergency planning is required to prepare for situations of great danger. Government operated information systems are necessary to allow endangerments to be recorded and gauged. Scientific and technical expert knowledge is required to permit any such dangers to be judged correctly (Bohret, 1993 : 91-95). Legal rules and regulations are needed to allow the population's behaviour to be controlled by compulsory means. Police, emergency and rescue services must be at hand. Suitable publicly-owned equipment, facilities and vehicles must be available. In addition to all this, the protection and accommodation of those affected must be ensured, even on the question of their official compensation. This subject covers a very complex range of administrative action (Konig 1991(b)).

If the characteristics of the post-industrial society include the ability to evolve a new quality of scientific and technical professions, this has an impact on the functions of public administration and, at the same time, triggers off reflex developments in those very civil service staff structures (Konig/Oechsler, 1987). Universities and technical colleges have to be expanded in order to provide for appropriate qualifications. However, this is not simply a matter of academicizing occupational life. A wide variety of options ranging from polytechnical training for medium-level job specifications to computer training for typewriting services are topics of discussion. The education sector's expansion has reactions on the civil service staff. Not only that, as explained above, new technical and scientific professions penetrate into the civil service, leading to a regrouping according to the branches of study like pharmacy, constructional engineering, mining, etc. In cases where the general public system of education does not provide for appropriate curricula and courses of study, specific intra-administrative institutions are established such as, for example, technical colleges for tax and customs administration, for the labour exchange authorities, or, at a higher level, academies for the further training of civil servants.

It being scientific and technical progress which, by its continuity, is the progenitor of the post-industrial society, it is understandable that the State promotes scientific research and technological development. Such promotion takes place both within and outside the universities. Large-scale extramural research institutions for nuclear research, space exploration, genetic research, etc. are established and administered by the State. A specific research administration authority, for instance in the form of a ministry of research, coordinates national and international activities. It is above all in the sphere of basic research, that one does not trust enterprises, the market, and competition to settle things properly. But over and above this, voices are heard time and again, which demand the promotion of application-oriented research. The borders between research and industrial policies become blurred, culminating as in the Japanese case, where research policies and industrial policies are steered in concerted action with the business sector.

Finally, if post-industrialism takes the shape of a services society, expansion of the civil service is a must anyway (Bohret, op.cit). In societies whose economic system features a highly differentiated market economy, State and administration have withdrawn more and more from the production of material goods, the relevant discussions even including subjects like water supply. The great majority of public tasks can be defined as services : from the educational system to health care, and from the traffic sector to the averting of dangers. A Welfare State is considered downright exemplary when it performs a maximum number of services as does the Scandinavian model, for instance (Jahn, 1993: 22). Accordingly, the theorists of post-industrialism stress the growth of the public sector and the expansion of public administration (Klages 1991 (b) : 556).

IV. On the System Rationality of Administration

After having dealt with the environmental conditions of post-industrialism and their relevance to public administration, let us turn back to the issue of whether a paradigm change from administrative management to entrepreneurial management in the state executive is approaching. At this point, a preliminary remark must be made : The epistemological characteristics of the post-industrial society concept are open to discussion. Some will lay stress on the idealist assumptions underlying such typification; others will emphasize its orientation to actual facts. Thus, it is an excess of ideas over actually observable trends, that is the point of concern for less optimistic theories. Critical references are made to unemployment and the refusal of performance, to the lack of standards and militant attitudes, entitlement mentality and mass manipulation, ecological limits and self-endangerment, and, not least, to the social psychological aspect of discrepancy between expectations and probability (Klages, 1994 (b)).

Indeed, life includes a wide variety of eventualities for which no allowance has been made in the concept of the post-industrial society. Among those relevant to the public administration are, for example, regionalism with its decentralized patterns of organization and precedence of responsibility on the part of lower-level units, citizen involvement in cultural and social affairs and even in averting of dangers, people's participation in public planning and decision-making as well as many other matters. All the same, post-industrialism allows for such a lot of socio-cultural conditions in the public administration's environment that it must be considered to represent a significant section of real life. Moreover, this section is the one with a considerable potential for the subject of entrepreneurial management in the public sector. For the post-industrial society is supposed to be ruled by economic calculations as well as by considerations of effectiveness and efficiency (Bell op. cit).

Let us, in this context, have a look at the assessments made by the theorists of post-industrialism themselves; they take for granted an increase of bureaucratization in public life and the technocratic elites in particular, while at the same time presuming a rise in the public sector (Hugger, 1987 : 88). Even for the scientific sector they state that — considering its strong expansion and its central position in the post-industrial society, the huge number of those concerned, and the enormous sums of money required — the bureaucratization of science is inevitable. The dangers implicit in this are patently obvious: the freedom of research might be stifled; the assessment of achievements might be distorted; the charismatic dimension of science might fail to be seen, etc. (Bell op.cit : 295-299). To avert such dangers one may initiate counter-institutions like a "Science Parliament" or even resist them in a counter-culture. However, the "bureaucratization of brainwork" must be stated as a fact.

Still, arguing that bureaucracy and operational efficiency are simply contradictory is inadmissible. When talking about the sums of money needed, it becomes obvious that money is a medium of communication in bureaucratic administration as everywhere else and that, concomitantly, cost-effective dealings with money become a standard of action in any money economy as is seen, for instance, from consulting the budget acts. However, this standard of action is not the only one: others include, for example, the binding force of legislation *et al.* The fact that the standard of cost-effective action in a bureaucratic administration is only superior to it in many situations precludes a solely entrepreneurial management in this type of administration.

The socio-cultural traits of post-industrialism do not suggest any greater likelihood of the adoption of principles like free market, competition and entrepreneurialism. If administration in the post-industrial society continues to be a Welfare-State administration, it will, to a large extent, be taken up with transfer payments, viz. in the private household sphere comprising children's allowances, housing subsidies, public assistance, training allowances, etc. In view of the fact that such payments are not made up for by an economic quid pro quo of equivalent market value; there is more, with the State as a guarantor of human rights, public assistance may not be administered as if one were dispensing charity (Klages 1994(a); 75 ff.). But, on the other hand, subjecting public assistance to situation-oriented entrepreneurial accounting by the administration depending on the prevailing economic situation, cyclical business activity or crisis, is not admissible either. Such benefits are intended to guarantee the survival needs of human beings; they must provide security and therefore be given a steady shape, for which reason they are defined in legislation and legal claims. So, in this respect, public administration is not a medium of transfer-economy-governed entrepreneurialism.

If we direct our attention to the focal status of science and research in post-industrialism (Bohret, 1988/89), it must be noted that, even in societies with a political majority giving priority to the yields of the market, the unreserved privatization of public universities, academies and research institutes is not brought up for discussion. As a matter of fact, no confidence is placed in the forces of the market in that area. Though, in the face of decreasing public funds, this does not prevent the management of such institutions from being urged to attach greater weight to cost effectiveness there (Kemmler, 1990; Reinermann, 1992; Seidenschwarz, 1992). Still, political wisdom implies the admission that scientific findings — even when reduced to their social benefits — contain such a lot of imponderables that economic efficiency considerations cannot turn the scale. Politicians may not, pointing to economic aspects, simply argue away the decisions that they have to take on scientific policies. Describing the role of a public university president as that of an entrepreneur is true only to a small degree, if at all.

That economic calculations are thus dismissed as subsidiary or inferior ranges of assessment becomes even more obvious when post-industrialism and risk society become associated with each other. Let us consider the case of genetic technology; at least in the great industries, the market forces are developing such a dynamic force that public subsidizing of industrial research appears expandable. As regards such transfer payments to private enterprises for applied research and development, evaluation in monetary terms and an appropriate administration of subsidies would be perfectly reasonable. However, precautions against dangers are given priority here. Through State regulations, i.e. acts on genetic technology, a framework in terms of safety and order rules must be established for scientific and technical developments in order to tie society's self-imperilment up with decision-making options, thus turning dangers into risks. The administration must then put such legal regulations into concrete shape, for instance, by its approval of genetic technology installations, and this above and beyond the entrepreneurial spirit. Similar considerations apply to the "information society". One may ask whether it is within the State's purview to instal data highways and manage them as a business. At any rate, however, ensuring data privacy protection in the interest of the people both by way of legislation and by administrative means is a public responsibility.

Model conceptions of a "new" administration have a great liking for the term "service". This extends from the definition of a local government as a service company (Banner, op.cit : 57) to the conversion of citizens into customers, who then expect State functions to be business services (Klotz/Mauch, 1994: 236). True, problems of perception arise when police arrest is termed a "service" although not regarded as such by those concerned (Hill/Klages 1993: 103). But all in all, the impression is created that the very category of service implies the entrepreneurial dimension. Yet, this would mean that post-industrialism, featuring the service society as one of its basic traits, would, from the socio-cultural viewpoint, represent an environmental condition of public administration which would suggest a paradigm change towards entrepreneurialism.

The term "service" can be of great help to State and administration. And so can a socio-cultural interpretation. Or, one may look into the question of whether the Swedish Welfare State is noteworthy because of its preference for services or the German Social Welfare State in giving priority to transfer payments, involving consequences in terms of public employment. This, however, makes it clear already that an interpretation of services merely making a point of their contrast with the production of physical assets, is of but limited help in the public sector. The focal point in appropriation for children's allowances, housing subsidies or supplementary welfare benefits does not lie in the immaterial advantage but in public assets. The market does not — fundamentally — make available such transfers. They can be valued in accordance with definite economic criteria and principles. But, in the final analysis, the procurement of public assets must be decided in the political and administrative sphere (Musgrave/Musgrave/Kullmer, 1990: 60). The authoritative and binding decision on granting of refusal of any such transfers is then the core of administrative action. We are discussing public services, and in this matter conclusions as to entrepreneurial management in the public sector may not be drawn unreservedly.

Now voices will be heard complaining that we were taking the slogan of entrepreneurial management too seriously. In reality, they say, this was only a matter of something like a third option between State and market (Reinermann, 1994 : 16). At this point, we must distinguish carefully between improvements in the application of the cost—effectiveness standard in politics and administration and that standard's upgrading as against other standards of action. Improvements in the economic handling of public affairs actually suit post-industrialism a great deal. But a general upgrading of economic efficiency vis-a-vis the standards of humanity, democracy and the rule of law would result in a paradigm of change. There are certain instances where such new priorities can be observed. The best-known case is probably that of the Grahamm Rudman-Hollings Act in the United States of America (Konig, 1993: 33 ff.). With the initial intellectual approach of a certain economic theory, an Act was passed incorporating some automatic economic curtailment mechanism in budgeting calculations so as to attain certain compensational targets. As it were, an economically governed procedure was given priority over politically determined proceedings. The result was many years of juggling in the estimates of public receipts and disbursements and not, however, any curtailment of the national debt.

So, the idea of outwitting politics by economic means does not appear to be enough. In conclusion, let us once again direct our attention to theoretical knowledge as the focus of the post-industrial society. Science also is a politico-administrative event. In post-industrialism, it is accused of bureaucratization. Accordingly, we have good reason to strengthen the application of operational efficiency standards in scientific matters. For instance, introducing some kind of controlling accordance with definite economic standards at the universities appears absolutely desirable (Reinermann, op.cit). Yet it would have to be confined to the assessment of secondary performance criteria (Hoffjan, 1994 : 293), namely labour force, infrastructure, organizational extent, material equipment, etc. The economic assessment standard may not be rated higher than the standard of evaluation relating to scientific quality itself. This, at any rate, is not the idea of the "axial principle" in post-industrialism. Public universities and also the public sector need something other than the entrepreneurial handling of the marketable goods. The socio-cultural environment in a post-industrial society relates to cost-effective modernization, but not to a change of paradigms towards entrepreneurial management in public administration.

REFERENCES

1. Aron, Raymond, *Die industrielle Gesellschaft.* Frankfurt a. M./Hamburg, 1962
2. Banner, Gerhard : Konzern Stadt, in : Hill/Klages S. 57 ff, 1993
3. Banner, Gerhard/Richard, Christoph (Hrsg.) : Kommunale Management Konzepte in Europa. *Anregungen Fur Die Deutsche Reformdiskussion,* Koln, 1993.
4. Beck, Ulrich Risikogesellschaft. Auf Dem Weg in Eine Andere Moderne, Frankfurt a.M., 1986.
5. Beck, Ulrich (Hrsg.) : *Politik in Der Risikogesellschaft : Essays and Analysen,* Frankfurt a.M., 1991.
6. Bell, Daniel : *Die Nachindustrielle Gesellschaft,* Frankfurt a.M./New York, 1976.
7. Bohret, Carl : Allegemeine Rahmenbedingungen und Trends des Verwaltungshandelns, in : H. Reinermann/H. Fiedler/K. Grimmer/K. Lenk/R. Traunmoller (Hrsg.), *Neue Informationstechniken Neue Verwaltungsstrukturen?* Heidelberg, S. 27 ff., 1988.
8. Bohret, Carl : Verwaltung und Universitat in der Bundersrepublic Deutschland vor den Herausforderungen der Neunziger Jahre, in : A. Frey/J. Bellers (Hrsg.), *Lateinamerika - Westeuropa. Annaherung oder Distanzierung,* Munster, S.11 ff., 1988-89.
9. Bohret, Carl : Folgen. Entwurf einer Aktiven Politik Gegen Schleichendekatastrophen, Opladen (Leske + Budrich), 1990.
10. Bohret, Carl : The Tools of Public Management, in K.A. Eliassen/J. Koeman eds., *Managing Public Organisations. Lessons from Contemporary European Experiences,* London u.a., Second Edition, S. 87 ff., 1993.
11. Bosengerg, Dirk/Metzen, *Heinz : Lean Management*—Vorsprung Durch Schlanke Konzepte, 4. Aufl., Landsberg, 1993.
12. Brokenshire, Peter. Kommunen als Konkurrierende Anbieter auf dem Markt fur Offentliche Dienstleistungen : das Britische Experiment, in : Banner/Richard (1993), S. 99-110, 1993.
13. Deutsch, K.W./Sonntag, *P. From the Industrial Society to the Information Society — Crises of Transition in Society,* IIVG/dp, S. 81 - 113, 1981.
14. Executive Office of the President. National Performance Review (Hrsg) : From Red Tape to Results : Creating a Government that Works Better and Costs Less, Washington D.C., 1993.
15. Forsthoff, Ernst. *Der Staat der Industriegesellschaft-Dargestellt am Beispielder Bundesrepublik Deutschland,* Munchen, 1971.
16. Fourastie, Jean. *Die grobe Hoffnungdes 20.* Jahrhunderts, Koln-Deutz, 1954.

17. Harbermas, Jurgen : *Legitimationsprobleme im Spatkapitalismus*, Frankfurt a.M., 1973.

18. Heady, Ferrel : *Public Administration. A Comparative Perspective*. 3. Aufl., New York/Basel, 1984.

19. Hennis, Wilhelm/Grafvon Kielmannsegg, Peter (Hsg.) : *Regierbarkeit. Studien zu ihrer Problematisierung*. Stuttgart, 1977-79.

2. Bande

1. Hesse, Joachim Jens (Hrsg.) : Die Erneuerung alter Industrieregionen. Okonomischer Strukturwandel und Regionalpolitik im Internationalen Vergleich, Baden - Baden, 1988.

2. Hill, Hermann/Klages, Helmut (Hrsg.) : Qualitats - und Erfolgsorientiertes Verwaltungsmanagement. Aktuelle Tendenzen und Entwurfe. Vortage und Diskussionsbeitrage der 61. Staatswissenschaftlichen Fortbildungstagung. 1993 der Hochschule fur Verwaltungswissenschaften Spayer, Berlin, 1993.

3. Hoffjan, Andreas : Effizienzvergleiche Offentlicher Theater. Cost Benchmarking als Strategische Erweiterung eines Theaterspezifischen Controlling, in : ZogU, Band 17, Heft 3/1994, S. 292 ff., 1994.

4. Hoffmann-Riem, Wolfgang (Hrsg.) : *Burgernahe Verwaltung? Analysen uber das Verhaltnis von Burger und Verwaltung*, Neuwied und Darmstadt, 1979.

5. Hood, Christopher : A Public Management for all Seasons? in : *Public Administration*, Vol. 69, Spring, S. 3 - 19, 1991.

6. Hugger, Werner : Szenarien Alternativer Gesellschaftsentwicklung, in : Konig/Dechsler, S.82-97, 1987.

7. Jahn, Detlef (1992) : Schweden - Kontinuitat und Wandel einer Postindustriellen Gesellschaft, in : Aus Politik und Zeitgeschichte, B43/92, 16. Oktober 1992, S. 22-35.

8. Kemmler, Walter : *Controlling fur Hochschulen* - Dargestellt am Beispiel der Universitat Zurich, Bern, 1990.

9. Klages, Helmut : *Die Unruhige Gesellschaft*, Munchen, 1975.

10. Klages, Helmut : *Uberlasteter Staat - Verdrossene Burger?* Zu Den Dissonanzen der Wohlfahrtsgellschaft, Frankfurt a.M., 1981.

11. Klages, Helmut : Stichwort "Industriegesellschaft", in : Nohlen (1991), S. 239 - 241.

12. Klages, Helmut : Stichwort "Post-industrielle Gesellschaft", in : Dieter Nohlen (Hrsg.), Worterbuch Staat und Politik, Bonn, 1991(b), S.555-556.

13. Klages, Helmut : Beurteilung der Sozialpolitik vor dem Hintergrund gesellschaftlicher Entwicklungen und sozialpolitischer Gestaltungsmaximen — Aus der Sicht der Wissenschaft, in : Bundesministerium fur Arbeit und Sozialordung (Hrsg.), Sozialstaat im Wandel, Bonn, 1994(a), S. 35 ff.

14. Klages, Helmut : Selbstentfaltung und Soziale Verantwortung. Eine Verteidigung der Gesellschaft Gegen ihre SelbstmiBverstandnisse, in : Manfred Henen/Michael Jackel (Hrsg.), Privatheit und Soziale Verantwortung. Festschrift zum 60. Geburtstag von Friedrich Landwehrmann, Munchen, 1994(b), S. 237 ff.

15. Koltz, Erhard/Mauch, Siegfried : Personalmanagement in Baden-Wurttemberg. Die Implementierung einer Konzeption in der Landesverwaltung (Teil 1), in: VOP, Heft 4/1994, S. 232 ff.

16. Konig, Herbert/Oechsler, Walter A. (Hrsg.) : Anforderungen an den Offentlichen Dienst von Morgen. Konzeptionen und Fallstudien zur Mittel - und Langfristigen Vorausschatzung, Regensburg, 1987.

17. Konig, Klaus : ZumVerwaltungssystem der DDr, in: ders. (Hrsg.). Verwaltungsstrukturen der DDR, Baden-Baden, 1991(a), S.9 ff.

18. Konig, Klaus : Krisenmanagement : Der Fall Tschernobyl in der Bundesrepublik Deutschland, in : Ant. N. Sakkoulas (Hrsg.), Administration - (Politique. Festschrift fur Athos G. Tsoutsos, Athen, 1991(b), S.263-274.

19. Konig, Klaus : Systemimmanete Und Systemverandernde Privatisierung in Deutschland, in : VOP, Heft 5/1992, S. 279 ff.

20. Konig, Dlaus : Zur Innenpolitischen Agenda - Die Amerikanische Bundesregierung am Beginn der Neunziger Jahre, Spayerer Forschungsberichte 121, Speyer, 1993.

21. Kouzmin, Alexander : "The Dimensions of Quality in Public Management." in : Hill/Klages 1993, S. 211 ff.

22. Kuhn, Thomas S. : *Die Struktur Wissenschaftlicher Revolutionen*, Frankfurt a.M., 3. Auflage, 1978.

23. Laux, Eberhard : Die Privatisierung des Offentlichen : Brauchen Wir Eine Neue Kommunalverwaltung? - Visionen und Realitaten Neue Kommunalverwaltung? - Visionen und Realitaten neuer Steuerungsmodelle -, in : Der Gemeindehaushalt 8/1994, S. 169 ff.

24. Luchmann, Niklas: *Soziale Systeme*, 2. Aufl., Frankfurt, 1985.

25. Marcuse, Herbert : *Der Eindimensionale Mensch*, Darmstadt, 1984.

26. Mascarenas, Reginald C. : "Building an Enterprise Culture in the Public Sector : Reform of the Public Sector in Australia, Britain and New Zealand", in : *Public Administration Review*, Heft 4/1993, S. 319 ff.

27. Moe, Ronald : "The "Reinventing Government" Exercise : Misinterpreting the Problem, Misjudging the Consequences", in : *Public Administration Review*, March/April 1994, Vol. 54, No.2, S. 111 ff.

28. Musgrave, Richard A./Musgrave, Peggy B./Kullmer, Lore. Die Offentlichen Finanzen in Theorie und Praxis, bd. 1,5. Auflage, Tubingen, 1990.

29. Nohlen, Dieter (Hrsg.), Worterbuch Staat und Politik, Bonn, 1991.

30. Osborne, David/Gaebler, Ted : Reinventing Government. How the Entrepreneurial Spiritis is Transforming the Public Sector, Reading, 1992.

31. Peters, Tom : *Jenseits der Hierarchien - Liberation Management*, Dusseldorf, 1993.

32. Reinermann, Heinrich : "Ein Zweieinhalbmal "Hoch" fur Controlling", in : DUZ, Heft 20/1992, S. 16-17.

33. Reinermann, Heinrich. *Die Krise Als Chance : Wege Innovativer Verwaltungen*, Speyerer Forschungsberichte 139, Speyer, 1994.

34. Ridley, Frederic : Verwaltungsmodernisierung in Grobritannien, : Hill/Klages. 1992, S. 251 ff.

35. Seidenschwarz, Barbara. *Entwicklung Eines Controllingkonzepts fur Offentliche* Institutionendargestellt am Beispiel Einer Universitat, Munchen, 1992.

36. Timmermann, Manfred : Wirtschaftliches Handeln Offentlicher Verwaltungen. Grundsatzliches aus Okonomischer und Verwaltungspraktischer Sicht. in : VOP, Heft 2/1993, S. 97 ff.

37. Wagener, Frido : Neubau der Verwaltung. Gliederung der Offentlichen Aufgaben und Ihrer Trager Nach Effektivitat und Integrationswert, 2. Aulf., Berlin, 1974.

11

Super-Optimizing Analysis and India's Industrial Policy

Stuart S. Nagel

Super-optimizing refers to a new and useful form of public policy evaluation. It seeks to find solutions to policy problems whereby conservatives, liberals and other major viewpoints can all come out simultaneously, ahead of their best initial expectations. The problem of industrial policy can serve as an illustration including the more specific problem of hand-crafted work versus assembly lines in India.

Background and Trends

India's textile policy and the informal sectors is almost an emotional topic in India because they are related to Gandhism and our freedom struggle. Gandhi is often pictured making thread at a handloom (charkha) in the informal sector in order to put down the idea of people working in textile factories like the one that exists in North Carolina. There are statistics with regard to how well the handlooms are competing with the Indian mills.

If one compares 1912 with 1939, the Indian mills progressed from about a million yards to 4 million yards. In comparison, the handlooms progressed from a million yards to a million and a half. However, if we look at the more recent figures, we come across an entirely different picture. In 1989, the mills were producing less than they were in 1939. They have dropped from 3.6 million yards to 2.6 million yards whereas the informal sector production has shot up from 1.5 million yards to 10.7. Yet, the data shows that there were only 15 power looms in 1942. The figure increased to

452 in 1980 and to 944 in 1989. If they have so many more powerlooms, why are the powerlooms not producing more cloth?

The conclusion is partly that Gandhism is working psychologically. There has been a phenomenal expansion of informal sector handloom output partly for ideological reasons. Probably no other developing nation has had that kind of development. It goes to show that people can get satisfaction out of things that may not be so productive but are probably more fun to do. Working on a textile mill assembly line in North Carolina is pictured in the Norma Rae movie as being very depressing, as contrasted to being one's own boss with the family loom.

This could be generalized a bit. There is no question that highly mechanized collective farms in Russia are not as productive as a bunch of farmers working their own plots as their own boss working into the night. Certain occupations or industries in certain cultures may be more productive by trying to take into consideration individual psyche more instead of treating people like machines.

If the mills were capable of running solely by themselves, like Japanese mills where there is no dehumanizing because there are not many humans around, then one gets a kind of super-optimum solution of high productivity and no dehumanizing. The North Carolina mills which are more like the Indian mills may give the worst of both possible worlds. They may be an example of a mill where productivity is down for lack of incentive, and dehumanizing is up due to regimentation. The Indian handloom is very humanizing, but is not as productive as the Japanese automated factory.

This is reievant to a section of African business development. At the 1991 Seychelles conference, that was one of the best debated subjects. Some people lauded the informal sector. Others said that it was only justifiable as a means towards more efficient factories and should not be considered as an end in itself but just a stepping stone.

There has been a big increase in the total productivity of household looms in India vis-a-vis factory looms. Prima facie, that seems rather strange. The explanation is that the household looms are not handlooms. They are machines, like sewing machines. They run on electricity. They constitute a compromise between home handicrafts and factory machines. They are home machines. They may seem like an ideal compromise. They may, however, sacrifice some potential productivity that could come from more factory automation. They may also sacrifice some equity and quality workplace that could come from home handicrafts, or more likely from a highly automated assembly plant.

Alternatives, Goals, and Relations

SOS stands for Super-Optimum Solutions. We have to focus on goals to be achieved, alternatives available for achieving them and indicators of relations between goals and alternatives. A few SOS tables involve two goals and four alternatives. Other more complicated SOS tables may involve more goals and more alternatives.

The problem in India lends itself well to a simplified SOS. The conservative alternative is handicrafted work by artisans, or just handicrafted work. The liberal approach is kind of Eli Whitney Henry Ford Assembly line that at one time was considered such a technological advance, which it was. The compromise is the current Indian situation which involves cottage industry using small machines.

We should call this home industry rather than cottage industry, although both sound like they could be referred to as sweat shops. That is one of the drawbacks to this kind of compromise. It easily leads to people working at home, but they are not their own bosses. They may be more wage slaves than if they worked in a factory. They do sweat it out at work, and someone shows up every day or so to pick up what they have done. They get paid a pittance for the work of life or control over their hours. The problem is not solved by trying to find a new word for cottage industry or home industry. Whatever it is, it could become a sweat shop. The Indian data does not say anything about the quality of life of these people working at home. It just says that they are producing a lot more cloth, which may have also been true of the sweat shops in the New York garment industry in the early 1900's.

The conservative goal is productivity, turning out a lot of cloth at a relatively low price. The liberal goal is a quality workplace in terms of (1) safety, (2) psychologically pleasant ambience (3) non polluted environment and (4) work that is not drudgery.

The handcrafted work involves a quality workplace. There is not much problem of pollution when one works with needle and thread. It is also pretty hard to get an arm chopped off by a power tool when one works with needle and thread. On the productivity side though, needle and thread is not so productive.

Assembly line work, one would expect would be more productive than cottage industry with small machines. However, if there are a lot of homes with a lot of small machines, they will outproduce a small number of assembly lines even though one assembly line produces a lot more than one home. It depends on how we define productivity. If it is defined in terms of effectiveness or total output, then the data shows the home industry is doing better. If productivity means output divided by some kind of inputs like money and effort, then the assembly line probably does better.

A Super-Optimum Solution

The super-optimum solution is to strive for the kind of factory that Japan has pioneered, that is highly productive and not dehumanizing because it involves only highly skilled humans in the form of executives and engineers, and nobody on the assembly line except robots. Somebody may be there on a console platform watching the robots. He or she may be watching television. Just like farmers in big harvesters having televisions in their cabs, are very different from working with a scythe to harvest wheat. We can refer to that as highly automated assembly plants. Japan does not even like to use the word 'factory' because it implies something that is constantly belching smoke. They call their automobile factories 'forges', which really sounds like belching smoke. The word assembly sounds like assembly line, but you can have things assembled without a line of people turning a bolt like Charlie Chaplin in the dehumanizing movie on the Ford Automobile Company.

Such a plant is better than a '3.5' score on productivity, may be even a '5'. It is a quality workplace with very few injuries or unhappy employees. The energy source is more likely to be reasonably clean rather than coal-burning. It may even be nuclear energy, although that raises safety issues for people outside the assembly plant rather than inside, or both. The safety of nuclear energy is a separate issue. One could have a highly automated assembly plant that does not use nuclear energy or coal. It could even use solar energy, although that is not likely with the current solar technology. It probably uses electricity, and if there are any chimneys belching, they are over the power company and not in the assembly plant.

Conservative in this context does not mean pro-business. It means preserving traditions and old ways of doing things. Likewise, liberal does not mean pro-labour. It means pro-technology, industrialization, rather than non-industrial lifestyles.

This is different from the Africa business development, although related. The Africa problem is basically large business versus small business rather than factory versus home. A better way to put it that does bring out the distinction is :

1. India's problem is handicrafts versus machines.

2. Africa's problem is small business versus big business (regardless whether they are handicrafts or machines). One could conceivably have a big business that employs a lot of people who work with their hands.

There are two different SOS solutions. One involves a technological fix with machines that does not involve assembly line workers, thus one has the productivity of machines without the dehumanizing of an assembly line. The other problem, i.e., Africa's problem involves a sequential SOS where small business leads to big business and is not an end in itself. That requires consciously encouraging small businesses that are not dead-ends, but are likely to be capable of being expanded. It especially means small businesses that manufacture something, rather than small businesses that sell groceries (manufacturing businesses and not trading ones).

Finding Other Super-Optimum Solutions

Finding SOS solutions is facilitated by the use of spreadsheet-based *decision aiding software.* It allows one to work simultaneously with many goals, alternatives and relations. That includes information and goals that are measured in multiple ways. Such software also allows for 'what-if' analysis to see how the tentative conclusions change as a result of changes in the inputs. SOS solutions are also facilitated by having *checklists* based on generalizations from previous examples. Such checklists and examples can be found in the growing literature on super-optimizing solutions. The literature includes win-win dispute resolution, growth economics, and non-zero-sum games.

REFERENCES

1. Majumdar Deepak, "The Issue of Small versus Large in India's Textile Industry", World Bank Working Papers, 1984.
2. Misra Sanjiv, "India's Textile Policy and The Informal Sectors" in Stuart Nagel ed. *India's Development and Public Policy,* 1992.
3. Chakravorty Sukhamoy, *Development Planning : The Indian Experience*, Oxford University Press, 1987.
4. Nagel Stuart S., *Global Policy India : International Interaction Toward Improving Public Policy,* of Marhn Press and Macmillan, 1991.
5. Nagel Stuart S., *Public Administration and Decision - Aiding Software : Improving Procedure and Substance,* Greenwood Press, 1990.

12

Systems of Technological and Managerial Education for 2000 A.D. and Beyond — A Perspective

M. Gopalakrishnan

The countdown to 2000 A.D. has begun. We have started taking steps consciously towards the 21st century. Very soon we step into the third millennium after Christ. The powers at the centre have given the green signal. What are our options?

Late Mr.Rajiv Gandhi, the then Prime Minister of India, in his Foreword to the VII Five Year Plan (1985-90) remarked "In the final analysis, development is not just about factories, dams and roads. Development is basically about people. The goal is the people's material, cultural and spiritual fulfilment. The human factor, the human context, is of supreme value. We must pay much greater attention to these questions in future. Outlays for human resource development have been substantially increased. Policies and programmes in education, health and welfare must also be restructured to provide a fuller life for our people. By 2000 AD the composition of the age groups will undergo (if our plans go well) vital changes. The persons in age groups 0-4 years, 5 to 14 years, 15 to 59 years and 60 plus will present a different picture in numbers." Let us take a look at the figures.

Age Structure of the Population 1980-2000
(as on 1st March)
(Per cent of total population)

Age group	*1980*	*1985*	*1990*	*2000 (projection)*
(O)	*(1)*	*(2)*	*(3)*	*(4)*
0-4	14.18	13.91	12.85	10.67
5-14	25.54	24.34	23.15	20.96
15-59	54.07	55.51	57.50	60.79
60 plus	6.21	6.24	6.50	7.58
Total	100.00	100.00	100.00	100.00

1. Seventh Five Year Plan 1985-90, Vol. I, Govt. of India, Planning Commission, New Delhi, 1985.

2. *Ibid*, p. 12.

A number of interesting implications will arise out of a study of the above Table. The number of females in the reproductive age group 15-44 will be 228 million in 2000 AD, up from 141 million in 1980. They will constitute 48.17 per cent of the total female population then. (The corresponding figure for 1980 was 43.4 per cent). The required administrative infrastructure for dealing with this group from the points of view of employment, industries, family welfare, education and health and so on is almost stupendous. Training requirements : as a function of the population apart, the quality of it needs to be intelligently conceived and dealt with. The major problem is to find the trained men and women who will do all these jobs.

(ii) The distribution of the labour force (male and female) in rural and urban sectors will also change drastically. The Planning Commission's estimates (in the VII Plan document) showed that by 2000 AD, 130 million (would join the unemployed list. Urbanisation which adds another dimension to this problem continues to grow in the next few years. It will add to urban unemployed at 3 to 4 millions per annum in the next few years.

Today about 60 per cent of the urbanites live in Class I cities (i.e. having over 1 lakh of population), about 26 per cent live in Class II and III towns (i.e. 20,000 to one lakh of people). The severe overcrowding that results will put a serious strain on the urban resources. We must thus train an enormous bureaucracy to administer the public utilities. This is a second major problem.

The leaps in science and technology fronts that are planned and anticipated are almost beyond comprehension today. New sectors that are brought into our fold in this respect are space and ocean technology, environmental upgradation, nuclear energy, information technology, to name a few. Though this country boasts of one of the major scientific and technological manpower systems of the world, conflicting views are being aired about the 'Brain Drain' we are suffering (that we are getting fat foreign exchange reserves from Non-resident Indians abroad is not to be forgotten). In the next 15 years, the world will have moved far ahead of us. Our Research and Development (R&D) systems; many feel, do not do justice to our expectations. Without entering into a controversy, it is suffice to say that we need to widen the foundations for R&D systems to be set up in the first decade of the 21st century. The broad steps to be taken in this field are :-

To firm up our links with international research— both fundamental and applied institutions. Such steps have already been initiated with France and Japan, two leading countries, of the developed world, soon after the former Prime Minister Late Mr. Rajiv Gandhi took over the office. Some of the important working groups and committees that were set up in the past two decades have made good recommendations in this regard. To recapitulate them:

(i) The working group on technical education set up in Nov. 1977 by Government of India and its subgroups have assessed manpower needs and submitted a report in Jan. 1978 giving detailed suggestions and recommendations (Report of Working Group on Technical Education,1978). These are valuable and action has already been initiated. (Details are given in Annexure—I.)

(ii) In June, 1978, Government of India (Ministry of Education) appointed a Review Committee under the Chairmanship of Dr. A Ramachandran (the Late Dr Nayudamma succeeded him) to review and evaluate foreign technical assistance and aid received by I.I.Ts, to assess the potential developed in I.I.Ts and to identify areas of further assistance from abroad. Other academic institutions were added to the terms of reference later. Its report, submitted in Jan.

1980 (without, however, an indepth study of non-I.I.T. institutions having been made), contained a number of valuable recommendations (Please see Annexure-II).

(iii) In June 1978 yet another Committee appointed by the Government of India under the Chairmanship of Late Dr.Y. Nayudamma to review the progress made till then in post-graduate education and research in engineering and technology, recommended measures for development. In its report submitted in June 1980 (See Annexure-III for details), it recommended measures for further changes. Its most important recommendation was to make the All India Council of Technical Education /Post Graduate Board a new National Statutory Authority. This has since been done.

(iv) In June 81, Government of India (Ministry of Education) published a 'guideline' document on the Scheme of Community Polytechnic in India started during 1978-79 on the basis of recommendations by the AICTE. The Council had recommended that a few selected polytechnics should act as focal points to act as agents for transfer of technology to the rural community and designated as Community Polytechnics. Consequently in the years that followed 35 such institutions were formed.

Let us take a look at another aspect of the higher level (degree and P.G)Technological and Engineering Institutions. Towards the end of 1984 there were in all 131 Colleges of Engineering and Institutes of Technology in which there were nearly 37000 seats (at degree level). For a population of 684 million this worked out to about 1 seat per 5.4 lakhs of people and 1000 seats for 11.2 per sq. km.

What should be the additional foundations to be laid in this regard by 2000 AD when the population will be nearly 1000 million? Sufficient thought does not seem to have been given to numbers in the government's plans, though, to do justice to the powers that be, qualitative improvements were planned in the VII Plan. The VIII Plan continued with same approach.

Forty new emerging areas of scientific education and technology have been identified including new ones such as Waste Management and Recycling Technology in the Report of the Working Group on Technical Education (1978) referred to earlier, while the list already got expanded to 66 areas in the next report (of the Review Committee on P.G. Education and Research in Engineering and Technology (1980) ! If one were to consider the addition of 26 new areas after a lapse of two years, what could be the level by 2000 AD? Apparently we need a triennial review and a crash programme of starting new centres of excellence (It will be of interest to know that the most advanced institutes of Technology we boast of today were started between 1950 (at Kharagpur) and 1961 (Delhi). In the last 25 years we can't refer to a single such institution that has been established in this area.

In the field of management-training we have today 9 institutions (See Annexure IV) of management and industrial engineering, founding and forge technology and technical teachers training institutes. The following emerging areas of technology and management seem to be of paramount significance today in the coming decade.

(1) Computer (hardware and software) technology.

(2) Application of appropriate technology in rural areas.

(3) Rural management.

In the area of rural development, a Council of Agricultural and Rural Technology (CART) has been set up. The Institute of Rural Management, (IRMA) at Anand Gujarat, has also made a good beginning. As for banking sector which has the most crucial role to play in activating and maintaining rural growth, we have to consider certain challenging lines of growth. In addition, an organised, countrywide attempt should be made to promote the growth of more training institutions in these areas. Given below is a set of presumptions (not exhaustive!), a list of some critical areas needing our attention and some policy issues. These do not comprise all that should be said but certainly give us enough food for thought.

Presumptions:

1. With outside help our rural systems have endogenous economic capability to treat the diseases of poverty, under employment and malnutrition.

2. This is assisted by a matching egalitarian social order. Alternately, the policy efforts and administrative structure for bringing this about should become critical very fast. That stage is yet to be reached.

3. The most critical action for the concerted efforts of all, in the long (next 15 years) and short run needs clear delineation as to the diversity of directions that are inevitable.

4. Both, the people's representatives and permanent civil service have a role to play in our plan for 2000 AD and beyond.

The increase in rural/urban poverty and discontent will not explode to cause a massive all India social upheaval : Technological changes will continue to help governments and enterpreneurs to solve almost any apparently insurmountable problem in the long run. Technology must be the main weapon in our armoury.

The critical fields	*Time-Frame in which it operates*
(a) Population control	Both in the long and short runs.
(b) Health and Family Welfare programmes	-do-
(c) (i) Agricultural productivity (intensive approach) to go up.	-do-
(ii) All marginal lands (and those not under the plough yet or lying as long fallows) need to be cultivated.	-do-
(iii) Increase in use of inputs, i.e. better seeds, more fertilisers, etc.	-do-
(iv) Better farming systems, particularly through lesser use of water in irrigational areas, retention of moisture in dryland agriculture, soil preservation and protection etc.	Long run
(v) Better ecological treatment	Long run
(a) by greater use of biofertilisers	
(b) increased use of non-traditional sources of energy and shift to renewable sources	
(c) forests (revival) through use of 'minimum forest areas" and increased social forestry concepts.	

Issues:

(a) Do we need a separate cadre of Rural Managers at

(i) Direct recruits' level in state and All India Civil Services?

(ii) Lower levels in state bureaucracy?

(iii) If so, what are the sources, their qualifications and training systems?

(b) Do we have adequate training systems?

We Need Staff in	*Level of Education*
(i) Agricultural sector	We need Degree holders and Diploma holders
(ii) CAD (Command Area Development and Irrigation Depts)	-do- -do-
(iii) Engineers	Degree holders and Diploma holders.

(iv) What sort of educational systems do we need for these degree holders and higher technical level staff on the one hand and diploma holders and lower level staff on the other?

(v) As Banks (commercial, cooperative, rural and regional) have a pivotal role to play, what should be their personnel systems to recruit, train and implant the personnel in rural areas for better and efficient working of rural development programmes?

(vi) How do we mesh the above administrative set-ups to usher in better educational (rural, adult and non-formal) systems and better rural health systems?

(vii) What legal systems (laws, codes, regulations, exemptions) do we need in this regard, inclusive of special treatment to encourage personnel recruitment from weaker sections (women included) of society?

(viii) What should be the role and type of non-official (or political) systems that should be encouraged and (changed or) ushered in? What should be their relationship with the bureaucratic element?

(ix) What administrative structure (of "specialists"vis-a-vis "generalists") will be suitable for various disciplines? For instance, there are problems in Training and Visit Systems where the dispute is between a single technical and administrative line of control from top to bottom and a generalist's administrative control at two intermediary levels in the line viz. at the block level and at a higher (command area) level.

(x) Are there limits to rural growth? If there are, what are the lower limits and what the upper limits by 2000 AD, in terms of:

(a) Rural population and emigration of households to urban areas?

(b) Rural population living below poverty line?

(c) Under-employed (and almost total unemployment for a certain period of time).

(d) Per-capita household income.

(e) nutrition status range of the poor.

(xi) Are our Land Reforms moving in the right direction? If not, how should they be changed/modified?

Priorities must be set. A rigid timetable for the next 1000 days needs to be outlined. A countrywide churning of the ocean of intellectuals needs to be done as was attempted for the Education policy by Government of India in the last twenty years.

ANNEXURE—I

1. Manpower Needs

(i) Present manpower supply-adequate for next decade.

(ii) Additional manpower needs to be met by increased efficiency and effectiveness.

(iii) New educational programmes to be based on well-established manpower needs.

(iv) Establishment of a National Manpower Information System.

2. Measures and Improvement

(i) Courses/Programmes - modification

(a) Flexibility in programmes through credit system and multi-point entry.

(b) Application-oriented research projects and consultancy centres tuned to needs of industrial and rural development.

(c) Integration of relevant management education in technical courses at all levels.

(d) Selected polytechnics ensuring transfer of technology to rural community to be designed as "Community Colleges".

(e) Advanced technician courses with Central Assistance.

(f) Continued review of curricula to cope with technological changes and manpower needs.

(ii) Staff Selection Development and Appraisal

(a) Staff selection based on merit and on All-India basis.

(b) Appointment to senior teaching positions on renewable contract basis.

(c) Personnel promotions to motivate deserving staff.

(d) Staff appraisal for developmental needs.

(e Pedagogical courses for teachers of degree institutions also.

(f) 'Adjunct professorship' for engineers from the Industry and 'Industrial residency' for teachers.

(iii) Students

(a) Selections based on aptitude and ability.

(b) Remedial programmes to help weak students.

(c) Student participation in academic bodies.

(iv) Instructional Support Services

(a) Improvement in library services through competent library staff and reprographic facility.

(b) Establishment of 'Learning Resource Centres'.

(c) Modernisation of laboratories—considering equipment obsolescence and curricula changes.

3. Management of the System

(i) A single agency to plan and organise technical education from the level of craftsmen to that of postgraduates.

(ii) A single agency to plan, organise and fund post-graduate activities in Universities, Indian Institutes of Technology, Indian Institute of Management and affiliated colleges.

(iii) Reorganisation of Directorates of Technical Education for effective professional and academic performance.

(iv) Administrative autonomy and powers of financial control to Government institutions for effective functioning.

(v) Academic autonomy to selected institutions.

(vi) Staff College for training and development of senior educators and administrators.

(vii) Setting up of a National Evaluation and Accredition Agency.

(viii) Statutory powers to the All India Council for Technical Education for maintenance of standards, on the pattern of the Indian Medical Council.

4. Financing of Technical Education

(i) Plan allocations for technical education to be commensurate with developmental outlay of user departments.

(ii) Expenditure by Industry on technical education to be totally exempted for income tax purposes.

(iii) Central share of assistance to be given direct to institutions - earmarking funds for technical education.

ANNEXURE—II

(a) "Foreign technical assistance to fill technological gaps that still exist and also to develop emerging areas in which adequate expertise is not yet available in the country. This would involve import of foreign expertise and equipment and also training of Indian faculty abroad."

(b) "Foreign collaboration on equal partnership basis in areas where we have already built up competence of very high levels. This sort of collaboration would be necessary for all times to come to keep ourselves abreast of scientific and technological developments all over the world."

(c) "Foreign capital aid by way of budgetary support to institutions to replace obsolete equipment etc. if adequate internal resources (including necessary foreign exchange components) are not available for this purpose".

The following are some of the main recommendations of the Review Committee:

(i) "The IITs should interact with their counterparts in advanced countries on a continuing basis to reduce the temporal phase-lag in developing emerging areas which are relevant to the national needs."

(ii) "It is unrealistic and unproductive to base development strategies on the availability of massive foreign technical assistance collaboration aid programmes. These programmes should be used only on a selective basis for new and emerging areas, for interaction in areas of excellence and for procuring sophisticated equipment not available indigenously."

(iii) "No foreign technical assistance programme should perpetuate our dependence in the area concerned on foreign expertise and support. Foreign technical assistance /collaboration /aid programmes should not be aimed at replacing existing indigenous endeavours; they should be directed at strengthening and upgrading them."

(iv) "Proposals for foreign technical assistance/collaboration/ aid received from the IITs and other academic institutions should not be considered in isolation. They should be considered on the basis of over-all national perspectives and in relation to what is happening in other departments and agencies in the country. All proposals for foreign technical assistance should therefore be considered by a National Screening Committee... Representatives of industry may also be involved in this exercise."

(v) "Foreign expertise / consultancy should be obtained only for absolutely essential areas of gaps in technology and that too only for short periods. But at the same time there would be a free flow of experts between India and other countries on equal partnership basis. Only sophisticated equipments, instruments not available indigenously should be imported under foreign technical assistance programmes. Efforts should always be to develop such equipment/ instruments in India."

(vi) "The IITs should not work in isolation. They should build and increase formal linkages with other academic institutions, R&D organisations and national laboratories."

(vii) "The IITs are competent and willing to give assistance-sans financial support—to institutions of lower formations in a variety of ways. Concrete steps should be taken to promote the flow of such technical assistance from the IITs to engineering colleges etc. The expertise available in the IITs to offer consultancy services should be fully utilised by the Educational Consultancy Company proposed to be set up under the auspices of the Government of India."

(viii) It is necessary to create in the IITs an infrastructure for training in the instrumentation area with particular stress on repairs and maintenance of sophisticated equipment.Each IIT should ensure that it is capable of maintaining and repairing its own equipment and also those of others in the region."

(ix) "There is need to establish Centres for Assessment and Transfer of Technology in the IITs".

ANNEXURE-III

(i) "...the Indian national investment in scientific and technological education and research should increase manifold to meet the growing needs of the changing social system."

(ii) "To ensure that only bright and motivated people are admitted to post-graduate courses, admission to these programmes should be restricted to only those who come through the GATE, as detailed in this report. The Government should impose on industry and Government departments the need to sponsor their engineers and technologists for post-graduate education, and research in the respective areas of their interest."

(iii) "The one-year post-graduate diploma courses have not been found to be popular and successful. They need not be offered as regular programmes unless they are specifically asked for and paid by the interested agencies."

(iv) "All ME/M. Tech. programmes should be of three semesters duration consisting of two semesters course work (including core and elective subjects) and one semester dissertation work."

(v) "The minimum duration for doctorate after ME/M.Tech. degree should be two years of full-time study and research. In exceptional cases when BEs/B. Techs. are admitted directly for doctoral programmes the minimum duration of the course should be 3 years."

(vi) "Introduction of part-time post-graduate programmes especially in Industrialised areas should be encouraged. New techniques and arrangements should be devised for extending high quality post-graduate education to engineers/ technologists employed at locations remote from established centres."

(vii) "It should be made mandatory to prescribe post-graduate degree as the minimum qualification for recruitment to many positions in the engineering profession in industry. R&D organisations, Electricity Boards, PWDs, Posts and Telegraphs, Railways etc. The present policy and practice of recruiting graduate engineers at the lowest levels (single point entry) to many services should be discontinued."

(viii) "A reliable national information system for the storage, updating, retrieval and analysis of manpower information should be established to assist technical education planning."

(ix) "All recruitments to teaching positions should be made only on all-India basis. Mobility and exchange of faculty between academic institutions, R&D organisations and industrial establishments should be encouraged to prevent in-breeding."

(x) "A rigorous staff appraisal scheme to assess teachers annually should be introduced in every post-graduate institution. Such staff appraisal records should be looked into at every stage of promotion. Suitable merit promotion schemes should be introduced in all institutions."

(xi) "Multi-disciplinary, trans-disciplinary and trans-organisation research with emphasis on design and development should be encouraged at all levels. Problems of industry should be documented and distributed to post-graduate institutions on a continuing basis. It is recommended that a national level R&D Newsletter should be published regularly giving information on all research projects for the benefit of post-graduate institutions, R&D organisations and industry. It would be good to organise atleast once in every two years an All-India Conference on post -graduate projects and to document them area/discipline wise."

(xii) "It is imperative that funding post-graduate education and research in engineering and technology in all engineering institutions including university departments should be a 100 per cent central government responsibility and that the existing dichotomies disparities in funding should be eliminated."

(xiii) "It is strongly recommended that a couple of National Data Centres with all the major data bases of S&T in the form of computer readable magnetic tapes should be established in India as a matter of urgency."

(xiv) "This committee's single most important recommendation linked to many other proposals in various sections in this report is that the Government should make the AICTE/ Post-graduate Board a new statutory organisation—a National Authority— with powers granted to it by Parliament to advance and promote the technological development of this country by maintaining high standards of engineering and technological education and research. The proposed Authority should optimise the utilisation of all available resources and provide impetus to all the centres engaged in Post-graduate programmes and research. Evaluation and accreditation of Post-graduate courses should be done atleast once in five years by a suitable national agency."

ANNEXURE— IV

1 to 4. Indian Institutes of Management, Ahmedabad, Allahabad, Bangalore and Calcutta.

5. National Institute of Foundry & Forging Technology, Ranchi.

6 to 9. Technical Teachers Training Institute, Bhopal, Calcutta, Chandigarh and Madras.

13

Emerging Themes and Perspectives in Development Administration : A Reflection

M. Bapuji

The term development administration which came into existence during 1960s as an approach in the field of comparative public administration represents those aspects of public administration, involved in the process of development or change in the new nations that emerged after the World War II. It gained rapid recognition and attention of the scholars who produced enormous amount of literature on the dynamics of development administration in the developing societies. As a result of the efforts of these scholars, the conçept 'development administration' has grown rapidly to attain the status of a distinct sub-field in the realm of Social Sciences.

In its earlier phase, as a distinct sub-discipline, development administration displayed a pronounced faith in the big government and the capabilities of bureaucracy in the promotion of social change and economic development. During those times, the government was regarded as the most efficient instrument of economic progress and social justice. Those were the 'hey days' of big government. Accordingly, the development administration which originated during those days demonstrated that the government could achieve the all round development of individuals and its weaknesses and lapses were controllable through the simple means of democratic process. This approach was uncritical of the orthodox postulates of rationality and maximisation but over-critical of the narrow boundaries of POSDCORB view of 1930s.

The first generation of scholars of this field looked upon development administration as a concept concerning the administrative systems of less developed countries in which the government and its bureaucracy occupy a central place. In the view of these scholars, the government /administration plays a multi-faceted role in these countries—the role of an innovator, change agent, catalyst, modernizer and so on. Even the pioneers and the most celebrated scholars of development administration such as F.W. Riggs, Weidner, Fainsod, Irwing Swerdlow etc., echoed this viewpoint. It can be safely assumed that development administration movement in its early phase is a movement in favour of big government.

The turn of 1970s saw a sea change in the conditions that existed during the previous two decades. As Esman succinctly puts it:

> Since the heady days of the early 1960s which gave birth to development administration, a generation has passed. A new environment has emerged which rejects most of the founding premises of the development administration movement undermining its original intellectual and political foundations.

In view of this far-reaching change in the context, since the early 80s there has been a shift in the approach and tenets of development administration theory. It moved from its original position to redefine its earlier premises and themes which were put to scathing attack by several scholars. Even the concept of development administration per se was subjected to vehement criticism which reflects that the development administration approach to comparative public administration tends to miss the hidden rationalities in the Third World administration, the means of being effective and respectful of human dignity in different cultures. It tends to downplay the effectiveness and humanity of pre-bureaucratic, informal social means of controlling behaviour and solving problems (e.g., crime control in Japan). It exaggerates the irrelevance of Third World studies to the understanding of the advanced world and downplays the potentialities for irrational bureaucratic performance in the advanced world. It produces the same unrealistic view of government-bureaucracy performance in the Third World as its objective correlative— the often idealized, just as often demonized, performance of advanced world bureaucracies.

After roughly two decades of its existence, the development administration came to deal with doctrinaire issues of privatization, popular participation, deregulation and liberalisation. Several Western intellectuals visualised the emergence of new school of development administration in 1980s which was based upon the perception that the Third World leaders have started rethinking about their earlier commitments to socialism, all pervasive government and hostility towards private enterprise. These leaders have learnt lessons from the collapse of communism in Eastern Europe and the success stories of newly industrialized countries of East Asia like China. Further, the 'perestroika' and 'glasnost' of the former Russian President Gorbochaev influenced the thinking of the Third World leaders. As a response to these perceptions, New Development Administration was advocated keeping in view the changed realities and settings of the Third World. The proponents of this school emphasised on the need for decentralisation, popular participation, limited government and incrementalism.

Earlier Approaches to Development Administration

Development administration like comparative public administration is a post-war phenomenon. As a concept it is rooted in the field's actual experiences, a context in 'which public administration theory is tested, validated or discarded. Comparative public administration, on the other hand, provides a framework for comparison of those field lessons, task complexities as well as contextual variations of the given problem. Despite differentiation, the study of comparative public administration and the study of development administration converge and appear complementary. Development administration, if and when it is preoccupied with the administration of development may be understood to mean the management of development programmes and projects aiming at changing the physical as well as social environment of developing societies. It is from this viewpoint that development administration has come to mean that it is a study of the administrative systems engaged in the process of development. A number of factors play their role in this definition. They include the needs of the developing societies, the structure of administrative systems, proper utilisation of human and physical resources, strengthening of the capabilities of administration, planning, innovative thrust and so on.

There are a number of approaches to the study of development administration. Some of them are reviewed here with a view to understanding the complexity of the field. The planning approach looks at development administration essentially as administration of planned change and development. Innovative thrust of the development administration was stressed by scholars like Fainsod. His approach reflects: Development administration is a carrier of innovative values. As the term is commonly used, it embraces the array of new functions assumed by developing countries embarking on the path of modernization and industrialization.

Fred Riggs's approach to development administration marks a distinction between development of administration and administration of development which are different yet interrelated aspects of development administration.

He further states

> Development administration refers to organised efforts to carry out programmes or projects thought by those who are involved to serve development objectives. The phrase (development administration) arises by simple analogy, with such expressions as agricultural administration, educational administration and social welfare administration, each of which involves organised efforts to implement agricultural, educational and social welfare programmes, respectively.

He also advanced the view that development administration refers to the administration of development programmes, to the methods used by large scale organisations, notably governments, to implement policies and plans designed to meet development objectives (and to) ... the improvement of administrative capacities. In operational terms, development administration is viewed as the process of guiding an organisation towards the achievement of progressive socio-economic goals. In the same vein, it is also looked upon as a goal - oriented and action- oriented administrative system.

Kempe Hope also shares a common ground as he asserts: "Development administration in contextual and operational terms implies efficient organisation and management of the development activities of a nation to attain the goals of development."

From the viewpoint of Waldo and others the temporal factor plays a dominant role in the large scale transfer of administrative technology. In the view of those who stress the importance of spatial factor the space orientation has considerable impact on the development of a society.

The managerial approach conceives the development administration as the complex of agencies, management systems, and processes a government establishes to achieve its development goals. It is the public mechanism set up to relate the several components of development in order to articulate and accomplish national, social and economic objectives... Development administration is the administration of policies, programmes and projects to serve development programmes.

Two more approaches to the study of development administration made their appearance in the field recently. The critical path approach of Packard assumes that the event and activity time of a project determine the shortest overall possible time of the project.

The regressive development administration approach advocated by Quah takes stand that the concept of development administration has a unilinear bias and does not take into account the possibility of failure and that development administration results not from the attempts of administrative reforms but from the ability of the organisation to get benefitted by such reforms.

The contents of development administration movement can now be summed up in the words of Schaffer thus:

> It has been a sense of the distinctiveness of administration for development programmes, policies, and plans in those conditions (traditional, transitional or newly independent, and less developed political systems) in which there are usually extensive needs (which could coincide with urgently expressed demands of political elites, modernizing ideologies and exercises in mobilization): precisely where there are peculiarly few resources and exceptionally severe obstacles to meeting the needs. The peculiarity of development administration lay exactly in that inconvenient combination: extensive needs, low capacities, severe obstacles.

Emerging Themes and Perspectives

A decade after the emergence of the concept of development administration a new environment emerged in the Third World which shook its earlier premises and intellectual foundations. Disenchantment with the poor results by the development administration during the 1960s and 1970s gave rise to a new wave of thinking regarding the role of government, particularly, development administration. It was realised in the intellectual circles that development administration is much more than implementation of development programmes and projects, creation of new institutional structures, adoption of new techniques and so on. They have also taken cognizance of the emergence of several new themes and issues in the socio-political contents of developing societies whose examination became essential for the understanding of the dynamics of development administration in the new context.

Some experts have adopted definite position and attempted to analyse the new currents for formulating new premises regarding the concept of development administration in the changed context. The proponents of this new school argued that the field of development administration in 1980s has moved beyond its voluntaristic interpretation of administrative phenomena prevalent in the early 1960s. Milton J. Esman echoed the sentiments of many scholars of development administration when he argued that the grand theory of development administration declined and the earlier enthusiasm and interest of the scholars waned. The grandiloquent theorizing and system building of 1960s dissipated. Esman also identifies the emergence of a number of new themes in the development administration literature at the level of middle range theory at the critical interface between concepts and social action. These themes represent considerable departure from the dominant spirit of development administration of 1960s. These new themes include:

1. Governments are limited in their capacity and these limitations should be incorporated into the design of public programmes.
2. As the governments cannot do it all, alternative and complementary channels need to be identified and fostered.
3. Programme designers recongnize and capitalize on the pluralistic properties of public administration.

4. Participation is an important dimension in the administration of public services.
5 Societal contexts provide both specific opportunities and special constraints for development administration.
6. Enhanced appreciation of the uncertainties and contingencies inherent in deliberate efforts at development change.

O.P. Dwivedi and Nef who examined the state of development administration during 1980s exposed the break down of the Western paradigm of development administration. They concluded:

As the Western paradigm of development administration was conceived as similarly, radical Third World initiative should be seen as attempts to create alternative models of development administation.

Further, they divided these indigeneous models into two groups:

1. Insurrectional models (eg. China); and
2. Fundamentalist non-insurrectional efforts (eg. India's Panchayati Raj, Tanazania's Ujamaa concept and Libya's People's Councils).

David Fashole Luke identified three new sets of persistent trends in development administration which present a formidable challenge to the efficacy of the post-colonial state in the management of development process. They are:

1. Building effective administrative capacity that is responsive and accountable; and

2. Equitable.

In his more recent analysis, Herbert Werlin concurred with the propositions of New Development Administration School proposed by Esman. More particularly, he supported the New Development Administration's emphasis upon minimal government, decentralisation and community development. Accordingly, he proposed the political elasticity theory which advocates that decentralisation, popular participation, privatization and minimal government require effective political leadership and bureaucracy and the ability to shift from soft (persuasive) to hard (coercive) forms of power.

Evidently, decentralisation has become one of the most popular and key themes of New Development Administration during 1980s.

Numerous scholarly studies have emphasized the importance of decentralisation and stressed that centralized bureaucratic administration model has failed. Indeed, to many, centralisation appears to be at best a wasteful enterprise. At worst, it is a primary instrument of the urban wealthy who heavily depend upon the rural poor. If one reviews the field's literature one can find ample criticism against the centralised bureaucratic and hierarchical organisational strategies which are dominant since independence in several Third World countries. Many consider them as responsible for the development stagnation of these countries over the past four decades. The appeal of these scholars for decentralisation is not difficult to understand. As Kempe Hope states:

> Administrative decentralisation promotes participation, access and responsiveness. Through administrative decentralisation it is possible to emphasise national standards to deal with problems that are national in scope, while at the same time to allow for adjustments to meet particular local needs.

Unfortunately, the results of decentralised efforts are somewhat disappointing. As Diana Conveyers exposes:

> In many cases the actual degree of decentralisation seems to have been very limited either because the proposed reforms have not been implemented as intended or the initial proposals did not provide significant decentralization.

Apart from the scholars of the West, few scholars of the Third World noticed new theorizing in development administration during the 1980s. As an analyst puts it:

> In 1980s development administration is less ethno-centric and less cultural in its western assumptions. Today development administration is characterised by context based theory which incorporates indigenous social, cultural, political and economic realities of the Third World.

Further, he identified two new trends in development administration during the 1980s. They are:

(1) A shift from a blueprint approach to a learning process approach. The blueprint approach emphasises advanced planning for administering a development programme. In contrast, the learning process approach emphasises flexible

planning strategy which adapts itself to the changing conditions; and

2. A shift from production-centred approach to people-centred approach—The former approach emphasised on the production of goods and services for maximization of profits while the latter approach gives precedence to people's needs over production of goods and services. This approach centres around the individual's needs and capacities.

Conclusion

The emerging themes in development administration during 1980s have undeniably started an important new trend in the realms of knowledge in this field. It is evident that development administration moved from its initial premises, in order to cope up with the changing context and complexities of the developing world. The socio-political currents blowing across the Third World have undermined many of its original premises including the master premise that public administration is an indispensable instrument of socio-economic development. Yet, development administration has survived and also acquired the label, New Development Administration (NDA).

Not only that, it has adopted several new presumptions compatible with the changing context of the Third World. Such a drastic 'paradigm shift' reflects that development administration while losing its initial appeal, has remarkable capacity of adaptability and can absorb any challenge. Defenders of the field like Luke argue that the increasingly secure status of development administration as a sub-specialization is manifested in the lively debates and exchanges on the relevant and poignant issues relating to the administrative phenomena of developing countries. Further, as an African proponent of New Development Administration suggests in the context of Africa:

> A New Development Administration focus is desperately needed, one which would prepare every young mind at every level of learning to the onslaughts and challenges of development as we enter the decade of desktop administration and development and a global market too complex to imagine where we cannot afford to be ill-prepared if the African generation of the next decade are to possess the skills, attitude and will to excel and compete.

The assertion of the above African scholar reflects the concern and commitment of the Third World scholars for revamping development administration as an academic discipline as well as a practical enterprise.

REFERENCES

1. Conveyers, Diana, "Decentralization: The Latest Fashion in Development Administration", *Public Administration and Development,* Vol. 3, No. 2, April-June 1983, pp. 97-103.
2. Dwivedi. O.P., and J. Nef, "Crisis and Countries in Development Theory and Administration: First and Third World Perspectives", *Administration and Development,* Vol.2, No.1, January-March 1982, : 59-79.
3. Esman, Milton J., "The Maturing of Development Administration", *Administration and Development,* Vol. 8, No. 2, April-June 1988, : 125-39.
4. Fainsod, Merle, "The Structure of Development Administration", in Irving Swerdlow ed., *Development Administration : Concepts and Problems,* Syracus, New York, Syracus University Press, 1963, p. 2.
5. Fried, Robert C., "Comparative Public Administration: The Search for Theories", in Naomi B. Lynn and Aron Wildavsky eds., *Public Administration : The State of the Discipline,* New Delhi : Affiliated East-West Press, 1992, : 329.
6. Gant, George F., *Development Administration: Concepts, Goals, Methods, Maidson* : University of Wisconsin Press, 1979, : 41.
7. Heapy, James, ed, *Spatial Dimensions of Development Administration,* Durham, N.C., Duke University Press, 1971.
8. Hope, K.R., "Development and Development Administration: Perspectives and Dimensions", *Administrative Change,* Vol.7, No.1, July-December, 1979, : 111-24.
9. Hope, K.R., *The Dynamics of Development and Development Administration,* Westport, Connecticut: Greenwood Press,1984, : 87-88.
10. Luke, David Fashole, "Trends in Development Administration : The Continuing Challenge to the Efficacy of the Post-colonial State in the Third World", *Public Administration and Development,* Vol. 6, No.1, January-March 1986, pp. 73-80.
11. Metwa, Mekki, "Development Administration Revisited", in Metwa, ed., *Contemporary Issues in African Administration and Development Process,* New Delhi : Allied Publishers, 1990, p. 43.
12. Pai Pandikar, V.A., "Development Administration: An Approach", *The Indian Journal of Public Administration,* Vol. X, No.1, January - March 1964, p. 35.
13. Quah, John S.T., "Regressive Administration: Some Second Thoughts on the Concept of Development Administration", *Administrative Change,* Vol.7, No.1, July-December 1979, pp. 25-36.
14. Riggs, F.W., "The Contexts of Development Administration", in Riggs, ed., *Frontiers of Development Administration,* Durham, N.C., Duke University Press, 1971, p. 72.

15. Schaffer, B.B., "The Deadlock in Development Administration", in Leys, E., ed., *Politics and Change in Developing Countries,* New York: Cambridge University Press, 1969, :184.

16. Singhal, Arvind, "Evolution of Development and Development Administration", *International Review of Administrative Sciences,* Vol. 57,1991, : 641-49.

17. Waldo, Dwight, ed, *Temporal Dimensions of Development Administration,* Durham, N.C., Duke University Press, 1971.

18. Weidner, Edward, "Development Administration: A New Focus for Research", in Ferrel Heady and Sybil Stokes eds., *Papers on Comparative Public Administration.* Ann Arbor, University of Michigan Press, 1962, : 104.

19. Werlin, Herbert, "Linking Decentralization and Centralization: A Critique to the New Development Administration", *Public Administration and Development,* Vol. 12, No. 4, October-December 1992, : 223-35.

14

Prospects of Panchayati Raj Institutions (PRIs) by the Year 2015 A.D.

S.N. Mishra and Lokesh Kumar

The Panchayati Raj Institutions (PRIs) in India are the prime instruments of decentralization at the grass-roots level. They assume importance due to the need to contain the relentless demographic pressures and optimum use of scarce resources for development. They act as vehicle in carrying back to the people the power that really belongs to them. In the din of economic liberalisation the PRIs are also one of the downright rationalisations to meet the challenges of development. An orderly scheme of central-decentral polity is then a crying need of the hour.

The success of the PRIs depend to a large extent on the proper mandate, self-governance and financial autonomy. Due to the lack of these factors, the PRIs in India, since their inception, have failed to evolve into a viable democratic structure at the local levels. So the question remains especially after the enforcement of the Seventy-third Constitution (Amendment) Act, 1992, which can be called as the watershed in the field of decentralised decision-making; what would be the prospects of the PRIs in India by the beginning of 21st century.

In our analysis, we would first like to discuss in Section I, the conceptualisation for the Panchayati Raj as envisaged by the founding fathers of the Indian Constitution as they lacked unanimity on this concept and how far the Seventy-third Amendment provided uniformity to the concept . In Section II, the focus would be on the various efforts taken by Indian Government to streamline the PRIs since independence upto the Seventy-third Amendment. But mere legislative enactment is not enough to provide viability to the so-called defunct PRIs, so Section III deals with the new Panchayati Raj in action (a State-wise scenario) in the post-Seventy-third Amendment period. Section IV deals with the prospects of the PRIs after the recent Amendment because the earlier legislative framework in relation to the PRIs failed at the operational level. The concluding remarks find place in Section V.

I

The concept of Panchayati Raj, since its inception,has faced various interpretations both from its protagonists and antagonists. This concept puts the emphasis on maximum local autonomy and minimisation of supervision and control by the higher authorities, especially the state government. However, its critics consider it to be a ruination for the country. Another controversy relates to the role of political parties in the PRIs. In this light, the Seventy-third Constitution (Amendment) Act, 1992 has provided a new dimension to the concept of Panchayati Raj.

The plea for greater autonomy to the rural bodies received conceptual strength with the advent of Mahatma Gandhi on the national scene and his enunciation of the doctrine of the national development through autonomous rural organisations modelled on the lines of panchayat system as it prevailed in ancient India. He envisaged a five-tier system of village panchayats, taluka panchayats, district panchayats, provincial panchayats, and all-India panchayats. The administrative system envisaged by him was that of a pyramid whose broad base was composed of numerous village communities of the country. It was envisaged that higher panchayats shall tender sound advice, give expert guidance and information, supervise and coordinate the activities of the village panchayats with a view to increasing the efficiency of the administration and public service. But it would be the basic units that would dictate to the centre and not vice versa. In fact, the whole system would turn upside down, the village shall become the real and moving unit of administration.

However, Dr. Ambedkar, who was primarily responsible for the Draft Constitution, gave no place to the panchayats in it. He spoke clearly and unequivocally condemning the village panchayats as "a sink of localism and a den of ignorance and narrow mindedness and communalism". He opined that the village republics spelled ruination for the country and played no part in the affairs and destiny of the country.

What followed was a middle path between the Gandhian concept of village panchayats and its condemnation by Dr. Ambedkar. There was only the formal acceptance of the idea of local autonomy, in juxtaposition, there existed a well-entrenched resistance to any radical change of balance of power in favour of local self-government institutions. The resultant of this was a mere incorporation of village panchayats in the Directive Principles of State Policy of the Indian Constitution.

Jaya Prakash Narayan, having his own concept of Panchayati Raj, had no place for political parties. He opined that the success of PRIs depended upon the extent to which political parties refrained from interfering with it and trying to convert it into their hand-maiden, and using it as a spring board to jump to power. "Self-government through faction-fighting will not be self-government, but self-ruination". Even Jawaharlal Nehru suggested for providing incentive for unanimous elections to Panchayats. Accordingly, as envisaged by him, there should be a Panchayati Raj system of two types, namely, those elected unanimously should be given more powers, and those elected by majority votes should be given less powers.

However, the concept of Panchayati Raj for the supporters of Parliamentary democracy assumes correlation between Parliamentary government and political parties. They feel that parliamentary democracy based on organised political parties and direct elections is the only and certain means of effective democratic government. The Principle of unanimity may lead to some form of totalitarianism. It is normally a 'visionary concept'. Now the Seventy-third Constitution (Amendment) Act, 1992 has added new dimension to the concept of Panchayati Raj by providing enough scope for direct elections and for political parties to contest elections and to play effective role by giving it a constitutional status.

In the present scenario, the concept of Panchayati Raj has come to be accepted as an extension of democracy up to the village, and has found favour amongst politicians. It is often said that mere exercise of the right to elect representatives to the central and the state legislatures is not enough for the ordinary citizen. In other words, the concept of direct participation of the people should be considered as an ideological commitment and therefore what is needed is legislative and structural changes to give legitimacy to people's participation.

The PRIs in India have travelled a long way to acquire a constitutional status from finding a mere mention of it in the Constitution in the form of Directive Principles (Art. 40). The Article 40 of the Indian Constitution states : "The state shall take steps to organise village panchayats and endow them with such powers and authority as may be necessary to enable them to function as units of self-government". This Article remained a dead letter for many years before finding a place of some importance in the form of the Balwant Rai Mehta Study Team report in 1959. The team had inter alia envisaged directly elected panchayats for a village or a group of villages, an executive body called panchayat samiti for a block with directly elected and co-opted members, and an advisory body, Zila Parishad, at the district level constituted indirectly with ex-officio members from the lower tier and others with the District Collector as the chairperson.

The situation prompted the Government to set up yet another Committee under the chairmanship of Mr. Ashok Mehta consisting of 13 members for suggesting the ways and means for strengthening of the PRIs. This Committee suggested the abolition of block as the unit of administration and recommended a two-tier set up at district and mandal levels covering a population of 15,000 to 20,000. The recommendations of the Ashok Mehta Committee were considered by a conference of the Chief Ministers held in 1979 which favoured the continuance of the three-tier system. They suggested the drawing up of a model bill which should be adopted and enacted by the states with necessary modification to suit the local needs.

In 1985, a 12-member Committee was appointed under the chairmanship of Dr. G.V.K. Rao for reviewing the administrative arrangements for rural development and poverty alleviation programmes. While recommending that the district should be the basic unit for policy planning and programme implementation, this committee emphasised the need for regular elections to the PRIs. The Seventh Five Year Plan document admitted the extremely peripheral status to which these institutions had been reduced and emphasised the need for radically changing the conventional methodology of planning for village and block level activities and for providing substantial funds and autonomy to the Panchayati Raj bodies.

Once again, in 1987, yet another Committee formed under the chairmanship of Dr. L.M. Singhvi to review the functioning of PRIs, recommended the reorganisation of villages to make village panchayats more viable. It also suggested that more financial resources should be made available to these institutions. The Sarkaria Commission on Centre-State Relations also observed that many of the local self-governing bodies were not functioning effectively mainly because elections to these bodies were not being held regularly and these bodies were being superseded on flimsy grounds. The need for uniformity of law in the states regarding holding of periodical elections and supercession of the Panchayati Raj bodies was also emphasised by the Commission.

A sub-committee of the Parliamentary Consultative Committee attached to the Ministry of Personnel, Public Grievances and Pensions was set up under the chairmanship of Mr. P.K. Thungon to consider the type of political and administrative structure needed in the district for district planning. The Committee felt that the PRIs should be constitutionally recognised and recommended that a constitutional provision should be made to ensure timely and regular elections to these bodies with their terms lasting for five years. The Zila Parishad should be the only planning and development agency in the district according to the opinion of this sub-committee.

The Constitution (Sixty-fourth) Amendment Bill, 1989, which, though passed by the Lok Sabha, could not be enacted as it was not passed by the Rajya Sabha. This Bill provided for constitution of panchayats in every state at the village, intermediate and district levels with the exception of states which have a population not exceeding 20 lakhs, where states may bypass the intermediate level.

In 1990, the Constitution (Seventy-fourth) Amendment Bill was introduced in the Lok Sabha but could not be taken up for consideration and since the Lok Sabha was dissolved, the Bill also lapsed. The Bill provided for 'Gram Sabha' in each village and also proposed that panchayats should be constituted at the village and other levels. Direct elections were suggested to all seats in the panchayats at the village level and to not less than 50 per cent of seats in panchayats at other levels.

The Constitution (Seventy-second) Amendment Bill was passed with near unanimity by the Lok Sabha on December 22, 1992 and by the Rajya Sabha on December 23,1993. After having been ratified by 17 state assemblies, this emerged as the Constitution (Seventy-third) Amendment Act, 1993, and came into force from April 24, 1993. So this Amendment Act is the culmination of various proposals made by the earlier committees or sub-committees on panchayati raj bodies, and thus gives PRIs a viable shape. The salient features of the Act are as follows:

— There shall be a gram sabha in each village exercising such powers and performing such functions at the village level as the legislature of a state may provide by law.

— Panchayats shall be constituted in every state at the village, intermediate and district levels, thus bringing about uniformity in the Panchayati Raj structure. However, the state having a population not exceeding 20 lakh have been given the option of not having any panchayat at the intermediate level.

— While the elections in respect of all the members to panchayats at all levels will be direct, the elections in respect of the post of chairperson at the intermediate and district level will be indirect. The mode of election of chairperson to the village level has been left for the state governments to decide.

— Reservation of seats for SCs\STs have been provided in proportion to their population at each level. Not less than one-third of the total membership has been reserved for women and these seats may be allotted by rotation to different constituencies in a panchayat. Similar reservations have been made in respect of the office of the chairperson also.

— A uniform term of 5 years has been provided for the PRIs and in the event of supersession, elections to constitute the body should be completed before the expiry of 6 months from the date of dissolution.

— The state legislatures have been given the power to authorise the panchayats to levy, collect, and appropriate suitable local taxes and also provide for making grants-in-aid to the Panchayats from the Consolidated Fund of the concerned state.

— A Finance Commission has to be constituted once in every 5 years to review the financial position of the panchayats and to make suitable recommendations to the state on the distribution of funds between the state and local bodies.

— With a view to ensuring continuity it has been provided in the Act that all the panchayats existing immediately before the commencement of this Amendment Act will continue till the expiry of their duration unless dissolved by a resolution to that effect passed by the state legislature concerned.

— The state legislatures should bring in necessary amendments to their Panchayat Acts within a maximum period of one year from the commencement of this Amendment Act so as to conform to the provision contained in the Constitution.

III

So far the Seventy-third Constitutional (Amendment) Act, 1992 has only provided the general guidelines for the effective and efficient PRIs in India. It has granted the PRIs a constitutional status, some sort of a uniformity by making three-tier system a permanent feature, a regularity by making elections imperative after the termination of the PRIs after every five years and the State Election Commission to conduct and supervise the elections, more financial autonomy with the constitution of the State Finance Commission etc. But the major question still remains: how the various states are responding and at what speed they are implementing the Panchayati Raj as envisaged by the recent constitutional amendment.

It can be said that India is on the threshold of a historic transition of political power to the grass-roots with all the states completing the process of enacting fresh legislation on strengthening of the PRIs on 23 April, 1994. As many as eleven states pushed through fresh legislation within 72 hours, some of them even in the early hours of 23 April, 1994 to beat the stipulated deadline of 23 April, 1994, the day panchayats became part of the Indian Constitution. However, the 73rd Constitutional (Amendment) Act is not applicable to Jammu and Kashmir, Mizoram, Nagaland and certain other Scheduled Areas of the country. But mere legislative enactments do not ensure effectiveness and viability of the PRIs in the states. What is more important is their operationalisation. So we will take up the state-wise assessment of the new Panchayati Raj in action to have a clear picture of the ground realities.

The Andhra Pradesh Panchayati Raj Act, 1994, became effective on 30th May, 1994. In the Gram Panchayats, the existing Sarpanchs have been re-nominated as "Incharge Sarpanchs". The cheque signing powers have been withdrawn from them and entrusted to Executive Officers through an ordinance. The Gram Panchayats are becoming nodal centres for development activities due to flow of funds from the Centre as well as the state government. A Village Panchayat in A.P. received on an average rupees 10 lakhs a year, besides the funds received under Jawahar Rozgar Yojana. The local bodies have been renamed as the Mandal Mahasabha (the middle level) and the Zila Mahasabha (the higher level). S.Karipandian was appointed as Election Commissioner for a term of 5 years on 5th June, 1994. With the enactment of the new Panchayati Raj Act 1994, the District Planning and Development Review Committees ceased to exist. A separate District Planning Committee is to be constituted.

The Assam Assembly passed the Assam Panchayat Bill on 9th April, 1994, though the PRIs are given more powers, under the new Act, the Government has the power to dissolve any Gram Panchayat, Anchalik Panchayat or Zila Parishad if they abuse power or are not able to perform their duties properly. Here, the PRIs are playing effective role in the developmental activities and in poverty alleviation programmes. A Gram Sabha of Holeswar Panchayat under Balipare Anchalik Panchayat held on 6th May, 1994 selected a total of 21 beneficiaries under IRDP for the year 1994-95. A series of intensive training courses for presidents and vice-presidents of 13 Gram Panchayats and Anchalik Panchayats were organised under the aegis of District Rural Development Agency (DRDA) in Bongaigaon. In the Total Literacy Campaign (TLC) launched in Kokrajhar district, panchayat presidents and members have taken an active role. In Tinsukia, 98 Gram Panchayats under 6 Development Blocks have undertaken the programme. Tapal Lal Barua has been appointed as the Chairman of State Election Commission.

The Bihar Panchayati Raj Act came into force on 6th August, 1993. The District Planning Committee has been constituted. Mr. K.K.Saha has been appointed as Election Commissioner. So far as election is concerned the then Chief Minister Laloo Prasad Yadav did initially make noises about holding early panchayat elections. However, no follow-up action was taken to fulfil the promise. Going by his utterances, it seems that he is disinterested in granting any real administrative or financial powers to the panchayats. The provision of reservation of seats is being utilised by him for creating vote banks for the forthcoming State Assembly elections.

The Gujarat Panchayati Raj Act became effective from 26th August, 1993, So far as Haryana is concerned, it has taken lead in the perpetuation of family planning programme. A candidate having more than two children will not be allowed to contest the Panchayat election. The state cabinet approved the setting up of the State Finance Commission and the State Election Commission in consonance with the provisions of Haryana Panchayati Raj Act, 1994. It is notable that Himachal Pradesh new Panchayati Raj Act, 1994 has made a provision for an independent audit agency and vigilance committees which would help in monitoring the functioning of the panchayats.

Karnataka was the first state to pass the new legislation on 7th April,1993 which became effective from 30th April, 1993. The Gram Panchayat elections were held on non-party basis on 29th December, 1993 which was a landmark in itself as 43 per cent of those elected were women and 32 per cent belonged to the SCs STs. However, the elections of Taluk and Zila Panchayat were delayed . Subsequently the election were held on party basis in August,1994. At the operational level it is interesting to note that the administrators of former Mandal Panchayats continue to function and conduct the day to day activities for Gram Panchayats without handing over the charge of their offices to the newly elected incumbents. There were widespread allegations that they had withdrawn funds from panchayats to be spent on continued basis as the financial year was coming to a close on 31st March, 1994. Even the Gram Panchayat annual plans/budgets for 1994-95 were prepared by the administrators in consultation with the local MLAs and sent to the Taluk Panchayat for formal approval. As a result, the newly elected members and functionaries of the Gram Panchayats will be forced to implement the annual plans prepared and approved by the bureaucrats. But subsequent developments and amendment in the Act of the state have provided bitting teeth to the PRIs.

The passing of the Panchayati Raj Bill by Kerala Assembly in the early hours of 23rd April, 1994 attracted widespread criticism from all quarters. This is well exemplified by the fact that as many as 3500 amendments were tabled by members belonging to both ruling and opposition parties. It is alleged that the Bill passed by the Assembly was virtually an empowerment to the bureaucracy rather than to the people.

As far as Uttar Pradesh, Rajasthan and Maharashtra are concerned, the legislative commitments of Panchayati Raj Act have already been fulfilled and operationalised. In Tripura, the Panchayati Raj Bill came into force on 7th November, 1993 and the elections were held in August, 1994 in which 76 per cent voters exercised their franchise.

In West Bengal, the panchayat elections were held in May, 1993, in which the left front, particularly the CPI (M), had romped home with a large majority. But it is notable that the overall domination of the privileged classes over the rural power structure remains unchallenged. The election also witnessed the spate of poll-related violence especially in Karanda village of Burddhaman district.

In contrast, the peaceful conduct of the panchayat elections in Punjab may be considered an important step towards restoration of the democratic process in this strife-torn state. Apparently enthusiastic participation of the rural section in the panchayat elections, with a turn-out of the more than 82 per cent, signifies not only a loosening in the hold of terror but also a break in the hitherto prevalent sense of alienation.

In the case of Orissa, it has been the first state to implement 33 per cent reservation of seats for women in panchayats, having 2500 representatives in the panchayats. A unique provision of Orissa Gram Panchayat Act is that if the Gram Panchayat Sarpanch who is elected or nominated is not a woman, the office of Naib-Sarpanch will go to a woman. Similar is the provision for the chairperson of the Panchayat Samities. The elected women members of the panchayat will supervise the various schemes meant for women and children at the village, block and district levels. In Orissa, the panchayats are having effective role in socio-economic development. The role of panchayats is being publicised through films, photographs, wall writings, group discussions etc. The area included 12 different blocks of Koraput, Raigada, Kalahandi, Nanpara and Phulbari districts. The Sarpanch of Dulki Panchayat (Jharsuguda district) took out a procession and held a meeting at the village level to create awareness regarding total literacy. The state government launched a scheme called 'Ama Gar' (our village). It aimed at upliftment of the rural people by providing them both funds and powers of decision-making for development works in villages.

The state of Madhya Pradesh requires a special mention because it is the first state to have had elections at all the three levels under the new constitutional provisions. The elections for Gram Panchayat, Janapad Panchayat and Zila Panchayat were held during May-June, 1994. The first meeting of the elected panchayats held in August, 1994 and 20th August, 1994 was observed as 'Adhikar Divas' as all the elected office bearers of the PRIs took charge of their offices. It is interesting to note that the office of Chief Executive Officer (CEO) will now be held by the elected district panchayat chairperson and the District Collector will function as its secretary. This significantly clips the wings of bureaucracy and in addition, a post of additional CEO will be created to which a Class I Officer will be selected through a competitive selection process. The state government has entrusted the newly-elected panchayats with the task of completing rural development projects. The training for setting up, running and marketing the products of the cottage industries and khadi will be undertaken by Janapad and Zila Panchayats. Besides, the panchayats have been given wide-ranging powers in the fields of social welfare, potable water supply, public health, family welfare, animal husbandry, dairy and poultry development, education, public distribution system etc.

Thus, the functioning of new Panchayati Raj reveals the fact that though the legislative formalities have been completed in almost all the states, yet, at the operational level, there are large variations between them. In some states like West Bengal, Madhya Pradesh, etc. the elections at all levels have been completed but some states like Bihar, Haryana and Rajasthan have postponed the panchayat elections. Still the high-handedness of bureaucracy, barring a few exceptions, over the local autonomy prevails. In addition to these, the fact that the principles of local self-government have not really percolated into the minds of rural people is evident from their lack of reaction when Panchayati Raj elections are not held in time.

IV

It is a sad affair for a democratic country like India that the basic ideology behind the Seventy-third Amendment to the Constitution of making panchayats the institutions of self-government has been largely ignored in the recent state legislations. What is required is that the legislators should cut across party lines and implement the laws in true spirit with the implicit purpose of transferring power to the people, and to plug the loopholes in the existing system. Only when the three-tiers of the Constitution—the Centre, the states, and the local bodies will function with regularity and efficiency and in close co-ordination the federal structure of the Constitution, the democratic nature of the polity will be preserved. Otherwise, the Constitution will become very much distorted in its content as well as implementation.

It can be said that the PRIs in India since their inception, have remained 'down to earth' without ever taking roots. But the fact that the PRIs have survived without regularity in elections show their inherent strength and, perhaps, make them the only institutions that live on despite ample conditions justifying their departure. So what is required is the "will" to make the PRIs viable democratic institutions on which the real democracy will thrive.

It is notable that the PRIs are the primary institutions of democracy where people from village, block and district level could participate. Except for them none of the other institutions can have direct participation of the local people. Devolution of power has to start here, and this is also where people at local levels got into the mainstream of development as well as public affairs. The PRIs, especially the "Gram Sabhas", make the concept of "direct democracy" like that of Greek City-States of Plato and Aristotle days feasible at present and also for centuries to come. The Gram Sabha has been designed to be the place where development issues should be discussed, development progammes initiated and beneficiaries of development schemes selected.

It may be added that the prospect of the PRIs would be on increase keeping in mind the pace of economic liberalisation in India. In fact, they would become the watchdog bodies ensuring proper implementation of the employment generation programmes like the Jawahar Rozgar Yojana (JRY), poverty alleviation and special programmes like IRDP, TRYSEM and area development programmes like DPAP, DDP, etc. all schemes falling under Minimum Needs Programme (MNP) and programmes of the nature of local development work. In fact, the PRIs would play an important role in accelerating socio-economic development in the rural areas.

Thanks to the 73rd Amendment Act, the PRIs are going to be vested with a lot of power and money in the coming years. The enhancement of the outlay for rural development to Rs. 30,000 crores in the Eighth Plan assumes greater significance in the context of this Act. The Ninth Plan has proposed outlay of Rs. 74,942 crores for rural development. In addition, the Panchayats are assured of a regular existence like any other democratic institutions enshrined in the Constitution and they will also have adequate powers, both administrative and financial for implementing the economic development programmes meant for people living in rural India.

It is heartening to note that the states will have to transfer 36 per cent of their total plan outlay to the sub-state level planning bodies from 1994-95. Of the proposed 36 per cent outlay to be earmarked for micro-level planning, 30 per cent will go to sub-state level planning bodies through lump-sum grants for expenditure on areas including rural water supply, roads, electricity, education and any other local schemes. The list of 29 areas included in the Eleventh Schedule of the Act is flexible giving discretion to the PRIs to select schemes depending on local resources and problems. The 5 per cent of the states plan outlay will be "united fund" — transferred to district or village bodies to be utilised at their own discretion. The remaining 1 per cent will be for poverty alleviation and employment generation programmes which are to be planned and funded at the village level. For the proper implementation of these, the activities and functioning of the PRIs will have to be closely watched and monitored so that they do not overstep their limits and cause irreparable damage to those living in their jurisdiction. What is needed is a consensual and uniform approach of auditing.

It can be observed that the democratisation of our pluralistic society cannot be ensured merely through legislative and administrative actions of the State. These enabling provisions will require massive mobilisational support and non-governmental organisations, academics and professional bodies, political parties and other groups should involve themselves in exerting pressure to restore power to the place to where it belongs. For the entire exercise of decentralisation, people like school teachers, progressive farmers, social workers and professionals should be involved. Above all, the PRIs elected representatives should also be trained in rising above their electoral rivalry. They should be made to understand that once the elections are over, the rivalry should end. In fact, elections to the PRIs must carry a look of 'Mela' (festival) to attract more and more voters.

To brighten the prospects of the PRIs in India, some suggestions are as follows:

The elected representatives of the panchayats should exercise superintendence and control over government officials, i.e. serving the panchayats instead of playing a subordinate role.

An inter-zila panchayat parishad should be constituted in every state with the Chief Minister as its Chairperson to thrash out legislative, financial and administrative matters of the panchayats. The planning set up at the zila-level should be headed by the Chairperson of the zila-panchayat.

The requirements of financial accountability should be designed and supervised by the Comptroller and Auditor General (CAG) and the power of dissolution as well as accountability of lower level panchayat units should rest with the next higher levels of panchayats and not with government officials in order to establish peer group accountability.

A constitutional amendment for ensuring elections to cooperatives is a must because a vibrant cooperative system is important for a successful Panchayati Raj.

In the end, we may raise the question : Do we seriously believe in democratic decentralisation or is it a mere paper exercise? It can be said that if the problems, both at macro and micro level are not solved; if the 'vested interests and the power brokers' are not knocked out of the system; if a half-hearted, uncooked, unplanned exercise is being done for the democratic decentralisation; if the financial autonomy conferred with accountability is not improved, we may land up in a situation, which a wise man once put it as 'Honey, I shrunk the People's Participation". If the policy of the government in giving impetus to the Panchayati Raj movement is implemented faithfully and fully, it will surely bring about the political, social and economic revolution which will not only strengthen the democratic character of our society, but will also prove to be a perennial source of throwing up energetic leadership which may change the entire face of the country and guide the destinies of the people most efficiently and effectively.

V

While concluding one more question comes to our mind which may be everybody's apprehension as to whât would be the fate of PRIs by 2015 A.D.? In regard to this query we are quite optimistic about the future of PRIs as the units of grass-roots democracy. No doubt success of the PRIs will depend upon the political will of the concerned state governments. However, making Panchayati Raj elections a regular phenomenon and giving them constitutional status may ensure their bright future. No doubt the elections at the state and central level are the regular phenomenon but still we have not been able to take our democratic polity towards a bright future. However, this situation, to our mind, is not going to affect rural political system in a substantive manner. The rural masses are, of course, illiterate and ignorant but very sensitive and capable of taking subtle decisions in the larger interest of the community. Moreover, due to mandatory and periodic elections, they will be in a position to shuffle and reshuffle the leadership of PRIs making them to realise that only those leaders could stay who are committed, non-partisan and take care of development of the village community. In such a way we hope that by the end of 2015 A.D., the Panchayati Raj Institutions may be deeply rooted in the rural community and may become the real vehicle of change and development in the country-side. The only danger which, we visualise, is from the side of the state governments. This apprehension is because of the fact that the 73rd Constitutional Amendment has provided maximum latitude to the states to make suitable amendments in their Panchayati Raj Acts as and when required and this process has, perhaps, only begun. And, as such, if such negative approach of the state governments continues then only God can save the Panchayati Raj Institutions from disintegration and stagnation.

REFERENCES

1. Bhargava B.S. *Panchayati Raj System and Political Parties* Ashish Publishing House, New Delhi, 1979.
2. Chaturvedi T.N. ed., *Panchayati Raj* IIPA, New Delhi, 1991.

3. *Economic Times*, 2nd October, 1993.
4. "My Vision of Village Swaraj", *Harijan*, 26th July, 1992.
5. 15-Point Programmes for Panchayats, *Hindu*, 21st August, 1994.
6. Imbanathan A., "Panchayati Raj— At the Crossroad" *Deccan Herald*, 29th November, 1993.
7. Inamdar N.R., *Functioning of Village Panchayats*, Popular Prakashan, Bombay, 1970.
8. Jain L.C., "Future of Panchayats", *Hindustan Times*, 4th October, 1991.
9. Jathar R.N., *Evolution of P.R. in India*, Institute of Economic Research, Dharmar, 1964.
10. Krishnamurthy B., "About Panchayati Raj", *Patriot*, 21st July, 1993.
11. Malviya H.D., *Village Panchayats in India* (AICC, New Delhi, 1956).
12. Mathur P.C., *Political Dynamics of Panchayati Raj*, Konark Publishers, New Delhi, 1991.
13. Mishra S.N. and S.S. Singh, *Road to Model Panchayati Raj* Mittal Publications, New Delhi, 1993.
14. Narain Iqbal et.al, *Panchayati Raj Administration: Old and New Challenge*, IIPA, New Delhi, 1970.
15. Sharma K.K., "Finance for Panchayati Raj", *Financial Express*, 13th September, 1993.
16. "M.P. Panchayat Bill Passed", *Statesman*, 31st December, 1994.

15

Establishing Linkages between Panchayats and Cooperatives for Sustainable Development

P.N. Sharma

The Panchayati Raj Legislation has come into force from 23rd April, 1994, throughout the country. This aims at decentralisation of power into the hands of the people at the grass-roots level so that they are brought into the mainstream of decision making process and are enabled to take decisions about their future according to their needs and aspirations. This legislation also aims at initiating the process of planning from below, coming in the wake of 73rd Amendment in the Constitution of India. The states are required to implement it or modify their existing laws to bring them in tune with the provisions in the above amendment. This is obviously a landmark in the history of democratic decentralisation and is expected to go a long way in building a strong institution at the village level which would look after all the functions of development and local self-governance at the village level.

The Government of Uttar Pradesh (U.P.) has made suitable amendments\modifications in the United Provinces Panchayat Raj Act, 1947 and U.P. Kshetra Samiti and Zila Parishad Adhiniyam, 1961 to fall in line with the 73rd Amendment. The state government, through the U.P. Panchayat Vidhi (Sanshodan) Vidheyak, 1994 have made even more radical provisions as compared to the 73rd Amendment and have prescribed reservation to the posts of pradhans for the members belonging to the Scheduled Castes, Scheduled Tribes and backward classes according to the proportion of the population of these castes in the population of the state as a whole. Also, at least one-third of the posts of pradhans have been reserved for women (including those who belong to these castes). The state government has included thirty subjects (instead of 29 in the Eleventh Schedule of 73rd Amendment) and each subject has been further disaggregated making the functions of a Gram Panchayat precisely defined. The major function of the Panchayat would be to prepare a plan for economic development of the village besides which it has been entrusted to look after the activities of women and child development. Similarly, it will continue to work for the promotion of dairy development and animal husbandry activities and maintenance of community land resources.

The state legislation in Article 36 has prescribed constitution of a number of committees for seeking assistance in performance of its functions. Besides the constitution of committees for ensuring social justice (Samta Samiti), and committees for looking after various sectoral functions, there would be a Development Committee (Vikas Samiti) which would be specifically responsible for the management of functions related to agricultural production, animal husbandry, village industries and poverty alleviation programmes. In this committee one representative of the cooperative societies operating in the area would be co-opted. Vikas Samiti is the most important committee of the Gram Panchayat and its chairperson would be the ex-officio member of all other committees whether it be education committee, health committee or public works committee. The Samta Samiti and Shiksha Samiti would compulsorily have one woman member besides one member belonging to the scheduled castes and tribes. Another important provision is that the Gram Panchayat can co-opt members from the NGOs approved by the state government.

Therefore, most remarkable provision made in Article 36 of the state legislation is the inclusion of a representative of the Cooperative Society in the Development Committee (Vikas Samiti) of the Panchayat which would be performing the crucial tasks of preparing the development plan on behalf of the Panchayat. It is for the first time that linkage has been provided between the two peoples' institutions which have been recognised as foundations of the democratic structure of the Indian polity. Needless to say that the roles of these institutions are complementary and supplementary to each other and if they work in unison the final outcome in the fields of economic and social development would be far better both in the qualitative and quantitative terms. The role of the co-operative was perceived not merely at ensuring provisions of credit and other economic inputs for improving the agricultural productivity of the member households but it also aimed at initiating a process of education of working together on a co-operative basis. This kind of co-operative development was to be reflected in other spheres of life. It was actually a process of developing a co-operative culture ultimately leading to common sharing of facilities as well as their benefits. For example, the mahila dairy project was to have the holistic development of women as its ultimate goal. Similarly, it was seen as an access to other rural development programmes. The Gram Panchayats on the other hand were supposed to look after the work of overall development of the village encompassing each and every household's needs and aspirations. The co-operatives can therefore be seen as an 'entry point' to the comprehensive and integrated development of the village as a whole and ensuring that the benefits of development reach the persons on the last rung of society.

Theoretically speaking, there are common principles which have been the motivating factors behind creation of these institutions. These can be summarised as under:

(i) Empowerment of the people especially the women and other underprivileged sections of society.

(ii) Self-reformation and a system of local government.

(iii) Rural transformation through utilisation of potentialities of the village society.

(iv) Providing opportunity on equitable basis for self-actualisation by each and every member of the community especially the women and the neglected groups of society.

As a matter of fact the ultimate goal has been to initiate a process of local development through these democratic institutions which would lead to creation of new social systems at the local level. These must embody participation and mutual cooperation among all groups besides national and state governments and non-governmental organisations. Ultimately, the success of local level development and its sustainability will depend on the self-organising capability of the people in a particular community. Development is always concerned with the way resources, ideas and organisation are combined to bring about a change. To a large extent, the self organising capability is shaped by the way resources are acquired by the individual households in the society. In this, the women and the underprivileged sections of society have to be given special attention so that they also become active partners in the development process as well as acquisition of resources. It is only then that the self-organising capability of the community can be built up and they can become decision makers and managers of their own affairs.

It is not merely that the underlying philosophy of the establishment of the above institutions is the same, there are other complementarities between the two:

(a) The organisation which is supposed to regulate the resources of the community is Gram Panchayat but the organisations that provide access to the resources outside the community are the cooperatives (including Mahila Mandals or Women's Groups etc.).

(b) The organisation that determines the meaning of resources in the community is Gram Panchayat. It also helps the people in establishing interlinkages of various programmes but the organisation and organisational activities that promote a sense of belonging among members of a community are the cooperatives including the women's groups, user groups and self-help groups. Equitable sharing of benefits is necessary to promote this sense.

Rural System

The complementary and supplementary relationship between the Panchayats and Cooperatives can also be analysed in terms of the rural system. In U.P., the Gram Panchayat comprises a number of hamlets which are generally caste based and within the hamlet, the traditional relationships still play an important role. In many cases the caste panchayats also operate and these are the most important social units. Although informally organised, these have a strong influence on all aspects of life including patterns of production and life styles. For any development effort to be launched the planners have to keep this fact in mind since the cooperative and collective activities take place through these groups. Sometimes, community land although vested in Gram Panchayat is also maintained by these groups where interests do not clash. In the existing situation what happens is that the facilities and amenities or assets created through government assistance are concentrated in the main village in whose name the Gram Panchayat is designated. The hamlets usually feel dissatisfied with this kind of decision of locating everything at the Panchayat headquarters.

The organised cooperatives do not have this kind of locational bias and members of different hamlets participate because of their own needs and availability of inputs. If taken into confidence they can provide a broad based locational pattern for the Panchayats and diversification of its activities.Through the cooperatives the Panchayats could dovetail the economic and social developmental activities also.

The local level administration is an integral and critical part of the rural system. The effectiveness of rural system depends to a great extent on the support and goodwill of the local administration comprising different field level functionaries. If Gram Panchayat is active and has developed good relationship with the field functionaries it is sure to secure larger number of schemes out of the kitty of schemes available at the block level. Since local level functionaries are also required to achieve their physical and financial targets, they also feel inclined to support good Gram Panchayats. This kind of relationship between the Gram Panchayat and local level administration can be utilised for increasing the efficiency and economic capacity of the cooperatives.

Sustainability

In the new system the Gram Panchayats are going to have their own financial autonomy and the devolution of finances will take place on an assured basis. The present system of flow of funds earmarked for different schemes through Gram Panchayat would continue and in addition they will have untied funds and their own income which can be utilised according to their own discretion. Therefore, if cooperatives (particularly women cooperatives wish to undertake income generating activities other than those in which they are currently engaged, the support of Panchayats would be crucial. The sustainability of such activities would depend largely on the attitude and contribution of Panchayats. The Panchayats and cooperatives have, therefore, to act in unison with each other if any activity has to be organised on a sustained basis. It would necessarily imply that a harmonious relationship exists between these two institutions.

Institutional Linkages

It may be either, the Co-operative or Panchayat, both these institutions can survive and prosper with the help of each other. It can be seen that most of the supportive inputs/services which are required for successful implementation of the activities of the co-operatives fall under the purview of Panchayats. Similarly in the case of the Panchayats with their increased developmental responsibilities, they will also require non-governmental resources, credit and other inputs and some of them may come from the co-operatives. These linkages between, activities, resources and elements of households have been shown in Table 1.1 which are self evident.

Convergence of Services

We have discussed earlier that the Co-operatives in the present are just concerned with the sectoral activity and in a sense it has been conceived as an end in itself. However, the economic activity, for example, dairy development should be seen as an entry point to the furtherance of larger objectives of improving the quality of life besides taking up other income generating activities. These can help in creating perceptible improvement in the levels of education and nutrition and other indicators of human development.

The above requires convergence of services and inputs delivered by different government and non-government agencies. This type of convergent planning can be done only through participatory planning at the village level. The community based planning, monitoring and evaluation will as a matter of fact provide the focus for unified sectoral actions at the village level. The cooperatives in collaboration with Gram Panchayat, will be able to move in the direction of convergent planning. This kind of covergence or coordination between different sectoral programmes cannot be achieved through the line agencies. Thus, the role of Cooperatives assumes greater significance in this context, the roles expected from the Panchayat and Cooperatives jointly can be summarised as below:

1. These organisations should provide active mechanism for securing government assistance.
2. They should be able to provide opportunity (equitable sharing of benefits) for collective action so that a base is created for succeeding forms of organisational endeavours.

3. They should make the goals of development operational in conformity with national or state priorities.
4. They should be able to develop a receiving mechanism for effective utilisation of external assistance.
5. Ultimately the above efforts should result in enhanced self organising capability based on the experience of working together for common goals which creates a snow ball effect for cooperative endeavour.

Measures to Achieve Integration of Panchayats and Cooperatives

The desirability and inevitability of the institutional linkages between the Gram Panchayats and the Cooperatives is obvious. The past experience shows that there has been a neutral relationship between the Cooperatives and the Panchayats except in those cases where the office bearers of both the institutions have come from the same affiliation. In some cases, however, Pradhans have been generous in extending facilities and support to some specific cooperatives like women's milk cooperatives. It may not be taken as a general feature. The cooperatives have been working mostly on limited sectoral lines and have seldom cared to work for the all round development of the village. It is not in their scheme of things.

It may be added here that since the two institutions have been created through different statutes and the socio-political background of the office-bearers of these institutions being different in many cases it would not be very easy to forge organic relationship between the two. Nevertheless, keeping in view the complementary and supplementary relationship between them and the common goal before them serious efforts need to be made to create an environment in which both these institutions work in coordination. The following are some of the measures which may help in fostering good relationship between the two institutions:

(i) A multi-disciplinary approach must be adopted which can address the question of how people with conflicting interests can make better decisions together particularly on difficult contentious issues. This can be done by organising frequent interfaces between the members of the two organisations to let them know each others activities. It would require better communication among the key members of the two organisations. The goal of maximising the welfare of the people should be the common meeting ground. Each institution can define what can it give and take from the other one.

(ii) A massive drive at conscientisation has to be organised. It should include conscientisation of the public in general and the opinion leaders in particular. It has to be brought home that Panchayati Raj is not merely an instrument of democratic decentralisation but is also a delivery system having complementarities vis-a-vis economic development and human resource development for it.

(iii) The training and education can play an important role in improving individual and organisational performance. The concern of training should be how those involved in decentralisation and cooperative management can acquire a body of knowledge, skills, attitudes and values essential for operating effectively a decentralised system of governance. The training should be concerned with learning rather than training in conventional sense.

(iv) The attitudinal changes have also to be brought about in the bureaucracy at all levels so that they start attaching credibility to the Panchayati Raj Institutions and Cooperatives. What happens is that efforts are made to change the attitudes of the field level workers while the top echelons in the government continue to maintain the same hostile attitude.

(v) The legislators and the members of Parliament also need to be convinced of the new system so that they can be prepared to reconcile with the new realities.

(vi) A proper environment for training at a massive scale should be created. Important features of this environment building exercise should include utilisation of mass media, preparation of training material in local language, distance learning, etc.

(vii) Creating gender sensitivity in the official and non-official functionaries by bringing together the men and women members on the common platform so that there are greater opportunities for exchange of ideas.

(viii) As mentioned earlier training is the most crucial aspect of the measures for successful developmental effort by both these institutions. Separate training courses should be designed for the non-official and official functionaries besides some combined /mixed courses.

Training of Development Functionaries

The key development functionaries are those officers/officials who are responsible to work directly with the communities to enable the democratic institutions work more effectively. The training of these workers can be more effective and result oriented if we are able to match their capabilities with their functions. The concept of preparing every worker as a multi-purpose worker does not always work well because there are certain jobs which require higher level expertise, e.g., helping the community in preparing a development plan. We have therefore divided the development tasks into three categories as also the key development functionaries workers. The first type is involved in Generic Tasks which are related to formulation of integrated village development plans by involving the local households, their organisations and other village level functionaries. These workers have to ensure sectoral, spatial as well as institutional linkages in the plan. They are then required to get the plan implemented through coordinated efforts of all the agencies.

The second type of tasks are operational (complex) tasks which involve direct community work. Here the worker establishes rapport with different agencies, co-operatives, self-help groups, women's groups, user-groups etc. and works as a catalyst. His goal is to motivate and mobilise the local communities so that they can build their own self-organising capability. These also assist in devising participatory monitoring and evaluation systems.

The third type of operational tasks in which the key workers are involved are more or less specialised line functions which are of routine and specialised nature. We are giving an illustrative list in Table-1.2 of these tasks and the concerned workers for providing some basis for designing training programmes for development functionaries.

Training of Non-officials

While designing training and orientation programmes of non-official development functionaries it would be useful to divide them in these (or similar) categories so that suitable programmes could be devised for different categories which will involve different kinds of knowledge and skills. It would also help in devising/designing suitable training methodologies for separate groups. The magnitude of training needs/problems can be gauged by the sheer number of peoples' representatives to be trained. In Uttar Pradesh alone 7,00,000 Panchayat members will require training.

Conclusion

The role of both the organisations, i.e., Panchayats and Cooperatives is important in convergent planning and sustainable development. For this, both the organisations need to be sustainable and integrated with each other. This would require attitudinal changes in the bureaucracy both at the higher levels and field levels and the political representatives at the central, state, district and village levels. The conflicting interests could be resolved only by adopting a multi-disciplinary approach. A massive drive of concretisation and similar dose of training, education and orientation would be required by delineating the expected roles and functions expected of them and designing programmes of training compatible with these functions at various levels. All methods of training and education should be included in the package such as workshops, seminars, distance learning, etc. The functionaries of Cooperatives and Panchayats have to work in unison to achieve their development goals.

Table 1.1 : Activities, Resource Aspects and Elements of Household Available Within the Community and From Outside

Activities	*Physical Aspect*			*Human Aspect*			*Monetary Aspect*		
	H.H.	*Comm.*	*O.S.*	*H.H.*	*Comm.*	*O.S.*	*H.H.*	*Comm.*	*O.S.*
Production Activity	Farm Land	Water	Control of erosion, Hydras Irrigation Channels, Water Harvesting,	Out migration of males	Sharing of labour on reciprocal basis	Supply of agricultural and other implements to reduce labour component and time consumption.	Nominal productive capital reinvested out of savings (very small)	Supply of wood and exchange of seeds	Employment Programmes, Supply of short-term and medium-term credit, agricultural inputs seeds and fertilisers, Animal Health Cover, IRDP grants.
	Animal Husbandry Drought animals and Milk animals.	Grazing Ground, Supply of Fodder	Cross-breeding, Market.	-do-	-do-				
Daily Life Activities	Housing	Timber for House Building, Drinking Water, Fuel	Construction of paths, Regeneration of Forests, Environmental Sanitation, etc.	Household members including those who send money from outside	Kinship groups, caste-groups helping in times of distress or celebration of festivals.	Health Education, Family Welfare, Activities to reduce drudgery of women, Mahila Mandal.	Money spent on Social obligations, Marriage of Children, Other Functions, Purchase of Consumer Goods, Radio etc.	Sharing of expenses on marriage through gifts in cash or kind, Arranging supply of timber for house building and exchange of labour.	Piped water supply, Electricity, Smokeless chulhas, Primary School Health Facilities, Nutrition, ICDS, Old age pension, Public Distribution System.
Management Activities	Limited right due to no control on most resources.	Distribution and regulation of benefits without disposal.	Laws and Rules for control and regulation of common resources.	Rights of assignment to household members.	Collective Action.	Create environment congenial to collective activity.	Rights of production welfare.	Accessibility of facilities and their utilisation.	Provision of facilities.

Note : H.H. = Household, Comm. = Community, O.S. = From Outside (including Cooperatives)

Anx- III A

Table 1.2 Key Development Functionaries by Categories of Tasks

Sl.No. Category	Designation of FLW	Expected Role (Illustrative)
I Generic Tasks	Asstt Project Director DRDA Subject Matter Specialist (Ag) Senior Horticulture Inspector, Soil Conservation Officer. Asstt Development Officer (Coop). Asstt Development Officer (MI), Asstt Develop. Officer (State), Asstt Development Officer (Panchayat).	(i) Identification of target villages within the area as a priority in terms of erosion status and needs of beneficiaries as per directions of senior staff. (ii) Developing an outline strategy for specific area after bench mark survey and situation analysis. (iii) Preparation of integrated plan based on participatory approach. (iv) Ensuring spatial and sectoral integration through coordination with line agencies, NGOs and outside agencies (v) Working out financial and technical details of the plan. (vi) Coordination, supervision and administration. (vii) Monitoring and Evaluation. (viii) Train the official and non-official functionaries in participatory planning methods.

Anx III B

Sl.No. Category	Designation of FLW	Expected Role (Illustrative)
(II)(A) Operational (Complex) Tasks	Village Development Officer, Village Panchayat Officer, Forest Range Officer, Cooperative Supervisor Secretary, Dairy Co-operative Women Group, Organiser Anganwadi Worker (ICDS), Village Level Extension Worker	(i) Working directly with the community as a catalyst and facilitator (ii) Understanding community group dyanamics and decision making process (iii) Understanding gender issues and conscientisation of the male members about role and status of women in society. (iv) Motivate and mobilise community members in organising user groups and

		other formal and informal cooperative arrangements (v) Mobilise groups, organisations to participate in planning and development process to achieve participatory development and achieve project objectives (vi) Helping communities in developing capability for development and an effective receiving mechanism (vii) Developing participatory monitoring and evaluation system (viii) Coordinating the functions of routine workers to achieve convergence of services (ix) Building integrated team approach
II (B) Operational (Routine) Tasks	Lekhpal (Revenue Record keeper) Stockman, Family WelfareWorker, Auxillary Nurse-cum-Midwife, Village Health Guide, Trained Dai Line Man (Hydel) Hand Pump Mechanic, Piped Water Supply Mechanic, Boring Mechanic, Hydram operator, Primary School Teacher, Kissan Sahayak (Farmer Guide)	(i) Performing their departmental tasks (ii) Delivery of inputs and services in accordance with project objectives. (iii) Maintenance and repair of facilities, amenities provided by the department.

16

Urbanisation Trends in India— A Critique of Remedial Measures

Dr. D.R. Sachdeva

Urbanisation, the process of movement of the rural population towards urban areas, is a global phenomenon. It has been going on at a highly accelerated pace in recent years. According to the estimates and projections of the United Nations Population Division, the urban population in the world had risen from 1361 million in 1970 to 2286 million in 1990 and is likely to be about 5 billion in 2025. In terms of percentage of urban population to the total world population, it implies an increase from 36.9 per cent in 1970 to 43.6 per cent in 1990 and 62.5 per cent in 2025. Very soon 50 per cent of the world population will be urban as against 29 per cent in 1950, 39 per cent in 1975 and 43 per cent in 1985. In other words, the urban population of the world which doubled between 1850 and 1975 will further double between 1975 and 2000. Massive urbanisation is engulfing the Third World. Within the span of the last two decades, towns and cities all over Asia, Africa and Latin America have been doubling and tripling in size. According to a U.N. forecast, by the end of this century, 41 per cent of the population in the developing countries will be living in towns and it will be about 80 per cent in Latin America, the most urbanised region.

In keeping with the global trend, there has been an accelerated growth of urbanisation in India. The total population of the country had doubled from 350 million in 1947 to 800 million in 1988 and it stood at 849.4 million on March 1,1991. During 1947-88, urban population had increased four-fold from 50 million to 200 million.

By the end of the century, the total population is projected to touch 1000 million and urban population 350 million. The Expert Committee of Registrar General (Census), however, projects urban population of 326 million in the year 2001. The National Commission on Urbanisation is of the view that the total population in India in 2001 will exceed 1000 million and the urban population will be in the range of 340 to 356 million constituting 35 per cent of the total population. According to the latest projections made by the United Nations, India's urban population is expected to be 330 million in 2001, 454 million in 2010, 591 million in 2020 and 658 million in 2025 when the total population of India is expected to be 1229 million.

Urban population is unevenly distributed in different states and Union Territories in the country. At the end of the spectrum, we have Arunachal Pradesh and Himachal Pradesh with 6.6 per cent urban population respectively, at the other end are Maharashtra and Tamil Nadu with 35 per cent and 33 per cent urban population, respectively. In between, we have states with proportion of urban population ranging from 11 to 32 per cent. The Union Territory of Chandigarh is 93.6 per cent urban while Union Territory of Dadra and Nagar Haveli is only 6.7 per cent urban.

Factors Contributing to Urbanisation

This unprecedented growth in urbanisation is attributed to migration of the people from rural to urban areas, natural increase in population and the reclassification of rural into urban areas. Factors contributing to migration from rural to urban areas are the push and pull factors, the former forcing or pushing the rural people to towns and cities due to population pressure on agricultural land and the lack of employment avenues and the latter attracting or luring the rural people to urban areas due to better jobs, comfortable standard of living etc. The other factors stimulating urbanisation are: industrialisation, economic growth, expansion of means of transport, increase in trade and commerce, establishment of new towns in the industrial zone, partition of the country and militant activities.

Challenges of Urbanisation

The phenomenal rise in urbanisation has posed serious challenges and grave problems for the urban governments in the form of shortage of housing, strain on civic amenities, haphazard growth of towns, growth of slums, scourage of urban poverty, scarcity of urban land, menace of pollution, lack of employment opportunities, social maladjustments, ruralisation of urban areas, encroachment on agricultural lands, various ills of city life, erosion of moral values, etc.

Major Policy Pronouncements in Relation to Urbanisation, Urban Planning and Development

In order to meet the challenges posed by the accelerated growth of urbanisation and the related problems created by it, it was only in the Third Five Year Plan that the National Planners had addressed themselves to the detailed study of urbanisation and its menacing impact on urban areas. The public policy issues in relation to urbanisation, urban planning and development as delineated in the various five year plans are as follows:

Third Five Year Plan (1961-66)

The Third Plan looked at urbanisation as an important fallout of the process of economic and social development. It had observed that there were many problems associated with urbanisation, such as rural-urban migration, standards of living in urban and rural areas, relative costs of providing economic and social services in towns of varying sizes, housing for different consumer groups, provision of basic facilities like water supply, sanitation, transport and power, pattern of economic development, location and dispersal of industries, civic administration, fixed policies and land use planning. It had attributed high costs of urban development to rising costs of providing housing, water supply, drainage, transport and other services. Unemployment, overcrowding, growth of slums and rise in the number of persons without shelter, all these tended to worsen the urban situation further.

In laying down the development policy, the Plan had suggested that:(a) as far as possible, new industries should be established away from large and congested cities; (b) the concept of region should be adopted in the planning of large industries; (c) the rural and urban components of development should be blended properly in community development projects or other areas within the district; and (d) diversification of occupational pattern should be attempted in each rural area in order to reduce the dependence on agriculture.

Fourth Five Year Plan (1969-74)

The Fourth Plan observed that for lack of financial and organisational resources, not much headway could be made with implementation of the development plans which the Third Five Year Plan had prepared for a large number of urban cities. It expressed concern about the alarming growth of population in the metropolitan centres and other large cities. For the metropolitan giants like Calcutta and Bombay, it suggested the policy to prevent future growth of population as well as to decongest them by a phased dispersal of population and for other cities to stabilise population at a desirable optimum figure and planning new towns in the region for absorbing the spill over population and to explore the development potentials of small towns in a region in this context.

The Fourth Plan laid special emphasis on the following important problems:

(1) In the rapidly growing cities, it was necessary to create planning regions and the jurisdictions of corporations or municipalities should coincide with the boundaries of appropriate planning areas; (2) Planning had to be supported by full legal structure for formulation and implementation. The importance of planning law had thus to be realized; (3) The administrative structure of the local implementation of development plans had to be streamlined; (4) Specific functional schemes on water supply, roads, etc. had to be cast within the frame-work of a long term plan, and in the long run, plans of development of cities and towns must become self-financing ; (5) Due to rapid increase in urban land values, land in urban areas had become a potent source of unearned income. Rising land prices, on the other hand, stood in the way of low income housing. So, a radical urban land policy had to be evolved to facilitate speedy and planned urban development;(6) To solve the housing problem in urban areas was an uphill task. Through proper planning and land policy, adequate supply of housing had to be attempted; and (7) So far as urban slums are concerned, the immediate attempt would be to ameliorate the living conditions of slums. Thus, the Fourth Plan suggested a much more cautious policy, taking due cognizance of the constraint of resources of all kinds.

Fifth Five Year Plan (1975-80)

The Fifth Plan had noted that despite growing awareness in the states regarding the problems of urban development, they had not been able to make much headway in taking comprehensive action for the adoption and implementation of master plans due, primarily, to financial and organizational bottlenecks at the local level. The Fifth Plan had identified the broad objectives of: (1) augmenting civic services in urban centres in order to make them fit for a reasonable level of living; (2) trying to deal with the problems of metropolitan cities on a more comprehensive and regional basis; (3) Developing the smaller towns and new urban centres to ease the pressures of urbanization on the larger metropolitan centres; and (4) Conceiving and pushing through projects of national importance, such as those relating to metropolitan areas or inter-state projects.

Sixth Five Year Plan (1980-85)

The Sixth Five Year Plan had emphasized on an Integrated Development of Small and Medium Towns (IDSMT) for which central sector was to provide Rs.96 crores with the concerned state governments making matching contributions. The Plan also provided for cluster of villages approach for provision of roads in the case of hilly, tribal, desert and coastal areas where the population was sparse and settlements were located far apart from one another. It had a definite approach to poverty issues, provision of additional consumption benefits and better and more equitable distribution of facilities in the fields of health, education, sanitation, housing and drinking water, slum upgrading and environmental improvement programmes. Housing programme for economically weaker sections formed another integral part of the Plan.

Seventh Five Year Plan (1985-90)

The Plan provided for the continuation of the scheme of IDSMT and revised the eligibility criteria to include towns with upto three lakh of population in it. It also laid greater stress on sites and services, slum improvement, Urban Community Development projects (UCD), Integrated Child Development Service (ICDS), and schemes of house and shelter upgradation. It made the first conscious effort to solve the problems of urban poverty in a coordinating manner by developing a package of programmes such as Nehru Rozgar Yojna, Urban Basic Services for the poor,

Environmental Improvement of Urban Slums, low cost sanitation, Night shelter scheme for footpath dwellers etc. It placed considerable emphasis on improvement in the living conditions of dwellers, a major thrust towards employment generation and creation of productive jobs, housing for economically weaker sections and low income groups with HUDCO support, expansion of nutrition programmes, public distribution system, National Housing Planning with assistance for National Housing Bank, etc.

National Urbanisation Policy Resolution 1975

The Town and Country Planning Organization of the Government of India had prepared the National Urbanisation Policy Resolution in 1975. Its main feature was the conscious recognition of the fact that rural development and urban development are complementary to each other and both have to be pursued together to promote healthy human settlement patterns throughout the country. The main objectives of the policy were identified as follows:

(a) Evolving a spatial pattern of economic development and location of a hierarchy of human settlements consistent with the exploitation of natural and human resources of the region, and ensuring functional linkages inter se; (2) securing the optimum distribution of population between rural and urban settlements within each region and also among the towns of various sizes; (3) Securing the distribution of economic activities in small and medium sized towns and in new growth centres in order to achieve maximum economic growth for the future; (4) controlling and wherever necessary, arresting the further growth of metropolitan cities by dispersal of economic activities, legislative measures and establishment of new counter magnets in the region; (5) providing a minimum level of services for improving the quality of life in rural and urban areas and reducing gradually the differences between rural and urban standards of living.

Despite many policy pronouncements discouraging further growth of industries in the metropolitan cities, new industries continued to be attracted toward these centres. Hence, a policy of decongestion of these cities and decentralisation of industries needed to be followed up by a proper industrial location policy that would provide incentives to new industrial units to move away from the metropolitan cities. Also such a policy would have certain disincentives for industries to come up in the already congested metropolitan centres.

Another method would be to extend the planning frame to a wide region surrounding the metropolis and to set up new towns to receive population spill-overs from the metropolitan cities. The intermediate cities which offered the second best opportunity for the development of large and medium industries, if developed within proper plan frames and endowed with necessary urban infrastructure, could also act as counter magnets to the metropolitan cities. As agriculture would continue to undergo a process of modernization, various farm and non-farm needs of the rural population could be met from the medium towns where agro-industries and small-scale industries could be located providing in the process opportunities for employment to the job seekers. The small towns at the bottom of the hierarchy would grow as rural service centres catering to the needs of their surrounding areas. The Policy Resolution had also suggested the regulation of urban land and improvement of living conditions of the urban poor.

Implementation of Urbanisation Policy Directives: Measures Taken to Meet the Challenge of Urbanisation

The urbanisation policy directives as announced in the successive five year plans and the National Urban Policy Resolution have been laudable but unfortunately they have not been fully implemented with the result that the process of urbanisation continues at an alarming rate; it presents a frightening spectre in the form of unplanned urban growth resulting in slums, deterioration in civic amenities to a breaking point and rendering cities and towns unliveable. Despite repeated policy pronouncements recommending location of big industries from the larger metropolitan cities, major new industries continue to be set up in around the metropolitan cities, the urban land policy has not been seriously pursued, and so on. Yet there is no denying the fact that urbanisation and its various problems have been receiving the attention of Central, State and local governments since the Third Five Year Plan period; and there have been some notable achievements in the field of urbanisation urban planning and development, as is evident from the following credit points :

(i) Town and Country Planning Organisation was set up by the Government of India in 1962, as the apex technical advisory body on matters relating to urban and regional planning strategies, research, monitoring and evaluation of central government schemes and development policies.

(ii) Master Plans have been prepared for all major towns and cities to promote orderly growth of urban areas and to check unregulated urbanisation.

(iii) The concept of Regional Planning is being promoted expeditiously in large metropolitan areas to reduce their burden of unmanageable population by arranging for the habitation of spill-over population in the new towns being set up in the region.

(iv) Efforts are being made to improve the infrastructural facilities in the urban areas, such as water supply and sewerage, transportation etc. under the centrally sponsored schemes for Integrated Development of Small and Medium Towns (IDSMT) with a view to reduce the migration of population from rural areas to major urban areas, to generate employment by creating resource generating ventures in small and medium towns and also to provide sufficient infrastructure facilities in these towns so that their hinterland is served better. The World Bank is also assisting various states in urban development programmes.

(v) The awareness about creating a healthy urban environment is growing day by day and pollution problems—water pollution and air pollution in particular, are receiving due attention at the various levels of government and community as is substantiated by the enactment of Water (Prevention and Control of Pollution) Act, 1974 and the Air (Prevention and Control of Pollution) Act, 1981 passed by the Central Government providing for the constitution of the Central Board for the prevention and control of water and air pollution and the setting up of similar Boards by the State Governments, and enforcement of these Acts by taking punitive action for the violation of the provisions of the Acts.

(vi) The problem of urban slums is being tackled vigorously. The initial idea of slum clearance has been replaced by the concept of slums improvement and efforts are being made to give the slum dwellers a better deal through the scheme of Environmental Development of Urban Slums for the slum population ranging between 51 to 56 million in 1990. The scheme was made an integral part of the Minimum Needs Programme (MNP) in 1976. The scheme aims at ameliorating their living conditions by provision of drinking water, drainages, community baths, community latrines, widening and paving of existing lanes, street lighting and other community facilities.

(vii) To meet the housing needs in the urban areas, the Housing and Urban Development Corporation (HUDCO) was set up in April, 1970 at the national level to provide capital funds for housing and allied urban development operations.

(viii) Administrative organisation for urban development is being revamped by providing more funds for municipal governments, improving their personnel structure and training the municipal employees through Regional Centres for Urban and Environmental Studies at Bombay, Lucknow and Hyderabad in addition to the Centre for Urban Studies, IIPA, New Delhi.

(ix) Urban Development Authorities have been set up in the major urban areas to devote exclusive attention to urban development. The achievements of these urban development authorities, such as Delhi Development Authority are commendable in tackling some of the urban problems in a safisfactory manner.

(x) Our policy makers have not been unaware of the problems of urban poverty. The Seventh Five Year Plan had taken explicit note of the growing incidence of poverty in urban areas and placed considerable emphasis on improvement in the living conditions of slum dwellers, employment generation and improving the access of the urban poor to basic amenities such as education, health-care, sanitation and safe drinking water.

(xi) The most notable development in the context of urbanisation in India has been setting up of Ministry of Urban Development in 1985 as the nodal ministry to oversee in totality, the process of urbanisation, to evolve urban policy and to try and to ensure that suitable plan priorities are assigned to urban development together with adequate funds.

(xii) The Ministry of Urban Development had appointed National Commission on Urbanisation under the chairmanship of Charles Cores to look into the issues of urbanisation. The Commission submitted its report in August,1988 in which it has made significant recommendations in respect of various facets of urbanisation and the management of urban governments with a view to effectively tackle the problems caused by the scourage of urbanisation and to ensure better administration of urban local bodies.

(xiii) The Government of India, in the Ministry of Urban Development, has passed the Constitution (Seventy Fourth Amendment) Act, 1992 for reconstituting, reclassifying, democratising and strengthening urban governments, by giving them more powers, more finances on the recommendations of State Finance Commissions, and management of elections by the State Election Commission and by granting them constitutional status.

(xiv) **National Capital Region Plan:** In order to check migration to Delhi and mitigate the problems arising out of continued migration, National Capital Region Planning Board was set up in March, 1985 to propose a plan for the National Capital Region. The plan is the only statutory plan of its own kind in the country providing for planned development of an inter state region which has been prepared with the active involvement of not only the participating State governments of Haryana, Rajasthan and Uttar Pradesh and the Union Territory of Delhi but also includes proposals which have been prepared in consultation with the concerned central ministries.

Reasons for the Failure to Check Urbanisation

Despite the remedial measures taken to halt the process of urbanisation, it continues unabated. The causes responsible for the failure of reversing urbanisation and solving urban problems can be identified as :

(i) Population Explosion: India's population is set to explode. Population growth at the rate of 2 to 3 per cent will inevitably lead us to an unmanageable 100 crore by the turn of the century. Twenty-five million urbanites in 1947 will have a zooming jump to 350 million in 2001, the parallel to which may be hard to find in the annals of history and civilisation. Demographers predict that the total land and water resources in the country will not be able to produce enough food for a population of "dreaded level". All this would bring with it a train of miseries, starvation, deaths, diseases, unrest, violence, law and order disturbances etc. Our population control programmes must succeed otherwise even the best of urbanisation strategies will fail.

(ii) Absence of National Urbanisation Policy: A comprehensive national urbanisation policy has not been evolved so far though piece meal methods to come to grips with the gigantic problem of urbanisation have been adopted by the Central and State governments and the connecting theme in all these efforts has been planned intervention in the process of urbanisation. A comprehensive national urbanisation policy is therefore required to be formulated and implemented to arrest migration to urban areas and render our towns and cities worth living.

(iii) Lack of Political Will: Population is not being controlled due to lack of political will notwithstanding the massive financial inputs. Similarly the planners tend to ascribe the failure to combat urbanisation to the lack of will on the part of the governments as in a democracy it is difficult to reconcile conflicting interests which influence implementation of decisions. The urbanisation policies and urban development plans, however, well intentioned these may be, cannot therefore be implemented.

(iv) Pressure of Interest Groups: Urban planning in its manifestations of master plans for various cities and redevelopment programmes failed due to conflict of interests and influence of interest groups. The zonal plans inspite of the care taken by the planners in identifying different areas of redevelopment erred in assuming that the people would be willing to shift— they discount or ignore the political influence that the business and the industry could wield as organised interest groups.

(v) Town Planning authorities lack statutory backing: The Town and Country Planning Organisation, Government of India and the Departments of Town and Country Planning in the States prepare plans for urban development including Master Plans which with their rigid land-use, zoning and development control has provided extremely poor instruments for regulating the dynamic process of urban growth. The core problems of Urban Planning are not only spatial but functional as well. A master plan fails to be truly comprehensive if its comprehensiveness is restricted to land-use allocations only. Moreover, Master Plans are violated with impunity by the vested interests. The Town and Country Planning authorities function as advisory bodies only and they lack any statutory backing to get their development plans implemented.

(vi) Low priority to urban development in the national planning process: After nearly four decades of planned economic development, urban development continues to remain isolated from the national planning process. In the five year plans so far urban development has been treated as an item of social expenditure, with the result that it accounts for a very small fraction of the total plan budget. There are compelling demands for plan funds. The investments on urban development have low priority, as these are generally looked upon as consumption oriented. Rural lobby is far more powerful and is naturally able to get more funds from the plan budget, as much as 50 per cent for rural development in the current plan.

(vii) Limited Role of Central Government: The country being federal, the central government can at best give policy leadership in urbanisation and the actual implementation would depend on the state governments in whose jurisdiction urban local government and urban development falls. Moreover, the plan funds directly expendible by the Centre on urban development are too meagre to good the states to fall in line with the central policy guidelines.

(viii) Financial Scarcity of the States: The States being in acute financial stress are unable to divert funds for urban development. Metropolitan cities like Calcutta, Bombay etc. require thousands of crores of rupees for their redevelopment and supply of basic civic amenities which they can ill afford but for the centre coming to their rescue. The gigantic problems of urban development have ultimately to be shouldered by the State governments. Yet there is general reluctance to face these problems. The State plans usually pay lip service to urban development since agriculture and other items have much more pressing claims. In general, the cities and towns are exhorted to pursue urban development tasks by raising more resources from their own domestic sources of revenue, without depending too much on state financial assistance.

(ix) Antiquated Organisation of Urban Bodies: The municipal bodies have antiquated organisations dating back to the 19th Century. The modernisation of their administrative structure and operation is long overdue. In most municipal organisations the political processes have failed to match the needs of growing urban problems. Nor has the quality and quantity of managerial personnel corresponded to the ever increasing administrative responsibilities. The Constitution (74th Amendment) Act, 1992 is expected to remove the existing deficiencies in the structure and organisation of municipal bodies and to revitalise and strengthen them to meet the challenges posed by urbanisation.

(x) Role of Politics: Politics has played a great role in determining the urban policies and in securing their implementation. Politics is viewed as an activity intended to make one set of interests prevail over the other, and as an attempt by various forces to maintain and establish supremacy over urban environment. It is because of the game of politics indulged in by various political parties at the helm of the affairs in the state and local governments that the urban bodies are superseded and the urban legislation aimed at the orderly development of urban areas is flouted by the vested interests.

Need for National Urbanisation Policy

Despite the care taken by the Urban Development policies since the planned development in our country began, the problems being faced by urban India are even colossal. The growth of cities and towns is not uniform. The infrastructural facilities are totally inadequate and in some cities are in a critical stage. The availability of urban land and housing especially for the poor is scarce. About 25 per cent of the urban population lives in slums and squatter settlements. Immigrants continue to flow in the urban areas and will continue to do so in future also. Hence, it is necessary to take a look into the long term perspective of channelising urbanisation to lay down a National Urbanisation Policy and to take effective measures for its implementation so that a healthy and orderly urban development takes place in the years to come. This was the view expressed by experts on urbanisation in 1975, but it holds good even today.

Essentials of National Urbanisation Policy

A comprehensive national urbanisation policy will have to cover all types of towns and cities. But because of the federal political structure of the country, as also the lack of a common national language seems well nigh impossible to frame any national policy of urbanisation that can be implemented in different parts of the country without resistance at state levels. Moreover Indians, by and large, are very informal people and, therefore, resent any kind of formal control or organisation. Anyhow, national urbanisation policy should have the following essentials. A national policy of urbanisation should be based on:

(i) Preventive measures: A strong agrarian base, to be developed to its full potential should be created by diversifying agricultural activity. This will also entail the location and planning of collection and distribution centres at appropriate places throughout the country.

(ii) Remedial measures: To relieve some of the existing cities from congestion, satellite towns should be built by decentralising industry and commerce.

(iii) Adequate infrastructure will have to be planned on a regional basis and suitably located in various parts of the country. Appropriate strategies will have to be worked out to ensure smooth implementation of the national urbanisation policy. Unless the Centre plays an active and helpful role in process of implementation, not much can be expected of any national plan and programme. It is, therefore, imperative that some of the key centres for providing implementational infrastructure on a regional basis should function under the care of the Central Government itself.

(iv) No national urbanisation policy can ever work in India unless it takes into account regional constraints, the most important of which will be geography and the chief occupation of the people of different States, for instance, in Punjab, the economy is based on agriculture, the concentration of population in isolated urban centres will be antithetical. Urbanisation based on ribbon development may be more appropriate here. Geographically, what works best in plains may not be workable on a hilly terrain. Topography of the hills precludes any large scale development that may be done as a matter of course in the plains. Similarly, due to its elongated geographical shape as well as sea-front location combined with fishery, coconut cultivation and coir industry, the state of Kerala requires a linear development. Besides, it has the unique virtue of having obscure urban rural boundaries.

(v) The national urbanisation policy should be subjected to a periodic review, say, every 10 years, so that it is continually updated in view of the new scientific and technological advancement.

(vi) Schools of architecture and planning can play a vital role in creating professional awareness of the need for food urbanisation policies at the national level and their implementation in the pursuit of making India a nation with a rich tradition of culture recreated in modern terms.

(vii) As a major strategy to achieve positive results, the decision making as well as implementing agencies will have to be made autonomous organisations with minimal political and bureaucratic interferences.

(viii) As the bulk of population to be affected by such policies will be rural, it will be in the fitness of things to associate more and more such experts— architects, planners, urban designers, environmentalists, economists, sociologists, demographers, etc. as they have a first hand experience and background of Indian rural life and culture.

(ix) A chain of data banks should be set up throughout the country for monitoring the urbanisation programmes and providing feedback for policy reviews.

Conclusion

The Government has been making major policy pronouncements in relation to urbanisation, urban planning and development in Five Year Plans. With a view to combat effects urbanisation necessary steps are being taken to ensure that large size cities especially cities with population range of one million should not be allowed to expand any further and as far as possible new industries and other economic activities which accentuate growth should be located away from these centres; new urban centres in proximity to the metropolitan cities should be developed as counter magnets so that the migrant population can go into these locations thereby reducing the pressure on the metropolitan cities; new urban nuclei should be planned in resource rich areas with a view to generate employment in these areas; the medium size towns should be provided with adequate services and amenities, and properly laid out industrial estates and industrial areas should be set up so that they could attract new avenues growth; the location of those various growth centres and focal points are to be chosen within the scope of integrated regional or area development plans.

Efforts have also been made to urbanise rural areas by providing them with electricity supply, roads, water supply, hospitals and dispensaries, educational institutions, means of communication etc. and thus improving the village life to bring the rural standards closer to the urban life styles. But despite all this, urbanisation trend is a worldwide phenomenon and irrevocable; it is rather difficult to halt it. Yet, if better and more job opportunities were created and better amenities provided, perhaps the rate of rural migration would fall considerably; the population explosion needs to be controlled effectively; and other issues such as the formulation of a comprehensive national urbanisation policy and its implementation, planned urban areas, enforcement of legislation relating to planned urban development, implementation of schemes especially Master Plans for various cities prepared by the Town and Country Planning authorities, execution of National Capital Region Plans, restructuring of the urban governments to cope with their ever increasing problems, establishment of urban development authorities in place of multiple urban institutions like Improvement Trusts, Water Supply and Sewerage Boards etc., provision of adequate finances to the State Governments by the Central Government and by the State Governments to Local Governments commensurate with at least their obligatory functions, dispersal of government offices and industries from metropolitan and capitals to other cities, alleviation of urban poverty; renovation of slum areas, research in urban governments and evaluation of urban development programmes etc. are addressed seriously with a strong political will, the process of urbanisation can be slowed down considerably and the urban areas made worth living.

REFERENCES

1. Bhattacharya Mohit, Urbanisation and Urban Problems in India-Some Policy Isues, *Nagarlok*, Vol. VII, No. 4, Oct-Dec. 1975, :13.
2. Gill S.S., Essentials of Urbanisation Policy, *The Tribune*, 6th June, 1990.
3. Government of India, *Five Year Plans*, New Delhi (1951-1990).

4. Government of India, Ministry of Urban Development, *Report of the National Commission on Urbanisation*, Vol. II, New Delhi, 1988.

5. Government of India, Projections made by the Expert Committee, Registrar General, Census.

6. Government of India, *Ministry of the Urban Development*, 1990-91 : 42-43.

7. Government of India, Ministry of Urban Development, 74th Amendment Act 1992.

8. Government of Punjab, *Annual Report of the Town and Country Planning, Deptt.*, (1988-89).

9. Town and Country Planning Organisation, *National Urbanisation Policy: An approach*, Proceedings of the Expert Group on National Urbanisation Policy, 8th Jan., 1975.

17

Law and Order Administration: Police Administration

R.S. Khanna

Maintenance of public order is essential for progress in a society, be it totalitarian or democratic. It implies that maintenance of public peace, ensuring safety to the people and property so as to enable them to pursue their occupations without fear for earning their livelihood. However, in a democracy "public order" is to be maintained according to the law of the land and in our case, the basic law of land is our Constitution. Its basic features are democracy, pluralism, federalism, secularism, socialism and judicial review. The Constitution is federal in nature with a bias towards the centre. It ensures the right to equality before law (Article 14). It also provides for prohibition of discrimination against citizens on grounds of religion, race, caste, sex or place of birth (Article 15). Equality of opportunity in matters of public employment is enshrined in Article 16 along with right to freedom of speech and expression, peaceful assembly, free movement within the territory of India and forming of associations or unions (Article 19).

It may be pertinent to mention that members of All-India Services particularly of Indian Administrative Service (IAS) and Indian Police Service (IPS), constitute an important link in the basic administrative structure of the country. They are appointed by the President, and they serve both the Union and the states but while working in the states they are under the administrative control of the state governments. There is division of functions between the Union and the states. Besides this, there is a concurrent list of subjects in which both the Union and the state can participate, though the will of the former will prevail in case there is a conflict between the two.

It is the responsibility of the state governments to maintain public order. Police (including railway and village police), a necessary adjunct to the maintenance of peace, is included in the State List. However, armed forces of the Union, or any other force subject to the control of the Union, could be deployed in aid of the civil powers under Item 2(a) (Schedule VII) of the Union List. Even Section 130 of the Criminal Procedure Code (Cr. P.C.) empowers the Executive Magistrates to requisition armed forces in aid of the civil powers but once they are requisitioned, their deployment depends upon the Commander of the armed forces. This item did not originally find its place in the Constitution but came to be inserted by 42nd Amendment, 1976 along with another Article 257(A) which provided for the deployment of forces of the Union by the Central Government for dealing with any grave situation of law and order in any state and the state governments were virtually deprived of all powers in this regard. But this Article was deleted by 46th Amendment though the Item 2(A) survived. However, keeping in view the provisions of the Cr. P.C., this amendment seems redundant. Deployment of forces is one thing and order to disperse unlawful assembly and use of force another. The latter is the prerogative of the Executive Magistrates. The crux of the matter is that the responsibility for maintaining law and order essentially devolves on the State Government though it could take the help, if necessary, of the Central Government.

The Constitution also distinguishes between "internal disturbance" (Article 355) and "public disorder". The former has the characteristics of "domestic chaos and, *inter alia,* endangers the security of the state. It may be man— made (e.g. a widespread and violent agitation or a communal flare up) or caused by nature (e.g. a natural calamity that paralyses administration in a large area of a state)." (Sarkaria Commission Report, 1988). The main objective of maintenance of law and order should be to see that the situation like internal disturbance does not develop. Prof. Bayley has suggested six objectives of this policy: (i) lessening the cost and disruption of social processes, (ii) preserving the legitimacy of government, (iii) defending the privacy of majority rule, (iv) protecting the sanctity of law, (v) off-setting disorderly and disruptive politics, and (vi) re-enforcing the sense of social discipline (Bayley, 1969).

At the state level, police station presided over by the Station House Officer constitutes the basic unit of the police administration. Its manpower strength depends upon whether it is located in a village, small town or a big town. A number of police stations are grouped into a sub-division and the sub-divisions are grouped into police districts. Police district is presided over by a Superintendent of Police, who usually belongs to the IPS. The jurisdiction of the police district and the revenue district usually coincides. The revenue district is presided over by District Magistrate, who usually belongs to the IAS. The relation between the District Magistrate and the Superintendent of Police is governed by Section 4 of the Indian Police Act, 1861, para 2, part of which reads thus "The administration of the police throughout the local jurisdiction of the Magistrate of the district shall, under the general control and direction of such Magistrate, be vested in a District Superintendent and such Assistant District Superintendents as the state government shall consider necessary." The expression "general control and direction" has led to conflicts between the two All-India Services officers. In order to smoothen the working of the police in the districts, the expression requires to be spelt out in detail. The intrusion of the District Magistrate in police affairs is resented as it is said to disrupt the vertical control structure of the police administration; the logic, however, is not understood. District Magistrate does not interfere in the day-to-day administration of the police force. He/she must take stock of the crime situation and the emerging trends and lend a helping hand in keeping law and order situation under control.

At present, District Magistrate acts as the co-ordinator, helping in making the various departments of governments in a district function towards the achievement of a common goal. The police cannot hold themselves aloof from the district team. Many problems of police arise because of the functioning of other departments; for example, education, labour, industry etc. and the existence of social tensions. It is the role of the Collector to bring the departments together in one forum to hear them and where agreement is not possible, to give a decision on the line of action to be adopted. Even though democratic decentralisation has been introduced by the enactment of 73rd and 74th Amendments to the Constitution, the Collector's role in this regard has not diminished as the Panchayati Raj institutions and urban municipal institutions have not been given the powers of local self-government. They are merely the agencies for carrying out municipal and development works. It is thus necessary that the Collector should not be made subordinate to any of the institutions under democratic decentralisation. Government essentially consists of two tiers— the Union and the states.

Recently, the law and order situation has deteriorated on account of several factors. There are three facets of criminal administration viz. investigation of the crime, its prevention and punishment of offenders. One of the basic principles of the rule of law is that the lowest functionary required by law to enforce this is permitted to do his duty without let or hindrance. According to this principle, investigation of crime must never be interfered with though his superiors can guide him in the matter. The concept of rule of law requires that police should act only as the agents of law and not of the state government which virtually is the political party in power. "Police investigation under certain circumstances is required as a part of judicial process and as such the court throws its ring of protection even at this stage by invoking the law of contempt." (Ghosh, 1963)

So far as giving instructions to the magistracy or police are concerned, Shri Govind Ballabh Pant in the debate on Article 356 in the context of imposition of President's Rule in Kerala in 1959 stated "No one has the right to ask a magistrate not to do what he is required by the law to do; no one can ask the policeman not to discharge his duty which the law has imposed on him". The same principle has been reaffirmed by the Calcutta High Court, thus "The authority and jurisdiction of the state government to issue administrative directions are limited, first by the Constitution, and, then by the laws of the land. There is no law which authorises the state government to issue directions to officers-in-charge of maintenance of law and order not to enforce the law of the land upon certain conditions being fulfilled and complied with. The provisions in Article 356 of the Constitution, which require that the executive power of every state shall be so exercised as to ensure compliance with the laws made by Parliament and any existing laws which apply in that state, are mandatory..." (AIR, 1968).

In December, 1992, Chief Minister of Uttar Pradesh issued an order to the District Magistrate, Faizabad not to use force. Obviously, this was an illegal order. In the absence of District Magistrate's order, central forces in the neighbouring places could not be deployed in Ayodhya to disperse crowds and prevent demolition of the disputed structure. The principle of non-interference also holds good in the case of withdrawal of criminal cases. It is the power of the executive to withdraw the prosecutions with the consent of the court. In its ruling (1972, *Criminal Law Journal*, 30) the Supreme Court made the following observations:

"The power contained in Section 494 of Cr.P.C. gives a general executive direction to withdraw from the prosecution, subject to the consent of the courts which may be determined on many possible grounds and is therefore wide and uncontrolled by any other provisions in the code... The essential consideration which is implicit in the grant of the power is that it should be in the interest of administration of justice which may be either that it will not be able to produce sufficient evidence to sustain the charge or the subsequent information before prosecuting agency would falsify the prosecution evidence or any other similar circumstances of each case. Nonetheless, it is the duty of the court also to see in furtherance of justice that the permission is not sought on grounds extraneous to the interest of justice or that offences which are offences against the State go unpunished merely because the Government as a matter of general policy or expediency unconnected with its duty to prosecute offenders under the law, directs the public prosecutor to withdraw from the prosecution and the public prosecutors merely do so at its behest." (Saxena, 1987)

Crime detection, crime prevention and maintenance of law and order are invariably linked. The traditional distinction between order maintenance and prevention of crime is artificial as every crime in a sense amounts to a breakdown of order Low emphasis on investigation work is not understandable. While practical intelligence can be obtained through secret services, criminal intelligence is mainly obtained by honest and painstaking investigation. When an investigating officer is engaged in tracing the accused in one crime, he often gets involved in the intelligence of several other crimes, quite often unconnected with the case in hand. The expeditious punishment of crime is also important as delay in taking decision in the matter shakes the credibility of the police and criminal justice administration. The criminal justice administration also depends upon the efficacy with which the challans are disposed of by the court. In this context, the separation of the executive and judiciary has resulted in accumulation of cases in the courts. In order to reduce the burden on the judiciary, it is suggested that the minor offences under the Indian Penal Code and other acts like excise, gambling, motor vehicles could be tried by the executive magistrates while serious offences could be tried by the judicial magistrates. In order to maintain the independence of the judiciary from the executive, some useful suggestions have been made by Shri M.N. Buch in his article on "IAS and IPS—Friends or Enemies".

In a representative parliamentary democracy, a question often asked is about the role of civil disobedience. It is assumed that dissent is reflected in the legislature. Then why should it be necessary to take extreme steps outside. Archibald Cox has examined the cult of directaction dissent:

"The core of the evil in true civil disobediences,' is that it weakens the bonds of law and compels the State to resort to power. You may object that this is a lawyer's viewpoint and that if a law is truly unjust, there is no reason to preserve it. My answer is that we are concerned with the basic idea of law—with a force binding all men— and that you can not pick and choose among good laws and bad laws according to each individual's conscience without destroying the whole concept of the rule of law. Nor do I attach value to the rule of law just because it is law. Law is a human instrument, constructed by men to meet men's own needs; it must justify itself by what it does for men in meeting their needs, including their ethical judgements and moral aspirations."

(*Encyclopaedia of Social Sciences*, Vol. IX, p. 52)

Justice V.R. Krishna Iyer had once stated in context of human rights and the law, "The capacity for change and growth is as essential an element of the rule of law as reason and voluntary compliance. When the pace of social change or the growth of social conscience is revolutionary, so must be the changes in the law. Social protest and even civil disobedience serve to make out the law's need for growth. Ideally, reform would come according to reason and justice without self-help and disturbing, almost violent forms of protest. Still, candour compels one here again to acknowledge that gap between the ideal and the reality. Short of the millennium, sharp changes in the law depend partly upon the stimulus of protest".

Every democracy which legislates with the backing of the majority is bound to recognize the voice of the minority, however small it may be. Therefore, in the technology of power politics, dynamic dissent by a group—even a one-man minority—has a seminal role.

"By engaging in civil disobedience a minority forces the majority to consider whether it wishes to have its actions construed in this way, or whether, in view of the common sense of justice, it wishes to acknowledge the legitimate claims of the minority...A further point is that civil disobedience is a public act. Not only is it addressed to public principles, it is done in public. It is engaged in openly with fair notice; it is not covert or secretive."

"Civil disobedience is non-violent for another reason. It expresses disobedience to law within the limits of fidelity to law, although it is at the outer edge thereof. The law is broken, but fidelity to law is expressed by the public and non-violent nature of the act, by the willingness to accept the legal consequences of one's conduct." "To be completely open and non-violent is to give bond of one's sincerity, for it is not easy to convince another that one's acts are conscientious, or even to be sure of this before oneself."

The appeal in civil disobedience is to the electorate. The forces of law and order are for the maintenance of status quo. The movement in society generates tensions in various spheres. How to reconcile the two?

The traditional responses to law and order situations are by imposing Section 144, closing the educational institutions, clamping curfew, rounding up a few miscreants, prosecuting those involved in violent activities, reaching some agreed settlements through negotiations and release of those arrested in the process after withdrawal of cases. Law and order situations are not sporadic. The police administration has to be vigilant and gather intelligence from all possible sources.

The important law and order situations could arise from : (i) students agitations, (ii) communal disturbances, (iii) caste conflicts, (iv) industrial unrest, (v) state-sponsored bandhs, and (vi) strikes by government servants in government establishments and public servants in public undertakings.

Student agitations are the most important as they comprise the young volatile group. The age limit for voters has been reduced to 18 years. This section comprises the youngest component of the voters. Students unrest arises from various causes, sometimes related to the unsatisfactory performance in the academic institutions, changes in curriculum, lack of basic amenities in schools and colleges, denying them any voice in the academic affairs, inter-union rivalry between various student unions etc. Sometimes these agitations arise as a result of governmental decisions like enhancement in reservation percentages in the educational institutions, enhancement of fees, change in the Vice-Chancellor of the University or Head of the college etc. The National Police Commission went into this question at length in Chapter 46 of its Report and proposed strengthening of proctorial system in the universities and also the creation of a separate protection force without arms for protection of property, guarding residential areas of universities, dealing with localised demonstrations by employees, students and teachers, providing adequate information base for ensuring security of individuals and property, carrying out searches at the instance of the university authorities and assisting university authorities during examinations etc. It would not only carry out the responsibilities mentioned in the foregoing but also prevent any agitation from escalating into violence.

Whenever the force is to be used, it should be timely but with maximum restraint, especially in the use of lethal weapons. Resorting to fire arms should be avoided as far as possible unless there is a provocation by the use of fire arms by the agitators. It is wrong to regard that the sanctity of academic campus is jeopardised by police entering its premises. However, whenever the police enters the campus, as a matter of courtesy, the academic authorities should be informed about it. In all campus interventions, the presence of a senior police officer is a must "so as to ensure that the force is firmly and fully under control and there is no vindictive action on the part of individual policemen." In cases of mixing of outside goondas and anti-social elements, police should interfere effectively. Student-police relationship requires development of healthy contacts between the two. Police-student interaction in non-conflict situations like participation in games, community projects and extra-curricular activities requires to be encouraged. The police should endeavour to remove the impression among the students that they are hostile to them. Special orientation courses covering student psychology, case studies of police handling of such cases, analysing the causes of police failures in dealing with students should be included as a part of the training curriculum of police cadres, particularly at lower levels. However, whenever student agitations have to be dealt with, though they require to be dealt with in a restrained manner, tact and firmness by the law enforcement agencies is absolutely essential. There should be no impression that students are above law.

The communal disturbances had virtually disappeared after the partition of the country, but in the last two decades, their incidence again increased. The National Police Commission has analysed the various causes which could give rise to communal riots and suggested certain remedial measures. The records at the police stations require updating in respect of communal and caste composition of the village, their occupational pattern, the names of influential people, places of worship, festivals etc. and also sensitive places, past history of such disturbances mentioning the causes which led to such situations. It is wrong to assume that a riot, if it occurs, remains confined to an isolated pocket having a communal history; it has a tendency to spread quickly to the neighbouring areas. Hence riot prevention measures should not only be applied to the isolated pocket but to the nearby areas also. It is well-known that rumours float freely in tense situations leading to further worsening of the situation. It is necessary that administration should itself disseminate correct and proper information to the public through all available means. Public co-operation should be sought by the formation of peace committees involving local people when tense environment is developing. The effectiveness of paramilitary forces gets blunted on account of the absence of the local knowledge. Thus even in peace times there should be interaction between the district authorities, the army and the paramilitary forces. There should be rehearsals to coordinate the law and order arrangements with the army and paramilitary forces during peace time as well, so that there is no misunderstanding or lack of coordination when they are called upon to aid the civil power. Action under Section 153-A should be firmly taken.

The police has to be trained to deal with mob control. An officer in the field has to be a good psychologist, capable of reading the mood of the mob and a good communicator capable of continuous dialogue with the mob and its leaders. He has to be sympathetical in dealing with the mobs. It will be futile if the mobs or its leaders discern any hesitancy or nervousness in his bearing and demeanour. The officer-in-charge has to take on the spot decisions. He cannot afford to look over his shoulders for guidance or instructions. It is his personal judgement of the ground realities that matters. If he takes time off to ponder over his future in the likely event of things going wrong, then things will most definitely go wrong. If in his thoughts the visions of a certain political master, an unscrupulous self-centered superior and an unjust and merciless press are brought up frequently during those tense moments, then he is bound to make a mess of things. (*Times of India,* Dec. 4, 1994)

It has been suggested that in order to make the police fully representative of the society in which it functions, reservation of vacancies should be made for minorities and other weaker sections of society in accordance with their proportions in population. This suggestion is totally unacceptable as its acceptance would go against the fundamentals of police philosophy that the police as a system has to function impartially as an agent of the law and cannot have any caste or communal approach to the problem dealt with by it. "A representative legislature is alright, but a representative bureaucracy is a dangerous mirage; if artificially enforced by legislations, it will be disastrous and is going to produce a state of civil strife." (Saxena, *op. cit.*)

In recent years, caste conflicts are emerging as another important law and order problem. These arise on account of backward classes (castes) asserting their rights over lands in the villages. The upper castes being powerful take revenge upon them knowing the weakness of the law enforcement agencies. Here also, the strategy to be followed is the same as in the case of communal disturbances.

The industrial unrest used to be an important item some years ago, but has now been overshadowed by other situations. The state-sponsored Bandhs are now becoming more important. The state governments are the upholders of law and order. It is strange that bandhs are called by them. However, the objective behind such bandhs is to press for their demands with the Central Government. In order to make them successful, covert coercion is exercised. It is worth recalling that the first state bandh was called in the pre-independence days by the Muslim League government headed by Suhrawardy in 1946 and we know with what results. It was the harbinger of communal riots which led to the partition of India. We tend to forget that daily wage earners/petty shopkeepers are the losers of their daily bread during such bandhs. Could not some other way be found for expression of views particularly by the ruling party? The experience uptil now has been that state-sponsored bandhs have been rarely peaceful.

Strikes by government servants and employees in public undertakings are quite frequent. They emanate on account of the delays involved in taking decisions, particularly in matters of revision of pay and other benefits like pension, etc. The employees are also aware of their pressure power and the threats announced by the governments do not have any impact. They are also aware of the terms on which strikes are usually called off. Such terms in negotiations involve withdrawal of departmental proceedings/ criminal proceedings and condonation of break in service. In government departments, the principle of "No Work No Pay" is seldom observed. The strike period is debited to leave account and where leave is not due, advance debiting of leave is allowed for. The softness of the political executive and the delay in government decisions are responsible for these situations. The police in such a situation cannot do much; it is for the political executive to act timely and firmly.

Law and order situations cannot always be dealt with purely as a police matter. The efficiency of district administration cannot be separated from the general health of the administration and this requires changes in the present practice of posting and transfers on political pressures. The faith of the people in the district administration and the police gets shaken because of frequent transfers. Loss of credibility in the police has serious repercussions. The posting of senior officers of the rank of Superintendents of Police and above are not always done on merit. The political executive interferes even in the posting of Station House Officers which is the prerogative of the head of the department, discarding the concept of neutrality of civil services in the posting and transfers and also the lower functionary exercising the powers vested in him. If law enforcement agencies are to be strengthened, selected, experienced, impartial officers are required to be placed in sensitive law and order districts. They should not normally be transferred before the completion of their tenure and in any case all district and police officers should not be transferred at the same time. Even though this is a well-known principle, it is frequently being observed in breach rather than in observance.

The head of the state police is often selected not because he is the best officer available for the job but because he is a man who suits the politicians. The police structure is of a semi-military type and if the head of the police is shunted off and on at the whims of the political executive, he cannot provide leadership. Of late, the posts at the Inspector General and Director General level have multiplied manifold with a view to provide promotion avenues, resulting in their devaluation. There are no avenues for promotion of the police constable; a ground level functionary is overlooked.

In order to provide leadership to the police, the selection of Director General of Police in an impartial manner is crucial and when selected he should be available for a period of three years. In this context, All-India Services Act, if necessary, may be amended. (*The Times of India*, Oct. 31, 1994) Further it is the state police which requires strengthening rather than creating more and more paramilitary forces at the state or the central level.

State police has more local information and knowledge. It should be provided with greater mobility by providing modern equipments like fast moving vehicles and telephone facilities, including STD. The responsibility for the survival of democratic government at the state level depends upon the law enforcement authorities. Large scale breakdown of the law and order could result in the imposition of the President's Rule (Article 356). Shri R. Venkataraman, former President of India, in his lecture (1993) stated that the power to order President's rule in states should be confined to cases like (i) Breaking or attempting to break the unity of India, (ii) Total breakdown of law and order which the ministry could not handle, and (iii) Refusal to abide by the Constitution, etc. The Supreme Court's judgement in S.R. Bommai and others etc. vs. Union of India and others etc. (Judgement Today, March 21, 1994, para 230) gives a more exhaustive though illustrative list of the likely Government of India's intervention. Even when President's Rule is imposed, the police are not divested of their responsibility for maintaining law and order. The focus of authority shifts from the state to the Centre.

The Civil Services, including the police, have to be politically neutral; their commitment is to the Constitution; they have taken oath of loyalty to abide by it. Even if no oath is taken, every citizen is to abide by the Constitution, respect its ideals and institutions. (Part IV A, Articles15-A, Fundamental Duties) "Committed Bureaucracy" does not mean commitment to a political party or a particular person. Adherence to this principle may be difficult and hazardous and involve frequent shifting of officers. The political scene is changing. The chances are that in the next decade with no party gaining absolute power at the centre or the state, the government may be less arbitrary. It may be realised that efficiency and honesty is more rewarding than inefficiency and dishonesty and probably therein lies our hope for a better future, though the interregnum could be difficult to bear.

REFERENCES

1. Amended Section 153A IPC has amplified the range of offences and enhanced punishment. The salient features are now : (a) several offences have been made cognisable and non-bailable, (b) offences committed in places of worship carry more punishment, (c) convictions under certain offences act as disqualification u/s 8 of the "Representation of the People Act".
2. Bayley, D.H., *Police and Political Development in India*, Princeton University Press, New Jersey, 1969, pp. 280-81.
3. Buch, M.N., "IAS and IPS - Friends or Enemies"— "Of Man and His Settlements", p. 290.
4. "Centre's note on police posts offends Bengal" in the *Times of India*. Oct. 31st, 1994, reg. Shri Pilot's suggestion for appointment of DG and Police Commissioner by a Committee of the Centre and the State. C.M. West Bengal regarded it as an infringement of State's jurisdiction.
5. Jay Engineering Works vs. State of West Bengal, AIR 1968, Calcutta. p. 407.
6. Judgement Today, March 21, 1994, para 230. "While it is not possible to exhaustively catalogue diverse situations when the Constitutional breakdown may justifiably be inferred from, for instance (i) large scale break down of the law and order or public order situation; (ii) gross mismanagement of affairs by a state government; (iii) corruption or abuse of its power; (iv) danger to national integration or security of the state or aiding or abetting national disintegration or a claim for independent sovereign status, and (v) subversion of the Constitution while professing to work under the Constitution or creating disunity or disaffection among the people to disintegrate democratic social fabrics."
7. Smt. Padmavati vs. R.K. Karanjia, 1963 (1) *Criminal Law Journal* 187 MP cited in Ghosh S.K., *Law and Order from the Police Point of View*, p. 112
8. Report of the Commission on Centre State Relations, 1982, Part I, Para 7.3.04.

9. "Mob Control is not Easy" Roberıo Julio, in *The Times of India,* December 4, 1994.
10. Saxena N.S., *Law and Order ın India,* Abhinav, New Delhi, 1987.
11. Venkataraman R., "The Crown of England and the President of India" Rajaji Birthday Lecture, 1993.

18

Public and Police Cooperation in Road Accidents

H.R. Bangia

1. On the one hand, effort is made in India to curb population and on the other, we find that the number of vehicles on the roads have increased manifold and consequently the number of road accidents have also increased tremendously. The Ministry of Health and Family Planning was renamed as the Ministry of Health and Family Welfare for better health and welfare of the people since the people in general were made aware of the small family concept. There was a time when the size of the family used to be so large that the names of the children were not known to all the members of the joint family, not to talk of the dates of birth.

2. In urban areas people are having individual dwellings not because the relations among the children and the father are not very cordial but because everyone wants one's freedom and comfort from one's own earnings. Everyone is busy to get one's own job done as there is a lot of stress and strain in work situations and in family life. Man of today sometimes is not even aware who are the neighbours residing to his left or right side. Self-aggrandisement is the motive of the human being of today. That is why the life of the individual has become very precious and everyone has a role to play in one's so called small circle.

3. Persons are on the move— may it be restaurants, hospitals, railway stations or airports, but they are not sure of the fate of their own lives because of mounting terrorism, kidnappings,

militancy, natural calamities and so on. Road accidents also claim a good number of lives in this scenario of increasing number of vehicles, maddening crowd and fast pace of urban life. People prefer to stay home before the TVs rather than going to theatres. The question that arises now is as to how best to save the precious life of the person who is on the road? It is not that the accident occurs due to the fault of the person who drives the vehicle but it may happen when one is hit by the other vehicle. Sometimes innocent poor persons sleeping on the pavements at night become the victims because some vehicle or the other run them over. Thus pavement-dwellers and pedestrians are also not safe. In certain cases, the only bread earner of the family could be the victim of a road accident.

4. With this end in view, what is the role of the government when the rule of the law is broken by the people who themselves are the ultimate sufferers? This apart, many accident cases are pending in the courts of law for decision for years together. Not that the individuals need compensation only but because the people seek justice as is expected from the legal forum. It is, therefore, high time that something concrete is done to safeguard the precious life of the people.

5. Clamping the vehicles parked at public places, on the roads and at places marked as "no parking" is a welcome step following an Amendment in the Section 122 of the Motor Vehicles Act, 1988. In Delhi alone there are about 25 lakh vehicles on the roads which do not find appropriate parking places in densely populated areas and shopping centres like Chandni Chowk, Karol Bagh, Connaught Place, Sarojini Nagar Market, Lajpat Nagar, Khan Market etc. Places where public gatherings are held occasionally also create a lot of problems for the general public as in the absence of manned parking facilities, the vehicles are parked haphazardly at any place and in any manner.

6. The role of public and police in this regard cannot be isolated as these are two facets of the same coin.

What the Public Should Know?

7. Accidents can be avoided if the public is aware of and observe the following :

— Obey all traffic rules and regulations.
— Drive pollution free vehicles on the roads.
— Keep half-blackened headlights.
— Keep indicators of the vehicles including two-wheelers functional.
— Underaged drivers are heavily fined.
— Two-wheeler drivers found without helmets are fined.
— Overspeeding vehicles during odd hours is an offence.
— Strict lane driving is essential even at red lights where drivers don't give way to left-side and right-side traffic.
— Indisciplined drivers are challaned as many times in a day as they disobey traffic rules and regulations.
— Number plates of approved size and in white and black paint are only used.
— Open trucks carrying labourers are not to display their hands outside the vehicles.
— No hanging of any element outside the vehicle is allowed.
— Crossing of single and/or double yellow border of the roads is an offence.
— Proper illuminating indicators and other allied precautions are required for bullock-carts/trucks carrying lengthy and bulging articles on highways.
— Above all, all possible cooperation is to be given to the traffic police.

Role of Traffic Police

8. Delhi Traffic Police have to also play a vital role to keep the roads worthy of safe-driving. The following are some of the measures which require its attention at all times :

— Ilumination of all dividers and removal of the dividers where not required.
— Broadening the crossings wherever required which would also eliminate the signal lights.
— Making one way entries of certain roads/lanes and making certain roads/lanes one way in peak hours.

— Immediate removal of elements of obstructive nature on or by the sides of the roads such as electric or any other poles, bulging or bending trees on the roads.

— Deployment of Special Traffic Squads to remove the obstructive elements on the roads and diversion of the traffic where the road is not safe for driving.

— Checking of spillage of POL (Petrol, Oil and Lubricant) menace on the roads.

— Senior Police Officials Squads to be on the move to solve arbitration on the spot.

— Illumination of speed brakers and traffic signs at appropriate places and distances.

— Instant impounding of the vehicles of indisciplined drivers.

— Seek public cooperation where necessary.

— Better cooperation of Traffic Police and Delhi Police.

— Public transport system to be streamlined.

9. Accidental cases should be attended on priority without wasting the time over the jurisdiction of the Police Stations. And above all, Delhi Police should not harass the general public when any accident case is brought to the police station.

10. All hospitals, dispensaries, private nursing homes should be encouraged to entertain road accident cases on priority. Rather incentive should be given to the person who volunteers to take the injured to the hospital and/or reports the matter to the Police.

19

Hospital Administration and Organization: Multi-Dimensional Aspects

Dolly Mathew

Modern Hospital System

Hospital is a twentieth century phenomenon. The early institutions from which it developed bore little resemblance to modern hospital. The hospitals earlier devoted rather generally to the care of the sick and it was the homeless sick for whom they were operated in the initial period. At that time hospitals were considered as a last resort for the treatment of patient and death rate was therefore terribly high. The last quarter of the nineteenth century was considered as the golden age of progress and development of hospitals. Laboratory examinations became an integral part of hospital services. The use of X-ray in the diagnosis of disease marked a major advance in specialization of various hospital services. Physicians recognised the unique service which the hospitals could render in modern diagnosis and treatment and sought staff appointments. The industrialization of the last two decades of the nineteenth century provided the required funds for hospitals on philanthropic grounds.

Hospitals are emerging as complex organizations with the variety of jobs to be performed by various personnel specialized as well as otherwise. Interactions of several heterogeneous groups constitute a great challenge to hospital managers and behavioural scientists. Besides, the environment in which the staff members have to work is very sensitive and constant tension exists. There are various different areas work including simple health checkup to detect disease, outpatient examinations, inpatient wards, operation theatres, intensive care unit, laboratory, x-ray unit and other diagnostic services. The problem of management becomes more acute where the needs are disproportionately higher than the available resources. The hospitals started becoming departmentalised with a aim of treating different diseases. Introduction of sterile techniques, use of antiseptics, confident surgical facilities, scientific medical and para-medical training and education, super functioning laboratories, operation theatres, specializations and super specializations all changed the appearance of the hospitals. Scientific gadgets, instruments and equipments along with new and ultra modern physical setting of the hospitals changed the face of the hospitals completely. This has required the management of the hospitals on scientific lines and has given way to a new and separate discipline in hospital administration.

Hospital administration can be well defined as a "continuing dynamic application of thought and action directed towards the structure, function and philosophy of an organized effort."

The term 'Hospital Administration' covers a large number of activities, as diverse as are the systems of hospital organization themselves. When occasion arises, the hospital administration fulfils very different functions, which may be roughly classified into three categories.

1. Preparation of hospital legislation, planning of the hospital system as a whole, determination of investment policy and of regulations for the operation of hospital, and establishment of architectural control and standards. These activities come within the State's legislative and executive power and are essentially the responsibility of the Department of Medical and Health which in coordination with other departments like Home, Finance, Public Works, Education, Labour, Social Security and Planning undertakes these activities.

2. Application of hospital legislation and of social assistance provisions by the authorities responsible for the management of hospital services, whether they be local or regional, public or private.

3. Daily running of the hospital by the administrative staff concerned with personnel, finance, accounts and technical services. The Director of the Hospital and other subordinate staff are responsible for these activities.

This distribution of responsibility naturally varies according to the degree of development and complexity of the hospital administration.

The principles of hospital administration as stated by McGibony are as under:

1. Objective analysis and evaluation of problems and resources.

2. Formation of objectives, policies, functions and their relationship.

3. Effective utilization of resources.

4. Management by methods and means to attain the objectives.

5. Continuing evaluation and accountability.

In India, there has been development in the medical and health services, with the preventive and rehabilitation aspects being added to the curative side but simultaneous and befitting development has not been made in the field of hospital administration. To quote Dr. O.N. Ghei in his book, 'Principles of Hospital Management', "In the field of health, we rarely have consciously trained executives... We have expected a vast army of professional care givers to fill individual human needs, mainly on a laissez faire basis, mostly without planning, without coordination, without sufficient concern for those who either do not look for care, cannot afford it or cannot get to it".

All the personnel in a hospital are directly or indirectly involved in its administration. The issue remains is of trainning these personnel in the art and science of hospital adminıstation. The administration has been running on the basis of age old practices and unscientific conventions. Thus, to acquaint the personnel with hospital administration, there is need to provide training and education in this field and the subject of hospital administration may also be incorporated in the syllabus of undergraduate and postgraduate medical and para medical education.

Distinguishing Characteristics of Hospital Organization

Hospital occupies a strategic mid-position and has a great opportunity and a corresponding obligation, not as an institution for the salvage of human wreckage, but as a coordinator of activities — professional, economic and social — in their application upon the problems of health.

Today's hospital is a unique organizational entity. To its patients, it is a place to receive care. To physicians and employees, it is a place to work. To its managers, it is a multifaceted organization embracing patient care and financial, custodial and food service activities. It is where sophisticated equipment, technology, and professionals and para-medical are combined to provide quality health services.

The main distinguishing characteristics of an hospital organization are :

1. The main objective of the organization is to render care and treatment to the sick rather than manufacture some uniform material object. The economic value of the product is secondary to its social and humanitarian value.

2. Hospital is much responsive to the society and its work is closely integrated with the needs and demands of its clientele. All the members work with a high degree of agreement with the objectives, as a result there is little conflict between their own needs and objectives of the organization.

3. The work at the hospital is of emergency nature and non-deferrable. This places a heavy burden of both secular function and moral responsibility upon its members. Correspondingly, the organization shows great concern for clarity of responsibility and accountability among its different members and very little tolerance for either ambiguity or error.

4. The nature and volume of work are variable and diverse and subject to relatively little standardization. Both the raw materials and end products of the organization are human.

5. The hospital has relatively little control over its workload and over many of its key members. In particular, it has little direct control over the doctors and over the patients — two of its most essential components. The patients are not only a very heterogeneous and very transient group, but are also in the hands of their doctors, who are not employees of the organization.

6. The hospital is a formal and a quasi-bureaucratic set-up, but at the same time it is highly departmentalized, highly professionalized and specialized organization which cannot effectively function without coordination amongst the organization

objectives and the individual needs, motivations, and informal adjustments.

7. Hospital follows an extensive division of work and involves many departments, offices, staff including medical, para-medical, technical and non-technical personnel. There is the medical staff, which is specialized and highly trained. There is also the nursing staff which include trained nurses as well as untrained nursing aides. The heads of department are responsible for the medical care and day-to-day running of their departments. Besides, there are also a number of medical technologists and technicians who work in the laboratory and X-ray departments of the hospital, as well as a number of miscellaneous clerical and secretarial personnel. Thus there is great degree of professionalization and specialization in the hospital organization.

8. All the persons working in the hospital depend upon each other for the performance of work. Specialists and professionals can perform their functions only when a considerable array of supportive personnel and auxiliary services is put at their disposal at all times. Without coordination, it is not possible for an hospital to perform its functions. It relies heavily on the skills, motivation and behaviour of the various functionaries for getting effective coordination. The flow of work is too variable and irregular to permit coordination through any mechanical standardization. Patient care is itself individualized rather than uniform or invariant. As the work is neither mechanized nor uniform or standardized and because it cannot be planned in advance, the organization must depend a good deal upon its personnel to make day-to-day adjustments which otherwise cannot be stated by way of rules and regulations. This is all the more required, especially taking into account that the patient is an unstable element who comes and goes very rapidly.

9. Taking note of the patients undergoing treatment in the hospitals, who require a human touch in their revival, the hospital organization tries heavily to effect coordination in the various activities of its functionaries. Yet, the hospital is also a highly formal, quasi-bureaucratic organization which relies on formal policies, written rules and regulations and specified job charts.

10. The day-to-day management of the hospital is conferred on the Medical Superintendent, who in turn delegates to the heads of various medical and non-medical departments. Their staff, that

is the doctors and nurses are not shown in the direct line of authority, but they definitely exert substantial influence throughout the hospital structure, enjoy very high autonomy in their work and have a good deal of professional authority over others in the organization.

The absence of a single line of authority however creates various administrative and operational difficulties and psychological problems. This makes coordination task difficult. It is not always clear where the authority, responsibility and accountability reside. The personnel like nursing staff have to take orders from their own nursing supervisors as well as the doctors. It further creates problems of communication and in resolving problems between the para-medical and the medical staff. It also leads to problems between the administration and doctors. The administration due to the fear of the intervention of doctors tend to become more and more bureaucratic, leading to bureaucratization of organizational operations of the hospital which is meant to adjust to everyday changing, unpredictable and emergent nature of working conditions.

HOSPITAL ORGANIZATION : SOME FUTUROLOGICAL PERSPECTIVES

In India, with the rapid increase in the population, the needs of health services are increasing at a fast pace. The Indian hospitals are still to cope with this pace of providing better medical and health services to teeming millions in quantity and quality. At least, one way to provide a solution to this problem, is that the present structural arrangement of the hospitals gives way to an alternative configuration that may be topped by an Institute of Medical Sciences, embracing the government run hospitals in each State. Hence, it would be pertinent here to mention some of the salient measures that would be required to make this conversion a meaningful reality.

1. The government run hospitals will have to be converted into a Referral Hospitals, in the nearest future. This step will be a prelude to the more serious and comprehensive efforts to follow. As soon as these hospital are converted into referral hospitals, the state governments will have to enhance the status and facilities of satellite hospitals.
2. The proposed institute will be a research oriented institution with competent and highly skilled doctors who would engage themselves in teaching, curative services and research, but

who would refrain from doing private practice. As a compensation, they would be paid attractive salaries and non-practicing allowance and provided residential accommodation.

3. The institute must be endowed with the most modern and well equipped library, with the latest chronicles, digests, journals, abstracts, theses and microfilmed material.
4. The institute faculty must be encouraged to attend national and international conferences, present papers, write articles and even organize conferences on behalf of the institute.
5. The institute should publish from time to time its 'proceedings' containing details about latest researches and results.
6. The institute must be autonomous in technical, administrative and financial matters. It must not be a regular part of the government system. It should have a large trust funding in the beginning and should be financially independent of the government subsequently.
7. To facilitate the generation of funds, the institute, on the pattern of Christian Medical College, Ludhiana, should developed profit centres and charge of its services from patients according to their financial worth. A fixed percentage, say 25 per cent, of patients should be charged only nominal prices for services, in case they are 'poor'.
8. The management of the institute should not be with bureaucrats of the present variety, but with professional hospital administrators who have earned diplomas and degrees-Indian or foreign-in hospital management.
9. The institute should be totally residential with housing accommodation made available to all its technical staff-senior or junior.
10. The institute will have to be located in premises which would be substantially spacious and at the same time ensuring accessibility to the majority of population. The hospital can be converted into a sub-centre of the institute with two or three specific specializations.
11. Instead of opening a number of new departments and units, it would be prudent to concentrate on the following areas in the initial phase:

A. Ophthalmology

B. Oncology

C. Orthopaedics

D. Neurosciences

12. The Medical Engineering Department will have to developed into a full-fledged organization with specialized staff, instruments and spare-parts. Only then, the problem of repair of machines will be resolved satisfactorily.
13. Ancillary departments will have to be organized at a large scale. These would be required for looking after the relatives of patients, religious needs of the patients and their relatives and the usual material needs through a shopping complex.
14. Adequate number of dharamshalas and guest-houses will have to be developed around the institute to enable the patients and their relatives to stay for longer treatment.
15. The institute should have a Department of Preventive and Social Medicine which would devote itself to the promotion of health education in the city and its neighbouring areas.
16. And above all, the institute should be able to develop and present a human face, shunning snobbishness that unfortunately becomes the characteristic of specialists in large research institutes. Patients and their relatives should be treated kindly and taken into confidence on their ailments. The doctors should be empathetic and sympathetic.

Rakich and Darr in their book, 'Hospital Organization and Management', have added certain futurological dimensions to a hospital organisation. According to them:

1. New hospital structures will be required to cope with the increasing complexities. This may be in the form of a matrix organisation setup to solve emergent problems consisting experts from different departments.
2. Future hospital organisations will focus on developing human resources.
3. Work accomplishment will be through mutual confidence.
4. There will be effective two-way communication.
5. Increased interaction with other health related institutions.

6. Increased decentralization of decision making area; and
7. New techniques of conflict confrontation by way of consensus and understanding among members.

REFERENCES

1. Davies R. Llewelyn and HML Macaulay, *Hospital Planning and Administration*, WHO, Geneva, 1966.
2. Ghei P.N., "Principles of Hospital Management", In *Selected Readings in Hospital Administration,* Indian Hospital Association, New Delhi, 1990.
3. Mc Gibony John R., *Principles of Hospital Administration*, G.P. Putnam and Sons, Second Edition, New York, 1969.
4. Rakich J.S. and K. Darr, *Hospital Organisation and Management,* Spectrum Publishers, New York, 1983.

20

A Framework for Environmental Management: Policy, Administrative and Training Issues

O.P. Dwivedi

I

The continuing and accelerating deterioration of our planet's ecological base poses a major threat to the viability of our world. And nowhere is the evidence of global ecological deterioration better argued than in *Our Common Future,* a Report by the World Commission on Environment and Development. But the real significance of this Report lies (1) in its thorough explanation of why we, the people inhabiting this planet are collectively destroying our resources; (2) in its thesis that we cannot save the environment without development and also we cannot keep on developing unless we save the environment; and (3) in its main recommendation that without restructuring the existing institutional arrangements and legal mechanisms, the fragmentation, overlapping jurisdictions, narrow mandates and closed decision-making processes will continue. And as "the real world of interlocked economy and ecological systems will not change, the policies and institutions concerned must." (World Commission on Environment and Development (WCED), 1987). To change the existing institutions and legal mechanisms, the Commission suggested that nation states should consider one of the two approaches establishing (a) "environmental policy, laws and institutions that focus on environmental effects"; and (b) "an approach concentrating on the policies that are the sources of those effects". (WCED. op.cit) Both approaches represent a distinct way of looking at solving environmental issues.

Most national governments have adopted the first approach—effect-oriented - by establishing environmental protection agencies without much change in existing institutional structures. Such environmental agencies were given jurisdictions mostly in those areas in which no other ministry or department could lay a concrete claim. However, as experience in some industrialized countries has demonstrated, the first approach has resulted in focusing exclusively on the effects and on reactive or remedial actions rather than on preventive measures. This has created some serious jurisdictional disputes concerning the environment which is seen by many ministries as a shared responsibility. In some cases, the environmental protection ministry/agency has taken a sharp stand against economic development policies being pursued by others. Thus, inter-ministerial jealousies have resulted in jurisdictional fights, policy fragmentation and pursuance of narrow objectives. The need of the day is not only to dwell on effects of environmental pollution but also on "sources and causes" of the same. It is essential that all government ministries whether dealing with economic growth, natural resources, human health, social development, or any other aspect of human endeavour are mandated to care for the environment. That is why the following recommendation of the WCED is key to the basic assertion of this paper : the necessary institutional framework for environmental management and an appropriate response by all governments :

> Environmental protection and sustainable development must be an integral part of the mandates of all agencies of governments, of international organizations, and of major private-sector institutions. These must be made responsible and accountable for ensuring that their policies, programmes, and budgets encourage and support activities that are economically and ecologically sustainable both in the short and long term. (WCED op. cit.).

There are four main sections in this paper: (a) outline of a policy framework for environmental protection; (b) institutional mechanisms needed and the related action plan to implement the policy framework suggested earlier; (c) a national strategy to train and upgrade the professional qualification and on-the-job experience of environmental administrators; and (d) some concluding observations on the entire issue. Further, the author has presented the case mostly from the perspective of Third World nations. (Dwivedi, 1994).

II

A Policy Framework for Environmental Protection

The issue of environmental protection has gained priority on the political agenda of many developing nations. Public awareness about the environment has succeeded in putting this issue at the centre of decision-making in government, industry and the home. During the past few years, but especially due to the Earth Summit meet in Brazil, public concern has become strong enough to compel a change in political rhetoric in all the nations. But it has not yet become strong enough to force real changes in the kinds of decisions that government and industry have always made — or avoided making. Policies on tax and fiscal incentives on energy, agriculture and forestry have not yet changed significantly. These continue to cause a steady depletion of the basic stock of ecological capital. Only recently in many Third World nations, the debate has begun on the policy and institutional changes needed to reverse environmental degradation and move towards sustainable development but obviously, real action is going to take time.

Each nation needs to bring the environmental issues from the margins to the mainstream of political thinking and decision making. This requires establishing of a national policy framework for environmental protection and management by each country. The framework, examined below, illustrates several interlocking mechanisms which should be considered by a nation in order to develop an integrated environmental policy and pollution control strategy. Such a framework should be based on certain approaches which are listed below, and may be used as a model for adoption by the Third World countries to tackle the environmental and natural resource challenge facing them.

(a) Policy Instruments: A country can utilize two types of policy instruments to attain its pollution control objectives: (1) regulatory mechanism or (2) effluent charge strategy. The regulation-enforcement instrument requires that the authorities must set out the following four steps : (1) set rules and regulations governing the behaviour of industries in each of the sectors (including environmental audits, effluent control devices, maximum allowable limits on discharges, etc.); (2) establish a set of penalties under the law to be imposed for non-compliance with the regulations; (3) continually monitor the actions of targeted industries so that the instances of non-compliance can be detected with spot-checks and regular audits; and (4) make timely use of the judicial process in seeking the imposition of penalties on the defaulting industries. The effectiveness of this approach is based mainly on the premise (a) even minor violations, if detected, will not be ignored by the enforcement authorities; (b) defaulting industries should first be given an opportunity to mend their ways before being forced to pay major fines or injunctions; and (c) the enforcement authority has sufficient budget and human resources to enforce the law.

The Effluent Charge Strategy: It uses economic taxes like effluent or emission charges; in order for this strategy to work, the enforcement authorities ought to consider the following three steps: (1) determine a set of charges or prices per unit of discharge of each polluting substance that is predicted to induce the necessary abatement actions on the part of dischargers; (2) continually monitor the level of discharges as well as establish a system of self-reporting with spot checks and environmental auditing mechanism; (3) levy a sum equal to the charge per unit of pollutant discharged during each reporting period. This approach provides a graduated cost to industries by making pollution itself a cost of production; and also it provides incentives for technological innovations.

Out of these two basic approaches (although there are other variations such as a hybrid of the two), most of the countries have followed, in general, the **regulation-enforcement** technique. Specially, in the context of many Third World nations, this approach could serve the cause better in contrast to relying on industries to innovate, self-regulate as well as to control pollution.

(b) Institutional Change: As the Brundtland report indicated, environmental protection and management can no longer be safely left to weak and underfunded departments or to several departments with overlapping responsibilities. The issue of integrated pollution control must be addressed responsibly; towards this end, all nations (specially the developing countries, if they have not already done so) should have established departments/ministries of environment as a structural response to the changing perceptions of the environmental challenge.

(c) Legislation/Laws Needed: To protect public health and the environment, effective legislation is needed supported by vigorous enforcement. Legislative and regulatory instrument set rules and regulations regarding the protection of the environment. For example, through the Environmental Impact Assessment (EIA) process, government should plan to ensure that environmental factors are considered in decision-making. This can be done through prohibition, standards, guidelines, permits and the like if each government is committed to make its enforcement capability highly effective.

(d) National Environmental Standards: National standards pertaining to water, air, effluent emission, noise, waste, pesticide residues, and odour should be established, in law, by all governments. It should be noted, though, that strengthened standards can only be achieved through increased investments from both public and private sectors as well as by concerted action on the part of the government regulatory agency.

(e) Laboratory Testing and QA/QC Procedures: To constantly monitor and detect the quality of industrial emissions, effluents, and other polluting substances (both organic and inorganic), a nation needs a network of environmental laboratories (both in public as well as in private sectors). To ensure that the procedures used by all the labs (specially those in the private sector, or even those operated by other ministries) for quantification are appropriate, and whether properly calibrated analytical instruments are being used, there should be a proper accreditation programme to maintain the necessary quality assurance (QA) and quality control (QC) procedures. Without such a programme, prosecution of an environment related offence may be difficult in the face of competency of the laboratory doing testing and analysis being questionable.

(f) Environmental Enforcement and Compliance: Securing compliance with environmental legislation and regulation is a mandatory activity for the government environmental ministry/ department. The success of environmental enforcement and compliance strategy of a nation, then, will depend on gathering of sufficient evidence and information relevant to the suspected violation. The evidence in the form of a sample is generally sent to an accredited laboratory for analysis and testing. Enforcement involves, then, regular inspection and monitoring to verify compliance, investigation of any violations, and applying measures to compel compliance. Prosecution and conviction is the final stage in the compliance strategy.

In addition to these main approaches, the following six points are equally important for use while developing a sound policy process and interacting institutional mechanisms for environmental protection.

(1) Long-term Targets

The traditional incremental approach to environmental protection needs to be replaced by a clearly defined long-term target-based strategy. For example, the ban of coral sand mining in our coastal waters and its replacement by basaltic sand within a time-frame of three years illustrates such a long-term objective on a delicate issue. The same may be said of the CFC's protocol to the Ozone Convention and the reduction of CO_2 emissions, albeit on a global scale.

(2) Integrated Pollution Control (IPC)

One of the toughest problems in dealing with the environment is the degree to which it is an integrated system— a delicate whole in which a change in one part affects all the others. This makes it difficult to set priorities for environmental action. Environmental problems do not easily lend themselves to this kind of ranking. If, for example, water pollution were to be the first issue tackled, what would happen to initiatives to deal with air pollution, which itself is a primary source of pollutant in water?

(3) Public Participation in Decision-making

There is now a growing recognition of the fact that the public has a right to information and that more direct citizen involvement will reduce conflict, enhance trust in agency decision and improve the quality of decision-making. Towards this, public input into decisions should be encouraged which will lead to substantive contributions to environmental protection by raising new issues and serving to counterbalance narrow agency biases. Active participation is necessary to ensure that policies reflect public preferences and procedural justice is necessary to foster public acceptance of government decisions.

(4) Economic Instruments

Economic instruments that reflect environmental costs will encourage decision-makers to take the environmental consequences of their actions into account. Possible measures include effluent taxes, tradeable emission rights, deposit/refund systems and user charges. Sustainable development, with its focus on anticipating and preventing environmental degradation before it occurs, means increased emphasis on appropriate resource pricing and economic instruments to achieve environmental objectives. Used properly, these instruments can ensure that the environment is more carefully considered in production and consumption decisions made at all levels of society.

(5) Changing Decision-Making Processes

It is not enough to improve the quality and availability of factors that affect decision-making process. The existing institutions and procedures must also be changed for the better. Environmental considerations must be formally recognized as essential decision-making criteria within government and private sector organizations. Improved decision-making process, which takes full account of environmental considerations, demands that all these partnerships be strengthened and expanded.

(6) Strengthening Partnerships

Better environmental decision-making will require co-operative efforts at all levels. There are many other important partnerships that need to be fostered. Business is an essential partner in the search for, and implementation of, effective solutions to environmental problems. Labour has an important role in changing the way decisions are made and in working with the government bodies and the business community to achieve environmental objectives. Women, individually and through the many organizations of which they are a part, also form a key to changed decision-making process. These partnerships will be essential to the long-term goal of achieving sustainable development.

The Environmental Non-Governmental Organizations (ENGOs) are already playing a crucial role in educating people about environmental issues and activities. They are essential to an active and balanced discussion of environmental issues.

Individuals and communities have the most important role to play in bringing about changes in our attitudes towards the environment and how we treat it and should care for it. Towards this end, governments should play an important role in encouraging individual and community actions towards environmental conservation. In this respect, it is a worthwhile idea to consider setting up of a National Environment Fund, for example, which could provide a springboard for co-operative government-community efforts to protect and preserve the environment; it might also assist in the promotion of environmental education and research, in the support of ENGOs, and in encouraging locally-initiated environmental programmes.

Today's youth are tomorrow's decision-makers. If they are to play any meaningful role in environmental decision-making and diplomacy, they must develop environmental literacy as well as leadership skills. There is a need to take measures to ensure that the nation's youth will have the opportunity to channelise their energy and talents toward achieving environmental objectives.

At the global level, problems require global solutions. Such solutions can be effective only if they are built on international partnerships, both bilateral and multilateral. This will require raising a collective consciousness among all the nations so that a concrete shape to the slogan "think globally and act locally" can be given.

This framework should be supplemented by an action plan which translates these perspectives into concrete policy, relevant legislation and institutional systems.

III

Action Plan for Environmental Protection

Today's environmental problems are the result of the failure of people at all levels of society—as individuals, in their business lives, and through decision-making — to make decisions that fully take the environment into account. This failure, especially in the developing nations, is not one of wilful irresponsibility. Indeed, only recently these people have started expressing their concern about environmental issues. Now the challenge is to integrate environmental considerations into decision-making in a more systematic, focussed and coordinated way. Therefore, for the governments of developing nations, their first priority should be to help change the way their certain policies are formulated, institutions are operationalised and decisions are made, especially with respect to establishing a national environmental investment programme which provides the goals, objectives, directions and guidance for governmental action with explicit linkage between environment and sustainable development. An action plan or framework should be drawn up which should include at least the following four policy areas for immediate action. These are: (1) a national physical development plan for the country; (2) a national environmental policy supported by the relevant administrative mechanisms; (3) a comprehensive legislation for environmental protection and management; and (4) an appropriate industrial policy. These aspects are discussed below:

(A) National Physical Development Plan

Many of the environmental stresses specially pertaining to urban development and location of industrial complexes result from ambiguous planning. Orderly and progressive development of land, towns and other areas whether urban or rural, are prerequisites for sound environmental planning. Towards this end, each of the developing nations should consider preparing a National Physical Development Plan (NPDP) for their countries. Such a NPDP should contain an assessment of development priorities with associated economic and financial costs coupled with the delineation of an appropriate institutional framework for the implementation of the plan. NPDP should be the first step in creating a sound environmental protection strategy for any nation. In the absence of NPDP, there would emerge inefficiency in land management, leading to further environmental degradation. In fact, to an extent development control and, by implication, environmental protection are functions of effective land management. The NPDP should consist of a map of the national territory, with supporting plans and documents, which would indicate the preferred spatial strategy, after taking into account all physical, social, historical, economic, environmental, political as well as international issues, and fundamental goals for its future spatial organization.

The main objectives of the NPDP may include : (a) the protection of agricultural areas, especially areas with the best potential; (b) the protection of the natural heritage, including the terrestrial and marine ecosystems, the coastline, historic and religious buildings and areas; (c) the judicious siting of all secondary and tertiary activities taking into consideration socio-economic as well as environmental issues; and (d) the improvement in the quality of life of all its citizens. This would include all the spatial aspects related to the educational needs, employment, social and leisure needs of the community as well as those related to transportation and communication sectors.

Based on the NPDP, or while it is being prepared, each government should consider preparing a **national environmental policy;** because these two policy instruments will assist the government in formulating an appropriate institutional strategy.

(B) National Environmental Policy and Institutions

It is suggested that the main goal of a national environmental policy of a nation should be : ***to foster harmony between quality of life, environmental protection and sustainable development for present and future generations.*** In addition, the policy should include the following specific features:

(a) Guiding Principles: These include conservation and preservation of the environment, accepting the stewardship role for mother earth, taking due care in planning economic development so that future generations will not be unduly harmed, undertaking preventive and anticipatory actions to control environmental pollution, recognizing the need and importance for collective decision-making process in environmental planning and management, providing for an appropriate legislation so as to establish adequate enforcement mechanisms, acknowledging the impact of international environmental issues on each state and their role in minimizing international pollution, promoting environmental code of conduct, and encouraging environmental education and awareness.

(b) Main Objectives Some specific objectives should be agreed upon so that the state is directed to act on items such as attaining industrial development while conserving the nation's natural resources providing to all people, amenities such as clean water and sewerage, promoting environmentally sound technologies, safeguarding occupational health and safety of workers, conserving and preserving the natural and cultural heritage of the nation, establishing and enforcing air and water quality standards, and cooperating with regional and international organizations for the global protection of the environment.

(c) Specific Attributes of the Policy In addition to the main objectives, the policy should have some specific characteristics. These may include : (1) meeting basic human needs without endangering the environment; (2) utilizing of natural resources in a manner which is ecologically efficient; (3) requiring environmental impact assessment of any major development project; (4) using economic instruments in achieving cost-effective environmental management; (5) controlling pollution at source and to the extent possible, requiring the polluter to pay; (6) government undertaking to provide clean water to all residents; (7) to prepare and implement a National Master Plan for Waste Management; (8) in order to reduce air pollution from exhaust, requiring vehicles to have fitted with exhaust control devices and to encourage the use of unleaded petrol; (9) controlling noise pollution; (10) creating green spaces around the urban settings and establishing national parks and sanctuaries for wild-life; (11) exploring means for energy generation by recycling household and industrial wastes, and establishing a recycling mechanism; (12) issuing nation-wide air and water quality standards, guidelines and codes of practice for use by all industrial and commercial concerns; (13) undertaking a qualitative study to assess pesticide residue in soils, foodstuffs, fish and animals; (14) promoting environmental education at all levels of schooling, promoting research on the causes and effects of environment—related diseases, assisting NGOs and cultural groups in enhancing environmental awareness and assisting in the training of scientific and technical personnel needed by the country; (15) introducing comprehensive environmental protection legislation; (16) prohibiting smoking in all designated public places; and (17) establishing a National Fund for the Environment. (White Paper on National Environmental Policy for Mauritius, 1990).

The above listed attributes of the suggested policy require some specific institutional and administrative mechanisms in order to implement, enforce and manage the recommended course of action as envisaged in the suggested policy document. Most important among these are : (a) establishment of a Ministry/Department of the Environment to be responsible for the administration of the environmental protection legislation, to design and develop environmental guidelines and standards, and to be a national focal point for information and research on all environmental matters; (b) incorporation of environmental considerations in the National

Physical Development Plan; (c) establishment of an Environmental Council representing industries, unions, NGOs, educational and research institutions, professional associations, cultural and religious groups, employers' federation, media, and others; (d) provision of a high level central coordination and policy approval mechanism to act as a pivotal body to see that the wishes of the legislature and the government as a whole are carried out by all government ministries and para-statal organizations; (e) a collaborative mechanism to be put in place to seek cooperation from the provincial, regional and municipal governments in areas of shared responsibilities and common concern for recreation, conservation and protection of the environment, management of land-fill sites, garbage removal, crisis management, enforcement of environmental laws and regulations; (f) requirement for environmental impact assessments on all developmental and industrial projects; (g) encouragement of media (television, newspapers and radio) to be a partner in enhancing environmental awareness in the country; and (h) establishment of an integrated and comprehensive national system for environmental protection and conservation.

(C) The Legal Context

A discussion about the institutional arrangements for environmental protection cannot be completed without addressing to the legal context of those institutions which are in existence or to be created under the enabling legislation. There may be some difficulties initially encountered in this respect because the combination of government institutions and legal arrangements may be very cumbersome. I am using the term "cumbersome" here because the laws, rules and regulations, orders, ministries, departments, divisions, para-statal bodies, commissions, boards, and councils create a complex web of inter-relationships which perplex even a citizen; nevertheless, it is essential that a review of the existing legal situation should be undertaken to determine the scope and extent of jurisdictional authority, gaps existing and remedial action suggested.

It is not necessary that all pollution control jurisdictions be centralized into one ministry/department. Decentralization, sometimes, is better than a highly centralized situation. This is the case when there exists a specialized agency, department or ministry which specializes in a particular sector of the environment. The best examples of this are the areas of fisheries and hazardous substances. In many countries, the decision has been made to have fisheries departments, rather than environmental protection departments, deal with marine pollution. The reason for this is that, prior to sophisticated analytical methods, fish are the best indicators of pollution : they either die or desert polluted areas. Fisheries officers and the fishermen they deal with on a daily basis can be the best marine pollution policemen since they know local fishing areas, the movement of local waters, and the behaviour of marine life in the area and they know immediately when something goes wrong.

For most of the nations, centralization of all forms of pollution control is neither necessary nor even desirable; nevertheless, the de-centralized system requires that where several ministries or departments are involved, there must be some means of ensuring that the environmental efforts of all are coordinated and do not duplicate, or still worst, contradict each other. Having two ministries perform the same or similar functions with respect to the environment is neither an efficient use of government resources and the taxpayer's money, nor it is good from the public viewpoint because it confuses the public as they do not know which set of standards or rules to follow. Duplication also creates legal problems since a person cannot be convicted twice for the same act or omission although the offence may have been committed under two separate legislations administered by two different ministries. Obviously, to exert the authority necessary to arbitrate between competing programmes of different ministries, the coordinating body would have to be a powerful agency most likely to be headed by either the Prime Minister or the President. Because, inter-ministerial coordination is less of a legislative problem than a matter of political and managerial issue.

Options for Securing a Legal Base for the Environment : For securing an appropriate legal base, a range of three options are suggested.

(a) The first option is to leave responsibility for environmental protection and management among the existing ministries but to strengthen the present laws. This option brings about the least change in the administration of the government. However, as environmental pollution control is generally fragmented among several ministries, the situation becomes more complicated and duplication as well as jurisdictional disputes get perpetuated.

(b) The second option is to opt for a comprehensive environmental legislation which would create a powerful central agency with overall responsibility for the environment. Any legislation which duplicates or conflicts with the new law would have to be repealed. In effect, this option would create a "super" environmental agency or ministry. This would mean radical changes in terms of the organization of the government and administration and the distribution of power among various ministries. However, this option may be easily implemented and will be more effective in a small nation rather than in a large federal state.

(c) The third option is a compromise between the first two. It involves the introduction of a comprehensive environmental law, with the power entrusted to an environmental ministry/department to set national standards on air and water quality as well as to give overall control and management of the environment. The new law may cover all the gaps in environmental protection, and also permit ministries and departments (with existing environmental responsibilities) to carry on and even strengthen their powers in their particular jurisdiction. The environmental law performs a "backstopping" as well as "audit" function for other ministries with existing responsibilities but would operate as the primary law for those areas of the environment which have no coverage. This option brings about relatively minor changes in governmental organization and structure, but needs an effective integrated system of coordination so that the risk of duplication of effort and enforcement is minimized. This option also entails a much more active role for the central environmental policy agency as apex decision-making body to act as the final arbiter of sectoral and jurisdictional differences.

There are, in general, two approaches to the enforcement of environmental laws. These are : the positive enforcement approach and the punitive approach. The positive approach is envisioned to provide corrective measures such as programme approval, enforcement and prohibition notices. The punitive approach seeks to go to the extreme of imposing the legal sanctions of the law. This authority is exercised by the courts with appropriate jurisdiction when criminal and civil aspects are involved. The very recent origin of environmental law and the consequent necessity to define new terms and concepts and to redefine old ones justify greater judicial participation. It is for these reasons that, instead of using administrative courts, it would be desirable to establish quasi-judicial bodies such as an Environment Adjudication Tribunal with the provision that judicial proceedings may be used to review the action of government environmental department/ministry and to see to it that the department performs its functions in a proper manner. Further, the penal sanction in environmental legislation should include a considerable range of fines as well as imprisonment. To be effective, fines must be tough enough to have a deterrent effect on the target industry. If the fines are moderate or low, they can easily be included in the overhead for the industry and thus passed on to the consumer as additional burden, first of having to bear the effects of pollution and second of having to pay for it.

(D) Industrial and Environmental Policy

The promotion of environmental protection techniques and low-waste technology is an essential preventive instrument in environmental policy, supporting efforts towards sustainable industrial development. (O.P. Dwivedi and V. Venkataswamy, 1992) Consequently, appropriate policies (fiscal or monetary) have to be formulated to encourage economical use through easy accessibility to soft loans. A consumer policy also has to be developed. The complexity of environmental choices for the consumer is quite confusing. The relentless increase in consumption contributes substantially to the pollution. This policy should focus on ways in which consumption of products— detrimental to the energy economy and harmful to the environment— can be regulated through taxes and charges as well as restricting the use and production of disposable products apt to spoil the environment. Both economic and ecological considerations deserve to be taken into account in industrial decision-making. An increase in the efficiency of energy and materials, for instance, would not only meet ecological objectives but also cut down on costs.

Countries lagging behind will find themselves eventually being compelled to choose between home markets and settling for a lower quality of environment or importing technologies developed by greener competitors. During the coming decade the approach to environmental issues looks likely to be governed by considerations to:

(a) Adopt practicable methods for controlling waste disposal right from the time of project formulation;

(b) Adopt clean technologies and encourage more effective re-use and re-cycling of waste in production;

(c) Implement a toxic and hazardous wastes management programme; and

(d) Implement demonstration projects in the control of industrial pollution with emphasis on clean technologies in specific industries, resource recovery, waste recycling and utilization as well as proper waste disposal.

Industrialization transforms raw materials into consumer products. Badly-managed firms are rarely kind to the environment. By contrast, efficiently-run firms try hardest to reduce environmental damage. The risks of the manufacturing activities spoiling the environment, wasting raw materials or dumping wastes haphazardly grow proportionately with the rate of industrialization and the absence of resource management. Fortunately, technology is available to mitigate these trends. But the cost associated with environmental degradation rarely, if at all, enter into our calculations. The time has come to include such costs to care for the health and security of nature. We need to improve our accounting system and modify our gross domestic product calculation, for instance, to reflect the new cost of economic activity. The protection of human health, water purification, or conservation of natural reserves parks, are taken to have a zero price in the absence of a market place mechanism determining their real worth through the operations of purchases and sales. This approach should be changed to integrate the environmental variables in economic planning.

Economic instruments aim at improving cost-effectiveness in achieving pollution control goals, reducing residuals and industrial wastes beyond mandated limits and stimulating technological innovation and relocation. Taxes and charges also represent an important source of revenue which can then be appropriated to protect the environment. Environment and industrial growth (and by extension economic growth) are intertwined. It is no longer possible to achieve growth and social development without maintaining the quality of the environment and the stock of natural resources, which in our case are the sea, streams, lagoons and forests. Preservation of the environment cannot, likewise, be achieved without changes in economic development, the expansion of industrial activities and technological innovations.

The above suggested **plan for action** should be studied carefully by the policy-makers of the developing nations so that each country has its unique set of policy and programmes created to strengthen institutions for environmental protection and management. But, effectiveness of this framework depends largely upon the level of preparedness and the availability of professionally trained environmental administrators, and their dedication in implementing the environmental policy and programmes of their respective nations. This aspect is examined in the next section.

IV

TRAINING OF ADMINISTRATORS FOR ENVIRONMENTAL MANAGEMENT

In general, there is a severe shortage of managerial personnel in all areas of governmental endeavours in Third World societies; the problem is really acute with respect to the management of the task of environmentally sound and sustainable development. Therefore, it is desirable that each of the developing nation draws a blue-print dealing with a national strategy to develop a team of environmental managers. This does not mean that other training programmes in place are to be overlooked or forgotten. On the contrary, such a strategy would integrate both aspects of training requirements.

It seems that in order to handle the administrative issues, a new paradigm ought to emerge (O.P. Dwivedi and J. Nef. 1985); it is suggested below :

I. Paradigm for an Effective Environmental Administration

In general terms, the suggested paradigm for environmental management could be configurated around the following traits.

(a) Complexity: Administration for environmentally sound development involves many and diverse elements. The importance of these as well as their interrelations are equally varied and diverse.

(b) Contextualism: Such administration occurs in a multiple and complex context : economic, social, cultural, political and technological. This context both affects and conditions the institutional arrangements and the administrative system created for the purpose. Further, the context gives the administrative system its specificity and content.

(c) Historicity: The milieu in which the administration for environmental protection takes place is not only structural; it is also historical. Existing institutions and the prevailing administrative culture and style conditions the process and procedures adopted for managing the sustainable development. For example, the colonial/imperial legacy affects the present and future circumstances.

(d) Relationship between Short and Long range Framework: Administration for environmental protection cannot be based on a short-term thinking; protection of the commons and our natural legacy requires a long-range perspective. In the past, it is the short-term gains which affected our vision with the consequence that we are facing the environmental crisis of planetary dimension.

(e) Relation between Micro and Macro Levels: Similarly, specific administrative practices and structures required for environmental protection have to be seen in relation to broader perspectives and vision.

(f) Heterogeneity: The concept of sustainable development envisions inter-relating and inter-locking forms and manifestations of administrative requirements. Interconnectedness among old and new institutions (created for environmental protection and conservation) is a key to the success of **environmental protection.**

II. Identifying Training Needs for Environmental Administrators

There is also a need to make a concerted effort in Third World countries to provide standard education and training for environmental administrators. In the past, training of public service administrators has tended to concentrate upon "generalists" to take care of more traditional "executive" law and order administration; this emphasis has to be changed so that training programmes are developed for very specific and developmental tasks. A training system for "environmental programme managers" can be constructed in the same way as more conventional scientific and technological systems in law, medicine or any other traditional careers are organized, or it can also be thoroughly innovative. For instance, it could integrate a series of levels in the system, from scientific to that of the practitioner. An important aspect here is the need to recognize that managerial skills required for the tasks ahead in the 21st century are more complex. Further, management — as programme implementation and problem-solving — is, in the case of underdeveloped countries, most crucial at the grass roots levels of the political process.

Another note should be added to the above commentary : public management involves essentially a public service. The essence of management here is not synonymous with business management. Thus, the training of managers for sustainable development cannot be just a transplant of the business experience and methods or the old-style public administration methodology into the realm of present-day governmental process readying to enter the 21st century. All too often this distinction is ignored when it comes to providing the initial training to administrators. Because, the distinction between the provision of a service to a member of the public or a public good and the profitable bottom line remains fundamental. This distinction must not only be understood but should be clearly ingrained in those who wish to enter the complex realm of development administration.

III. Towards a New Administrator for Environmental Protection

The above discussion has very direct implications in defining the tasks and the training programme of the new type of administrative cadre. For this, we may have to look at a new scientific and technological system necessary for the creation and extension of appropriate administrative know-how. If such administrators are to be a new breed of managers, a number of formative conditions along the lines of the paradigm outlined earlier must be met. In operational terms, this entails the necessity to combine techniques with training not only in social sciences but also in natural science disciplines as well so that these administrators are ready to analyze and act upon the needs of sustainable development. In other words, an environmental administrator becomes a policy analyst with equal capability for operationalizing and problem-solving; this may be possible only when such an administrator is equipped to appreciate the scientific and technical issues (including even rudimentary knowledge of environmental sciences and engineering), and balance these by integrating with policy sciences. Furthermore, given the globalization of environmental and sustainable development issues, such an administrator would have to think in terms of global implications of his/her local issues. Thus, an environmental administrator would need to acquire an international perspective and be capable of seeing global and regional trends which affect the process of development within his domestic realities. Acquiring such a perspective would be a prerequisite for a properly trained environmental administration.

V

CONCLUDING OBSERVATIONS

In conclusion, the following three observations are presented :

(A) Environmental Crisis and Administrative Vision

Although environmental concern has achieved considerable global acceptance and popularity, the perception of crisis is not shared by all in various ministries and the administrative sphere. As a matter of fact, those who articulate this sense of crisis are considered sometimes as emotional and irrational lot and sometimes as power-grabbers and empire-builders. But then the magnitude of environmental crisis demands a more measured and systematic response than name-calling alone. Specifically, it demands institutional coordination, policy adjustments and structural adaptations. And when this demand has to be responded, the existing governmental structure has no capacity to face a challenge so pervasive and complex as potentially disturbing the administrative edifice of a nation. And so, where it is not implemented yet, it is not surprising to see individual ministries trying not only to protect their turf but also to expand their power-base by claiming more administrative capability and vision relating to environmental protection. In such an atmosphere, the task of coordination becomes extremely difficult as the agency which has been entrusted with this task is seen by others as an undesirable intruder and obstructionist in their normal functions. One result is futile gestures or withdrawal symptoms at worst, or unenthusiastic support at best. Often, the resisting administrative agency employs such techniques as prevention, curtailment or circumvention of anticipatory policy pronouncements. Finally, when a new ministry/ department of environment has been established, even then the new department does not do better than to be accorded a marginal position in the administrative hierarchy. Compounding the situation is the perception among many administrators that environmental policy and management still is a discrete function, something added to an administrative structure whose basic mandate has not been altered.

(B) External Inducement for Institutional Capability Building

During the late 1980's, many international aid agencies (both the international organizations such as the World Bank and UNEP, as well as those belonging to individual industrialized nations) started showing great interest in a nation's capacity to manage its own environment. These external inducements helped in expediting the process of institutional acceptance and administrative accommodation relating to capacity building for environmental protection; nevertheless, the initial hesitation about the role of this "new kid on the block" is still continuing. For example, this was clearly evident in India when the Department of Environment was formally established in 1980, or in Mauritius where the new Ministry of Environment and Quality of Life was constituted in 1991. It was not surprising to note that some officers of other ministries harboured concern about the new role of such an agency. Of course, this is nothing new because the same happened in other countries when a new multi-disciplinary-oriented environmental protection agency was created. Institutional strengthening takes a back seat when doubts (possibly to the point of outright resistance) persist among the key ministries about the new organization. In such a situation, direction from the office of the Prime Minister or President becomes crucial for ordering cooperation, integration, and coordination.

As environmental problems cut across ministerial responsibilities and jurisdictions, there is a need for more forceful articulation of environmental concerns in national planning and policy making as well as in improved coordination, institutional structures and legal instruments in the implementation of policies involving environment and development. (The World Bank, 1988) For example, in the case of Mauritius, the World Bank, in its Report *Economic Development with Environmental Management Strategies for Mauritius* noted that it endures "diluted authority and diffused legislation" which has implications for rational, efficient and sustainable natural resource management, a concerted effort is required to systematicaly review the "institutional, legal and regulatory arrangements, and the establishment of a comprehensive national policy for environmental protection and management". (The World Bank, op. cit) A similar situation also exists in many Third World countries.

A note of caution is desirable here. Externally induced changes, while easily instituted, must be given time to gain acceptance by the body politic and the existing administrative and legal mechanisms. Placing too much faith on instantaneous changes as well as expecting a "magic wand remedy" for bringing requisite organizational effectiveness and motivational changes in the administrative apparatus has sometimes proved counter-productive. And when the expected results do not follow the action, the recipient country turns against those organization(s) which induce such recommended changes. That is why a great care should be taken and externally suggested changes should be instituted at a slow pace giving time to adjust to changes locally. Like a human body, the governmental institutions too require time to accept foreign organs; at the same time, one should be ready for rejection from the body. It will be beneficial to all the Third World nations to undertake an assessment of the "induced change" in the administrative, institutional and legal mechanisms pertaining to environmental protection.

(C) Implementation and Action

Policy and legislation for environmental protection by themselves are not sufficient conditions for implementation and enforcement. These must be followed by necessary institutional arrangements; but even institutional mechanisms must await the setting of priorities of programmes which the government wishes to implement. Thus, after the policy has delineated areas for governmental action, and after legislative review and framework have identified those areas which require legislative action, it is desirable for a government to set in motion a programme review process to determine what priorities can be given to emerging issues requiring governmental attention in the near future and in the long run.

One major institutional arrangement required by a government is to formally establish a coordinating mechanism to be responsible for overall coordination and implementation of government policies and programmes. One such body suggested may be called an inter-ministerial Environment Coordination Committee with the following objectives and functions: (a) to ensure early and effective consultation on environmental protection; (b) to ensure a full and open sharing of information among the ministries and para-statal bodies on all matters related to the protection of the environment;

(c) to advise the Minister of the Environment on matters related to environmental quality guidelines, national standards, codes of practice, regulations, and other control measures in order to avoid duplication and to ensure proper enforcement to protect the environment; and (d) to maximize cooperation and coordination and minimize conflict and duplication among government ministries and para-statal bodies on activities dealing with environmental protection.

There is no doubt that our existing and surviving institutions for environmental protection are probably unsuited to new tasks. For example, old public health criteria are no longer sufficient for present-day circumstances; hence the job cannot be done unilaterally by a Ministry of Health alone. Similarly, an array of single-purpose agencies each being responsible for one resource such as water, or agriculture, etc., cannot be expected to voluntarily accept subordination or relinquish their specific mandates to a vague goal such as enhancing environmental quality or the quality of life. Further, it is not easy for the older institutions to submerge their interests so quickly to a new institution which may appear to tackle environmental protection problems cutting across the existing administrative and jurisdictional boundaries. Moreover, the preference of some that all aspects of the environment ought to be handled by a "super ministry" is equally troublesome to the existing governing institutions. Hence, the solution lies in adopting a realistic approach based on compromise and mutual adjustment among the older ministries and the newcomer. The sooner this realization is accepted, the better it is for the environment and for the community. Because the central theme that should determine the task of environmental protection is the prevention and control of factors or situations in advance of crises. If preventive measures are taken in advance, the community and the nation can be spared from the possible disasters. Treatment or other after-the-fact remedies should be regarded as failure by governmental agencies to achieve this objective.

Nowhere would a real environmentalist argue against economic development except that it must not only avoid disasters but must also be done in an ecologically sound and sustainable climate. This can be achieved if each country, to the extent that it is capable on its own, puts its house in order by bringing necessary changes in its institutions and in its attitudes towards nature. This is an obligation that each country owes not only to its citizens but also to the world at large of which it is a constituent part; because all nations contribute to ecological deterioration and all nations are affected by it. Thus, each country, irrespective of its size and economic status, must set a good example at home before it demands that others respond to the global ecological crisis.

REFERENCES

1. Dwivedi, O.P. and J. Nef "Training for Development Management : Reflections on Social know-how as a Scientific and Technological System" in *Public Administration and Development,* Volume 56, Number 3, 1985.
2. Dwivedi, O.P. and V. Venkatasamy ed., *State of Environment in Mauritius Ministry* of Environment and Quality of Life, Port Louis, 1992.
3. The World Bank Report on Economic Development and Environmental Management Strategies for Mauritius, November 1988.
4. The Report of the World Commission on Environment and Development, Our Common Future, Oxford, New York, 1987.

21

Administrative Corruption: A Framework of Analysis

Dhrubajyoti Bhaumik

Public administration texts have rarely dealt with corruption, let alone analysis. Researchers who persisted in un-covering corruption often found themselves persona non-grata not only in official circles but also among academia because they supposedly tarnished the image of public administration and tainted public officials. Every country has its own specific forms and patterns of corruption and it is hard to generalise about experiences of different countries within a common framework of analysis.

A study of administrative corruption seeks to unravel causes of preventable public maladministration and helps in restoring public confidence in administrative ethics. While delivering lecture on Morality and Administration in 1957, Paul Appleby favoured a code of Administrative Ethics for US Public Service. (Bailey, 1986) Reporting in 1989 National Commission on the Public Service in U.S.A. in pursuance of identical perspective called for rebuilding public trust on public officials by way of removing "public perceptions of corruption, waste and ineffectiveness in government". (Report of National Commission, 1989). Today this is the acknowledged agenda of the governments all over the world.

Definition of Corruption

What exactly is meant by unethical public behaviour under the rubric of administrative corruption? It consists of "behaviour which deviates from the normal duties of public role or violates rules because of private gains or reasons— regarding family, close private clique, pecuniary or status gains regarding (influence). This includes such behaviour as bribery (use of rewards to pervert the judgement of a person in a position of trust); nepotism (bestowal of patronage by reason of ascriptive relationship rather than merit); and misappropriation of public resources for personal gains." (Nye, 1967) Thus it includes all abuses of public role for private advantage that deviate from established norms. Added to this should be all abuses of public position such as lying and conflicts of interests that offend notions of how officials should act, business and other extraneous improprieties that influence official acts (fraud, favour and threat) (Caiden, 1994). Pragmatically, no administrative system is entirely free of corruption; in case of isolated occurrences the system should quickly trigger automatic institutionalised fail-safe devices to arrest potential damage. In the modern administrative state, corruption appears to be pervasive, routine, irrespective of scale and regime. In western democracies, scandals occur encompassing such venerated institutions as Scotland Yard and the Dutch royal family (Caiden, op.cit). Elsewhere spread of corruption is all too common and public officials plunder public purse. Administrative ethics is disdained and touches the bottomline in ex-communist regimes (as revealed now), poverty stricken Indian sub-continent, African dictatorships and populous Latin American countries (Mellow, 1991)

Corruption: Four Perspectives

From the above definition four broad perspectives of corruption may be identified : a) Legal, b) Historico-cultural, c) Public Interest, and d) Market-centered. While legal perspective defines corruption in terms of deviations from legal norms of public office, (Nye, op. cit) historico-cultural perspective takes traditional practices and perceptions as a basis for identifying corruption. (Abhueva Jose V. in Heidenheimer ed. Political Corruption, 1989). In public interest perspective, corruption is identified in terms of sacrifice of public interest for private gains, (Arnold A. Rogow and H.D. Lasswell in Heidenheimer ed. Political Corruption, op. cit). Market centered perspective views corruption as a "maximising mechanism", that enables public official to use his official domain to serve himself in accordance with principles of demand and supply and that, at the same time benefits corruptee in a situation of scarcity (Klaveren in Heidenheimer, op.cit). Legal perspective enables a broad agreement over the definition of corruption and therefore over the scope of its study, "but it does not allow looking into the actions or inactions which corruption laws do not cover, yet which need to be included" (Arora, 1993). In reality, provisions and gaps in the corruption laws may breed corruption in some systems. Public interest is an Achilles heel; it may be twisted and there exists scope for disagreement on what can be taken to contravene public interest especially when the state authorities, quite often try to justify even the most unworthy action/inaction under the umbrella term 'Public Interest'.

According to historico-cultural definition, corruption thrives under the cloak of traditional values and norms of behaviour. While laying excessive emphasis on history as the prime determinant of people's attitude towards corruption it seeks to relate corruption to the nature of society "making it difficult to see the role of state authorities in colonising these values to promote and perpetuate other more modern issue-based exchanges." Market-centered definition of corruption rests on transaction involving two parties and the system "because of its capacity to correct imbalances in demand and supply of goods, it tends to undermine the coercive aspects of corruption transactions on the one hand and non-conjunctive corruption on the other." In the light of limits and scope of the perspectives as stated it seems important to integrate them into a broad framework so as to attain a holistic approach to the study of administrative corruption. Hence the need is to : (a) explore the inter-relationship of different perspectives as emphasized by specific empirical contexts; and (b) extend their focus to the questions which have escaped them (Arora, op. cit).

Analysis of corruption embedded in the framework of state-society relations is useful in some important ways. For this purpose, corruption implies actions or inactions of state elites who indulge in distorting the framework of state-society relations for personal benefits. Following the definition, corruption may be divided into three types : coercive, collusive and non-conjunctive. Understanding various types of corruption as well as strategies for their perpetuation will surely help in directing efforts towards eradication of corruption. In the dynamics of state-society relations the concept of corruption may be placed broadly in terms of (a) power and authority; (b) law and policy (Arora, op. cit.).

Corruption: Power and Authority

Corruption here is viewed as the craft used by state elites-political as well as administrative — for transforming authority into power which can be exchanged for other kinds of power in society to favour or disfavour to specific individuals or groups therein. Discriminatory exercise of power flowing out of authority and the mode of taking power beyond the limits of authority are its two forms (Arora, op. cit). While the Santhanam Commission in India (1962) had gone, inter-alia, into corruption as 'discriminatory exercise of power', the Shah Commission of Enquiry appointed in 1977 scathingly criticised 'the mode of taking power beyond the limits of authority' i.e. excesses committed during the Emergency by those in position of power. In both these capacities corruption may result in contrasting reactions, a sense of helplessness among sufferers and confidence in beneficiaries. Besides these two forms, administrative corruption may take other forms as well. To Heidenheimer (1989), administrative corruption is inseparable from political corruption. One complements the other. If politicians do not tolerate corruption and revelation of wrong doings is accompanied by swift and stiff retaliatory measures, any failure to take such action would provoke an immediate public outcry.

Administrative corruption contaminates everyone who comes into contact with it. Being its fountain head politicians wink or connive at corruption knowing that they will be protected and shielded by their entourage. Somehow administrators will silence accusers, incriminating evidence will be unavailable and possible prosecutors bought off. The public too has to go along with it. On the one hand, they rely on politicians who crank public agencies to their service, on the other, expect law enforcement officials to prosecute politicians and public office holders and sweep the house clean. Public sector cannot be isolated. The nature of the modern administrative state is that it penetrates into all social activity and merges into other institutions and other sectors. (Official corruption contaminates the administrators and any corruption in these administrators contaminates the public sector). (Heidenheimer, op. cit) This can best be seen in the operations of international organised crime which sucks every country into its influence and permeates even into international organisations that would be beyond its grasp and above suspicion (Arluckhi, 1992). All these presuppose freedom of information and free mass-media willing to report and investigate corruption without fear or favour. Undoubtedly this is a very tall order. Corruption presents a serious challenge to the integrity, well being and stability of the global society in which everyone is a victim of its distortions of power and governance. Of late, the international community has come to realise this and it is intended to take up this dimension seriously.

There are no two opinions that centralisation of authority is the cesspool of corruption by making both alignment easier for those in power and access difficult for those without power. It is not however true that corruption is the characteristic of the higher echelons of authority alone. Power that belongs to authority becomes real at the points of operation which are widely dispersed in a centralised system. Thus, corruption at the centre of power percolates into all other points of power too. At the points of operation benefit of high level corruption is not only shared but also actualised. Robert Wade (1982) in his study of canal irrigation in South India provides an insight into the extent of linkages between corruption at lower and higher levels of authority. "Politicians... nearly forced junior engineers to raise illicit funds through distribution of canal water and allocation of maintenance contracts and offerred them a share of these." Corruption is thus interlinked with patterns of power organisations in the system or in the manner power tends to organise its relations between State and society. Perhaps multiplicity of power centres is not its remedy; it may rather contribute to its proliferation.

Panchayat as an institution for decentralising power is alleged to have been responsible for decentralising of corruption: The experience in Karnataka which introduced one of the most successful decentralisation programmes in 1980 is a pointer in this direction. While studying the Panchayati Raj in West Bengal, Neil Webster (1992) noted the existence of widespread corruption. In 1987, it was officially stated in the Legislative Assembly that out of 120 cases filed, 4 or 5 ended in conviction, the rest were at different stages of proceedings. 90 to 95 Pradhans were expelled from CPI (M) or Left Front partners on proven charges of corruption. Writing about implementation of development programmes by PRI in West Bengal, Ross Mallick (1993) mentioned that although checks were officially applied at every stage, malpractices like false entries of names in muster rolls, insufficient work than prescribed were still reported by the local people. Even if some workers did not work upto the prescribed extent, they managed to get the certificate of satisfactory work. It was also reported that at times the Modified Ration Shop (MRS) dealer supplied very bad quality of wheat. It was suspected that the dealer sold out the better quality foodgrains in the open market and distributed the worst quality of grains purchased at lower prices. The trading of favours and contacts alleged to have become a way of life in rural India. It is said of Indians and Bengalis in particular that "next to the interests of his family the public interest does not exist." (Lelyveld, 1975)

Corruption: Law and Policy

In State-society relations, law and policy provide an important dimension. Corruption emerges outside the framework of law. It is extra-legal or illegal which in turn distorts the very basis of power. In fact, corruption seeks to neutralise or manipulate law, if necessary, for the desired outcome. The beneficiaries and the victims thus created are not according to the intent of the law. According to the National Police Commission, extortion by police of periodic payments or hafta from shopkeepers, platform vendors, brothal keepers, promoters of gambling dens, and other illegal traders etc. is the price paid to escape the network of unfavourable laws. Neutralisation or by-passing of law is well-known in other spheres too, ranging from traffic rules to tax laws. In essence, even though power elites may be incapable of capturing the (legal institutions or law-making process, corruption as a channel helps them at the implementation spaces not undermining the authority of power-holders but significantly adding to it). Umpteen regulatory laws aimed at keeping the powerful economic interests in check contribute to their growth in view of their capacity to use corruption for changing the very nature of law. Corruption not only has the capacity to neutralise or secure redefinition of law but contributes to the creation of law as well. In order to get an insight into the structure of situation as stated, there is the need for a thorough examination. It is important not only to examine how the purposes of law are frustrated but also why laws 'meant to be defeated' are enacted at all.

What has been said of law is applicable to policy and programmes as well. Alongside the expansion of state sponsored policies and programmes there has been pari-passu increase in the programme failures to achieve their objectives. It is widely believed that elites camouflage their vested interests in both regulatory policies and beneficiary-oriented programmes; they are hell bent to strengthen their own position as well by exploiting possibilities of programme failure through corruption. This becomes evident from the enormous benefits cornered by politicians and administrators in the process of programme and policy-execution. Thriving on corruption, the nouveau rich in most of third world countries constitute a class and seek to storm the citadel of power in the system.

Corruption: Its Typology

Traditional view is that administrative corruption is individual and therefore incidental. By punishing or dismissing an individual it can be tackled. But increasingly corruption is recognised as systemic and rooted in mores and institutions of society. (As mores and institutions differ, practices considered corrupt in the western world might actually fulfill economic, political and administrative needs better). So called corruption appears to be consistent with customs and traditions while the law and bureaucratic ethics that make it illegal and immoral are alien or superimposed. In the midst of systemic or institutional corruption individual stands helpless in spite of one's self-control and honesty. He is likely to be battered just as gale lashes the lonely but in an open field. Such systemic corruption may be found whenever societies prize organisational loyalty over the public interest, where standards of public rectitude and integrity have been eroded and where notions of public responsibility and trust have been thrust aside by the exploitation of public office for private gain. (Caiden, op. cit) In systemic corruption identifiable features are : (a) the organisation professes an external code of ethics which is contradicted by internal practices; (b) internal practices encourage, abet and hide violations of the external code; (c) non-violators are penalized by foregoing the rewards of violation and offending violators; (d) violators are protected and when exposed treated leniently; (e) accusers are victimized for exposing organisational hypocrisy and are treated harshly; (f) non-violators suffocate the venal atmosphere; they find no internal relief and much external disbelief; (g) prospective whistle blowers are intimidated and terrorized into silence; (h) violators become so accustomed to their practices and the protection given to them that on exposure they express surprise and claim innocence and unfair discrimination against them; (i) collective guilt finds expression in rationalisation of internal practices and without strong external support there is no serious intention of ending them; (j) those formally charged with revealing corruption rarely act and when forced by external pressure to do so excuse any incident as isolated, rare occurrence.

Arguably, if corruption is institutionalised or systemic it can no longer be considered corruption. It is merely the operational norm of public administration that does all manner of beneficial acts for society. Numerous knots of rules and regulations, for illustration, for setting up an industry in India may be cut off by way of 'Speed Money'. In other words, plan for corruption finds support to quicken the pace of development. But closely examined, systemic corruption far from being functional is dysfunctional to society; (a) it perpetuates closed politics and restricted access preventing social change; (b) it suppresses opposition contributing to increased resentment. Instead of becoming an alternative to violence, it may escalate far more violence; (c) it perpetuates and widens class, economic and social divisions contributing to societal strain and prevention of cohesion; (d) it prevents policy intended to protect public interest; (e) it blocks administrative reform; (f) it siphons off huge public resources and contributes to private affluence and public squalor; (g) it contributes to social anomie; (h) it subverts trust and cooperation in the administration.

In respect of systemic corruption results are alike in western and non-western countries. To explain it by way of Gunnar Myrdal's 'Soft State' (1968) in the context of non-western under-developed countries, is no phoney argument. In a 'Soft State' the governing apparatus is hollow, riddled with self-promoting, self-interested groups that have little agreement on what is in the general interest, the government is incompetent, inefficient, inconsistent and arbitrary, the State siphons off potential wealth into heavy security expenditures, conspicuous consumption and privatised assets and it becomes a prime source of corrupt exploitation. This calls for getting into the roots of governance system to discover why individual integrity is deliberately compromised in pursuit of objectives in-consistence with values of the community. The organisational culture in which systemic corruption is embedded has to be revamped with systematic reforms in the administrative system.

An interrelated issue is the question of public accountability and trust. Law cannot always prevent perversion and abuse of power. In a sense, public accountability of persons in high places begins where laws governing their duties and responsibilities end, when degenerations are institutionalised, loss of faith in political leadership becomes obvious. The harm is not just in taking advantage of public trust but also in abuse of public accountability. All diversions of public funds, all public money spent on things not officially sanctioned, disbursed and allocated, every misuse and abuse of public office fall into this category. There may have been the absence of criminal intent or actual breach of the law, but there may be deliberate evasion of public accountability and trust.

Another identifiable typology of corruption runs thus : collusive, coercive and non-conjunctive. Under collusive corruption, corruptees actively participate in corruption and use it as a means for deriving benefits greater than the costs of corruption for themselves "by jumping the queue or by obtaining undue attention or avoiding problems that others face because of their incapacity or unwillingness to resort to similar methods." (Arora, op. cit) Noting the prevalence of corruption in India, Santhanam Commission observed "we are told by a large number of witnesses that in all contracts of construction, purchase, sales and other regular business on behalf of the government, a regular percentage is paid by the parties to the transaction and this is shared in agreed proportions among the various officials concerned. We are told that in the constructions of P.W.D., seven to eleven per cent is usually paid in this manner. In all cases, failure to pay the percentage results invariably in difficulty and delay in getting the bills paid." Involvement of high government officials in this kind of corruption cannot be gain-said. Janakiraman Committee Report on Bank Securities Scam established charges against a number of top officials including Directors of Public Sector Banks for helping out Harshad Mehta by flagrant violation of rules. *(Statesman, July 7, 1992, Calcutta)* Another variant of collusive corruption is also present. It admits to the role of inter-personal relations or more precisely, relations of loyalty. Although there is no immediate transaction involved in this case, the power holder in exercise of his authority is often influenced by considerations of primordial loyalties, such as, caste, religion and even regional considerations and with the object of retaining his social position finds support in handy procedures.

Coercive corruption is interpreted as one-sided victimising corruption inflicted upon the corruptee by those in authority. Coercion implies not just physical violence alone; it includes mental torture (through threats of punishment) as well. These two situations bear the characteristic of those structures of authority upon which the capacity to execute coercion rests, as for example, the Police. The Third Report of National Police Commission observed "Corruption in police, as in any other branch of public administration, is clearly (linked with the scope for exercise of power to the advantage or disadvantage of one or the other.) It is, however, qualitatively different in police because of the predominance of extortion and harassment as compared to collusive corruption that prevails in several other departments, particularly those connected with collection of taxes or issue of permits and licences." Both inaction and undue action constitute the tactics of such corruption. A corruptee is found to adopt it as a last resort. Santhanam Commission held the view that corruption is largely contingent upon willingness to corrupt and capable of corrupting and interestingly "both willingness and capacity to corrupt is found in large measure in the industrial and commercial class."

Non-conjunctive corruption is markedly different from two other types mentioned earlier. "While the operationalisation of both coercive and collusive corruption involves the conjunction of actors, the non-conjuctive corruption does not even involve a transaction between those in authority and those outside it." (Arora, op. cit) An individual in authority exercises the power to bestow benefit upon himself as a private person, as, for instance, by assigning contracts to himself, making false claims or acquiring goods or wages etc. The Reports of Vigilance Commission pointed out misappropriation of public resources by those in authority and they are illustrative of such corruption. In its Annual Report 1984-85, Vigilance Commission indicated that 27 per cent of Vigilance cases in the Department of Telecommunication related to misappropriation of government store materials. Pilfering of materials and store items by inserting false entries in the registers, claiming wages of labourers by entering fictitious names in the muster roll and pocketing the wages of labourers meant for disbursement illustrate non-conjunctive corruption. In P & T Department out of 225 cases handled by it nearly 23 per cent were connected with misappropriation of store materials. Public reaction to these types of corruption vary widely. Admittedly, collusive corruption is closely guarded both by state-elite and those who enter into it. Such corruption does not impose any cost on those unwilling to enter into collusion. Coercive corruption, however, is not opposed by those in position to collude. People are not averse to making routine payments which they regard as saver of time and effort. Besides, people are largely unaware of non-conjuctive corruption and their attitude towards it is generally of indifference. Peoples' concern finds expression only when they are directly affected or incur loss because of such corruption.

Corruption: Its Strategies

An outline of strategies which in effect form the basic elements of corruption system is relevant in order to help in analysing reality of corruption, the reasons of its tolerance by the people and factors that weaken peoples' resistance to it. There are five important strategies; mystification, distancing, folklore, colonisation and pacification.

Mystification: As the most effective strategy of the corruption system it has three worth mentioning aspects : First, it involves the power of the State. Usually authority holders seek to spread the mystique of their power. People are given the impression of unlimited ambit of authority coupled with the role of discretion involved in the exercise of such authority. National Police Commission testifies mystification of authority thus : "Certain police power which involve the exercise of discretion in the day to day working of the police... give scope for corruption and malpractices accompanied by extortion and harassment to the public." (Third Report of the NPC, op. cit) Second, such strategy is interwoven with the rights of the people. Rights are reduced to insignificance as a result of denial of information coupled with ignorance about the possession of the rights. A Parliamentary Committee attached to Personnel Ministry in 1988 pointed out that the bulk of public budget was spent on printing literature on Anti-Poverty programmes ignoring the fact that roughly 60 per cent of the country's population is illiterate. Most people in remote forest villages do not know what they can collect legally from the forest. Third, Mystification is linked with official acts covered under Official Secrets Act which withholds from public certain kinds of information. Undeniably, public authorities are often inclined to hide even that information which need not be hidden. Under the Act the entire process of decision-making is covered. Kickbacks involved in Bofors deal were veiled in secrecy till the media exposed it to the public. Sugar scandal which has been brought to light now also falls into this category. In such cases, the question of raising objection to the exercise of power does not arise at all.

Distancing: It is a type of strategy adopted to create a distance between persons of authority and those without it often reducing the latter into a state of subjugation and helplessness. Distancing implies exclusion of society, meaning people from operational structure of State and absence of participatory rights of the people. The failure of the large number of rural development programmes is attributable to this type of distancing between State and society. In such a framework of State-society relations, middlemen operating from outside or inside the State structure can bring benefits of access to individuals or groups through corrupt exchanges. Middlemen or brokers are not interested to close the gap between the people and authorities; rather they try to sustain it for better pay off. Distancing of society from State may assume dual role of authority holders: they operate simultaneously as a private person and as a public person. The public person becomes accessible only when approached as a private person directly or through middlemen.

Folklore: Myrdal noted 'Folklore of corruption' in India as a highly effective strategy for reaping benefits. Words are spread like bushfire about pervasiveness of corruption i.e. about its being systemic and impossibility of moving the system without corruption by those in authority themselves or by interested parties. Not only it induces the people to take resort to corruption but legitimises corruption of individual authority holders in view of its systemic character as well. 'Folklore of corruption' is a canopy under which collusive, coercive and non-conjunctive corruption grow and thrive. Now-a-days people talk of contracts being sold, transfer and postings offered through 'greasing of the palms', deals being struck for kickback, public goods being misappropriated and privileges being misused. 'Folklore of corruption' generates a sense of despondency among the people and helps those who indulge in it. Happily it provides a congenial atmosphere for the middlemen to carry on brisk trade.

Colonisation: Essentially, it denotes the use of innocuous practices of the people in traditional settings as instruments of corruption. In reality colonisation of traditional values and norms is the outcome of the modern system of authority and power. This explains why several corruption studies highlighted the need for taking note of traditions and historico-cultural evolution of societies while defining corruption strictly according to norms and practices in a given structure of society.

Pacification: As a strategy it seeks to perpetuate the state of corruption. Those in authority weaken the possibilities of resistance or challenge to corruption, through actions, mostly symbolic, in order to convey the message to the people that they are serious in eradication of corruption. Unkept promises to give clean government to the people, appointment of Investigation Commission, preferably headed by judicial personnel for the sake of impartiality and integrity, Departmental enquiry into official lapses, transfer of cases to Vigilence Cells etc. are some of the devices adopted for pacifying the people. Those in authority also manage to make an impression related to prevention of recurrence and spread of corruption.

Corruption: Global Perspective

Corruption is a global phenomenon (*Statesman*, Dec 6, 1994). It is not confined to dictatorships or impoverished societies or capitalist countries alone. Corruption appears to be a regular, repetitive, integral part of the organizational society and the Modern Bureaucratic State, common to all political systems. It is endemic, chronic and pervasive, a universal and enduring problem (Scott, 1972). It can only be tackled on giobal basis, as the corruption of one country spreads to its neighbours and contaminates the international order. (Caiden in Ramesh K. Arora's et al *Universe of Public Administration,* 1994) Until a global agreement on anti-corruption activities is arrived at, it is perhaps not possible to adopt strategies for fighting corruption. Moves in regard to the strategies to combat corruption throughout the world are afoot. By and large there has been an agreement on Joseph Nye's definition of corruption as behaviour which deviates from the formal duties of a public role because of private-regarding influence. (Nye, op. cit) Exactly what kind of behaviour should be covered by corruption is still a subject of contention between moralists and pragmatists. (Heidenheimer, op. cit) As the line between acceptable and unacceptable practices varies in so many countries, the existence of a grey area in between cannot be ruled out.

Presently, attention is getting diverted from individual corruption to systemic corruption which is "cancerous and disintegrative to the administrative state, to the legitimacy of the polity and to the authority of government itself" (Johnston, 1986). Caiden has suggested the following efforts to fight against systemic corruption: Global fostering of: (a) a democratic ethos; (b) a universal ideology of public service; (c) public service codes of ethics; and (d) public service ethics education and training.

(a) Fostering of a Democratic Ethos

Corruption breeds in a ground where people are made to feel alienated from public officials who refuse to recognise the sovereignty of the people. The aim of fostering democratic ethos is to restore public identification with polity and to restore people's sense of ownership at the same time impressing public responsibility and accountability on public officials. (Wright, 1973 and Marican, 1972) Not only should the political arena reflect public opinion but the public bureaucracy should also be a fair reflection of social structure. Representative bureaucracy should accompany the representative government. (Krishlov, 1974) For socializing public in regard to their role in protecting and advancing public integrity and propriety against corruption, the need for highlighting institutions cannot be ignored. Array of socializing institutions in this regard are : home, religion, school, youth club, Armed Services and International mass media.

(b) Fostering of a Universal Ideology of Public Service

Together with the democratic ethos has arisen a concerted attempt to internationalize an ideology of public service among professionals and career officials, ingrained in the declarations of the French Revolution consisting of following edicts : (1) government is a public trust to be used in the general interest, not for a sectional interest; (2) Public officials are to abide by the law in the same way as everybody else; (3) Public officials are servants of the people; (4) Public officials should be the embodiment of all public virtues i.e. they should be qualified, honest, hardworking, impartial, wise, just, trustworthy, responsible and their conduct should be irreproachable; (5) Appointment to public office should be based on merit, not on privilege or discrimination; (6) Public officials should perform their duties efficiently and economically and guard against corrupt practices.

(c) Fostering of Public Service Codes of Ethics

Codes of right official conduct which have been established in many countries are remarkably similar. A list is provided below regarding public service laws. Nearly every country has an anti-corruption department, but complains of its inherent inadequacy, first, because of the prevailing climate of corruption in the society, the department itself becomes corrupt, and second, such a department tends to be ill-equipped for thorough and rigorous investigation. Perhaps the single greatest advantage of a code of conduct is the measure of certainty it provides as to the standards of ethical conduct expected from civil servants.

In 1978, International Association of Schools and Institutes of Administration (IASIA) established a code of Public Service Ethics for guidance to member countries. Since then it has been subjected to considerable debate. "Since the roles of public servants are too diverse and varied to allow any one code to be applicable to all to serve any purpose, a code should be as role-specific as possible while allowing for flexibility in order to serve as an instrument of control over administrative action." (Caiden, op. cit)

(d) Fostering of Public Service Ethics Education and Training

As public administration Schools and Institutes vary widely in their purposes and arrangements, the study of public service values and ethics has different applications in different countries. Yet, the IASIA has discovered substantial international agreement that private gains in the public service should not be pursued at the cost of public interest. During the last two decades, the IASIA has emphasised the need for the inclusion of values and ethics in education and training programmes for public managers. Despite the plea for cultural distinctness and maintenance of traditional institutes and moves, the majority of association members maintain that the IASIA should propose international public management training standards for values and ethics. The adopted standards include :

(a) Instruction in a governmental system which fosters and protects the responsiveness and accountability of public servants to direction and control by the public through its representatives;

(b) Instruction in a system of public communications which fosters citizen understanding of and participation in the process of governance;

(c) Instruction in the purposes and limitations of government as an institution for fostering economic and social progress and cultural values; and

(d) Instruction in the rights, obligations and responsibilities of individuals and groups within the social and political systems (Dwivedi and Englebert, 1983).

The IASIA's Ethics Working Groups offer an ongoing unique international forum for dialogue about bureaucratic ethical standards including systemic corruption. According to the IASIA, instruction of public administrator should include :

a) The prevailing system of laws, regulations and practices governing the conduct of all public officials and employees

(b) Standards of conduct which prohibit the use of public office for self interest or private gain or for improperly giving preferential treatment or disclosure of confidential information;

(c) Standards of conduct embodying respect, fairness and justice by public officials and employees in their individual and group relationships and in their contacts with the public;

(d) Modes of behaviour by public officials and employees which reflect the need for responsiveness and loyalty to professional colleagues and for the support of legitimately established governmental and departmental policies and programmes within a framework of conscientious observance of established rules and procedures ensuring that public resources are utilized in an effective and efficient manner. (Dwivedi, op. cit).

An attempt has been made for presenting a close study of corruption identifying specific corruption contexts and the strategies adopted for sustaining it. This is intended not to foreclose other possibilities of theorising but to sensitize theorists to undertake studies with suitable alterations.

REFERENCES

1. Arlucchi, P. : 'Corruption, Organised Crime and Money Laundering World Wide' a Paper Presented in the Fifth International Anti-Corruption Conference. Amsterdam. 1992.

2. Arora Dolly, Conceptualising the Context and Contextualising the Concept : Corruption Reconsidered' in *Indian Journal of Public Administration,* Volume XXXIX, No. 1, 1993.
3. Bailey Stephen K. 'Ethics and Public Services' in Stillman ed. *Public Administration : Concept and Cases,* Houghton Mifflin, Boston, 1986.
4. Caiden Gerald E.,*Handbook of Administrative Ethics,* Mercel Dekker, New York, 1994.
5. Caiden Gerald E. and Naomi J. Caidene. "Administrative Corruption Revisited" in *Phillipine Journal of Public Administration,* Volume XXXVIII, No. 1, 1994.
6. Caiden Gerald E. et al. "Further Light on Combating Administrative Corruption" in Ramesh K. Arora's *The Universe of Public Administration,* The Centre for Administrative Change, Jaipur, 1994.
7. Dwivedi, O.P. and Kenneth Kernaghan, *Ethics in Public Service : Comparative Perspective.* Inter Institute of Administrative Services. Brussels. 1983 (Dwivedi and Ernest A. Englebert on "Education and Training for Values and Ethics in Public Service" in the same book).
8. Heidenheimer Arnold J. et al., *"Political Corruption : Readings in Comparative Analysis,* New Brunswick, 1989.
9. Johnston Michael, "The Political Consequences of Corruption : A Reassessment" in *Comparative Politics,* Volume 18, No. 4, 1986.
10. Krislov Samuel, *Representative Bureaucracy.* Englewood Cliffs. N.J., 1974.
11. Lelyveld Joseph, Calcutta The Perennial Press, Hongkong, 1975.
12. Mallick Ross, Development Policy of a Communist Government : West Bengal since 1977, Cambridge University Press, 1993.
13. Marican Y. Marsoon, Bureaucratic Power in India and Japan in *Philippine Journal of Public Administration.*
14. Mellow C., *The Wages of Sin.* CEO. International Strategies, 1991.
15. Myrdal Gunnar, *Asian Drama, An Enquiry into the Poverty of Nations :* Vol. II, New York, 1968.
16. Nye J.S., "Corruption and Political Development : A Cost Benefit Analysis" in A.J Heidenheimar et al., *Political Corruption,* Transaction Books, New Brunswick, N.J., 1989.
17. Scott J.C., *Comparative Political Corruption,* Prentice Hall, Englewood Cliff, N.J., 1972.
18. Wright Maurice, The Professional Conduct of Civil Servants in *Philippine Journal Administration,* Volume 51, Spring 1973.
19. Webster Neil, *The Panchayati Raj in West Bengal,* Bagchi, Calcutta, 1992.

22

Administrative Corruption: Its Causes and Effects on Socio-Economic Development—The Case of Tanzania

N.J. Sola

Abstract

"In all governments, rich and poor, capitalist or socialist, the problem of misuse of public funds is a serious one. It is confined not to one level of government but transcends all levels from the centre to the local, down to the village level" (*The Times*, January 11, 1986). This article is an attempt to discuss the problem of corruption within the context of Tanzania by looking at the possible causes, the forms and effects to the achievement of socio-economic development. The article also briefly discusses the attempts made by the government to curb the problem and concludes by suggesting strategies that could be used to minimize it.

Introduction

The pressure mounted by the international donor community on developing countries to improve their governance is not unfounded. Evidence has shown that efforts made by these countries to revive their economies cannot succeed because, among other things, of bad management and corruption. Certainly as *The Times* puts it, corruption is common place everywhere but the pace and degree at which it has been spreading its tentacles in the developing countries has drawn the concern not only of the international donor community but governments of developing countries as well. In Tanzania, the problem reached a critical condition in the 1970's prompting the formation of the anti-corruption squad and formulation of laws to deal with it. This as it seems, has proved to be a failure as evidenced by the recent move by the government to form a special committee to investigate the leaders alleged to be corrupt.

Defining Corruption

Because of global social and economic diversities, it is difficult to give a definition of corruption that will fit universally. What one community might see as a normal practice, to others it might be a corrupt practice. Nye's definition quoted in Heidenheimer (1970:5), describes corruption as, "...behaviour which deviates from normal duties of public role because of private regarding...pecuniary or status gains, or violate rules against the exercise of certain types of private regarding influence. This includes such behaviour as bribery,...nepotism,...and misappropriation..."

Others describe corruption as, "Illegal or unethical use of governmental authority as a result of consideration of personal or political gains" (Benson, 1978) "Illegal use of organizational power for personal gains" (Sherman, 1978). However since this article focuses on bureaucratic corruption, we could simply describe it as the abuse of authority by a civil servant or government employee for attaining private gains. It manifests itself in various forms such as the embezzlement of public funds, fraud, nepotism, theft, misrepresentation, to mention but a few.

Causes and Types of Corruption

Although it is argued that corruption exists in all the countries, causes might not be the same. If we agree that the problem is a creation of the social, economic and political conditions prevailing in a country then we must also agree that different social, economic and political systems create different types of corruption. It is not within the scope of this article to discuss in depth the causes and types of corruption but we may agree with Klaveren (1970) that it is caused by human weaknesses. That, its root lies exclusively in the *apetitus divitiarium infinitus* or the insatiable avarice. This weakness which is common to all human beings can be revealed by the individual when provided with opportunities to conduct vice or when there is no effective mechanism for checking on individual behaviour.

Corruption can be of different types. These types are classified according to the kind of people who are involved in it, as well as the level of its spread in society. In this case one might talk of political corruption if it is the politicians who are involved or administrative or bureaucratic corruption if those involved are bureaucrats/administrators. Similarly, when there is a deviation by a handful public employes from their normal duties and roles because of private gains, we may term this as "individual corruption". At least at this level, it is still easy to control. But when corrupt practices become part and parcel of life in any society, it becomes difficult to control. When it reaches such an advanced stage, it no longer becomes "individual" but "systemic". This is best described by Caiden (1977) as, "Deviant conduct which is so institutionalized that dysfunction is actually protected." Unlike individual corruption, this type is difficult to control and poses a threat to the social, political and economic well-being of a nation.

The Tanzania Experience

Like in many other developing countries, corruption in Tanzania can be described as "systemic." It is a behaviour elaborately rationalized by those who practice it. Those responsible for ensuring that employees' adherence to established norms and professional code of conduct express their concern not because of necessarily seeing corruption as an evil but, mostly because of external pressure. Very few seem committed to fighting this evil and to make matters worse, they lack the support of the ruling party and government. No wonder there is a twist in meaning of several acronyms used for the various bureaucratic institutions/agencies and the new vocabulary pejoratively used to refer to the behaviour of government officials is emerging. For example SU an acronym for Shirika La Umma (a para-statal organisation) is nicknamed Shirika La Ulaji or meaning an organization where people can achieve individual gains; ST (government of Tanzania) Serikali Tajiri, a mockery meaning the government is rich; CCM (Chama Cha Mapinduzi— the ruling party) nicknamed Chukua Chako Mapema meaning take what is yours while early. New vocabulary that has sprung out with the escalating level of corruption includes among others Mtukula, Chai, Chau Chau, Mlungula, Ulanguzi etc. This is a reflection on people's experience of the decline in moral values of those charged with the responsibility of running the government.

On tracing the causes and nature of administrative corruption in Tanzania, one has to look at the trends in the economic and political development of the country and their effects on the country's bureaucratic structures. In the 1960s and early 1970s, corruption among government employees did exist but not at such an alarming state as it is today. By then, one might argue, the type of corruption that existed was "individual" corruption. The situation started to worsen after the Arusha Declaration and as the economy started to plunge into decline, these provided opportunities to those in power and those with the means to practice it.

Bureaucratic institutions created before and after the Arusha became manned by political appointees characterized by personality relations rather than devoted responsibility and ability. With this, the politicians could intervene in the decisions to determine who should be hired or fired, who should be promoted or demoted, where contracts should be awarded, how the resources should be utilized etc. This in turn, resulted into having bureaucracy suffering from the problem of personalization, incompetency/inefficiency and corruption. As Staudt (1991) observes, "Patronage based recruitment foster rapid growth in public employment and can result in a costly, blasted bureaucracy filled with excess incompetents."

When these incompetent political appointees muddle in one organization, often the best the government does is to transfer them to other organizations, in many cases in their same capacity and sometimes with extra responsibility/promotion. This is an undeniable reality that one must not feel inhibited to point out. What would one conclude when the President defends a decision not to fire a senior government officer who had squandered worth millions of government money simply because he feels sympathetic towards the officer's family? How can one person with limited educational background serve in more than four management boards or be retained for some years after retirement? In one of the BBC interviews, one ex-government official was asked this question and he being on the defensive, argued that experience is the determining factor. If experience was the criterion used, hopefully no concern would have been raised about the way government agencies are run. The crux of the matter is as Hope (1985) pinpoints that the bureaucracy has been politicized and "With the politicization of the bureaucracy... has come bureaucratic corruption" (Quoted in Agarah, 1990:28). This is the outcome of political rationality undermining technical rationality.

The government has until recently continued to give financial support (subsidy) to organizations even when there have been allegations or evidence of incompetence and corruption. The best the government does is the selection of probe committees whose constitution does not follow any stipulated criteria. For instance, if there are allegations levelled against the management of a government agency, a probe committee is usually formed. Occasionally some members of these committees are drawn from among members of the governing bodies of the organizations to be probed. It is difficult therefore, to comprehend the inclusion of such members as they might defend the management so long as they have some vested interests. Again, since patronage dictates the selection, the inclusion of incompetent, biased and corrupt elements is inevitable. Consequently, the probes are not thoroughly carried out, take long time to end and of course consume lots of financial resources. Moreover, most findings of the probe committees are either made secretive or shelved, altogether in a bid to arson to the offices of the Bank of Tanzania, the Ministry for Home Affairs and the Ministry for Land and Urban Development. If the findings come out, majority of them defend the management against the allegations and even when the allegations are proved to be right, it takes the government long to take action and in most cases the action taken involves transfer, forced retirement or any other such lenient punishment. This practice of showing leniency, makes the government look weak and therefore encourages those involved in corruption and others to think that getting involved in such vice is worth risking.

The economic decline that started in the late 1970s intensified the problem. Memories still linger on peoples' minds, of the period of scarcity and hiking of prices of almost all essential commodities. The period when one arriving home from abroad had to bribe a customs officer to be allowed in three pieces of toilet soap and some toothpaste! When one had to offer a drink to an employee of the Regional Trading Company (RTC) to get a kilo of sugar, or bribe the district trading officer to get a permit to buy rice from the National Milling Corporation for a wedding or Christmas function!. The escalating prices of the scarce commodities and the stagnation of workers' salaries could not enable the survival of the wage earner. Consequently, many had to look for alternate means to supplement their meagre income. Looting and selling of public property, demanding bribes for the free services, involvement in dubious dealings, poor attendance at work, non-compliance of professional ethics, job procedures and regulations became a common behaviour of most government bureaucrats. There are some people who argue that the Arusha Declaration is the one that led the government to become oblivious to the welfare of its employees, therefore exposing them to temptation of corruption, embezzlement of public funds and abuse of power (*Sunday News*, October 10, 1993).

Besides, the bureaucratic procedures, rules and regulations used in many government offices as means of control provide the opportunity for corruption. For instance, import taxes are so high and the procedures to follow to claim one's goods released are very tedious. It should not be forgotten that the higher the taxes are set the more likely it is that people will try to avoid it. As one article in the *Daily News* of October 13, 1994, pinpoints, "One of the most fertile areas for corruptive practice is the tax system because the process of tax assessment and payment presents ideal and multiple temptation for fraud and embezzlement". It further went on to note that "...the more complicated the tax system, the greater are the chances of corruption." The procedures used for clearing goods imported from outside the country for example, are so unnecessarily complicated that one is tempted to bribe to have them out through the back door. The notorious "long room" (customs house) is a case in point. Those who have had goods or articles from abroad will still remember the hurdles they had to endure to have them cleared. Undoubtedly, some regulations and procedures are devised less from altruism than from bad intentions.

In Tanzania, administrative corruption exists in several forms and is difficult to list them all in this article. However, a few are worth mentioning.

(i) Bribing so as to Achieve a Personal Goal or Demanding for Payment

The goals range from receiving a would be free service to those services that one has to pay for. Examples, bribing to get employment, to win a tender, to pass an exam, to go for training, to get promotion, to pay less or evade paying income/import tax, to get a driving license, to get tax exemption etc. The payment can be in kind or in cash. Normally it is the government official who solicits or directly or indirectly makes the demand, or someone with the financial power who lures and bribes an official to get whatever is desired without adhering to procedures. For example, the chronic problem of tax evasion is said to be resulting from collusion between businessmen and unscrupulous customs officials (*Daily News*, November 3, 1991; January 18, 1992). Another example is that of senior officers at the prisons headquarters who are alleged to have been demanding 15 per cent from tenderers as a condition for payment for groceries supplied to prisons (*Daily News*, Friday, July 23, 1993).

(ii) Fraudulent Spending of Public Funds

This takes various forms such as paying salary to non-existing workers (ghost workers), spending money on non-existing projects or services, making claims for assignments not undertaken or double claims for undertaken assignments, inflating figures on money spent on various projects or official activities, dubious purchases, unvouched expenditure and many others. At least on every other day there is a heading in one of the local newspaper reporting vices such as, **"418m/=Embezzled; 12 Bn,/=Lost in Dubious Payment; Education Ministry Embezzled 300m/=; 44bn/=in mess up"** (*Daily News*, Friday, November 18,19 & 21, 1994). This means the salaries paid to these non-existing workers were being pocketed by individuals. Phony quotations of prices of commodities bought by government departments or ministries is a common practice. For example, it was recently reported that most secondary schools in the country have spurious outstanding debts for money spent on food. The price quotations made for certain items whether bought or not are derisive. One banana @ Tsh 500, a kilogram of vegetables (mchicha) @ 3,000!

(iii) Fraudulent Use and Plundering or Sabotage of Public Property

Most public property in Tanzania is deceitfully used by government employees. This ranges from the selling of office equipment or machinery, stationery and other supplies to using them for purposes other than the intended ones and without permission. It is common, for example, to find a government vehicle being used to supply or ferry building material to a private building site either owned by a government official or a businessman. If the owner is a businessman the money paid is pocketed either by the driver or his superior depending on who masterminds the dubious mission. Fradulent use of public property also includes sabotaging, commandering and/or taking as private what is supposed to be the public property. For example, the transfer of drugs from a government hospital by a hospital worker to his privately owned chemist shop or the transfer of building materials intended for building a public clinic, health centres or primary school to build a private house. In many organizations the maintenance units or building and estates departments are sabotaged because tendering out the maintenance function is a lucrative activity to the officials.

(iv) Hiding and Destroying Information and, Averting Responsibility

The disappearance of documents from government offices is a common practice. Often important government documents have been destroyed on the pretext of electrical fire faults (the case of the Ministry for Home Affairs and the Ministry for Land and Urban Development), and others have disappeared under mysterious circumstances. Headlines such as "Tax exemption papers untraceable" feature often in the local dailies. Instances of case files in courts of law and personal files in registry offices disappearing are not something new either. A registry clerk hides a personal file so as to solicit bribe from the person looking for it. Here the person will be someone making a claim for say a transfer, leave pay, etc. If one wants to see the "boss" manager, personnel officer etc. for official reasons, one has to arrange with the secretary first. At least one should expect answers such as "He is busy; Come tomorrow; He is not in," from the secretary, but if one gives the secretary a "tip" there will be no such answers.

There is a saying that to get quick service in a public office one has to put on a "long sleeved shirt" meaning you can not get a service if you are stingy "Mkono mtupu haulambwi", literally meaning, "an empty hand can not be licked". What it all means is that one has to part with something to be attended to even if the service is free. The government employee will try to use every means possible to get paid illegally. For example, cashier may decide not to write cheques on the pretext that there are other things that will include the person being attended to part with something or promise to do so. In the case of courts of law files are lost or evidence tempered with as long as the defendant or plaintiff is ready to pay.

(iv) Nepotism, Regionalism, Ethnicity and Religious Considerations

The problems of nepotism, regionalism and ethnicity are very common practice in hiring, placing, training and executing other related personnel function. Complaints of selection, promotion and training of employees based on where one comes from or who is who to who are very common. This has given rise to an assumption in many people that one has to have a "godfather" if one is to succeed in getting a job or else one has to bribe to achieve a desired goal. Perhaps nepotism is the result of the extended family problem where as in the African tradition and culture one is expected to help members of his or her family or relatives whenever he or she has the opportunity to do so. This is taken to be an obligation and failure to do so normally results into being blamed or even being considered as of no use to the community. Staudt (1991 : 90 op. cit) puts it that, "Ties of kinship, affection, etc. determine access to favours of power holders". Consequently, one is forced to do everything possible to make sure that a relative gets "fixed" somewhere no matter what qualifications, experience and ability one has. Of late, there have been some undocumented complaints of appointments being made not on merit but on religious background of the individual. However true this is, the problem might not be considered as very serious.

Effects of Corruption

The effects of corruption in Tanzania can easily be seen by anybody, Tanzanian or non-Tanzanian. Nobody will refute the fact that self-interest in maintaining power and privilege has led to a situation where bureaucrats corner most of the nation's resources to themselves. Facts speak for themselves. A visit to many urban centres, particularly the so-called low density posh areas today will reveal some of the most exquisite buildings one can think of. (We are not suggesting here that people should not live in decent houses). Ask the owner how much he/she earns per month and you will get the surprise of the year. You will even be more surprised to learn that the building was completed in less than a period of one year. Where does the money come from? Obviously this is the tax payer's money! Now, therefore, one of the effects of corruption is the diversion of public resources to the private.

In addition, corruption widens the social division as only those who can afford to bribe, benefit. This is the case, for example, of the problem of tax evasion where Asians benefit more compared to indigenous Tanzanians because of the former's financial ability. The social division is also widened by the fact that it is only the few who are involved in corruption that can lead decent life and/or survive the hardships caused by the economic decline. These are the ones who live on the sweat of the poor tax payers and send their kids to study abroad or to international schools.

We could also link the increase in crime with the increased level of corruption. Let us ask ourselves a few questions. What happens to today's school and/or college leavers from poor families in a situation where freezes on employment are now inevitable? They do not have "godfathers", nor do they have the money to bribe so as to be employed. What about the employee who has neither a "godfather" nor the ability to bribe so as not to be included in the list of employees to be retrenched or be readmitted into the service clandestinely? No doubt these people will do anything possible to make both ends meet. They cannot bribe but at least they can be involved in other criminal activities as an alternative So increased crime rate could be taken as an effect of corruption.

Corruption affects the performance of any organization making it impossible to attain the set goals or objectives. This is so because it normally results into administrative inefficiency. Caiden (op. cit) argues that, "Corruption acts as a brake on organizational change by preventing policy changes, blocking administrative reform, increasing resentment among certain groups and may foment unrest." For example, it is difficult to envisage success in achieving the objectives of the ongoing administrative and economic reforms. How can the economic reforms succeed while the principles governing the reforms are being violated? How can the government maintain an efficient and productive civil service or workforce, while the retrenchment exercise has always been conducted subjectively? Moreover, the criteria used and the employee performance review systems provide opportunities for corruption. That is why there have been many complaints from the employees. For this reason, some members of the international donor community have decided to withhold their promised financial aid. More to this is the fact that the image of the country is tarnished.

Of late, Tanzania has been witnessing friction between employees and management in several work places. There have been cases where the managements have been locked into or out of their offices (management lockouts), like in the Kilimanjaro Tools. The Dares-Salaam Group, Morogoro Canvas, and many others. In most of these cases the managements are alleged of being corrupt. We have also been witnessing the public taking the law into their hands. For example, thieves being subjected to mob justice. At Mnazi Mmoja in Dar es-Salaam the public pulled down the material fencing of a construction site to an illegally acquired piece of land. At Kibasila in the same city, students destroyed bricks, property of one businessman who was illegally given permit to operate his business on the school premises. (The Ministry for Lands and Urban Development is one of the most notorious ministries with the most corrupt employees). After the Kibasila incident, the president while condemning the current trend of invading school or institutions premises for individual gains also concurred that plot misallocation was one of the causes of social disruption and distrust among the public (*Daily News*, November 17, 1994). The question to ask is why are all these things happening and what is their effect? The answer is obvious. Public trust has been eroded and this is another effect of corruption. Their confidence in national leaders and government agencies has decreased and so is their cooperation. This might culminate into serious social disruption that will be beyond State control. We have to remember that "Where there is smoke, there must be hidden fire."

Corruption can also discourage investment and enterprise. People with the entrepreneurial skills and ability find it expensive to go around bribing so as to win a permit or a trading license or operating business in an atmosphere of uncertainty. This in turn might have an effect on the national economy. The possibility is that the few investors we have so far might have decided to do so because of the opportunity they see of surviving through corrupt means and reaping the wealth of this country.

5.0 Efforts Made by the Government to Curb Corruption

Measures taken by the government to check on the problem of corruption came into force from the time of independence. For example, there is the leadership code that restricts political leaders and also government employees from engaging in dubious activities.

A section of this code that has been amended, prohibits public officers from engaging in extra income generating activities such as owning a company, guest house or hotel, being double employed, or owning shares in a private company. In this respect, the leadership code covers both the political and administrative leaders. The fact is that before the introduction of multiparty democracy, party scrutiny has played a significant role in determining the advancement of the individual at the workplace.

Later in the 1970s as mentioned in the introductory part, the government established the anti-corruption squad. This squad was created following the establishment of the Prevention of Corruption Ordinance of 1970. This Ordinance covered public officers in the general sense in that it included members of the national assembly, members of local authorities and government employees. It authorized the Director of Public Prosecution through police officers of the rank of superintendent and above to search any person suspected to be in possession of property acquired by corrupt means.

As the economy continued to decline, corruption increased and economic sabotage started taking its toll. This prompted the government to establish yet another Act, the Economic Sabotage Act of 1983, later amended to Economic and Organized Crime Control Act of 1987. For example, in outlining the Economic Recovery Strategy in February 1983, the then Prime Minister announced major steps to be taken. These included among others to "Ensure that all economic saboteurs are eliminated and that every person lives on his or her own sweat. The government was not to tolerate a person or group of persons living through racketeering" (*Daily News,* Monday, February 28, 1983). People thought to be involved in activities violating foreign exchange control, causing loss to government or para-statal organization, trade conduct that violated the laws governing trade, price regulations or any conduct violating the laws preventing corruption, were treated as economic saboteurs. A special tribunal was formed to deal with cases of suspects of economic sabotage and racketeering. In one of its hearings for example, a manager with one of the Regional Trading Companies (RTCs) was alleged to have sold an electricity generator to himself at a cost of Tshs 29,000 instead of Tshs 40,643 (*Daily News, Monday,* May 30, 1983). With the above, the mass-media specifically the radio started a special programme to sensitize and educate the public; a programme that is still being aired.

Important to note however is that, despite the government's declaration of war against this evil, the pace with which the war started slowed over the period of time. Worse still, those who were assigned this noble task took it as a golden opportunity to make themselves rich. In other words, those organs entrusted to fight corruption, became the most corrupt. Corruption therefore did not decrease; on the contrary it increased. Proof to this is the recent move by The President to form a team to tackle corruption. This team or committee is given powers to question government leaders suspected to be corrupt or involved in squandering public funds. No doubt such a move signifies the failure of earlier efforts to curb the problem. Tanzanians are also not convinced that the move will bear any promising results.

6.0 What Needs to be Done

Combating administrative corruption in Tanzania has proved difficult because of the influence of politics on public administration. Consequently there is now little respect for official rules and the law. Political considerations have been the criteria for appointing civil servants to man government ministry, departments and other state organizations. The result is incompetence and immorality, by public administrators. To make matters worse, the law enforcing organs like the judiciary and the police are all involved in this wicked behaviour.

Fight against corruption cannot succeed unless the government does something to change the system under which it has been operating particularly in the area of public administration. The bureaucracy has to be depoliticized and be left with the authority and power to operate according to the requirements of the professions. Sometimes administrators fail to discharge their responsibilities because of political interference. The success or failure of government depends upon the efficiency of public administration but, public administration can not be efficient if it is interfered with or forced to act contrary to laid down procedures.

Simultaneously, the welfare of employees has to be taken care of. The need for a realistic salary structure is obvious. Conditions of extreme inequalities, absolute poverty and widespread lack of basic needs satisfaction are enough incentives to corrupt employees

(Blunt and Popoola, 1985). The basic salary of majority of Tanzanians is hardly enough to enable them to survive for a week despite efforts by the government to increase it. The problem of administrative corruption will persist unless what they earn is enough for meeting their basic requirements.

Screening of top civil servants before being appointed to head ministries or government departments should also be given priority. Certainly, there is some screening but such screening has been based on the loyalty of the employees' job ability and potential. Equally important is the employees' command of moral authority. This is important since the situation in which our public administrators operate today, depicts a culture that is tolerant of unethical behaviour, a culture in which the bureaucratic virtues of specialization, expertise, neutrality and efficiency have eroded, and this is detrimental to good governance.

Lastly, commitment of the politician is of paramount importance. However, this can only be possible when the political leadership has emancipated from all forms of debauchery including the problem of evading procedures so as to procure appointments for their followers. The fight against corruption therefore, should start by removing all corrupt political leaders. This so far has proved to be difficult because of lack of accountability and transparency by the national leaders. The fight should be waged by indiscriminately punishing the guilty. Corrupt leaders are known to the public but the problem has always been the system of harbouring evil doers by the top leadership. However, with mounting pressure from the public and the international community, there is optimism for transparency and responsibility by the political leaders.

REFERENCES

1. Agarah, T., "Checks and Balances of Bureaucratic Excess and Corruption in Nigeria: An Assessment of the Public Complaints Commission" in *African Administrative Studies,* No. 35, 1990.
2. Banfield, E., "Corruption as a Feature of Governmental Organizations" in M. Ekpo. ed. *Bureaucratic Corruption,* 1979, : 75-99.
3. Bayley, D., "The Effects of Corruption in a Developing Nation" in, Heidenheimer ed. *Political Corruption: Readings in Comparative Analysis.* Holf, New York, 1970, : 521-33.
4. Benson, G., *Political Corruption in America,* Lexington Book, 1978.
5. Blunt, P. and O.Popoola, *Personnel Management in Africa,* Longman, London, 1985.

6. Caiden, G.E. and N.J. Caiden. "Administrative Corruption" in *Public Administration Review,* No. 37, 1977, pp. 3:01-9.

7. *Daily News,* February 28, May 30, 1983, 1992, 1993 and 1994.

8. Sherman, L., *Scandal and Reform : Controlling Police Corruption,* Barkeley, California University Press, 1978.

9. Soal, A., "Bureaucratic Corruption in Nigeria : The Continuing Search for Causes and Cures", in *International Review of Administrative Science,* No. 1.

10. Staudt, K., *Managing Development : State, Society and International Context,* Sage Publications, London, 1991.

11. Mzalendo, and Uhuru, October and November, 1994.

12. *Sunday News,* 1991/1992/1993 and 1994.

13. *The Express,* September 22-24, 1994.

14. *The Family Mirror,* June, 1994.

23

Role of Ethics in Public Administration

Alka Dhameja

Introduction

In the post-independence period, India has taken giant strides in pursuit of its Constitutional goals of social justice, equality and economic development. The public administrative set-up of the country has served as an important instrument in this process. However, over the period of time, its functioning has witnessed many deviations from the defined ethical path. Much has been asserted time and again regarding the need for administrative ethics. From the Mundhra scandal of 1957 to the more recent security, fodder, housing and hawala scams, our politicians have simply had their hands full. The rising political corruption and its nexus with criminals has been intricately linked with administrative malpractices. The articles and write-ups on 'ethics and public administration' have generally thrown light on various reasons for unethical activities and proposed different forms of remedies to combat them. Corruption has often been projected as the most visible form of unethical conduct and the so-called forte of the political and permanent executive, quite oblivious to the fact that this growing menace has manifested itself far and wide in almost every profession, the non-governmental and the other para-statal bodies are also not insulated from it. It is too early to comment that the process of liberalisation would change the scenario for the better, because as we expand globally and open our doors to the multinational corporations and other types of foreign capital, the virus of venality might just get even more opportunities to feed on.

In this changing ambience, when we talk of ethics we cannot help but talk of the maladies of corruption, favouritism, flouting of rules and role of vigilance committees. Though the indispensability of these factors to this topic cannot be overlooked, we would just cursorily address these issues and try to deal with the problem in a different perspective. The role of public administration has become complex and all-pervasive, administrators are constantly engaged in making policies and solving conflict situations at different levels of hierarchy in order to cope with the increasing demands and expectations of the target groups. Emphasis is therefore needed on those aspects of ethical guidelines that could provide the administrators, especially the bureaucrats, some assistance in identifying a problem, choosing an alternative and implementing the best course of decision. Our service conduct rules lay stress on penalties and punishments for different aberrations and departures from the underlined guidelines but disregard the pertinence of the factors that lead to such situations.

It is essential that administrators are familiar with the process of ethical decision-making: they should know how to handle a problem situation, the role of facts and values in solving them and recognise the ways of protecting themselves from extraneous pressures, identifying alternatives and projecting consequences. 'What should not be done' needs to be replaced by 'what should be done' in different work situations. Though no ethical code can provide answers for every decisional dilemma, it could give a broad outline of what would be the best possible way of dealing with them through instances and examples based on past experiences and established conventions. Thus, without getting into the debate on the causes and remedies with regard to corrupt practices, let us concentrate on the need for evolution of an ethical code of conduct that would help in dealing with the ambiguities that arise because of obsolete rules and contradictory guidelines.

The types of unethical activities, universally recognised, are bribery, nepotism, graft, patronage, influence peddling, use of official property, documents or position for private gains, non-adherence to official rules etc. The service conduct rules of administrators prohibit them from indulging in these activities through their various sections and clauses. It is often assumed that administrative personnel who do not involve themselves in these activities are the ethical ones. These conduct rules only talk of the 'Don'ts' and not so much about the 'Do s', they do not speak of any behavioural norm that can be followed at the time of conflict and indecision. (Dwivedi, 1978). Major part of the service rules book deals with classification of posts, conditions of service, penalties, appellate authorities and forms of appeal etc. Provisions of 'choice' and 'option' in cases of decisional dilemmas do not receive any mention. This may create chaos in the day to day functioning of public administration and give rise to situations that are not easily comprehensible.

Some Ethical Dilemmas

O.P. Dwivedi raises several fundamental questions that can arise out of unclear conduct norms. He calls them ethical dilemmas. These are :

1. What favours are acceptable without being considered discourteous and rude. Should any and all kinds of gifts and hospitality be avoided? or should it be limited to a specified minimum? If so, what should be that minimum?
2. Is a public servant only a public servant during office hours? or ethical norms should be practiced outside office hours also?
3. Should the public servants interpret policies and programmes according to their individual perceptions of right and wrong or should they only adhere to the values of the institutions they are serving?
4. What should the public servants do if their personal honesty and integrity appear to be out of place in their work environment?

Absence of clear-cut guidelines could lead to some more problems such as :

(a) Should every kind of favour extended to a friend or relative be considered unethical? There are various conditions that transform a gift into a bribe. In a system that tends towards ascriptive rather than achievement-oriented pattern of working, favours from people of the same caste or region are not considered unethical by anyone.

(b) What if the public servants are forced to indulge in unethical behaviour because of stringent rules and procedures of the organisation? At times, bypassing the rules becomes very essential.

(c) Sometimes political pressures, legal guidelines, tight deadlines, media exposure and expectations of the people who are directly affected by the policies force the administrators to overlook ethical norms, too many pressures can interfere with administrative demands of efficiency and quick results.

The service conduct rules were made years back and cannot provide solutions to the above mentioned conflict situations. The nature of public administration has changed beyond recognition and so has the definition of ethics. What is now required is a serious updating of these service rules and guidelines in the backdrop of the changes in order to provide some answers to these very important questions. Bureaucrats are often perturbed over the growing politicisation of administration, manipulation of their promotion avenues and transfers by the politicians whereas the politicians allege over-bureaucratisation of the system. The first step in the direction of solving these problems would be a clarification of the role and the mandate of the administrators vis-a-vis those who come in direct contact with them.

Changing Role of Public Administrators

Public administration is no longer concerned with just implementation and monitoring of government policies, it cannot be expected to take neutral stands on the issues that confront development programmes and policies. The legacy of anonymity, neutrality and commitment to the rigidities of administrative regulations and the party in power is slowly being relegated to the background. Administration is now beginning to focus more on innovativeness, new concepts of problem-solving and effective citizen-administration interaction. Today's administrator has to skilfully anticipate policy needs, identify choices and alternatives and decide on the instrument of implementation and monitoring. Different organisational sub-cultures are emerging, administrators are experimenting with various ways of doing a particular task. There is no one organisational culture or one best way of performing a task. The administrators have vast discretionary powers that call for fair utilisation, moreover the influence of private corporate sector in the areas that were hitherto in the domain of public administration is forcing them to lay more emphasis on flexible procedures, qualities of decisiveness, self-regulation, answerability and achievement-orientedness. Administrator's behaviour that entails personal choice, biases, values, likes, dislikes and capacity for reasoning should now play a distinct role in tackling decisional dilemmas.

Max Weber made a clear distinction between the 'private' and 'official' life of a bureaucrat. He stressed that bureaucrats were personally free in the sense that they were subjected to legal rational authority with respect to their impersonal official obligations. The heads of departments in the civil service would normally have a clear schedule of duties for which they were responsible and this would normally exclude activities outside those listed (Wallis, 1989). This view was later refuted by thinkers such as Robert Merton, Elton Mayo, Peter Blau and others. Administrative behaviour received a different treatment at the hands of Chester Barnard, Chris Argyris, Rensis Likert, Doughlas Mcgregor and other socio-psychologists. Behaviouralists like Herbert Simon also dealt with decision-making and problem-solving functions of the administrators at length, in fact, administrative behaviour remained an area of serious research till 1980s, yet, clear-cut guidelines for administrative functioning have not been able to emerge. The recommendations of Reform Committees have also not been sincerely implemented. Ethical performance, thus, has to be seen in the present context. It must now assume wider connotations.

Defining Ethics and Ethical Behaviour

It is true that we cannot coin a definition of ethical performance in public administration that could be uniformly applied and enforced. It is also difficult to set standards for judging what is ethical and what is not, although a laid down list of unethical activities is already available for reference. We even subscribe to the view that morality and ethics are relative terms. Still, a responsible public administration is imperative for any democratic set up and it should include ethical functioning. We cannot simply bifurcate the two by saying that ethics deals with morals and values while public administration is about actions and decisions. A broad definition of ethics would be 'A systematic enquiry into human conduct in order to discover both the rules that ought to govern our actions and the goals we should seek in life' (Johnson, 1984). In other words, ethics aims at developing the standards for human conduct. According to Terry L. Cooper, "Ethics involves substantive reasoning about obligations, consequences and ultimate ends" (as quoted in Denhardt, 1988). Though ethics is the science of morals, a theoretical examination of morality, it is not just confined to the right rules of conduct, now it is widely being associated with professional standards rather than being merely debated at a philosophical plane. The different ideas on ethics can help define administration if concentration is shifted to meaningful research.

In public administration, ethics focuses on how the public administrator should question and reflect in order to be able to act responsibly. Ethics requires inquiry and contemplation into truth, that is seeking the right answer to one's question with the help of ethical deliberations, the administrator questions the 'adequacy' and 'meaning' of proposed action in the light of obligations to the organisation as well as to the public. In the words of Gibson Winter, 'Ethical reflection means that ethics looks to the future, it is concerned with the goodness and rightness of a person's doing and making; it is concerned with the constituted social identity only for the sake of the project being constituted, it looks to the past for the sake of the future. It judges the past because the future bears new possibilities' (Jun, 1986).

In order to keep pace with the demands that are being made on public administration, an administrator has to draw a line somewhere between what ought to be allowed and what not. Kathryn G. Denhardt feels that to be ethical, an administrator has to independently engage in the process of :

(i) Examining and questioning the standards in the light of which administrative decisions are made,
(ii) Relating with the social concerns and organisational goals and reflecting a commitment to these goals,
(iii) Adapting to the changes in the environment; and
(iv) Preparing to be held responsible and accountable for the decisions made in the individual and professional capacity.

In the present administrative set up, these type of guidelines governing ethical behaviour are conspicuous by their absence. There is also no mechanism to ensure that the administrators function in a situation that can help them in making appropriate decisions, keeping in view the interests of the people, the environment and the overall objectives of national policies. Such an atmosphere would denote an organisation that can help them in participating in ethical deliberations without being conditioned by external pressures, a workplace which can facilitate conflict resolution by attaching right priorities to the given values and obligations and finally an ambience that can assist them in tackling every type of behaviour and rules deviation without much difficulty. This is very essential if administration has to be made more responsive and accountable.

Issues Confronting Problem-Solving and Decision-Making

Decision-making is a complex task even in a more or less conducive atmosphere. Administrators are faced with new problems and situations every now and then, some of them being routine while other are non-routine. The non-routine situations require designing of effective alternatives and divergent problem-solving so that administrators responsible for making public choices are able to design as many answers as they can. The pattern of problem solving also varies from a reactive to a proactive orientation. In an organisation that is stable and predictable, administrators can afford to be reactive, but in conflict situations, they have to be proactive because in such situations, anticipation of future tasks and creation of viable alternatives becomes essential. As our perceptions influence the process of defining a problem and its content in reality, we also have to think about ways of solving the problem. Our approaches to problem-solving are also related to our values. It has been pointed out that the values may be explicit or implicit and they often manifest in cultural norms and beliefs or psychological needs. Understanding the values of the individuals (read administrators) helps one understand their actions towards problem-solving (Jun. op. cit.).

Multifarious factors affect the values of an administrator which in turn affect his/her problem-solving and decision-making ability. As we all know, public administrators are generally influenced by their country's Constitution, legal norms, organisational rules, ruling party's pressures, caste and family obligations, public interest, exposure to press and time constraints at the time of making policies/decisions. These factors somehow overshadow their own perceptions of right and wrong. There is therefore a need to agree upon a broad framework of guidelines which could assist them in the event of conflict so that they could weigh the pros and cons in each situation and arrive at a solution. Actually, it is not easy to determine as to which values should be given precedence and which ones should be ignored. It is often difficult to establish a straight connection between the facts and the values, sometimes facts and values demand different kinds of response behaviour in specific situations. As has been highlighted, the administrators work in a world of facts and values. There is no bridge between the two elements. Facts are the raw data that serve as the knowledge base for decisions, they just simply exist. Values, on the other hand are always a matter of conflict between individuals or groups. Values are at the core of moral choices. In cases of ethical dilemmas, administrators have to choose between competing and mutually exclusive values (Cooper, 1994).

Application of facts and values to the decision-making process is a very complex exercise. According to David Hume, no 'ought to be' (value) type of conclusion follows directly from an 'is' (fact) type of proposition. He believed that reason could not alone serve as the foundation of morality. Reason is unable to grasp moral differences, such differences engender responses that are felt or sensed. And, while morality by its very nature involves active agents, reason is "perfectly inert" and quite unable to motivate agents to act (Norton, 1993). Immanuel Kant, on the other hand, held that if we think of ourselves solely in empirical terms, we will necessarily think of ourselves as heteronomous, as moved by our desire for this and that and never solely by respect for law. This thought would be debilitating to our efforts to be moral, Kant called this the primacy of practical reason and this reason requires us to accept beliefs that can neither be proven nor disproven theoretically (Guyer, 1992). Thus, irrespective of all objects of the faculty of desire, the action has to be performed. This definitely makes the decision-making process rather complicated, the administrators are moved by their desires, biases, perceptions and attitudes to achieve particular tasks and tend to get influenced by their responses to specific situations, and the codified values, underlined guidelines and the reasoning process may not come in handy in solving problem areas demanding moral decisions. Still, even when it is not possible to arrive at a suitable decision every time, in the words of Herbert Simon (1945), administrators should try at reaching atleast a 'satisficing solution' that is the near best solution if not the best one.

All types of reforms and ethical training should now attempt at making public servants identify decision-making rules, project positive and negative consequences, understand the appropriateness of ethical principles, and their value assumptions and underlying moral basis. Values are always needed to determine whether one condition or fact is better than the other, written guidelines can solve the matters to some extent. C. Wright Mills (1959) observed that it is easy to see that most social issues involve a tangled up mess of factual errors and unclear conceptions as well as an evaluative bias. There is a need to logically untangle these and restate the issues in order to determine what it is that we value most and what are their implications. Herbert Simon also laid emphasis on the dichotomy between facts and values. According to him, each decision involves selection of a relevant goal and a behaviour (value judgement) and its implication (factual judgement) but he concluded that ethical or value laden propositions have admixed within them certain factual elements. He felt that to determine whether a proposition is correct, it must be compared directly with experience or the facts. And again since factual propositions according to him could not be derived from ethical ones by any process of reasoning nor could ethical propositions be compared directly with facts since they asserted the 'oughts', he laid down that it was essential that decision-making process must start with some given ethical premise. For an ethical proposition to be useful in rational decision-making :

(a) The values taken as organisational objectives must be definite, so that their degree of realisation in a situation can be assessed; and
(b) It must be possible to form judgements as to the probability that particular actions will implement these objectives.

Evolving a Code of Conduct

Against this backdrop, it is somewhat tedious to evolve guidelines that could make provisions for dealing with conflict situations. It is widely felt that it is not easy to legislate morality, still a code could help in regulating ethical behaviour by providing greater degree of precision and refinement needed for conduct of administrative matters. It could incorporate provisions that would clearly state standards, help in anticipating problems and developing some broad solutions. There is a need to evolve such a code because without it evaluation of performance becomes difficult, and also since actions of the administrators need to be gauged against certain set standards. Moreover, as many administrative practices and behaviours as possible should be brought under the purview of written laws,; unwritten laws and practices leave much room for arguments, conflicts and manoeuvring. A code of ethics could thus serve as a written standard of behavioural norms. Major characteristics of any code should be :

(i) It must serve as a norm of behaviour according to which fresh entrants could be counselled,

(ii) It must serve as a comprehensible guide for everyday behaviour at the work place, a standard on which sanctions could be based and by which behaviour could be evaluated; and

(iii) It must serve as tool of administrative control. (Denhardt. op.cit).

Administrative culture is an integration of various factors, beliefs, interests, viewpoints of not just the public servants but of all those who come in contact with them. The entire gamut of administrative culture and sub-cultures has to be kept in view while attempting any reforms and evolving any code. Reforms in public administration cannot be effective unless sincere endeavour to revamp each and every rung, level and area of administration is made. In fact, many efforts in the past have gone awry for want of an integrated approach to the problem. It also has to be kept in mind that the administrators join the public service with an already well-defined bent of thinking, attitudes and ideas, they already possess an ethical code. No type of ethical training can erase what they have imbibed in their early years of life. All that can be done is to condition and mould these attitudes in the interest of the organisation and the people they are meant to serve. A systematic code of ethics could be of crucial use in this exercise. Again, it has to be remembered that since every behaviour cannot be codified, a written code would also carry along with it an unwritten code that would include administrator's discretionary domain and people's expectations of it. Moreover a written code might imply that what has not been covered under it is allowed or can be considered ethical, it would also always remain an external disciplining device whereas what is required is an introspective attitude and a desire for 'self-cleansing'.

Some may still argue that a code of ethics would turn out to be just another set of rules like the service conduct rules that many would not even care to read, let alone follow. After all we do have ethical codes for professions like medicine, journalism etc. but not many take them seriously. Standards of ethics are deteriorating day by day, instances of misconduct can be cited from different fields and professions. It has also been felt that we must resist moralising and be practical about accepting moderate levels of immorality in life (Ralph Clark Chandler's views quoted in Terry L. Cooper's Handbook, 1994). In fact, ethical standards of public servants can in no way be divorced from the standards of the society in general. Can we actually have a set of ethical norms and values for administrators which others who come in their contact never think of adhering to? Some may also feel that it is not possible to formulate an everlasting code of ethics since values and norms keep changing with time. It has been observed that if administration is based on a permanent value frame-work, new developments, conflicts and problems will also be judged on the basis of that frame-work, it therefore becomes difficult to apply same set standards of morality on a rapidly changing administrative structure and functions. (Denhardt. op.cit)

Certain moral norms like honesty, truthfulness, discipline, fairness, tolerance, justice etc. are a part of moral order of any society and the code of ethics has to be based on them. To say that it is impossible to agree on a basic moral foundation leaves public servants without any ethical guidance for solving their decisional problems and they become free to operate in a state of confusion, ambiguity and amorality. According to Kathryn Denhardt, the intention is not to evolve some static and never-changing moral standards for all times; while the broad moral order remains the same, the understanding and interpretations of these standards change with time. With every new development, we can neither have a new set of moral standards, nor can we change the broad outline of existing standards, we can only try to adjust the implications of the moral standards with that of new developments.

The problem is further compounded because of the prevalence of various approaches to ethics and evolution of an ethical code. While the deontologists (Kant, Hume, et al) would insist on including all the activities that are performed as a duty, as a principle, as per a universal maxim under what could be defined as ethical behaviour. They believe that moral norm has to be chosen irrespective of the desire to achieve an end. The teleologists on the other hand would like to include all those activities that maximise the good of people, they insist on results and consequences, public interest and utilitarianism being top-most in their priorities. The believers of communitarian ethics do not believe in credibility of universal ethics, they would rather opt for a more local ethics. The ethical relativists detest rigid codification of morals since they believe in 'situationism' and are not in favour of universality of ethical standards. The Anti-foundationalists and the post-modernists are also in the same league but for different reasons, they do not recommend any long-term ethical codes. They believe that such meta-naratives marginalise concepts of difference and otherness (Cooper, op. cit).

Evolving a code of conduct is therefore quite an arduous task. It is just not possible to provide an exhaustive list of what a code must entail. A lot of spadework has to go into the task of formulating a code, the areas it should cover and the norms it must include, and the exercise must be undertaken at the central, state and local levels of the government. The 73rd and 74th Amendments have given extensive powers to the panchayats and urban local bodies but they would not serve any purpose unless they are enforced sincerely as per certain guidelines. In addition to the clear and strict regulations on acceptance of gifts, post-retirement employment restrictions, nepotism, improper use of public property and official powers and the activities already categorised as unethical by our service conduct rules, the new code of ethics should also include :

1. Norms identifying conflicts of interest (in course of administrative processes as well as between administration and other non-government and private sectors).
2. Priorities guiding discussions in cases of conflict and indecision.
3. Areas of commitment, fairness, honesty, justice and impartiality towards the service and fixing of responsibilities (inter-departmental, intra-departmental and between departments of public administration and other bodies they associate with).
4. Requirements for defining the administrator's mandate.
5. Norms governing participation and consultation of different groups during administrative processes.
6. Methods of evaluating, and disseminating the information contributed by the participating groups of administrators.
7. Definition of limits of permissible secrecy (in the changing context, policies and decisions that were always kept under the carpet have to be brought out in the open, more

transparency in administrative functioning has to be emphasised).

8. Extent of obligations of administrators in cases of external pressures especially in cases of political manoeuvring (for circumstances requiring swift action, a definition of the administrator's responsibility to disclose information could be formalised).
9. Extent of accountability at different levels with respect to the duties performed.
10. Extent of duties and obligations in cases of pressures from family and peer groups.
11. Norms governing enforcement and evaluation of decisions and policies.
12. Nature of monitoring mechanism for administrative tasks which would include resource allocation and audit.
13. Areas of citizen-administration interaction, norms governing such interaction and definition of limits of permissible secrecy even in this case.
14. Rules governing administrative processes, especially in the areas of recruitment, training and career development with emphasis on flexibility and adaptability, (Benveniste, 1984, emphasis added).

Enforcing the Code

An ethical code based on a collectively worked out moral order cannot produce desired results unless it is implemented effectively. The bureaucrats have strongly asserted the need to initiate structural reforms in the I.A.S., they feel that the main areas of malaise are 'political interference', 'lack of transparency', 'stagnation' and 'insecurity' which are forcing officers to submit or resign (*The Sunday Times*, July 23, 1995). It is not possible to bring into force a code of ethics if it is self-serving and is subject to constant external interference and manipulation, a certain degree of autonomy is a pre-requisite for any code to be successful. We are witnessing a change in the pattern of authority, obedience and discipline. People no longer want to remain at the receiving end, they are learning to reason, question and assert themselves with much more intensity. Now, almost every rung of administration is involved in decision-making, the conflict between individual values, organisational standards and societal norms is thus clearly visible. Expansion of para-statal bodies and the private sector has made it mandatory that a framework of rules which lays down the role and obligations of public servants, be formulated and enforced.

Ethical analysis is usually sidelined because it goes against the interests of both the politicians and the civil servants. It is essential that the citizens are also made aware of the nature and content of the code for the public servants. It would make the task of ethical evaluation and enforcement of the code much simpler. Though the code may not reflect a consensus of opinion on ethical issues, it can still provide direction and advice with regard to ethical conduct and assist the administrators in analysing their options and alternatives. No code can be a foolproof set of guidance for every decision and situation, the administrators themselves have to be innovative, perceptive and adaptive in order to fit in the broad guidelines to the new situations and problems. We cannot undermine the role of the code from within which has to be adjusted with the code from without.

Moral and value judgements are not mere preferences and certainly require reasons or justifications, they must be subjected to some degree of rational analysis. We are now in the domain of a change-oriented administration that is constantly experimenting with new concepts and ideas. Analysing the laid down rules and disputing their applicability should thus become a necessary part of administrative process. It has been rightly observed that in order to inculcate a sense of ethical judgements among the administrators, they must make certain individual judgements regarding the issues affecting administration even in their professional capacities. A better approach would be not to substitute institutional arrangements for individual judgements but to attempt at simultaneous and complementary reforms of the institutions and individuals (Denhardt, op.cit).

In the U.S. in 1978, the Congress passed the Ethics in Government Act which among other things attempted to consolidate responsibility for conflict of interest issues within the Office of Government Ethics. In 1988, it was made a separate branch agency to provide overall direction to execute branch policies related to preventing conflict of interest situations (Gidman, 1992). The Ethics Committee within American Society for Public Administration developed a code of ethics for public administrators some years back. Recently, a code of ethics for Italian doctors has also come into force. Transparency International is a non-profit organisation that has been set up in Germany with branches in many countries to oppose corruption in business transactions and to strengthen the process of good governance. Research Committee on Political Corruption of International Political Science Association, the International Institute of Administration Sciences concentrate on different aspects of official misconduct and formulation of professional code of ethics (Caiden, 1995).

At the home front, Sadachar Bharati, an organisation of eminent citizens has prepared a code for political parties and poll candidates highlighting the need for maintaining discipline, high standards of morality and electoral reforms (*Hindustan Times,* Dec. 3, 1995). But, apart from a few rhetorical attempts, serious efforts have not gone into evolving a code of ethics. All that can be said is that nothing should be discarded without being given a fair trial. Public Administration departments must also not be left behind in this reform process. As pointed out before, ethical behaviour of public administrators cannot be sustained in a vacuum, their functioning is linked with the people around in more ways than visible, they come in close association with citizens, members of the private sector, voluntary agencies, foreign corporations and most importantly the political representatives in their every day working. There is thus a need to formulate ethical norms and extend them to other professions since it is not possible for the administrators to act ethically if everyone else keeps violating the code. We cannot conclude by saying that the solution lies only in the introduction of a code of ethics. It can no way be a substitute for vigilance bodies like the Central Bureau of Investigation, Lokayukta, Central Vigilance Commission etc., but if enforced and monitored with honest zeal, it can act as a much needed remedy for the crises-ridden administrative system.

REFERENCES

1. Amy, Doughlas, J., 'Why Policy Analysis and Ethics are Incompatible' in *Journal of Policy Analysis and Management,* Volume 3, No. 4., 1984.
2. Andrews, Kenneth, R., 'Ethics in Practice' in *Harvard Business Review,* Volume 83, No. 5, 1989.
3. Benveniste, Guy., 'On a Code of Ethics for Policy Exports' in *Journal of Policy Analysis and Management,* Volume 3, No.4, 1984.

4. Caiden, Gerald E. and Naomi J. Caiden, 'More on Official Misconduct' in *Indian Journal of Public Administration,* Volume XLI, No. 3, 1995.
5. Cooper, Terry C. ed., *Handbook of Administrative Ethics.* Marcel Dekker, New York, 1994.
6. Denhardt, Kathryn G., *The Ethics of Public Service: Resolving Moral Dilemmas in Public Organisations,* Greenwood, New York, 1988.
7. Downie, R.S., *Government Action and Morality : Some Principles and Concepts of Liberal Democracy,* Macmillan, New York, 1964.
8. Dror, Yehezkel, 'Administrative Culture Desiderata' in *Indian Journal of Public Administration (IJPA)* Volume 36, No. 3., 1990.
9. Dubashi, P.R., 'Public Accountability and Ethics in Administration' in *IJPA*. Vol. 24, No. 3., 1983.
10. Dwivedi, O.P., *Public Service Ethics,* Institute of Administrative Science, Belguim, 1978.
11. Dwivedi, O.P., 'Ethics and Administrative Accountability' in *IJPA*, Volume 24, No. 3., 1983.
12. Gilman, Stuart C., 'The U.S. Office of Government Ethics' in *Bureaucrat.* Volume 20 (1), Spring Edition, 1991-92.
13. Guyer, Peter ed., *Cambridge Companion to Kant,* University Press, U.S.A., 1992.
14. Jain, R.B., 'Political and Bureaucratic Corruption in India' in *IJPA,* Volume XLI, No. 3., 1995.
15. Johnson, Oliver A. *Ethics : Selections from Classical and Contemporary Writers.* CBS, New York, 1984.
16. Jun, Jong S., *Public Administration: Design and Problem Solving,* Macmillan, New York, 1986.
17. Maheshwari, S.R., 'Emerging Profile of India's Administrative Culture, in *IJPA*. Volume 36, No. 3., 1990.
18. Maheshwari, S.R., 'Ethics for Civil Service in India' in *IJPA,* Volume XLI, No. 3., 1995.
19. Meehan, Eugene J. *'Ethics for Policy Making' : A Methodological Analysis.* Greenwood, New York, 1990.
20. Mills C. Wright, *The Sociological Imagination,* Oxford, London. 1959.
21. Norton, David F. ed., *Cambridge Companion to Hume,* University Press, U.S.A., 1993.
22. Palmier, Leslie, *The Control of Bureaucratic Corruption : Case Studies in Asia.* Allied, New Delhi.
23. Rohr, John A., 'Problem of Professional Ethics' in *Bureaucrat,* Volume 20, (1). Spring Edition. 1991-92.
24. Simon Herbert A., *Administrative Behaviour,* MacMillan, New York., 1958.
25. Weber, Max, *The Protestant Ethics and the Spirit of Capitalism,* University Books, London: (IX edition). 1968.
26. Wallis, Malcolm, *Bureaucracy : Its Role in the Third World Development.* Macmillan, London. 1989.

24

The New Policies: Some Emerging Challenges of Public Administration in India

V. Bhaskara Rao

The nature, scope and significance of Public Administration is determined by the historical, social, cultural, political, economical and external factors (Hakim, 1993). But today in India, particularly the external factors seem to be playing a dominant role. In fact, it is the external factor which has been shaping the destiny of Public Administration in India, both before and after independence.

Recent Changes

The recent widespread changes have altered the international social and economic order and demanded the administration including economic planning (Dandekar, 1994) to "Respond and adjust to the changes quickly and creatively vis-a-vis the market economy" and "without tearing out socio-cultural fabric".

The most important change in Public Administration in India in 1990s is its reduced scope and significance. It has been addressed to change its nature with certain 'publics'. The recent changes are:

1. New Economic Policy—privatisation—Market friendly economy—GATT Agreement.
2. New Social Policy—Higher percentage of reservations, facilities to BCs/OBCs in public employment and educational institutions.
3. New Political Policy—Constitutional status to the local governments and reservations to women, BCs, SCs and STs.
4. New Labour Policy—Golden Handshake, Exit policy.

5. New Administrative Policy—Deregulation, Delicencing, Debureaucratisation—Use of para-military forces and the new Disruption of Terrorist Activities Act.
6. New Educational Policy—Science, Computer, Professional and Management Education through private institutions and Distance Education.

Implications of the "New Policies"

It is pertinent to note that all these "new" policies have to be carried out by the administration "without tearing the socio-cultural fabric". It is important to note that until the beginning of the 90s, the Indian socio-economic fabric was essentially anti-market and its concern was for the poor, the weak and the downtrodden. There was greater emphasis on social justice and development. But neither social justice nor the development was possible without a change in the 'socio-cultural fabric'. Therefore, even the new policies cannot be implemented without educating the people and the ruling elite, to the extent that the economic and political restructuring requires restructuring of the traditional values and behaviour in every field. (Dandekar, op.cit)

There are strong feelings against certain aspects of privatisation and the market philosophy. For the new economic policy has, in a way, whittled down the power of the State and the poor continue to expect that they can use the State power and policies to uplift themselves. "In fact, their hope and ambition to do so are now rising higher than ever before." (*The Hindu,* August 24, 1994)

Privatisation or liberalisation of economy results in less governance but it is obligatory to have a better social State in India. For the Constitution of India entrusted the State with the special obligation for achieving the "socio-economic transformation" to ensure "socio-economic justice" to the masses. The new policies reduce the significance of the positive State and enhance the scope of the negative State. The negative State cannot achieve the objectives enshrined in the Constitution. It may also reduce the power of the parliamentary democracy and lead to executive dominance. The contemporary democratic State could not devise effective mechanism to make bureaucracy accountable. (Kuldeep Mathur, 1991) In spite of it the role of the positive State and the bureaucracy cannot be minimised.

Bureaucracy might be ineffective and inefficient but to argue that public servants are not interested in the efficiency and effectiveness of the public sector is not logical. Bureaucracy, if proved incompetent in the discharge of economic tasks, and in the light of a further division of economic functions between public and private administration on the principles of economy and to reduce the burden on the public exchequer is felt necessary, might find its role mitigated. But, such a new division cannot absolve the government of its ultimate responsibility. The government is required to monitor the privatised economy and its effects. It is expected to defend the public interests and the tradition of financial incorruptibility and better State-society relations.

Privatisation may lead to a better performance of economy, but private sector in India which has not yet proved its social responsibility in ample terms may cause problems in distribution leading to more inequality. Bureaucracy will have to play very crucial new role in tune with the new economic policy and securing socio-economic justice through market forces. In this context, State intervention becomes necessary in a large number of areas of human concern. If the administration cannot meet the new demands and leaves the matters to the market forces, the police will have its hands full to control the discontented mobs and oppressed mass movements. Consequently, the underworld may gain control over the public. To take care of the security, para-military forces and armed services may gradually replace the police and the civil service and the civilian administration. The roots of the rule of law, democracy and equity would be threatened. Already in some places violent gang behaviour has made the mark of fascism. The State, though democratic is found in the middle of severe imbalance between the concentration of economic and social power in the hands of a relatively few and the enormous spread of ballot-box power. (*The Hindu*, op.cit)

The appointment of the National Human Rights Commission in 1994 at the instance of external factors brings to light many things that are taking place during recent years. The Commission in its recent visits to states expressed displeasure against the misuse of the TADA act and irregularities in the system. (*The Hindu*, August 28, 1994)

Political and Administrative Reforms/Changes

For public administration to provide good governance to society and exercise political power to manage the nation's affairs, it is necessary to get on to the chosen path of democratic decentralisation and socialist economic planning. We should work towards the success of the new local governments which empower the people at the grassroot levels. The success of the new social policy and the new economic policy depends largely on the relations between politics and the administration in order to maintain the correct balance of power between the contending social groups. The calls for certain reforms in the existing politico-administrative set-up. Some of the reforms that should be brought immediately are :

1. Introduction of electoral reforms for cleaner and free elections to all public bodies and to eschew influence of money and muscle power.
2. Amendments to the Anti-Defection Law to plug loopholes in order to prevent defections of whatever nature.
3. Amendments to the Official Secrets Act for demystifying the policy process.
4. Exposure of the unholy nexus between politicians, bureaucrats and criminals.
5. Creation of effective public grievances redressal system at every level.
6. Creation of a regular Human Rights Commission at all levels.
7. Establishment of quasi-judicial bodies in every statutory organisation for regular resolution of conflicts.
8. Training professionals, educating semi-professionals in the theory and philosophy of public administration at regular intervals.
9. Conscious efforts on the part of the academic discipline of public administration to educate and train the citizens to be an effective human resource.

Summation

The present model of public administration in India needs to be modified. Nothing much can be done at any stage "without tearing the socio-cultural fabric". The role of the State need not be minimised based on the external factors. The State, today, needs to be a better State, making the bureaucracy accountable. A more open government is suggested for better participation of all the concerned in the policy process. The urgent need of the hour is to evolve a political consensus and develop the political will and skills. The new public governance should deal mainly with democracy, human rights and the institutional functioning of the new panchayati raj and urban local governments.

REFERENCES

1. Barush, Amit, 'The 'Harsh' Side of the Law', *The Hindu*, August 28, 1994.
2. Chopra, Pran, 'The Crisis of Democracy', *The Hindu*, August 8, 1994.
3. Dandekar, V.M., 'Role of Economic Planning in India in the 1990s and Beyond', *Economic and Political Weekly*, June 1, 1994, : 1457-64.
4. Hakim, Mohammad A., Determinants of Administration in Developing Countries A Review and a Basis for Analysis. *The Indian Journal of Public Administration*, April-June 1993, : 111-22.
5. Mathur, Kuldeep, Bureaucracy in India: Development and Pursuit of Self-interest. *The Indian Journal of Public Administration*, Oct-Dec, 1991, : 637-48.
6. Resumussen, Public Enterprises and Privatisation : A Study of Canada and India, in Pradeep Saxena ed. *Comparative Public Policy*, Rawat, Jaipur, 1993, : 167-72.

25

Situational Leadership: A Model for Cross-Cultural Influence

Paul Hersey and Dewey E. Johnson

Introduction and Purpose

How does the situational leadership model offer a viable leadership model for effective cross-culture influence? This is an important issue of concern to forward looking scholars and practitioners.

Focus of the Discussion

Several concepts and terms must be clarified for the purposes of this discussion. The most fundamental issue is: What is leadership? In our view, leadership is a broader concept than management. Management is thought of as a special kind of leadership in which the attainment of organizational goals is paramount. The key difference between the two concepts, therefore, lies in the work organization. Leadership occurs any time one attempts to influence the behaviour of an individual or group, regardless of the reason. It may be for one's own goals or for those of others, and they may or may not be congruent with organizational goals. For the purpose of this discussion, leadership will be thought of within an organizational context.

How does one influence? Through power! Power cannotes influence potential — the resource that enables a leader to gain compliance or commitment from others. Amitai Etzioni suggested that power is derived from an organizational office, personal influence, or both. Individuals who are able to induce other individuals to do a certain job because of their position in the organization are considered to have position power; individuals who derive their power from their followers are considered to have personal power. Some individuals can be considered to have both position power as well as personal power. These categorizations are consistent with decades of behaviour science research that suggests that task and maintenance activities are the key determinants of effective group.

There have been a number of attempts to classify position and personal power. Position power can be divided into legitimate, reward, connection and coercive which are the bases of power while personal power can be divided into expert, information and referent.

The central issue then is whether or not leadership is "culture-free', that is, generalizable and capable of being transferred from one geographical and social context to another. Before we address to this issue, some background information on situational leadership is needed.

Situational Leadership

Situational leadership is based on an interplay among (1) the amount of guidance and direction (task behaviour) a leader gives; (2) the amount of socio-economic support (relationship behaviour) a leader provides; and (3) the readiness level that followers exhibit in performing a specific task, function or objective. Why the emphasis on followers? As Fillmore H. Sanford has indicated, "There is some justification for regarding the followers as the most critical factor in any leadership event." Followers in any situation are vital because individually they not only accept or reject the leader, but also as a group they actually determine whatever personal power the leader may have.

It should be noted that situational leadership is a model and not a theory. A theory attempts to explain why things happen as they do. A model, on the other hand, is a pattern of already existing events that can be learned, and, therefore, repeated. Situational leadership's concepts, procedures, actions and outcomes are based upon tested methodologies that are practical and easy to apply.

Basic Concepts of Situational Leadership

According to Situational Leadership, there is no one best way to influence people. Which leadership style a person should use with individuals or groups depends on the readiness level of the people the leader is attempting to influence.

It is important to understand leadership styles as they are used in the model and the idea of follower readiness. Leadership style is the behaviour by the leader as perceived by the followers. This behaviour can be classified into the two broad categories of task and relationship behaviour.

Task behaviour is defined as the extent to which the leader engages in spelling out the duties and responsibilities of an individual or a group. These behaviours include telling people what to do, how to do it, when to do it, where to do it, and who should do it.

Relationship behaviour is defined as the extent to which the leader engages in two-way or multi-way communication. The behaviour includes listening, facilitating and supportive behaviour. Task behaviour and relationship behaviour are two separate and distinct dimensions. They can be placed on separate axes of a two dimensional graph, and the four quadrants can be used to identify four basic leadership styles. Task behaviour is plotted from low to high on the horizontal axis while relationship behaviour is plotted from low to high on the vertical axis. This makes it possible to describe leadership behaviour in four ways or styles. These four quadrants can be used as the basis for assessing effective leadership behaviour. No one style is effective in all situations. Each style is appropriate and effective depending on the situation.

It is important to note that while task and relationship are used in their operational definitions, different words representing the same underlying definitions may be used in different settings. For example, guidance and supportive behaviour or directive and facilitative behaviour.

Readiness of the Followers or Group

As noted earlier, there is no one best style of leadership; it depends upon the situation within which the attempt to influence takes place. The more the leaders adapt their behaviours to the situation, more effective are their attempts to influence the outcome. The situation, in turn, is influenced by the various factors that are present. Some of these factors include: leader, followers, supervisor, key associates, organization, job demands, decision time.

The relationship between leaders and followers is the crucial variable in the leadership situation. If the follower decides not to follow, it doesn't matter what the supervisor or key associates think or what the job demands may be. There is no leadership without someone following.

Readiness Defined

Readiness in situational leadership is defined as the extent to which a follower has the ability and willingness to accomplish a specific task. People tend to be at different levels of readiness depending on the *task* they are being asked to do. Readiness is not a personal characterstic; it is not an evaluation of a person's traits, values, age, and so on. Readiness is how ready a person is to perform a particular task. This concept of readiness has to do with specific situations, not with any *total* sense of readiness. All persons tend to be more or less ready in relation to a specific task, function or objective that a leader is attempting to accomplish through their efforts.

The two major components of readiness are ability and willingness.

Ability is a function of the knowledge, experience and skill that an individual or group brings to a particular task or activity.

Knowledge—Knowledge of the task.

Experience—Experience with or related to the task.

Skill or Performance—Demonstrated skill and/or performance in successfully completing similar tasks.

Willingness is a function of the confidence, commitment and motivation that an individual or group has to accomplish a specific task.

Confidence—the person's or group's feeling that, "I can do it".

Commitment—the person's or group's feeling that, "I will do it."

Motivation—the person's or group's feeling of "I want to do it."

Willingness is only one word that describes the issue. Sometimes, it is not that people are really unwilling, it's just that they've never done a specific task before. Perhaps they don't have any experience with it, so they are insecure or afraid. Generally, if it is an issue of never having done something, the problem is insecurity. The term 'unwilling' might be most appropriate when, for one reason or another, the individuals have slipped or lost some of their commitment and motivation. It ought to imply that they are regressing.

Even though the concepts of ability and willingness are different, it is important to remember that there is an interacting influence system. This means that a significant change in one will affect the whole. The extent to which followers having willingness into a specific situation affects the use of their present ability. And it affects the extent to which they will grow and develop competence and ability. Similarly, the amount of knowledge, experience and skill brought to a specific task will often affect competence, commitment and motivation.

Readiness levels are the different combinations or ability and willingness that people bring to each task. The continuum of follower readiness can be divided into four levels. Each represents a different combination of follower ability and willingness or confidence.

Readiness Level 1 (R1)

Unable and Unwilling—The follower is unable and lacks commitment and motivation, or

Unable and Insecure—the follower is unable and lacks confidence.

Readiness Level 2 (R2)

Unable but Willing—The follower lacks ability, but is motivated and is making an effort, or

Unable but Confident—The follower lacks ability, but is confident as long as the leader is there to provide guidance.

Readiness Level 3 (R3)

Able but Unwilling—The follower has the ability to perform the task but is not willing to use that ability, or

Able but Insecure—The follower has the ability to perform the task, but is insecure or apprehensive about doing it alone.

Readiness Level 4 (R4)

Able and Willing—The follower has the ability to perform and is committed, or

Able and Confident—The follower has the ability to perform and is confident about doing it.

These combinations correspond to the readiness levels directly below. To use the model graphically, if required, identify a point on the readiness continuum that represents follower readiness to perform a specific task. Then construct a perpendicular line from that point to a point where it intersects with the curved line representing leader behaviour. This point indicates the most appropriate amount of task behaviour and relationship behaviour for that specific situation.

In selecting the high probability combination of task behaviour and relationship behaviour, it isn't necessary to be exact. As one move away from the optimal combination, the probability of success gradually falls off, slowly at first and then more rapidly the further one moves away. Because of this, it is not necessary to score a direct hit, a close approximation keeps the probability of success high.

Application of Situational Leadership

Use of the situational leadership consists of five well-defined and inter-related steps. Since there are many variables which affect organizational performance, the process focusses on those variables that empirical research and managerial practice have identified as the most critical variables. To determine what leadership style or pattern of behaviours the leader should use in a given situation, several key decisions must be made.

1. What objective(s) do we want to accomplish?

First, the leader must determine the task-specific outcomes the followers are to accomplish on an individual and group basis. Without creating clarity on outcomes, objectives, sub-tasks, milestones, and so on, the leader has no basis for determining follower readiness or the specific behavioural style to use for that level of readiness.

Without specific objectives, the leader will be in the same position as Alice in Lewis Caroll's *Alice in Wonderland.* Recall for a moment when Alice was in a dilemma and she had to ask the Cat who was sitting on a tree for advice :

"Would you tell me, please, which way I ought to go from here?"

That depends a good deal on where you want to get to," said the Cat.

"I don't care where..." said Alice.

"Then it doesn't matter which way you go," said the Cat.

"...so long as I get-somewhere," Alice added as an explanation

2. What is the readiness of the situation?

Once objectives have been created, the leader must then diagnose the follower's readiness to accomplish these objectives. The key issue might be : "How ready or receptive is the follower to accomplish a specific objective?" If the follower is at a high level of readiness, only a low amount of leadership intervention will be required. If, on the other hand, the follower is at a low level of readiness, considerable leadership intervention may be required.

3. What leadership action should be taken?

The next step is deciding on an appropriate leadership style. Suppose the leader has determined that the follower's readiness level, in terms of accomplishing a given objective is high; that is, the follower is able, e.g. has high amounts of knowledge, skill, experience and resources and is willing, e.g. has high amounts of confidence, commitment and motivation. The appropriate leadership style would be one of delegating since the follower has high amounts of both ability and willingness. If the follower's ability and willingness were low, a more directive leadership style would be appropriate.

These steps reduce the constraints of culture. For example, when an objective is set within the organization' external and internal culture, the readiness of the follower to achieve an objective is based on an assessment of the follower's readiness at that time and place within the culture. Further, the leadership style is determined by the interplay between that objective and its cultural context. Therefore, the model obviates many of the potential problems arising from importing a "foreign" leadership model and attempting to apply it to that specific culture.

4. What would be the result of the leadership intervention?

This step requires assessment to determine if results match expectations. Individuals and organizations learn a little bit at a time. Development is positively reinforcing successive approximations as the individual or organization approaches the desired level of performance. Therefore, after a leadership intervention, the leader must assess results through rechecking the objectives, rediagnosing readiness, and ascertaining if further leadership is indicated.

It is critical that the willingness component be carefully assessed. Leadership is more than a creation of objectives: it is achieving those objectives. Most leaders focus on the "what to do" and forget about the "doing it." When one looks at their plans, they are 96 per cent structures. The main reason they do not work is that leaders do not consider the implementation process.

5. What follow-up, if any, is required?

If there is a gap between present performance and desired performance, then follow up is required in the form of additional leadership interventions and the cycle starts again.

Is Situational Leadership Culture-Bound?

Our response is a resounding, No! it is not culture-bound. Each of the five key steps discussed above are not only task, objective, goal, and so forth specific, they are culture specific. Therefore, the conceptual integrity and operational usefulness of the model cuts across cultural boundaries. This has been demonstrated because the model's basic ideas and concepts that have been proven effective throughout the world in more than 128 countries for almost three decades. Further, the primary reference, ***Management of Organizational Behaviour*** (Prentice-Hall Publishing), now in its sixth edition, has been translated into fifteen languages. A seventh edition is now in preparation. This acceptance by academics and practitioners confirms that situational leadership provides a common sense way of blending all the different resources within an organization so that they can function as a powerful unit. The key elements combine in a manner to help individuals and groups move ahead, powerfully and confidently, to meet the leadership and management challenges of the future.

Summary and Conclusion

Because the situational leadership model is not person bound, team bound, culture bound, or environment bound, it has enormous flexibility. This is a powerful benefit when we are talking about leadership in a global environment. We have in this model a situational technology based process of translating objectives into actions. What a powerful idea! An idea that will make it possible for many individuals and organizations to create and to achieve their aspirations.

26

Budget Deficits in China: Calculations, Causes and Impact

Huaping Luo and Robert T. Golembiewski

Every public function-personnel, finance and so on—is seen as intimately linked with its cultural and Constitutional contexts in developmental cycles whose understanding will challenge the best that is in practitioners and researchers. Ideally, research can inform action; and action always help set the agenda for research, whether that elemental fact is recognized or suffers neglect. Generalizations typically are dangerous, but we cannot here go wrong in assigning a high priority to public budgeting and financial administration. This was true in the United States of the 1970s and 1980s; it remains appropriate for the 1990s; and one can even now raise reasonable claims for the continuing stability for financial administration as we move beyond the year 2000 A.D.—the Chinese year of the Dragon.

Cross-national studies on public budgeting and financial administration typically involve many challenges but, as a scholar points out, individual case studies and analyses constitute a key step in the right direction (Guess, 1992). This essay deals only with selected aspects of China's financial administration and full-blown comparative analysis. This essay does not hide its ambition, but it can now claim the label "comparative" only in the narrow sense of an early exploration of the synergy between the training, methods, and experiences of the two co-authors.

Comparative methods and research designs have a special power. Although development phases will often differ, good comparative research is relevant for many governmental units. In sum, such research can inform policy-makers about where their jurisdiction is, has been or may be going.

Budget deficits are a main theme for disciplines like public administration, political science and economics (Wildavsky, 1988 : 205-290; Schick, 1990 : 70-74; Kettl, 1972; Savage, 1988: 14-17; Eisner and Pieper, 1984). The People's Republic of China provides a window through which students of comparative and development administration can have a glimpse at how one developing country deals with budgetary deficits. This essay has four emphases: it discusses the calculations of deficits in China, analyzes the causes of budgetary deficits, assesses the impact of deficits and predicts the future of deficits in China.

Calculating Budget Deficits in China

Budget deficits are simply a fact of life for most of the countries in the world, and they are similarly understood. A budget deficit is simply the amount by which a government's expenditures exceed receipts. There are no important differences in the way oriental and western scholars generally define budget deficits (Chen, et al, 1984 : 123-35; Kettl, 1992 : 16). However, a general definition of deficits does not resolve the problem of how to estimate or calculate deficits (Courant and Gramlich, 1986: 8-12). To illustrate, the calculation of deficits by the Chinese government uniquely dealt with debt revenues before 1994. In the Chinese calculation, a budget deficit equalled expenditure minus the sum of debt disbursements and current revenues. In other words, in China, debt disbursements constituted revenues rather than a means of financing deficits. As a result, the officially published deficits were much smaller than the ones calculated by the method accepted by most countries. For instance, suppose that in a fiscal year the government's expenditures were 500 billion yuan, debt revenues were 50 billion yuan, and non-debt revenues 400 billion yuan. For the Chinese government, the deficit was 50 billion yuan (500 billion – [400 billion + 50 billion]). But for most countries, the deficit would amount to 100 billion yuan (500 billion – 400 billion).

Note another feature associated with this unique calculation. The official deficits were totally financed by "loans" or "overdrafts" from the central bank—the People's Bank of China. In China, until today, the People's Bank cannot refuse overdrafts by the Ministry of Finance because the government budget is approved by the top leaders. Of course, no one expected that such "loans" would be repaid by MOF to the People's Bank, and in fact such "loans" have never been repaid. The official or "hard" deficits were simply financed by printing more money. Consequently, the financing of deficits in China was different from that in America where financing deficits through direct loans from the Federal Reserve is prohibited by law, although for the latter, the Federal Reserve monitors a very small share of the government deficit through open market operations (Kettl, 1992 : 28; Courant and Gramlich, 1986 : 20; Shahin, 1992 : 74).

The Chinese official deficits were often called "hard" ones because of their great impact on the economy. They were financed by printing money, which increases the supply of money undesirably and exerts inflationary pressure on the economy (*People's Daily*, March 28, 1993). Unlike the U.S., where money supply is controlled by the independent Federal Reserve, Chinese money supply nominally is controlled by the People's Bank, but is very responsive to the commands of top party and government officials.

If judged from standard international practice, in China, "soft" deficits had also existed, although they were not reported by the government. Those deficits were "soft" because they were completely financed by the government's domestic and foreign debts and exert less inflationary pressure on the economy than "hard" deficits. "Soft" deficits approximately equalled the net of debt revenues (new issuances minus repayments). This is not the place for details, but calculations suggest that about 58 per cent of the actual deficits (calculated by international standards) from 1979 to 1993 are "soft".

The unique Chinese official calculation of deficits further encouraged an always-tempting illusion—that the government can spend without discipline. On the maturity of government debts, and as debt repayments reach their peak, the government has simply but constantly increased the size of the new debt issuance. The illusion was a dangerous one, even if all stakeholders agreed to play that game.

The official calculation of deficits, although rather peculiar, had a major political advantage—it underestimated the size of deficits and hence overestimated the performance of the government. The Ministry of Finance (MOF) loved this definition because deficits were believed to be a negative indicator of MOF's performance. In addition, because Chinese "hard" deficits had an inherent linkage with inflation, when (as often happens) inflationary pressures became a concern of the society, the government and elite leaders tended to prefer underestimated even if illusory deficits over a real but larger one because no one wanted to take the responsibility for inflation.

Note that, since the early 1980s, the government's attitude toward budgetary deficits has changed from complete rejection to that of limited acceptance. Prior to 1980, China's budgetary policy produced or even faked an annual balance between revenues and expenditures, plus a small surplus (Ge, 1982-83). This budgetary policy was required by China's traditional command economy, in which the government controlled all economic activities. Micro-economically, the government specified what to produce and how much to produce by State-owned enterprises, which accounted for more than 80 per cent of all goods and services. In this command economy, producer sovereignty reigned. Consumers had few choices in addition to purchasing whatever the State-owned enterprises produced; they could risk dilution of their funds by inflation, or go extralegal or illegal. Macro-economically, the government tried to keep a balance, although illusory between the quantity of money in circulation and the quantity of commodities in order to avoid a "hidden" inflation—commodity shortages. This was a losing game. The planned economy, inevitably, more or less, resulted in shortages because price signals did not play an effective role in allocating resources. A planned economy failed because no government, even aided by modern computers, had the capacity to predict individual consumers' demands and accordingly, to plan production. Budget deficits were believed to be a factor aggravating shortages. When prices were controlled, an unduly expanding supply of money would demonstrate itself by creating shortages of supplies and commodities. Of course, it is incorrect to attribute all shortages to budget deficits.

In addition, the Chinese government tried to avoid deficits because they were believed to symbolize government inadequacy. Since the government had tried to maintain a picture of being omnipotent, it had claimed the ability to balance its budget. Budget deficits would erode the credibility of the government.

Consequently, the government tried to avoid deficits, or at least to camouflage them. Although deficits actually existed in ten of the thirty years during the period from 1950 to 1979, all of them occurred as a result of overestimating revenues or underestimating expenditures due to uncontrollable factors such as natural disasters (Sheng and Chen, 1981). In other words, not even a single deficit was planned. Rather, expenditure controls were weak and/or arbitrary. In China, for example, supplemental appropriations needed no approvals from the legislature. Typically, when an agency faced an urgent unplanned demand, it could obtain extra appropriations if its request was approved by the main party and government leaders. If no revenues available could meet the agency's demand, the Ministry of Finance would overdraw from the People's Bank of China.

In the early 1980s, as noted, the Chinese government policy featured a limited acceptance of budget deficits, related to 1979's unprecedently-large deficit—17.9 billion yuan, or 14 per cent of expenditures. This resulted from several sources: a revenue decline caused by wage increases to State-owned enterprises' staff and workers; an increase in capital outlays resulting from the government's ambitious development programmes; an increase in defense expenditure due to the Sino-Vietnam border conflict; and a one-time repayment to government employees of salaries postponed by the Cultural Revolution. In Financial Year (FY) 1979, while revenues decreased by 1.78 billion yuan, the wage bill, capital outlays and defense expenses increased by 6 billion yuan (Zhang, 1982: 1-38). The 1979 deficit, due to its immensity, shook the government's confidence in its ability to balance its budget in the short run, given the demands for government investment to fund long-term development. In 1980s, the government planned a deficit for its budget for the first time (Wang, 1980). Ever since, all deficits have been planned rather than as a result of unexpected influences in the implementation process, except for those in 1981 and 1986, when planned balanced budgets ended up with deficits. The correlation between budgeted and actual deficits seems both high and positive.

This change in budgetary policy might be said to symbolize a shift in fiscal philosophy in China (Hsiao, 1987: 46) but, to a greater degree, it reflected tough trade-offs between political and economic alternatives. Although accepting the deficit budgets was hardly easy, they did have their economic and political advantages, given China's context at that time. Economically, the government's dominant role in economic development was inevitable, given the tiny non-public sector, and government capital spending had been a major engine for China's economic development. However, limited budget resources became a severe constraint on future development: it seemed impossible to raise tax rates further and profit contributions. Compared to slowing economic development, deficits were politically attractive. Rapid development is very helpful in building top leaders', credibility. Because of a lack of personal stature like Mao Zedong's, the Chinese leaders in the post-Mao period were eager to establish the trust of the people. People were tired of unfulfilled promises made by the government in the past. They strongly supported those who could help reduce poverty. As a result, development became a top priority. Between reforms and a balanced budget, the leaders chose economic reforms. Hence, to post-Mao leaders, the political attractiveness of reforms even with unbalanced budgets was larger than that of no reform with balanced budgets.

As noted above, the official estimates underestimated the size of deficits in China because debt disbursements were counted as revenues. In order to have a clear picture of China's deficits, the official deficits need to be adjusted against the background of a normal definition of deficits. It needs to be pointed out that China's deficits were modest even when adjusted according to internationally accepted practice. The ratio of adjusted deficits/GDP and the ratio of adjusted deficits/expenditures were 2-3 per cent and about 10 per cent. Those two ratios were only about half of the average levels for other developing countries (Shahin, 1992 : 29-31). However, although declining in the middle 1980s, thereafter increased in absolute size. The causes for the sharp increases in deficits are analyzed in the next section.

Causes for Sustained Budget Deficits

The growth of budget deficits was linked to market-oriented reforms and to the way they were carried out, but some political considerations were involved. In the post-Mao period, especially during the late 1970s and early 1980s, competition continued between two political cliques : one favouring reform and development, and the other insisting on maintaining the status quo (Short, 1982 : 227-251).

The reform faction's chief asset was popular support because the people expected to live a better life through economic reforms. It was very clear to those favouring reform that people were no longer satisfied with the planned economy because it led to serious commodity shortages. However, in the beginning, the reform lacked strong power base. The status quo faction was dominated by conservatives, who objected to reform either because they feared losing their vested interests, or because they had a deep commitment to Mao's policies (Shirk, 1993 : 145-149).

To counteract the conservatives, the reform faction had to obtain support from local bureaucrats at the provincial level and below, as well as from ordinary people. Those in this group proposed to decentralize or delegate as well as to increase profits retained by State-owned enterprises. Pro-reform leaders at the top won support from local bureaucrats because the latter gained power in the decentralization process. Besides its political advantage, decentralization was economically justified as improving efficiency in that the central government had never effectively controlled State-owned enterprises.

Decentralization was implemented in two ways. Thus, the central government delegated to local governments, discretion concerning planning, investing and budgeting. In addition, reforms increased profits retained by State-owned enterprises and gave them more management discretion. The State-owned enterprises (SOEs) accounted for more than 80 per cent of total output in China and hence any improvement in their efficiency would trigger China's economic growth. Delegating management discretion was the first step to revitalize SOEs via increasing their responsiveness to markets. This discretion focussed on input procurement, production, decision-making, pricing and marketing of products, as well as the use of retained profits.

Fiscal decentralization is yet another important dimension of decentralization. Under the new fiscal system—the fiscal contracting system, provinces were encouraged to develop their economies by keeping a larger share of revenue increases, in sharp contrast with the previous fiscal system. Under the pre-reform inter-governmental fiscal relationship, the budgets of all provinces had to be approved by the central government, which dictated a specific percentage of the revenues in such a way that each province could retain for each new fiscal year (FY). The percentages varied from province to province. Some poor provinces, whose own-source revenues were insufficient to cover their expenditures, received grants from the central government. Although this system was designed to reduce fiscal disparity among provinces, it often proved counter-productive because it encouraged provinces to spend money rather than save or boost revenues. Under this system, the more you spent relative to your own-source revenues (excluding grants) in FY_{t-1}, the higher the sharing ratio of retained revenues to total own-source revenues in FY_t. Of course, provinces' expenditures must be authorized, but the problem was that not all expenditures, once authorized, were justified. For example, even if some expenditures were no longer necessary due to unexpected changes after the budget was approved, provinces had no inclination to cut them.

Under the fiscal contracting system, the sharing ratio for a province's own-source revenues was fixed for a three-to-five-year period. This longer period was designed to stabilize the fiscal expectations of provinces and, hence, to reduce opportunistic behaviour by them. In any case, the sharing ratio varied widely from province to province. Shanghai, the largest industrial city in China, was required to transfer three-quarters of its own-source revenues to the central government. In contrast, about eighty per cent of Tibet's expenditures were funded by grants from the central government (Agarwala, 1992 : 74).

The fiscal contracting system stimulated the development of local economies because it stabilized the expectations of local bureaucrats. Under the fiscal contract signed in 1979, for example, Guangdong province was required to transfer one billion yuan to the central government every year. Because it could keep 100 per cent of marginal revenues beyond one billion yuan, it was motivated to develop revenue-yielding industries, and in turn the increased revenues supported many development programmes. As a result, Guangdong's economy showed very rapid development for more than a decade.

However, the fiscal contracting system has reduced the growth of the central government's revenues since it was implemented more than a decade ago. In the post-Mao period, provinces' interests and independence were strengthened and they got opportunities to bargain with the central government. In the negotiations with provinces, the central government did not have as much leverage as in the pre-reform period. In fact, the central government often had to make concessions, with the major consequence that the growth rate of transferred revenues from provinces to the central government was low, as compared with both economic growth and inflation. According to the fiscal contracts for 1988-1990, the nominal growth rate of transferred revenues from provinces to the central government ranged from 3.5 per cent to 9 per cent while, in the same interval, GNP grew annually by 14 per cent (Agarwala, 1992 : 264). Because fiscal contracts were fixed for three to five years, the central government could not adjust the sharing percentages annually, as it did before. When the economy grew rapidly, the central government's revenues did not increase at the same pace, and provinces got windfalls. As a result, the growth of local government's revenues was larger than that of the central government's revenues, and the ratio of the central government's revenues to consolidated revenues went down with time (Wong, 1991). While local governments could always find items on which to spend, the central government had to fund its increasing expenditures even if its revenues grew slowly because it seemed to lag in transferring expenditure responsibilities to provincial governments. This inevitably led to an increase in national deficits.

Another negative impact of decentralization on balanced budgets was abuse of discretion, including the granting of tax reductions and exemptions by local governments. Although in China all taxes belong to the central government by law, provincial and country governments enjoy important discretion — e.g., in granting tax reductions and exemptions to enterprises under their jurisdictions. Decentralization reinforced provincial motivation to seek their own interests. In the post-Mao period, performance on local economic development and popular support became more important than rewards from Beijing.

In order to protect their own interests, rich provinces used both illegitimate and legitimate means to reduce the tax liabilities of their enterprises. Those provinces with a high revenue-remitting percentage would reduce the tax liabilities or profit remittances of their own enterprises rather than transfer revenues to the central government (World Bank, 1990 : 17), often excessively. In this way, revenues were kept in their own enterprises and later would be "voluntarily" donated for local expenditures. Ningbo, a city of Jiangsu Province but under fiscal contract with the central government, was required to remit 72.1 per cent of its own-source revenues (Agarwala, op.cit : 74). For instance, if it reduced the tax liability of one of its enterprises by 100 yuan, the central government's revenues would decrease by 72.1 yuan and Ningbo's government revenues would be reduced by 27.9 yuan. After that, the Ningbo government could ask those enterprises that had been granted tax reductions to contribute 40 yuan to those programmes financed by Ningbo's budget. In this game, the central government lost 72.1 yuan, but the Ningbo government and the hypothesized SOE "gained" that sum : 12.1 yuan to the Ningbo government, and 60 yuan to the SOE. Such abuses of tax reductions and exemptions contributed to the growth of central budget deficits (Liu, 1993).

Another factor contributing to the growth of budget deficits was the reform of State-owned enterprises. In the pre-reform period, taxes and transferred profits from SOEs accounted for 85 per cent of the consolidated government's revenues (State Statistical Bureau [SSB], 1992 : 191). However, SOEs operated inefficiently due to stifling management system. SOEs acted as a government agency in relationship with central or provincial or county governments. Besides paying taxes, SOEs transferred nearly all profits to the government. At the same time, almost all expenses — including working capital and investment—were financed by government budgets. In addition, SOEs would receive subsidies from governments for their operating losses. The lack of linkage between SOEs' profit performance and the disposition of financial resources, although contributing to equal income distribution among workers, eroded the motivation of SOEs to seek efficiency. As a result, from the beginning of the reform, the government decided to strengthen the linkage between the amount of profits made by SOEs and their spending.

Since then, two major profit-contracting systems—the profit-retaining system (PRS) before 1986, and the contracting responsibility system (CRS) since 1987— have been carried out in SOEs. Under either system, if the actual profits made by an SOE are smaller than or equal to the target profits set by the government, the SOE retains profits up to 10 per cent. If the actual profits are more than the target profits, as much as 70 per cent of the excess profits could be kept in the SOE. This put pressure on the negotiation of targets, but otherwise encouraged profit-seeking.

A higher marginal retaining percentage for increased profits over targets was an incentive for SOEs to improve efficiency. As China's economy showed rapid growth due to the reform and flow-in of foreign investment, government revenues did not grew rapidly as expected due to low performance of SOEs and the weaknesses in the profit-sharing method. Furthermore, the more rapid the economic development, the lower the ratio of the government's revenues/GNP, as SOEs had a higher marginal retaining percentage for surpluses over the targetted profits (World Bank, 1990 : 16). Consequently, both PRS and CRS tended to lower the growth of government revenues.

The profit-contracting systems sparked off controversies between the players in the decision-making process, based on their conflicting interests. In general, the systems were welcomed by managers and workers of State-owned enterprises. With increased profits retained by SOEs, managers could control more funds and workers received more bonuses and improved welfare. In contrast, the Ministry of Finance (MOF) officials emphasized the importance of a balanced budget, and therefore opposed the profit-contracting system. In the opinion of MOF, the systems were often tilted in favour of SOEs at the expense of the government's revenues. MOF advocated implementing a tax-for-profit system, under which each SOE would pay taxes rather than remit profits to the central or local governments, because taxes are not subject to negotiations. In contrast, other central industrial administration departments—e.g. Oil, Railroad Transportation, Chemical and Non-ferrous Metal Industries—advocated the profit-contracting system. Under the profit-contracting systems, these ministries could play a role in setting ratios or quotas of remitted profits for enterprises under their supervision, and could even receive contributed funds from them.

MOF officials could generate a strong argument. Although fiscal decentralization and the profit-contracting systems provided institutional incentives for rapid economic growth, the government's revenues as a percentage of GNP declined from 34 in 1978 to 15.3 in 1993 The consolidated government revenues grew more slowly than GNP from 1978 to 1993, with the former growing at the rate of 9.7 per cent, and the latter at 15.3 per cent (SSB, 1992 : 28-29).

As government revenues declined, budget deficits could have been moderated by reducing expenditures, but expenditure pressures were sustained. China's reforms were carried out in an incremental style because they had no precedents to follow (World Bank, 1992 : 37-42). Incremental reforms were intended to reduce risks and social shocks, but they had their disadvantages—Primarily, the failure of the decision-makers to estimate in advance the fiscal impacts of reform programmes and to integrate them into a comprehensive plan. More often than not, the government increased discretionary expenditures to compensate citizens for the increasing living costs arising from price adjustments and liberalizations, with the hope of mitigating popular discontent but with the reality of budget deficits. Main expenditure pressures have been on subsidies, education and technology as well as administrative spending. Expenditures as a whole increased a bit more rapidly than revenues, with the former growing at 10.1 per cent and the latter 9.7 per cent (SSB : 191-92).

The differing increases in revenues and expenditures resulted from a particular reform style, contextual factors and development strategy. Since reforms were initiated in 1979, for example, the government's spending for subsidies has constituted a large share of total expenditures—from 9.3 per cent in 1979 to 17 per cent in 1993. The subsidies included two categories : one for essential daily consumer goods and the other for funding SOE operating losses.

Subsidizing consumers for essential goods was a strategic choice for gaining popular support for the reforms. It had been very clear to Deng Xiaoping and his supporters that, even if reforms brought benefits to people in the long run, they would be doomed to fail if carried out at the cost of lowering the living standards of most people, as cases-in-point, economic reforms in the East European socialist countries such as the former Yugoslavia were accompanied by inflation and increased living costs that led to social chaos. In order to reduce dissatisfaction with several redistributions arising from reforms, essential consumer goods were subsidized. The subsidized consumer goods included food grains, edible oil, meat, vegetables, cotton, and household coal (Wulf, 1986).

Reforms were often a matter of one step forward, in sum, and then one backwards. In order to stimulate agricultural development, for example, the government raised the purchasing prices of agricultural goods several times after 1979. Since an overall wage increase without efficiency improvement would reduce the profits of SOEs and probably also would induce inflation, wage increases were delayed. Consequently, in order to prevent the living standards of most citizens from going down due to inflation, essential agricultural products had to be sold to urban dwellers at prices lower than the purchasing prices paid to farmers.

The losses caused by the price gap between purchasing prices and reselling prices were subsidized from the government budget. Although price subsidies protected the vested interests of most citizens, they induced a perverse phenomenon: the greater the agricultural production, the more the government's spending on subsidies. If further reforms on marketing and pricing of agricultural goods are carried out, and if citizens accept upward-adjustments of the prices of consumer goods, price subsidies will tend to decline.

The other kind of substantial subsidy compensated for SOE losses during the course of market-oriented reforms and the bill is large. Overall, 45 per cent of SOEs operate at losses (*China News Digest*, October 28-29, 1994). In order to avoid serious unemployment and social riots due to the possible bankruptcies of SOEs, the government paid large subsidies to loss-making SOEs. A top leader even said, if all loss-making enterprises were allowed to go bankrupt, the resulting 20 per cent unemployed might well hit the streets in demonstrations, and the government would be paralyzed. The net contributions to government revenues from SOEs' profits decreased from 52.7 per cent in 1978 to just 5.0 per cent in 1993, a decrease due in part to the rapid expansion of the private economy. Recently, the government has made every effort including passing the Bankruptcy Law and the Enterprise Law—to make SOEs responsible for their financial performance. These laws are designed to reduce government subsidies to SOEs, but their effects to date have been limited. Those subsidies have more or less stabilized at a historic high level.

Chinese leaders understood the positive relationship between increasing subsidies and deficits, but they preferred reforms to a balanced budget. In 1985, when a price reform plan was discussed at a meeting at the top decision-making group, an MOF official argued that the country could not afford such an ambitious price reform programme, Premier Zhao retorted fiercely, asking MOF not to use its budgetary problem to slow reform.

Even if these subsidies to SOEs are unavoidable, they have serious consequences. Although increased government subsidies were not surprising given China's institutional context and reform strategy, ironically, administrative spending as a percentage of the government's total expenditure increased from 4 per cent to 8.4 per cent in 1992. While government has been reorienting from micro-management to macro-management, and as the tasks of government have been reduced, the size of government employment has increased by 8 per cent from 1978 to 1990. This compares with the growth rate of 2.9 per cent in the total social labour force (SSB, 1992 : 80). Undoubtedly, this growth is counter productive. It suggests that the government met difficulties in its attempts at "streamlining". For example, government employees were reluctant about non-government employment because Chinese public bureaucrats enjoy high status, job security and benefits such as public housing. Some top leaders also wanted to protect their pet ministries. For instance, two industrial departments—Machine Manufacture and Electronic—were merged in 1987 only to be separated in 1993, soon after Li Peng became the Premier. Not incidentally, Li Peng had worked in the Ministry of Electronic Industry.

The fast growth of spending for education and science as a percentage of expenditures—from 7.3 per cent in 1978 to 13.1 per cent in 1992 - was supported by Deng's preference and China's economic development strategy. Unlike Mao, Deng studied abroad in the 1920s and accepted the significance of knowledge and technology to economic development. He walked that walk, rather than merely talking about it. Indeed, when Deng was rehabilitated as Vice Premier for the second time in 1977, he chose to take charge of national educational and science affairs.

Virtually all Chinese leaders believed that it was impossible for China's economy to take off without major improvements in human capital. The economic objective is to make China a middle-income country in the next fifty to seventy years. Sustained economic growth based on quality human resources and technical progress is indispensable, if this objective is to be achieved. Hence, increases in government's expenditure on education and science were inevitable strategic choices and their short-run contribution to deficits intended to serve continued economic development.

The Impact of Budget Deficits

In sum, the growth of deficits in China involved not only economic factors but also political dimensions. Politically, budget deficits supported the reforms and hence strengthened the power of the pro-reform leaders. Realistically, few reform programmes could have been implemented had China stuck to the balanced-budget principle.

Nonetheless, conservative leaders often used budget deficits as a pretext to attack market-oriented reforms. Chen Yun, whose personal stature may not be lower than Deng's, is a stubborn proponent of balanced budgets. He attributed the growth of deficits to the reforms advocated by Deng, and saw them as a symptom of a deteriorating economy. Deng replied: "Why be afraid of small deficits? The United States has had large-sized deficits, yet its economy is still expanding." In November, 1990, after the Tiennenman pro-democracy movement, conservative leaders-using budget deficits as evidence-tried too recentralize the fiscal system but failed due to strong resistance from local leaders.

Despite the persistence of deficits, the political pressure has been strong enough to encourage certain flexibilities in economic reporting. In 1987, when many people complained about high inflation and attributed it to budget deficits, Premier Zhao ordered MOF to produce a phantom balance, a strategy often used in the American budgeting process (Mikesell, 1991 : 84-94). MOF delayed reporting until expenses actually incurred in 1986.

Budget deficits may have positive economic impact under some conditions (Heilbroner and Berstein, 1989 : 132), and China's deficits as a whole has contributed to the development of bottle-necked sectors such as energy, transportation and communications. These areas are very important to China's long-term economic growth, but they are underdeveloped as compared with other industries. The government has been the main investor in these sectors over an extended period, due to several deficiencies. Basically, capital markets are underdeveloped, and large investments in infrastructure are hard to obtain. In addition, non-government entities pour their capital into arenas producing high profits in the short run, but have far less interest in low return sectors, even if strategic. Although government investment has declined sharply, it has concentrated on the bottle-necked sectors. If China balanced its budgets by cutting capital expenditures as it did in the past (Luo, 1988a, 1988b), the investment on energy, transportation and communications would have to bear the brunt and their development would lag even more. Balancing budgets by cutting capital expenditures can be penny-wise and pound-foolish (Colm and Young, 1968).

Seen from another point of view, China's deficits also have troubling impacts. Because most of China's deficits (adjusted for debt revenues) are financed by "loans" or overdrafts from the central bank, the deficits directly contribute to inflation from 1979 to 1993, the correlation coefficient between the size of deficits and the rise in the retail price index is 0.93. This correlation is not perfect, but neither is it very distant from 1.0.

The Outlook for Budget Deficits in China

Will China's deficits continue into the foreseeable future? The answer is yes, probably. Let us review the positive as well as the negative impact of possible future developments on both the revenue and expenditure sides of the government's budget. Positive developments include a higher growth rate of the government's revenues and a decline in subsidies. Here, the early signs seem favourable. Beginning in 1994, a new inter-governmental fiscal relationship—a division of taxing power—came into effect (*People's Daily*, Sept. 14, 1993). Under the new framework, the central government divides taxing power between itself and the provinces in order to strengthen its fiscal position. Provinces are deprived of the right to grant tax exemptions or reductions if the tax in question is administered by the central government. Moreover, a new tax system, through which the central government tries to control most important taxes—e.g. profit taxes and value-added taxes—was implemented in 1994 (*Beijing Review*, March 14-20, 1994). According to this tax system, SOEs will no longer remit profits to the central or local governments. Instead, they will pay a profit tax, whose rate is 33 per cent. All enterprises in a few industries have to pay a value-added tax. A consumption tax also exists. In addition, spending on price subsidies might be further reduced. In 1993, many provinces liberalized the prices of daily necessities and the government made no commitment to pay for possible increases in future living costs (Beijing Review, August 1-22, 1993).

However, bad news concerning possible deficits also exists. Although the growth of the government's revenues may improve in the coming years, expenditure pressures will remain. As noted above, it will be impossible to reduce capital outlays appreciably without negative effects. A study of deficits showed that in the pre-reform period, the government tended to balance its budget by cutting capital outlays in FY, if the FY budget ended with a deficit (Luo, 1988b). However, this deficit-reduction strategy may result in more losses than gains in the long run. As analyzed above, investment in highly-desirable sectors such as energy, transportation and communications would be reduced sharply if the budget were to be balanced. A lag in the development of these sectors will constrain China's economic growth in the long run.

Another expenditure pressure on the government budget comes from pay increases to government employees. Since 1986, the pay levels of the staff and workers in the sectors of administration, education, science, health and culture have been lower than the average wage level. It seems impossible for the government to delay pay increases in these sectors any longer. The government increased pay by a small scale to government employees in 1994, but a strong pressure for continuing increases to guarantee the salary gap in a reasonable range between the government and non-government sectors is still on. Finally, SOE losses will continue to be a heavy burden with nearly one-half of them reporting losses (*China News Digest,* October 28-29, 1994). In short, deficits may increase rather than decrease.

Summary

China's deficits reflect serious conflicts in the course of market-oriented reforms. The government had to retreat from overwhelming monopolization of resources, but its role in economic development was not assumed by other organizations. Due to decentralization in pursuit of market-oriented reforms, the government's revenues as a percentage of GNP went down, at least in the short run. An inherent weakness in the inter-governmental fiscal relationship—the abuse of tax reductions and exemptions by provinces—exaggerated the decline of revenues. At the same time, the government faced difficulties in shifting expenditures and spending on subsidies which has increased at a high rate. Here, there is a deep dilemma : reforms have reduced the control of resources by the government, especially the central government but sustaining development requires investment by the government. Consequently, budget deficits became critical to the Chinese government. Political compulsions are another important reason why China abandoned the balanced budget principle and turned to budget deficits as a means of financing development. The political costs of deficit reductions will be prohibitive, and the probability of success seems small. People's expectations about living standards have escalated, and this implies a sustained and stable development. Slow development based on a balanced budget might lack support from the people.

Can China recentralize its fiscal system? That probably is doomed to be an exercise with a high potential for civic unrest. Early reforms empowered a particular interest group—local bureaucrats—and they would strongly oppose this attempt.

In sum, balanced budgets do not seem probable in China's future. This prediction has to be discounted a bit, however. Recently, the government initiated a series of reform programmes concentrating on adjusting inter-governmental relationships, and especially the tax system. Some of them are designed to increase the government's revenues as a percentage of GNP as well as to increase the central government's revenues as a percentage of consolidated revenues. In addition, price reforms may reduce the government's spending on subsidies.

Notes

1. The Ministry of Finance reports a consolidated budget for all governments in China. Similarly, a province's budget consists of the budget of the provincial government and the budgets of all county governments. This budget practice is common in centrally planned economies (Premchand, 1993).

2. Beginning with the FY 1994, the government has changed the practice used since 1949: the government budget now sees public debt as a means of financing deficits, but printing money is still an important source for funding deficits.

3. The famous economist Janos Kornai denied a linkage between budget deficits and shortage. See Kornai (1979, pp. 931-35). However, Kornai's conclusion is valid only when deficits are financed by debts, or when financing deficits by loans from the central bank does not lead to a simple increase in supply of money. Neither of the two conditions is satisfied in China.

4. Mao deprived hundreds of thousands of dissidents of their jobs from 1960s to 1970s. In 1979, Deng rehabilitated them and paid them owed salaries in the past years due to the deprivation of jobs.

5. In the Chinese context, adjusted deficit = (revenues + SOEs' subsidies) + (expenditures + subsidies) + (debt disbursements — payments of principal and interest). (See International Monetary Fund, 1986 : 91-92).

6. State-owned enterprises are administered by either the central or local governments.

7. The percentage for FY_t is the ratio of authorized expenditure in FY_{t-1} (E_{t-1}) to provinces' own-source revenues in FY_{t-1} (R_{t-1}). If the ratio for a province were larger than one, it meant that the province received grants from the central government. If the ratio for a province were smaller than one, it indicated that the province remitted some of its own-source revenues to the central government. For developed provinces, E_{t-1} is smaller than R_{t-1}, the ratio of the retained revenues to the total own-source revenues is E_{t-1}/R_{t-1}. Suppose that a province's own-source revenues are 1,000 million yuan and the authorized expenditures are 650 million in FY_{t-1}, and are 1,500 million yuan for FY_t. The retaining ratio for that province for FY_t would be 0.65, and retained revenues would be 975 million yuan (1,500 million x 0.65). The transferred revenues to the central government would be 525 million yuan (1,500 million x [1-0.65]). For poor provinces whose E_{t-1} was larger than R_{t-1}. The gap was filled by grants from the central government.

REFERENCES

1. Agarwala. R. *China : Reforming the Inter-governmental Fiscal Relationship*, World Bank, Washington, D.C., 1992.
2. "China adopts a new tax system," *Beijing Review*, 37 (11) March 14-20, 1994 : 11.
3. "State to Ensure Steady Price Reform," 36 (33) *Beijing Review*, Aug. 16-22, 1995 6.
4. Chen, Gong, Hou, Menchan and Yuan, Zhenyu, *Public Finance*. Beijing, China: China Financial and Economic Press, 1984.
5. "State Enterprises Continue to Lose Money,"*China News Digest (Electronic News)*, October 28-29, 1994.
6. Colm, Gerhard, and Marilyn Young, "In Search of a New Budget Rule," : 186-202, in R.T. Golembiewski eds. *Public Budgeting and Finance : Readings in Theory and Practice*. Itasca, 11 : F.E. Peacock Publishers, 1968.

7. Courant, P.N. and E.M. Gramlich, *Federal Budget Deficits : America's Great Consumption Binge.* Prentice-Hall, Englewood Cliffs, N.J. : 1986.

8. *Country Report: China and Mongolia,* the 2nd quarter, UK Business International, Economic Intelligence Unit, 1993 and 1994.

9. Eisner, R. and P.T. Pieper, "A New View of the Federal Debt and Budget Deficits, *American Economic Review,* 74 (1) 1984: 11-29.

10. Ge, Zida, "On the Issue of Balancing the State Budget," *Chinese Economic Studies,* 1 (Winter), 1982-83 : 107-23.

11. Guess, G.M., "Comparative Government Budgeting," : 95-124, in J. Rabin ed., *Handbook of Public Budgeting.* Marcel Dekker, New York, 1992.

12. Heilbroner, R. and P. Berstein, *The Debt and the Deficit : False Alarm/Real Possibility.* W.W. Norton and Company, NY, 1989.

13. Hsiao, K.H. *The Government Budget and Fiscal Policy in Mainland China.* Chunghua Instituation for Economic Research, Taiwan, 1987.

14. *A Manual on Government Finance Statistics.* International Monetary Fund, Washington, D.C., 1986.

15. Kettl, D., *Deficit Politics: Public Budgeting in its Institutional and Historical Context.* Macmillan, New York, 1992.

16. Kornai, J., *Economics of Shortage.* Institute for International Economics Studies, Stockholm University, 1979.

17. Liu, Zhongli, "A Report on the Implementation of the 1992 State Budget and the 1993 Preliminary State Budget, *Beijing Review,* Aug. 19-25, 3 (1) : 19-22, 1993.

18. Luo, Huaping, "The Rigidity of and Control of Government Expenditures" (in Chinese). *Zhongginnian Jingji Luntan* (Young Economist Forum), 3, : 58-62, 1988

19. "A Comparative Analysis of Fiscal Deficits in the Pre-Reform and Reform Periods" (in Chinese). *Caijing Lilun Yu Shijian* (Public Finance in Theory and Practice), 8 March, 1988(b): 17-20.

20. Mikesell, J.L. *Fiscal Admistration: Analysis and Applications for Public Sector.* Ca: Brooks/Cole Publishing, Pacific Grove, 1991.

21. *China's Fiscal Statistics.* Ministry of Finance, Department of Comprehensive Planning, Science Press, Beijing, China, 1992.

22. "The Government's Revenues Exceeded the Budget Target." *People's Daily,* March 28, 1993 : 3.

23. *People's Daily.* "A New Plan for Reforming the Inter-governmental Fiscal Relationship Released." Sept 14, 1993 : 1.

24. Premchand, A., "A Cross-national Analysis of Financial Practices," 1993, : 87-102, in T.D. Lynch and L.L. Martin eds. *Handbook of Comparative Public Budgeting and Financial Management,* Marcel Dekker, New York.

25. Savage, J.D., *Balanced Budgets and American Politics.* Ithaca, Cornell University Press, New York, 1988.

26. Schick, A. *The Capacity to Budget.* Urban Institute Press, Washington D.C., 1990.

27. Shahin, W.N. *Money Supply and Deficit Financing in Economic Development,* Quorum, West port, 1992.

28. Shen, Jingnong and Chen, Baosen, "China's Fiscal System." 1981, : 634-54, in Economic Research Center, the State Council of the People's Republic of China eds. *Almanac of China's Economy.* Modern Cultural Company Limited, Hong Kong.

29. Shirk, S.L. *'The Political Logic of Economic Reform in China.* University of California Press, Berkeley, 1993.

30. Short, P., *The Dragon and the Bear : China and Russia in the 80s.* William Morrow and Company, New York, 1982.

31. State Statistics Bureau (SSB), *China Statistical Yearbook.* China Statistics Publishing House, Beijing, 1992.

32. Wang, Binqian, "A Report on the Implementation of the 1979 State Budget and the 1980 Preliminary State Budget." *New China Monthly,* Sept. 1980 : 11-18.

33. Wildavsky, A. *The New Politics of the Budgetary Process.* Scott Foresman and Company, Glenview, 1988.

34. Wong, P.W. Central-local Relations in an Era of Fiscal Decline : The Paradox of Fiscal Decentralization in Post-Mao China." *The China Quarterly,* No. 128, 1991: 691-714.

35. World Bank, *China: Revenue Mobilization and Tax Policy.* World Bank, Washington D.C., 1990.

36. World Bank, *China: Reform and the Role of the Plan in the 1990s.* World Bank, Washington D.C. 1992.

37. "Xiaochu Vingchizhi Jinnian Zhongtuxi co Eliminate "Hard" Deficits is a Challenge to the Implementation of this Year's Deficit, *World Journal,* March 11, 1994.

38. "Jingnian Caizhengchizhi Jiangjin Qibaiyi (This Year's Deficit will be nearly 70 Billion Yuan)." *World Journal,* March 12, 1994, : 11.

39. "Guoqi Shangshi Nongtu Zhuoyong (State-owned Enterprises Lose their Dominance), *World Journal,* April 23, 1994 : 10.

40. Wulf, L.D., *International Experience in Budgetary Trends During Economic Development and Its Relevance to China,* World Bank, Washington D.C., 1986.

41. Zhang, Zhuoyuan, "Introduction: China's Economy after the Culture Revolution." in Lin Wei and Arnold Chao eds. *China's Economic Reforms.* University of Pennsylvania Press, Philadelphia, 1982.

27

A Suggested Approach to the Study of Bureaux

Saugato Sen

Introduction

The purpose of the present paper is to suggest a line of inquiry into the nature and functioning of the generalised bureau. I shall argue that *methodological* individualism, articulated through rational choice methods is the most promising approach to the study of bureaux. Two basic premises inform this approach. First, individual actors, and not the system, are the elementary units of study. The system is more or less an aggregate of the individual actors. Secondly, individual actors display rationality. I shall presently discuss the notion of rationality. There have been some rational choice analyses of bureaux, which I will spell out. However, the existing and usual analyses of bureaux using rational choice methods will have to be extended and modified, to incorporate and take into consideration more recent concepts and ideas being used primarily in economics, particularly in industrial organisation theory.

Two questions naturally pose themselves at this point. First, what does *economics* have to say about bureaucracy? After all, other social sciences like sociology and public administration are considered the usual disciplines for the study of bureaux. Secondly, what does economics have to say about *bureaucracy*? Does not economics concern itself with, and limit itself to, the study of topics sucn as production, income, consumption, investment, money and so on? Related to this is another question: *why* should economics attempt to analyse bureaux? This paper attempts a partial answer to these questions. It attempts to show the economics can fruitfully analyse institutions.

It would perhaps not be out of place to mention here that there is often a misplaced resistance on the part of some social scientists to methodological individualism as a tool of analysis. The usual reason adduced is that the use of methodological individualism and taking a rational choice approach is thought to necessarily imply an espousal of individualism as a social philosophy and *ideology*. This is simply unfounded; indeed, there is a rational choice approach even to the study of *Marxian* political economy (see for instance, Elster (1985), Morishima (1973), and Roemer (1982)). The other reason given for not adopting a rational choice approach, and which is quite related to the first, is the view that social phenomena are holistic in nature, in that the whole is greater, or at any rate quite different from, the sum of the constituent parts, much like the relationship of the human body with its constituent organs. In other words, the macro picture is somehow different from the sum of the individual units of study.

In economics, this is seen in some interpretations of the Keynesian approach to the study of the macroeconomy, that is, the economy as a whole. It is true that while talking about social and individual preferences, Rousseau had distinguished between the 'general will' and the 'will of all'. Nevertheless, it is equally true that in *Economic and Philosophic Manuscripts of 1844*, Marx had emphasised that the 're-establishment of 'Society' as an abstraction *vis-a-vis* the individual' must be avoided. In some interpretations of Marx, though, Marxism is seen as a holistic or a systems theory; but then, so is the ideologically antithetical *functionalism*.

Weber, Simon and Rationality

The pioneer in the analysis of internal dynamics of organisations must surely be taken to be Max Weber. He saw the central characteristic of the industrial society to be the rise and eventual dominance of the formal organisation. The defining feature of industrial society in terms of behavioural trait Weber took to be rationality and rational action. Weber, however, made a distinction between *zweckrational*, or rationality with respect to goals, and *wertrational*, or rationality with respect to values. Bureaucracy would be infused with the former and would be the institutional articulation of rational action. Weber put forward rationality both as a prescriptive as well as a descriptive-predictive feature about the industrial society. It was the main organisational form for handling complex tasks, he felt. The main elements of the bureaucratic office, according to Weber, were that the office would be organised on a hierarchical principle and there would exist abstract rules of functioning.

The important point about Weber's analysis is that he clubbed all types of formal organisations together, the common feature being rational action. Government administrative departments, business firms, the military, even educational institutions and hospitals are all organised on the same lines, that of rational action. Similarly, Weber saw very little to distinguish between organisations in capitalist and socialist societies. This is a key limitation that we concentrate on further ahead, and we argue that the key factors distinguishing a government administrative bureau from a business firm must be identified and focussed on in the analysis.

Given that rationality (albeit in an extended sense) was a central feature of the Weberian analysis, did Weber use methodological individualism as a mode of analysis? Two crucial aspects about Weber's method are *interactionism and verstehen*. Weber did not consider the whole system as a unit of study but focussed on interactions among small groups of social actors. The concept of *verstehen*, which was also stressed by Dilthey, states that economic actors give *subjective* meanings to their lives and situations. However, the social scientist should *objectively* study these perceptions of the actors. It is the concept of Ideal Type that was perhaps Weber's most profound contribution to social science methodology. The theory of bureaucracy that he propounded was of an ideal typical bureaucratic organisation. The important point here is that an ideal type is supposed to capture at once the features of an *ideal* or perfect representative of the object under study and the characteristics of *typical* specimen of the object under study.

Probably the most important contribution after Weber which uses the concept of rationality is Herbert Simon's, through his wide body of writings (for example, Simon, 1957). Simon made it possible for a dialogue to take place between public administration and the behavioural sciences. He gave the study of bureaucracy a scientific approach and a much-needed rigour. He made decision-making the focus of attention, looked at behaviour of organisations in terms of their goals, and stressed cognitive aspects and rational choice as objects of study. It is sometimes asserted that Simon followed a systems approach, but he sought to explain organisational behaviour in terms of the goals of the *individual* members of the organisation. He thus kept the goal at the level of the individual but contended that *interaction among the individual members* determines the organisational goals (thereby hinting at the structure of modern Game Theory).

What are the salient features of Simon's decision-making approach? There are three components: first, the individuals list the alternative actions available to them. The set of actions or strategies available to an individual may be called her strategy set. The second component is determining the consequences of these actions. The third is comparative evaluation of the consequences. It is important to mention these because the terminology in modern Game Theory is remarkably similar. What is called consequences in Simon's approach is called outcomes, and the utility or benefits (which allow a ranking of alternatives) accruing from these outcomes is called a payoff. The advantages of using Game Theory will be discussed presently but suffice it to mention at this point that Game Theory is used to study situations of interactions. However, in decision theory, the process of an individual decision-maker operating under uncertainty is usually depicted as a 'game' between this individual and 'nature'.

The intricacies of decision theory need not be elaborated. It is, however, essential to point out the difference between Simon's notion of rationality and that usually used in several social sciences, particularly economics. A simplistic view of rationality would equate it with maximising behaviour. This is not incorrect, but a preference relation is supposed to underlie choice or behaviour. This preference relation defined over the set of alternatives supposedly satisfies certain axioms. The two most important ones are the following. First, if action *x* is preferred to action *y*, which is preferred to action *z*, then *x* must be preferred to *z*. Secondly, between two alternatives *x* and *y*, either *x* must be preferred to *y*, or vice versa, or both must be equally preferred, that is, the individual must be indifferent between the two alternatives. Another important component of rationality is consistent behaviour: faced with similar circumstances and alternative courses of actions, if the individual preferred and chose action *x* over action *y* in the first situation, then she must not choose *y* over *x* in the second situation, given that the two situations are identical. Roughly speaking, rational behaviour means that the individual is doing the best she can, given her constraints. Notice that this notion of rationality is broad enough to incorporate Weber's *zweckrational* as well as *wertrational*. It only asks that behaviour is consistent and utility (it can serve as proxy for whatever the individual is trying to maximise) is maximised. What gives the person utility is not important to the conceptualisation of rationality—it may be goals, it may be values, it may be commodities, or whatever else. The individual should choose those actions which best satisfy her objectives.

Simon changed the notion of rationality—or rather, said, in effect, that rationality in the sense described above is seldom used in practice. He adduced the concept of 'bounded rationality'. The individual, Simon said, seldom has total knowledge of the actions available to her and the consequences therefrom. She also has incomplete information and is usually in an environment of uncertainty. Hence, she displays not maximising but *satisficing* behaviour. It is often thought that this term means aiming satisfactory gains, but the word is satis-*ficing* and the suffix is from 'sacrificing.' Thus, the individual sacrifices some gains and aims for satisfactory returns to chosen actions.

It is possible to argue that this notion is more or less about rational behaviour under uncertainty and imperfect information, which can be easily handled using modern concepts in economics, without having to jettison or even amend the notion of rationality. One such concept is *rational expectations*, which means that the subjective expectation that individual actors have about uncertain outcomes coincides with the mathematical expectation of the variables in the model that the social scientist is using. In other words, the individual actors in the story know the probability distributions of the variables in the model that the researcher is using (this in a way stands the concept of *verstehen* on its head). We shall not dwell further on Simon's notion of rationality except to say that this sense of rationality is used in what is called transaction cost economics, which as we shall see is one of the approaches to modern institutional economics.

While Simon has demonstrated the importance of rationality, decision-making and choice in the analysis of administration and organisations, he has also shown the need to keep the organisational and institutional framework in perspective as setting when using the rational choice methods to analyse behaviour. For his combining cognitive, behavioural and institutional aspects in the analysis of administrations and organisations, Simon richly deserved his Nobel Prize in economic science. He in a sense started the interface between administrative theory and economics.

The Public Choice Approach to Study of Bureaucracy

Till about 1965, the scholarly body of work on the bureaucracy was carried on in the spirit of Weber and Wilson, notwithstanding Simon. In 1965, Gordon Tullock published his book *The Politics of Bureaucracy*. This book marked the beginning of work, within the public choice framework, on the analysis of bureaucracy. Till that time, the public choice literature had busied itself with analysing and developing models of representative government and the executive. The father of the public choice approach is generally considered to be Duncan Black who investigated the rationale of group decision-making (Black, 1948). From this a few years later, it branched off, mainly due to the work of Kenneth Arrow, into what is called social choice theory (Arrow, 1963). This is concerned with the relationship between the individual and society, or more specifically, with how to aggregate individual preferences and the ranking of alternatives into a social preference and choice, and to see under what conditions this can be done at all. For an overview of social choice theory, see Sen (1986, 1988); the classic expository work in social choice theory is Sen (1970). Public choice theory veered off in a different direction and concentrated on providing a rational choice approach to *political processes and institutions*.

The classic work in the public choice literature on *bureaucracy* is, of course, Niskanen (1971). This work started an onrush of future contributions on bureaucracy from a public choice perspective. Niskanen formulated his theory in a framework of what economists call bilateral monopoly or a situation where there is a single seller of a product confronting a single buyer of the product. Consequently, both come to have considerable power, control, and bargaining strength. In his model, the novel innovation was a new theory of bureaucratic supply. The bureaucracy sells its services to the representative government. In the model, the government and not the public is the buyer of bureaucratic services. The bureau is the only seller of its services and the government is its only buyer. This is a 'market' which involves an exchange of the 'output' of the bureau. This exchange of the output is for a budget and not a per-unit price. Here Niskanen brings in the rational choice aspect of his formulation. In any rational choice model, agents are expected to optimise some behavioural function; in this model, bureaucrats are supposed to want to maximise their budget. On the buyer's side, the behaviour and preferences of the government are derived from conventional models of representative government and majority rules which already existed in the public choice literature. In a later paper (Niskanen, 1975), Niskanen added a more basic maximisation exercise underlying budget maximisation. Bureaucrats are pictured as being utility maximisers, with utility taken to be depending, among other things, on expected remuneration, patronage, discretionary power, ease of management and ideological factors. Tullock (1965) and Downs (1967) have indirect allusions to some of these points.

Niskanen's theory is in an exchange paradigm. It talks of the exchange of output for a budget, between the individual bureau and the government. What is relevant is also how work is organised *within* the bureau. Even here economic theory has much to contribute as a lot of work has been done within economics on the internal organisation of firms. For a long time, much of economic theory had proceeded taking institutions as given. Although classical writers such as Adam Smith talked of work organisation within business firms and indeed, Smith related efficiency with division of labour in his famous example of the prototype pin factory, it was left to economists of much recent vintage to undertake systematic study of internal organisation of firms.

Transaction Cost Economics and the Economics of Information

Two strands of analysis have been forwarded. The first stresses transaction costs, the nature of contracts, governance structures and property rights. The other approach emphasises information—its nature, use and distribution within the organisation. Ronald Coase set the analytical ball rolling (Coase, 1937, 1960) regarding the first approach. He first posed the question regarding business firms: if the market is such an efficient allocator of resources, why do organisations such as firms need to exist? He suggested that there are costs to undertake any transaction, and institutions evolve to minimise these transaction costs. At the same time economic historians like Alfred Chandler (1977) described how the business firm changed over time in terms of structure and organisational principles. Douglas North (1981) has argued that development of institutions takes place primarily due to changes in property rights. For an outstanding account of transaction costs economics, see Williamson (1985). Transaction costs economics posits that each type of organisation—market, firm or bureau—is characterised by a distinctive form of set of contracts, incentives and control structures This line of analysis utilises the concept of bounded rationality, and acknowledges that a rational individual can display guile.

The reason why economists should pay attention to institutions and governance structures can be presented by an illustration that is actually a bit of a digression. Early in this century there was a protracted debate between economists Ludwig von Mieses and Friedrich Hayek on the one hand and Oskar Lange and Abba Lerner on the other regarding the operational feasibility of socialism. The former group argued that a central planning authority under socialism would be informationally constrained and would not be able to provide incentives, unlike the market mechanism, and would therefore be a poorer allocator of resources and consequently less efficient than capitalism.

The latter group argued, in effect, that the state need not be articulated through an overcentralised planning mechanism. In fact, resources under socialism can be allocated on the lines suggested by the theory of perfectly competitive firm, which in the sense of not being able to influence prices in the market and taking them as given and selling a homogeneous product as other firms in the market, is not likely to exist in actual capitalist societies. The socialist state can mimic this firm, which in economic theory is considered more efficient than firms under less competitive conditions, like monopolies and oligopolies. This was the first articulation of what is called market socialism. Lange and Lerner are generally considered to have had the upper hand in the debate. Although Lange recognised that the main danger under socialism was growth of the state and over-bureaucratisation, he suggested that an analysis of the bureau was not the province of the economist. It should be noted that both sides in the debate conducted the debate around resource allocation and economic efficiency and did not consider the governance problem under socialism (see Williamson, 1994). Now when the formerly socialist (or what was passed off as socialism) countries embark on the path of liberalisation, governance structures and design of efficient administrative set-ups and organisations are receiving a great deal of attention from economists. This is also with regard to analysis of developing countries as several among them are currently engaged in liberalisation and globalisation. Framing of laws like contract laws, designing incentive structures and articulation of property rights are among the most crucial topics in the economics of development today. The work and results of economists are increasingly likely to be of use in the study of government administration and bureaux.

Information economics is an area of economics that is of recent vintage, having come into use for application only since about 1970, although there were a few stray and sporadic articles earlier. The central concept in this branch is, of course, information. The origin stemmed from the idea that unlike what economic theory was suggesting then, every economic agent or party to a transaction did not have an equal amount of private information regarding resources, endowments and so on. Information is imperfect. This renders the exchange or transaction process sub-optimal, even when other conducive conditions are present. In some situations, there may be an assymetry of information, such as in the market for second hand cars where the seller of the car has more information about its condition than the buyer. Presence of assymetric information may lead to what is called adverse selection, or choosing of something of a lower quality which would not otherwise be chosen. Often in organisations, there may be what is called moral hazard, which is a term originally borrowed from the insurance literature. This means that one party, called the agent, takes actions which cannot be or are costly to monitor by another party, called the principal which has an interest in getting the agent to do something of use to the principal. In organisations, the employer or the superior officer is the principal and the worker or the junior officer the agent. Moral hazard can be lessened through optimal mechanism design. A discussion of this will be taken up in the section on game theory. Using the concept of moral hazard, we can discuss the old problem of *beamtenherrschaft* (rule of officials) that Weber referred to, which he feared would undermine the bureaucratic goals and objectives.

The Theory of Teams

The theory of teams addresses a set of questions midway between those addressed by individual decision-making theory and theories of collective choice. A team is taken to mean an entity made up of a number of decision-makers who have a common objective and have common interests and beliefs, but who control different areas of decisions, and they base their decisions on possibly different information. As such, a bureau is a prime candidate for analysis using team theory. Team theory was first expounded systematically in Marschak and Radner (1972). Other notable early contributions include Groves (1973) and Groves and Radner (1972). The theory of teams seeks to study how different decision sets and tasks (as well as information) can be allocated among different members of a team and how to devise working methods that are efficient. Several studies within the team theory literature delve into these questions. There are several issues germane to the study of teams. How is information to be evaluated? What should be the degree and extent of centralisation within the team (organisation)? Complete centralisation would mean that all members do not have the same information structure. If it is totally decentralised, efficiency can fall. To avoid problems, either it should be the case that everyone totally communicates to everyone else, the random stochastic elements that he or she observes or that every member communicates information to a central agency, which then communicates the corresponding individual action, required, to each member. This would be complete centralisation. There can arise serious efficiency loss due to such over-centralisation. For a discussion on this point, see Arrow (1974). In practice, there is incomplete sharing of information within the bureaucratic organisation. Hence, there are reports, task forces, committees, and so on.

Game Theory

Another important tool for the analysis of bureaucracy is Game Theory. The term is misleading because it is actually a theory of human interaction and does not necessarily have to do with actual games. Whenever rational people undertake some action or make a decisions the outcome of which also depends on the action and/ or the decisions of other rational people, it becomes a situation where game theory could be applied. Although it is most widely used in Economics, it has been applied in Political Science, Sociology, Moral Philosophy, Management, and has even had writers in the Marxian tradition urging its use in Marxian Political Economy (Bose, 1975; Elster 1985).

A game is simply a list of the players, the sets of strategies available to them, and the outcomes resulting from the actions and their payoffs. Games are traditionally divided into cooperative and non-cooperative games depending or whether or not binding and enforceable contracts can be made among the players. Games are also distinguished based on whether moves by the players are made simultaneously or sequentially. The former type is called games in strategic form. The latter type is called games in extensive form. Cooperative games are depicted in what is called characteristic function form. In the early literature on game theory a distinction used to be made between two-person games and general n-person games as well as between zero-sum games and non-zero sum games but these distinctions are not terribly important nowadays. Games that take place over time are called dynamic games; others are static games. One of the most important solution concepts in Game Theory is what is called Nash equilibrium. This is a set of strategies for each player that is optimal, given that all other players are using their optimal strategies. Nash strategy equilibrium for a player is an example of a dominant strategy, which is a strategy that does not give a lower payoff as compared to any other strategy for that player. There have been several refinements of the Nash equilibrium concept, like sub-game perfection. These concepts extend the theory of games to situations of uncertainty. There is also a large body of literature within game theory that ties it with information economics. For an incisive analysis of bureaux applying game theoretic concepts, see Tirole (1986).

One of the most fruitful areas of applications of game theory and which can be very useful in analysing bureaux is a combination of game theoretic concepts with that of social choice theory. This is the area of what is called Mechanism Design. This has basically to do with attempts by a planner, or say a controlling authority, in a bureau to devise certain incentive structures and mechanism whereby each individual finds it to be her dominant strategy to reveal her true preferences and choices. The individual does not find it gainful to free ride on the efforts of others in an organisation. This is called the Revelation Principle. Game theory thus has much to offer for the study of bureaux.

Cooperative Game theory has thrown much light on situations where of a total of say n individuals in a group or organisation or even a political party, a smaller group or subset forms a coalition, and when it is profitable for these coalitions to be formed. Cooperative Game Theory also has a lot to say about situations of bargaining. Unfortunately, many social scientists consider Game Theory to be applicable only to situations of conflict or competition, when it has applications in almost any situations of human interaction and interdependent decision-making.

Conclusion

This essay was a tentative statement regarding some tools that modern economic analysis has to offer towards analysis of bureaux. The approach is basically to begin with individual actors, to see who does what, which objective functions are optimised, what are the payoffs, and what is the information structure. Underlying all this is the implied rationality of actors. We merely catalogued some important tools that ought to be in the toolkit of the analyst. In conclusion, we may state that for a long time the economic approach was taken to mean simply the weighing of benefits against costs, or to undertake a 'pleasure-pain calculus' (actually it is benefits at the margin against marginal costs, and even the benefits would be expected benefits). This is broadly true but within this framework is a rich body of analytical tools can be applied even to situations that have traditionally not been considered economic (mainly by non-economists) because there was not an explicit mention of money. The approach and the tools used therein and discussed above can provide a self contained and coherent set of techniques which can deal with the relation of the individual and the group; with decisions, goals, and objectives; with information, incentives and motivation, with contract collusion and teams. The additional virtue would be that the approach provides a common set of tools, a common framework and expresses itself in a common language that is precise.

Several points could be added to the discussion. First, how do we measure outputs and inputs in the case of bureaux? How would questions of efficiency be addressed? How are the 'consumers' of bureaucratic services be considered? One point that immediately suggests itself is that the concept of moral hazard is immediately applicable with the consumer as the principal and the officials the agent. Most of the concepts we have outlined find easy application in any extended discussion of bureaucratic organisations.

REFERENCES

1. Arrow, K.J., *Social Choice and Individual Values, second edition,* New Haven: Cowles Foundation, 1963.
2. Arrow, K.J., *The Limits of Organisation,* New York, Norton, 1974.
3. Black, Duncan, 'On the Rationale of Group Decision Making' *Journal of Political Economy,* 1948, Vol. 56, 23-34.
4. Bose, A., *Marxian and Post-Marxian Political Economy.* Harmondsworth, Penguin, 1975.
5. Chandler, A., *The Visible Hand.* Cambridge, Massachusetts, Harvard University Press, 1977.
6. Coase, R.H., 'The Nature of the Firm' *Economica.* 1937, no. 4, pp. 386-405.
7. Coase, R.H., "The Problem of Social Cost' *Journal of Law and Economics* 1960, no. 3, pp. 1-44.
8. Downs, A., *Inside Democracy,* Boston, Little Brown, 1967.
9. Elster, J., *Making Sense of Marx.* Cambridge, University Press, 1985.
10. Green, J. and Laffont J.-J., *Incentives in Public Decision Making,* Amsterdam, North Holland, 1979.
11. Groves, T. 'Incentives in Teams' *Econometrica* 1973, Vol. 41, pp. 617-31.
12. Groves, T. and Radner, R., 'Allocation of Resources in a Team' *Journal of Economic Theory* 1972, Vol. 3, pp. 415-44.
13. Marschak, J. and Radner, R., *Economic Theory of Teams,* New Haven, Yale University Press, 1972.
14. Morishima, M., *Marx's Economics: A Dual Theory of Value and Growth,* Cambridge: University Press, 1985.
15. Niskanen, W.A., *Bureaucracy and Representative Government.* Chicago: Aldine-Atherton, 1971.
16. Niskanen, W.A., 'Bureaucrats and Politicians' *Journal of Law and Economics,* 1975, December, vol. 18(3), pp. 617-43.
17. North, D.C., *Structure and Change in Economic History,* New York: W.W. Norton, 1981.
18. Roemer, J., *A General Theory of Exploitation and Class.* Cambridge, Massachusetts: Harvard University Press, 1982.
19. Sen, A., *Collective Choice and Social Welfare,* San Francisco, Holden-Day, 1970.
20. Sen, A., 'Social Choice Theory' In *Handbook of Mathematical Economics* Vol. 3. in K. Arrow and M. Intrilligator(eds.), Amsterdam: North-Holland, 1986.
21. K. Arrow 'Social Choice' In *The New Palgrave* Vol. 4, in J.Eatwell, M. Milgate and P.Newman, (eds.) London: Macmillan, 1988.
22. Simon, H., *Administrative Behaviour (second edition),* New York: The Free Press, 1957.
23. Tirole, J., 'Hierarchies and Bureaucracies: on the Role of Collusion in Organisations' *Journal of Law, Economics and Organisation* 1986 Vol. 2, no. 2, Fall, pp. 181-214.

24. Tullock, G., *The Politics of Bureaucracy,* 1967.

25. Williamson, O. *The Economic Institutions of Capitalism.* New York: The Free Press, 1985.

26. Williamson, O., 'The Institutions and Governance of Economic Development and Reform' in *Proceedings of the World Bank Annual Conference on Development Economics,* 1994.

Index